Fifth Edition

The Crosscultural, Language, and Academic Development Handbook

A Complete K–12 Reference Guide

Lynne T. Díaz-Rico
California State University, San Bernardino

PEARSON

Boston • Columbus • Indianapolis • New York • San Francisco • Upper Saddle River
Amsterdam • Cape Town • Dubai • London • Madrid • Milan • Munich • Paris • Montréal • Toronto
Delhi • Mexico City • São Paulo • Sydney • Hong Kong • Seoul • Singapore • Taipei • Tokyo

Vice President and Editor-in-Chief: *Aurora Martínez-Ramos*
Editor: *Kathryn Boice*
Editorial Assistant: *Michelle Hochberg*
Marketing Manager: *Krista Clark*
Production Editor: *Mary Beth Finch*
Projection Coordination, Editorial Services, and Text Design: *Electronic Publishing Services, Inc., NYC*
Manufacturing Buyer: *Linda Sager*
Art Rendering and Electronic Page Makeup: *Jouve*
Interior Design: *Electronic Publishing Services, Inc., NYC*
Cover Designer: *Diane Lorenzo*
Cover Photo: *Rob Marmion/Shutterstock*

Library of Congress Cataloging—Cataloging-Publication Data

Díaz-Rico, Lynne T.
   The crosscultural, language, and academic development handbook : a complete K–12 reference guide / Lynne T. Díaz-Rico. — 5th edition.
      pages cm.
   Includes bibliographical references and index.
   ISBN 978-0-13-285520-4
   1. English language—Study and teaching (Higher)—Foreign speakers—Handbooks, manuals, etc.   2. Multicultural education—United States—Handbooks, manuals, etc.
3. Language and education—United States—Handbooks, manuals, etc.   4. Education, Bilingual—United States—Handbooks, manuals, etc.   I. Title.
   PE1128.A2D45 2013
   428.0071'73—dc23   2012051129

10 9 8 7 6 5 4 3 2 1

PEARSON

ISBN-10: 0-13-285520-8
ISBN-13: 978-0-13-285520-4

Dedication

I dedicate this edition to Kathryn Weed.
Her devotion to excellence,
her generosity of spirit,
and her daily cordiality
set a standard for what it means to
be a true colleague.

—LTD-R

About the Author

Lynne T. Díaz-Rico is a professor of education at California State University, San Bernardino (CSUSB). Dr. Díaz-Rico obtained her doctoral degree in English as a second language at InterAmerican University in Puerto Rico and has taught students at all levels from kindergarten to high school. At CSUSB, Dr. Díaz-Rico is coordinator of the Masters in Education, Teaching English to Speakers of Other Languages Option program. She is actively involved in teacher education and gives presentations at numerous professional conferences on such subjects as intercultural education, critical language analysis, and organization of schools and classrooms for educational equity. Her current research interest is the use of language in complex, particularly crosscultural, contexts.

Contents

3   Learning about Second-Language Acquisition   46

PART TWO Instruction   69

Oracy and Literacy for English-Language Development,
Content-Area Instruction, and Bilingual Education

4 Oracy and Literacy for English-Language Development   70

5   Content-Area Instruction   114

6 Theories and Methods of Bilingual Education 147

PART THREE Assessment 183

7 Language and Content-Area Assessment 184

PART FOUR Culture   217

Cultural Diversity in the United States, Culturally Responsive Schooling, and the Role of the Family in Schools

8 Cultural Diversity   218

PART FIVE   Policy   311

Language Policy and Special Populations of English Learners

11   The Role of Educators in Language Policy   312

12 Culturally and Linguistically Diverse Learners and Special Education 333

Introduction

The presence of many linguistic and ethnic minority students in the United States has challenged educators to rethink basic assumptions about schooling. School models and methods based on the notions that students share the same cultural background and speak the same language are no longer sufficient to meet the needs of today's students. The urgent need to provide a high-quality education for students in the United States whose native language is not English calls for increased expertise on the part of classroom teachers, administrators, and community leaders.

In the past, schools were designed for native speakers of English. Today's students come from diverse cultural and linguistic backgrounds. But the cultural patterns of schools and classrooms may not ensure that all students have equal opportunity to succeed. Culture is a part of the educational process that has been invisible but that can no longer remain so. By understanding the influence of culture, educators can avoid inadvertently advantaging those students who share the dominant culture while neglecting those students whose cultures differ from the mainstream. Culture includes more than the habits and beliefs of students and teachers; the school itself is a culture in which the physical environment, daily routines, and interactions advantage some and yet may alienate others. Educators now need a foundation of cultural awareness and second-language acquisition theory in order to adapt schools to the needs of multicultural and multilingual students.

Crosscultural, Language, and Academic Development: A Model for Teacher Preparation

Much has been written about the effect of culture on schooling, second-language acquisition, and ways to help English learners achieve access to the core curriculum. To synthesize this wealth of information, a means of organizing this knowledge is needed. The figure on page xvi represents the central elements of this book and their relationship to one another.

In the figure, *learning* occupies the central area (Part One). Understanding the learner, the language to be learned, and the process of learning a second language helps teachers to meet the needs of individual learners.

Instruction is the second major area that organizes knowledge about teaching English learners (Part Two). Instruction for English learners falls into three categories: oracy and literacy for English-language development, content-area instruction (also known as "sheltered" instruction or specially designed academic instruction in English—SDAIE), and theories and methods for bilingual education.

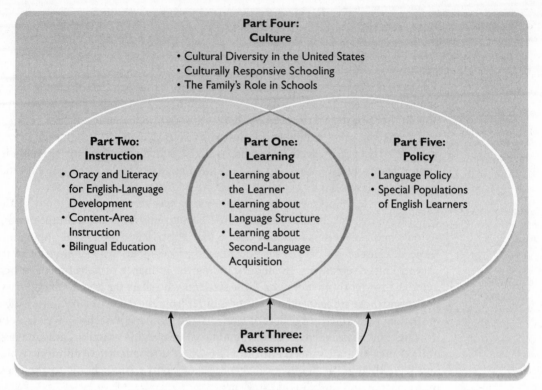

Theoretical Model for Crosscultural, Language, and Academic Development

Assessment practices are influenced by instruction and policymaking, and, in turn, assessment affects learning. Assessment of students is the way to determine if curricular content is appropriate and teaching methods are successful. Through assessment, one can ascertain what learning has taken place. The placement of students as a function of assessment affects the organization and management of schooling; thus assessment involves not only issues of pedagogy and learning but also policy. Assessment is covered in Part Three.

Culture permeates all activities of learning, instruction, and policymaking. Fundamental insights into cultural diversity in the United States, the role of the intercultural educator, the means for creating culturally appropriate pedagogy, and ways to augment the role of the family in schooling are provided in Part Four.

The fifth area, *policy*, denotes the organization and management of schooling, elements that affect the operation of schools. Because the policies affecting schooling can be better understood with a background on the influence and importance of culture, policy for English learners is discussed in Part Five.

Chapter 12 discusses policies and practices in the relationship between English-Language development (ELD) and special education. This chapter addresses effective curricula, teaching methods, assessment, organization, and management of instruction.

Teachers can be resources within their schools and districts on matters pertaining to English-language and academic development for their multicultural and multilinguistic students. A framework that organizes crosscultural, language, and academic development in terms of learning, pedagogy, and policy contributes to teachers' abilities to describe, communicate, and teach others about this field.

New With This Edition!

In addition to changes in the model (see figure on page xvi) and updated information, this fifth edition expands the classroom-related vignettes (Example of Concept) and instructional modifications (Adapted Instruction) to help the classroom teacher work successfully with culturally and linguistically diverse students. The concepts and information provided in this text encompass those necessary for examinations such as California's CLAD, California Teacher of English Learners (CTEL), and numerous other state requirements.

Care has been taken to use acceptable terminology to denote school students whose primary language is not English, as well as terms to denote various racial and ethnic groups. The terms *Hispanic* and *Hispanic American* denote those whose ancestors originated in Spain or Spanish America, and who now represent twenty-six separate nationalities and a variety of racial groups (Bruder, Anderson, Schultz, & Caldera, 1991). Research has shown that the ethnic labels for Hispanics are complex. In open-ended interviews, Latino adolescents were asked for their ethnic label preferences. In many cases, they did not commit to a specific label, instead indicating that they ascribed to more fluid, flexible labels. On average, students selected "Latino," "Mexican American," "Hispanic," and "Mexican," when asked to choose only one label. When selecting "American," "Chicano," "Salvadoran," or "Guatemalan," students always added a second term (Zarate, Bhimji, & Reese, 2005). *European American* is used in preference to *White* or *Anglo* to denote those whose ancestral background is European. *African American* is similarly used to refer to those whose ancestors came from Africa. Other ethnic group labels follow a similar logic. In some cases, data are cited that classify groups according to other labels; in these cases, the labels used in the citation are preserved.

Like the changes in terminology for racial and ethnic groups, terminology for students learning English as an additional language has undergone change. Over the years, these students have been called *language minority, limited-English proficient (LEP), non-English proficient (NEP), English-as-a-second-language (ESL) learner, English-language learner (ELL),* and *learners of English as a new language.* In this book, both the terms *English learner* and *culturally and linguistically diverse (CLD) student* are used. The term *English-Language development (ELD)* is used to denote classrooms and programs that promote English learners' language and academic learning.

Burgeoning information in the areas of culture and linguistic/academic development has made *The Crosscultural, Language, and Academic Development Handbook* a difficult yet useful synthesis. The result, I believe, is a readable text that brings into focus the challenges and possibilities in educating new Americans. Principles and practices that promote crosscultural understanding are relevant for all.

Help your students get better grades and become better teachers.

MyEducationLab™   MyEducationLab (www.myeducationlab .com) is a research-based learning tool that brings teaching to life. Through authentic in-class video footage, interactive simulations, rich case studies, examples of authentic teacher and student work, and more, MyEducationLab prepares students for teaching careers by showing what quality instruction looks like.

MyEducationLab is easy to use! At the end of every chapter in the textbook, you will find MyEducationLab videos that correlate with material you've just read in the chapter. The assets in MyEducationLab include:

- **Video.** The authentic classroom videos in MyEducationLab show how real teachers handle actual classroom situations.

- **Case Studies.** A diverse set of robust cases illustrates the realities of teaching and offers valuable perspectives on common issues and challenges in education.

- **Simulations.** Created by the IRIS Center at Vanderbilt University, these interactive simulations give you hands-on practice at adapting instruction for a full spectrum of learners.

- **Lesson Plans.** Specially selected, topically relevant excerpts from texts expand and enrich your perspectives on key issues and topics.

- **Classroom Artifacts.** Authentic PreK–12 student and teacher classroom artifacts are tied to course topics and offer you practice in working with the actual types of materials you will encounter daily as teachers.

- **Lesson and Portfolio Builders.** With this effective and easy-to-use tool, you can create, update, and share standards-based lesson plans and portfolios.

Acknowledgments

A book like this could not have been written without the help and support of numerous individuals. The teachers and students with whom I have worked have given me insights and examples. My colleagues have shared their experiences and expertise. In addition to those who gave so much support to previous editions, I would also like to thank those who have made this fifth edition a reality. It goes without saying I owe homage to the California Commission on Teacher Credentialing for their work in designing California's CLAD credential and its revision, the CTEL authorization.

I want to thank the teacher education and TESOL master's students at CSUSB as well as my colleagues in TESOL and in the Department of Language, Literacy, and Culture at CSUSB who have enriched my understanding of the teaching–learning process as it relates to second-language learners, and who have participated with me in research and curriculum development.

I am grateful also to those who provided helpful reviews of the manuscript for this edition: Nikki Ashcraft, Shenandoah University; Camie Modjadidi, Moravian College; Terah Moore, George Fox University; Nilsa Thorsos, Azusa Pacific University.

To all those who have provided linguistic and cultural support not only to English learners but also to those who have struggled to adapt to a new culture, I salute you. To the researchers and authors who provided valuable insights into this process, my deepest thanks for your pioneering efforts. Finally, I thank series editor Aurora Martínez Ramos, my editors Erin Grelak and Kathryn Boice, and the rest of the Pearson editorial staff for their efforts in producing this book.

Learning

Learning about the Learner, Language Structure, and Second-Language Acquisition

Part One represents learning the foundations of instruction: knowledge about the learner, about the structure of language, and about the process of acquiring a second language. Chapter 1 explores the learner, with a focus on the psychological factors in language learning that make individual language learners unique, as well as the sociocultural factors that situate the learner in the context of cultural patterns that may influence groups of learners to react in similar ways to classroom instruction. Chapter 2 introduces language structure and functions. Chapter 3 offers insights from classic and contemporary research in language acquisition and development, particularly in the context of the classroom. The accompanying figure highlights Part One of the theoretical model presented in the introduction.

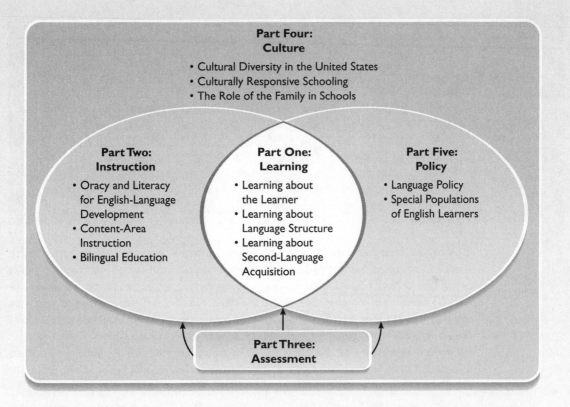

Theoretical Model for CLAD Learning: Learning about the Learner, Language Structure, and Second-Language Acquisition

1

Learning about the Language Learner

English learners comprise a growing proportion of school children in the United States.

© Zurijeta/Shutterstock

In sixth grade, I had one of the first in a lucky line of English teachers who began to nurture in me a love of language, a love that had been there since my childhood of listening closely to words. Sister Maria Generosa did not make our class interminably diagram sentences from a workbook or learn [a] catechism of grammar rules. Instead she asked us to write little stories imagining we were snowflakes, birds, pianos, a stone in the pavement, a star in the sky. What would it feel like to be a flower with roots in the ground? Sister Maria filled the board with snowy print . . . until English . . . became a charged, fluid mass that carried me in its great fluent waves, rolling and moving onward, to deposit me on the shores of my new homeland, I was no longer a foreigner with no ground to stand on. I had landed in the English language.

Julia Alvarez (2007, p. 34)

Because of her English-language development teachers, Julia Alvarez is a writer. She can communicate her memories, her joys, her terrors—those ideas and feelings that make her human. Learning a second language connects people across cultures, making it possible for immigrants to achieve their dreams and aspirations. This cross-cultural process enriches everyone.

Teachers in the United States are increasingly expected to educate students whose native languages are not English and whose cultural backgrounds vary considerably from that of the American mainstream culture. Although the teaching profession includes educators from minority cultures in the United States as well as from other countries, the core of the profession remains the white, middle-class, usually monolingual teacher who can benefit from teacher education that includes specialized methods and strategies for the effective education of culturally and linguistically diverse (CLD) students.

Moreover, research has documented the effectiveness of long-term primary-language education. However, numerous classrooms contain students speaking various home languages. Thus English-language development (ELD) classrooms that require modified instruction in English become increasingly important. Teachers with a strong interest in language acquisition and a sense of compassion for the difficulties faced by CLD students are often the most successful in promoting their academic success.

Common Beliefs about Teaching English Learners

Before beginning to explore the multiple factors that create complexity in teaching English learners, it is important to address four key misconceptions (see Harper and de Jong, 2004).

Misconception 1: Exposure and Immersion Are the Answer

Many teachers believe that the mind of a child, left to its own resources, will automatically learn a second language given enough time. This may stem from the parallel misconception that the first language is learned easily. However, before reaching kindergarten a five–year-old child has had more than 25,000 hours of family life in which to learn the primary language—but attending school for 180 days amounts to about 1,000 hours of English per year. Even if a second language were learned like the first, this would be nowhere near an equivalent exposure to language. Krashen's insight is that exposure must be comprehensible; school, on the other hand, often features abstract and decontextualized language.

Misconception 2: One Size Fits All

Learners do not all progress at the same rate in acquiring English. Differing levels of literacy in the first language as well as differing success in prior education, learning-style diversity, and differing social skills are just a few of the ways in which learners vary.

Misconception 3: Specially Adapted Instruction in English Is "Just Good Teaching"

Teachers may resist acquiring pedagogy designed to incorporate second-language-acquisition techniques because they think they can simply use techniques that are tried-and-true for native speakers of English—or they use remediation techniques designed for low-achieving students. In fact, neither approach is justified. For example, English learners may need modified instruction just to gain the confidence necessary for a minimal level of oral participation; silence does not indicate a lack of understanding. Teaching English learners requires a specific set of skills that are addressed in this book.

Misconception 4: Effective Instruction Means Nonverbal Teaching

Making instruction comprehensible by providing pictures and teaching using gestures are techniques designed to enhance understanding when language must be augmented—but this does not replace the need to teach language. Conceptual understanding and language are intertwined—one supports the other. The expert teacher takes responsibility for both.

Teaching in a second-language-acquisition context does not become simpler by reducing its complexity, but rather by acquiring the teaching skills required to operate effectively. Misconceptions undermine the motivation to learn how to succeed in a difficult teaching domain.

Schools, as institutions within a society, perform an important role in socializing students and helping them gain the knowledge, skills, roles, and identities they need for success. Students who enter school must develop a high level of English proficiency, and teachers are challenged to develop students' English skills during the K–12 period of schooling. The first part of this chapter presents current demographic trends. The chapter then introduces the English learner and offers ways for teachers to inform themselves about these learners' needs.

English Learners: Demographic Trends

The profession of teaching has changed dramatically in the early twenty-first century; many more classrooms contain English learners, students whose home language is not English and who are not classified as "fluent English proficient" based on test scores and other criteria. By 2025, one in every four students will initially be classified as an English learner. A quick overview of the demographics of English learners in the United States can help teachers to visualize the numbers of these learners and their distribution in the schools.

In 2010, 25.2 million (9 percent) of the U.S. population over 5 years of age was limited-English proficient (LEP) (Pandya, McHugh, & Batalova, 2011); six states

(California, Texas, New York, Florida, Illinois, and New Jersey, in order of LEP population) had more than 1,000,000 each. In 2008–2009, 49,487,174 students were enrolled in K–12 schools in the United States. Of these children, 21 percent spoke a language other than English in the home; 4.3 million are reported to speak English with difficulty (NCES, 2011). In all, 5,346,673 were English learners (NCELA, 2009). This represents a 51 percent increase since 1997–1998.

In nine states (California, Oregon, Nevada, Colorado, Arizona, New Mexico, Texas, Illinois, and Florida) more than 10 percent of students are English learners. The greatest growth in percent of population, however, has taken place in ten states, mostly clustered in the South: Alabama, Georgia, Arkansas, North Carolina, South Carolina, Virginia, Tennessee, and Kentucky, as well as Indians and Colorado (NCELA, 2009). Five states—California, Texas, New York, Florida, and Illinois—are home to almost 70 percent of all English learners in elementary schools (Cosentino de Cohen & Clewell, 2007).

California had the largest population percentage of non-English-language speakers; 37 percent of students enrolled in school speak a language other than English at home. Following California in percent of non-English speakers are New Mexico, Texas, New York, Hawaii, Arizona, and New Jersey. Other states—Florida, Illinois, and Massachusetts—also have large populations of non-English-language speakers. The majority of English learners in the United States are Spanish speaking (28.1 million); Asian and Pacific Islanders constitute the second-largest demographic group of English learners.

The National Clearinghouse for English Language Acquisition and Language Instruction Educational Programs (NCELA) put the number of children of school age with a home language other than English at 9,779,766—one of every six children of school age—and 31 percent of all American-Indian/Alaska Native, Asian/Pacific Islander, and Hispanic students enrolled in public schools (National Center for Education Statistics, 2005). Of these language-minority students, in 2005–2006, 5,074,572 do not yet have sufficient proficiency in English to be able to succeed academically in tra-ditional all-English-medium classrooms (NCELA, 2007). Los Angeles Unified School District leads all other school districts in the nation both in the number (220,703) of English learners, number of languages (92), and percent of total enrollment (33 percent), followed by New York City at 154,466 students (2011), or 41 per-cent of total students, with 168 home languages represented. Following Los Angeles and New York City are Dade County, Florida; Chicago; Houston; Dallas; San Diego; and Long Beach. In 2011, California, with a school enrollment of approxi-mately 1.4 million English learners, led the states in need for English-learner ser-vices at the K–12 level. In California, English learners constitute 23.2 percent of the total enrollment in California public schools. Almost 1 million more students speak a language other than English in their homes. This number represents about 37.4 percent of the state's public school enrollment. Although English learner data are collected for 59 language groups, 82.7 percent of the state's English learners speak Spanish (www.cde.ca.gov/ds/sd/cb/cefelfacts.asp).

Taking a closer look at the largest source of English learners, according to the latest U.S. Census data, there are 50.5 million Hispanics in the United States, comprising

16 percent of the total population. Adding the nearly 4 million residents of Puerto Rico, the total number of Latinos surpasses 54 million. Of those speaking a language other than English in the home, 62 percent (35,468,501) are Spanish-speaking (Shin & Ortman, 2011). Between 2000 and 2010, the Latino population increased by 43 percent (15.2 million), accounting for more than half of the 27.3 million increase in the total population of the United States. In the coming decades, Latinos will account for 60 percent of the nation's population growth between 2005 and 2050 (U.S. Department of Education, 2011).

In today's American public education system, Latinos are by far the largest minority group, numbering more than 12.4 million in the country's elementary, middle, and high schools. Currently, nearly 22 percent, or slightly more than one in five, of all preK–12 students enrolled in America's public schools are Latino. There are 17.1 million Latinos ages 17 and younger in the United States; therefore as they mature, their children will comprise a large group of students in the schools for many years to come.

The national distribution of English learners by grade levels is as follows: Grades PreK–3, 44 percent; grades 4–8, 35 percent; grades 9–12, 19 percent; and alternative schools, 2 percent (Rahilly & Weinmann, 2007). Of children who speak a language other than English at home, 81 percent are U.S.-born or naturalized U.S. citizens (Lapkoff & Li, 2007).

These population demographics indicate that all states need to provide services for English learners, with the need greatest in California, New Mexico, New York, Florida, Illinois, and Texas, serving Hispanics or Asian/Pacific Islanders. The linguistic and cultural variety of English learners suggests that more and more teachers serve as intercultural and interlinguistic educators—those who can reach out to learners from a variety of backgrounds and offer effective learning experiences.

Psychological Factors That Influence Instruction

Learners do not learn language in a vacuum. They learn it by interacting with others. Psychological and sociocultural factors play important roles in a learner's acquiring and using a second language. Teachers who are aware of these individual (psychological) and group (sociocultural) factors are able to adapt instruction to meet the individual needs of the learners so that each student can achieve academic success. Figure 1.1 offers an outline that can help teachers organize the factors they know about a given learner.

Psychological factors are traits specific to individuals that enable them to acquire a second language (L2). Learners use the assets of their personalities to absorb the ambiance of the culture, to process the language they hear, and to create meaningful responses. Psychological factors can be divided into three categories: *background* factors, *social–emotional* factors, and *cognitive* factors. Teachers can help students be aware of those psychological factors that further their language learning and can work with students to ensure that these factors promote rather than impede their learning.

Figure 1.1 English-Learner Profile

Psychological Factors

The Learner's Background

Learner's name _____ Age _____ Gender (M / F)

Grade _____ L1 proficiency _____

Type of bilingualism _____

Previous L2 experience _____

Assessed L2 level: Reading _____ Writing _____ Listening _____ Speaking _____

Prior academic success _____

Likes/dislikes _____

Social–Emotional Factors

Self-esteem _____

Motivation _____

Anxiety level _____

Attitudes toward L1/L2 _____

Attitudes toward the teacher and the class _____

Cognitive Factors

Stage of L2 acquisition _____

Cognitive style/Learning style _____

Learning strategies _____

Sociocultural Factors

Family acculturation and use of L1 and L2 _____

Family values _____

Institutional support for language-minority students _____

Sociocultural support for L1 in the classroom environment _____

The Learner's Background

Naming Practices and Forms of Address. A learner's name represents the learner's individuality as well as a family connection. People feel validated if their names are treated with respect. Teachers who make the effort to pronounce students' names accurately communicate a sense of caring. Students may be asked to speak their names into a tape recorder so the teacher can practice privately. Expecting students to say their names again and again so the teacher can rehearse may be embarrassing for both parties.

Naming practices differ across cultures. The custom in the United States is to have a first (or given), middle, and last (or family) name. On lists, the first and last names are often reversed in order to alphabetize the names. In other parts of the world, naming practices differ. In Vietnam, for example, names also consist of three parts, in the following order: family name, middle name, and given name. The names are always given in this order and cannot be reversed because doing so would denote a different person—Nguyên Van Hai is different from Hai Van Nguyên. In Taiwan the family name also goes first, followed by given names. Puerto Ricans, as well as other Hispanics, generally use three names: a given name, followed by the father's surname and then the mother's surname. If one last name must be used, it is generally the father's surname. Thus, Esther Reyes Mimosa can be listed as Esther Reyes. If the first name is composed of two given names (Hector Luis), both are used. This person may have a brother who is Hector José; for either to be called simply Hector would represent a loss of identity.

In many cultures, adults are referred to by their function rather than their name. In Hmong, *xib fwb* means "teacher," and Hmong children may use the English term *teacher* in the classroom rather than a title plus surname, as in "Mrs. Jasko." Middle-class European-American teachers may consider this to be rude rather than realizing this is a cultural difference.

Osgood (2002) suggests ways to enlist native-English-speaking students to make friends with newcomers: Challenge them to teach a new student their names and to learn the new student's first and last names, using recess, lunchtime, or free time to accomplish this task.

Adapted Instruction

Students' Names

- Understand the use and order of names and pronounce them correctly.
- Don't change a student's name, apply a nickname, or use an "English" version of a student's name (even at the student's request) without first checking with a member of the student's family.

Age. Second-language acquisition (SLA) is a complex process that occurs over a long period of time. Although many people believe that children acquire a second language more rapidly than adults, recent research counters this notion. While it is true that the kind of instruction varies greatly according to the age of the learner, there is little evidence to indicate that biology closes the door to learning a second language at certain ages (see Singleton & Ryan [2004] and Han [2004] for further discussion of age-related issues in SLA, as well as the Point/Counterpoint box on pages 9–10).

First-Language Proficiency. Research has shown that proficiency in the first language (L1) helps students to achieve in school. In order to learn a student's strengths in the first language, a teacher, primary-language-speaking aide, or parent who is fluent in the language of the student may observe a student working or playing in the primary language and take notes on the child's language behavior, or schools may rely on formal testing.

Acceptance of the first language and use of the first language to support instruction promotes a low-anxiety environment for students. A lower anxiety level in turn promotes increased learning.

Adapted Instruction

First-Language Proficiency

- Monitor students' fluency in their primary languages and share concerns with parents if students appear to be dysfluent in their home languages.
- In cooperative groups, allow use of the first language so that students can discuss concepts.

Types of Bilingualism. Cummins (1979) analyzed the language characteristics of the children he studied and suggested that the level of bilingualism attained is an important factor in educational development. *Limited bilingualism*, or subtractive bilingualism, can occur when children's first language is gradually replaced by a more

POINT COUNTERPOINT

What Is the Best Age for Second-Language Acquisition?

For adults, learning a second language can be a frustrating and difficult experience. In contrast, it seems so easy for children. Is there a best age for learning a second language?

POINT: Children Learn Second Languages Easily Those who argue that a child can learn a second language more rapidly than an adult generally ascribe this ability to the *critical period hypothesis*—that the brain has a language-acquisition processor that functions best before puberty (Lenneberg, 1967)—despite the fact that the critical period hypothesis has not been proved.

Evidence from child second-language studies indicates that the language children speak is relatively simple compared to that of adults; it has shorter constructions with fewer vocabulary words and thus appears more fluent. Moreover, adults are often unaware that a child's silence indicates lack of understanding or shyness, and they underestimate the limitations of a child's second-language

acquisition skills. One area that seems to be a clear advantage for children is phonology: The earlier a person begins to learn a second language, the closer the accent will become to that of a native speaker (Oyama, 1976); age of L2 learning appears to be the most important predictor of degree of foreign accent (Piske, Mackay, & Fiege, 2001).

COUNTERPOINT: Adults Learn Languages More Skillfully Than Children Research comparing adults to children has consistently demonstrated that adolescents and adults outperform children in controlled language-learning studies (e.g., Snow & Hoefnagel-Hoehle, 1978). Adults have access to more memory strategies; are, as a rule, more socially comfortable; and have greater experience with language in general. The self-discipline, strategy use, prior knowledge, and metalinguistic ability of the older learner create a distinct advantage for the adult over the child in second-language acquisition.

Marinova-Todd, Marshall, and Snow (2000) analyzed misconceptions about age and second-language learning and reached the following conclusions: "[O]lder learners have the potential to learn second languages to a very high level and introducing foreign languages to very young learners cannot be justified on grounds of biological readiness to learn languages" (p. 10). "Age does influence language learning, but primarily because it is associated with social, psychological, educational, and other factors that can affect L2 proficiency, not because of any critical period that limits the possibility of language learning by adults" (p. 28).

Implications for Teaching

Teachers need to be aware that learning a second language is difficult for children as well as for adults. Helping children to feel socially comfortable reduces their anxiety and assists acquisition.

dominant and prestigious language. In this case, children may develop relatively low levels of academic proficiency in both languages. The most positive cognitive effects are experienced in *proficient bilingualism*, when students attain high levels of proficiency in both languages. This is also called *additive bilingualism*.

Adapted Instruction

Promoting Additive Bilingualism

- Seek out or prepare handouts that encourage families to preserve the home language.
- Make sure classroom or community libraries feature books in the home language and encourage students to check out books in both languages.
- Welcome classroom visitors and volunteers who speak the home language, and ask them to speak to the class about the importance of proficiency in two languages.

Previous L2 Experience. English learners in the same grade may have had vastly different prior exposure to English, ranging from previous all-primary-language instruction to submersion in English—including students with no prior schooling at all. Moreover, no two students have been exposed to exactly the same input of English outside of class. Therefore, students' prior exposure to English and attainment of proficiency are often highly varied.

Although students at the beginner and early-intermediate levels seem to acquire English rapidly, research has shown that progress between the intermediate and advanced levels is slower (Goldenberg & Coleman, 2010). This may account for the difficulties experienced by the "long-term" English learner (Olsen, 2010).

Students who have been overcorrected when first learning English may have "shut down" and be unwilling to speak. It may take time for a more positive approach to L2 instruction to produce results, combined with a positive attitude toward L1 maintenance.

Assessed L2 Level. An important part of the knowledge about the learner that a teacher amasses as a foundation for instruction is the student's assessed level of proficiency in listening, speaking, reading, and writing in English. This can be obtained during the process of assessment for placement. In California, the California English Language Development Test (CELDT) (online at www.cde.ca.gov/ta/tg/el) is the designated placement instrument; other states have other ways to assess proficiency. The student's L2 level is the beginning point of instruction in English.

Adapted Instruction

Assessing L2 Proficiency Levels

- Be aware that a student's listening/speaking proficiency may surpass that of reading and writing, or vice versa.
- Assess each language skill independently.
- Use a measure such as the Student Oral Language Observation Matrix (SOLOM) to assess students' oral proficiency.
- Use *The English–Español Reading Inventory for the Classroom* (Flynt & Cooter, 1999) to provide a quick assessment of reading levels in two languages, or the *Cooter Flynt Cooter Comprehensive Reading Inventory* (2006) for English proficiency.

Second-language learners are individuals who vary greatly in their acquisition of a second language. However, there appear to be some generally accepted stages of development through which learners progress. These stages include *preproduction, early production, speech emergence,* and *intermediate fluency.* In preproduction— also called the silent period—the learner is absorbing the sounds and rhythms of the new language, becoming attuned to the flow of the speech stream, and beginning to isolate specific words. In this stage, the learner relies on contextual clues for understanding key words and generally communicates nonverbally.

Once a learner feels more confident, words and phrases are attempted—the early production stage. In the third stage, speech emergence, learners respond more freely. Utterances become longer and more complex, but as utterances begin to resemble sentences, syntax errors are more noticeable than in the earlier stage ("Where you going?" "The boy running."). Once in intermediate fluency, students begin to initiate and sustain conversations and are often able to recognize and correct their own errors.

Regardless of the way one labels the stages of second-language acquisition, it is important for the classroom teacher to use this level as the basis for instruction.

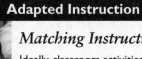

Adapted Instruction

Matching Instruction to Students' L2 Levels

Ideally, classroom activities match the students' second-language acquisition levels.

Beginning Level (preproduction stage)
- Provide concrete activities featuring input that is augmented by pictures, real objects, carefully modified teacher speech, and frequent repetition of new vocabulary.

Early Intermediate and Intermediate Levels (early production and speech emergence)

- Ask questions that evoke responses of single words and brief phrases.
- Provide opportunities for students to use their primary language as they acquire the second language.

Early Advanced Level

- Engage students in opportunities to speak with greater complexity, read several pages of text even though they may have limited comprehension, and write paragraphs.
- Offer a curriculum that supports and explicitly teaches learning strategies (see Chapter 5).

Prior Academic Success. A valid predictor of school success is prior academic success. By reading a student's cumulative academic record, a teacher may get a sense of the student's strengths and weaknesses. This can be augmented by observations of the student during academic activities and interviews of family members and former teachers. It is important for the current teacher to assemble as complete a record of students' prior schooling as possible to best inform instructional decisions.

Likes/Dislikes. Inquiring about students' favorite academic subjects, television shows, and extracurricular activities is one way of bridging adult–child, teacher–student, or intercultural gaps: Who/what is your favorite [native-language/culture] singer? Actor? Video game? Outdoor game? Storybook? Grocery store? Holiday? What do you like about it? Students can write about favorite subjects, and teachers can then use these culturally familiar ideas in math story problems and other content.

Psychological Factors: Social–Emotional

The affective domain, the emotional side of human behavior, is the means through which individuals become aware of their environment, respond to it with feeling, and act as though their feelings make a difference. This emotional dimension helps determine how language acquisition and communication take place. The affective factors discussed here are self-esteem, motivation, anxiety, and learner attitudes.

Self-Esteem. A large part of one's feelings revolve around how one feels about oneself, one's self-esteem. High self-esteem may *cause* language success or *result from* language success. Self-esteem enhancement, such as efforts to empower students with positive images of self, family, and culture, may facilitate language learning.

Self-esteem is particularly at risk when learning a second language, because so much identity and pride are associated with language competence. Schools that honor the primary languages and cultures of students and help students to develop additive bilingualism foster strong identities; schools in which students face disrespect and discrimination hinder students' social and emotional development (Cummins, 2001).

Children who do poorly in school face daily degradation to their sense of self-esteem as they often receive low grades, and experience disapproval from their teachers and even social ostracism from peers (McKay, 2000). A healthy sense of success is necessary not only to master academics, but also to feel valuable to society.

Example of Concept — *Building Self-Esteem*

Anita Alvarez was a Spanish-speaking first-grade student at the beginning stages of English-language acquisition. She was shy and retiring, and Mrs. Figueroa noticed that she seldom took advantage of opportunities to chat with her peers. Anita seemed to have good sensorimotor abilities and to be particularly adept at building three-dimensional models following printed diagrams. When Mrs. Figueroa observed that Mary, another student in the class, had a lot of difficulty in constructing objects, she teamed Anita with Mary; and, with Anita's help, Mary completed her project successfully. Noting this success, Mrs. Figueroa publicly praised her to the class and referred students to her for help. Mrs. Figueroa was pleased to see that, subsequently, Anita talked more with other students and seemed to acquire English at a faster rate.

Many classroom activities can be used to enhance students' self-esteem. In the Name Game, students introduce themselves by first name, adding a word that describes how they are feeling that day—using a word that begins with the same letter as their first name (the teacher may provide English learners with an alphabetized list of adjectives). Each subsequent person repeats what the others have said in sequence. Another activity, Name Interviews, lets students work in pairs to use a teacher-provided questionnaire. This includes questions such as, "What do you like about your name? Who named you? Were you named for someone? Are there members of your family who have the same name?" and more (Siccone, 1995).

Example of Concept — *Motivation for Acquiring a Second Language*

I began learning Spanish in middle school, just because it was part of the curriculum. But when I entered college, I began to develop a real interest in Spanish and learning more about Chile, about my mom's culture. I knew that I needed some sort of challenge in order for me to become more proficient in Spanish, so I decided to study abroad in Chile, to learn more about the Chilean culture and be able to understand it first-hand. I was motivated also because I believed that learning Spanish would help me advance in my career of international education.

—*Darlene Peceimer (2013)*

Motivation. "The impulse, emotion, or desire that causes one to act in a certain way" is one way to define motivation. Gardner and Lambert (1972) postulated two types of motivation in learning a second language: *instrumental*, the need to acquire a language for a specific purpose, and *integrative*, the desire to become a member of the culture of the second-language group. Most situations involve a mixture of both types.

Generally, in classrooms, teachers may believe that motivation is a trait or a state. As a *trait*, motivation is seen as being relatively consistent and persistent and is attributed to various groups: parents, communities, or cultures. Students are motivated to learn

English by such incentives as the desire to please—or not to shame—their families or by the drive to bring honor to their communities. As a *state*, motivation is viewed as a more temporary condition that can be influenced by the use of highly interesting materials or activities, or by contingencies of reward or punishment. Pittaway (2004) describes ways that teachers can increase students' motivation by investing in their success.

Adapted Instruction

Motivating Students

- Give pep talks to remind students that anything worth doing may seem difficult at first.
- Provide students with a list of encouraging phrases to repeat to themselves as self-talk.

Anxiety Level. Anxiety when learning a second language can be seen as similar to general feelings of tension that students experience in the classroom. Almost everyone feels some anxiety when learning a new language—that is, they have feelings of self-consciousness, a desire to be perfect when speaking, and a fear of making mistakes. Using a foreign language can threaten a person's sense of self if speakers fear they cannot represent themselves fully in a new language or understand others readily. Anxiety can be debilitating. As one student recalled,

> During these several months after my arrival in the U.S.A., every day I came back exhausted so I had to take a rest for a while, stretching myself on the bed. For all the time, I strained every nerve in order to understand what the people were saying and make myself understood in my broken English. I sometimes have to pretend to understand by smiling, even though I feel alienated, uneasy, and tense. (Barna, 2007, p. 71)

Because anxiety can cause learners to feel defensive and can block effective learning, language educators strive to make the classroom a place of warmth and friendliness and where peer work, small-group work, games, and simulations are featured. Highly anxious learners must divide their attentional resources into both learning and worrying about learning. Accepting English learners' use of both languages during instruction may help reduce their anxiety about speaking English (Pappamihiel, 2002).

Adapted Instruction

Ways to Deal with Excessive Student Anxiety

- Monitor activities to ensure that students are receiving no undue pressure.
- Avoid having anxious students perform in front of large groups.
- When using a novel format or starting a new type of task, provide students with examples or models of how the task is done.
- Teach test-taking skills explicitly and provide study guides to help students who may need extra academic preparation.

Source: Woolfolk (2007).

Attitudes of the Learner. Attitudes play a critical role in learning English. Attitudes toward self, toward language (one's own and English), toward English-speaking people (particularly peers), and toward the teacher and the classroom environment affect students (Richard-Amato, 2003). One's attitude toward the self involves cognition about one's ability in general, ability to learn language, and self-esteem and its related emotions. These cognitions and feelings are seldom explicit and may be slow to change.

Attitudes toward language and those who speak it are largely a result of experience and the influence of people in the immediate environment, such as peers and parents. Negative reactions are often the result of negative stereotypes or the experience of discrimination or racism. If English learners are made to feel inferior because of accent or language status, they may have a defensive reaction against English and English speakers.

Students' attitudes toward the primary language vary; some students may have a defensive reaction or ambivalent feelings toward their own primary language as a result of internalized shame if they have been made to feel inferior. Peers may incite attitudes against the L1 or may try to tease or bully those who speak the same primary language with a different dialect.

Attitudes toward the teacher and the classroom environment play an important role in school success in general and English acquisition in particular. One way to create a sense of belonging is to assign a new student to a home group that remains unchanged for a long time. If such groups are an ongoing aspect of classroom social organization, with rules of caring, respect, and concern already in place, then the home group provides an ideal social group to receive newcomers and help them develop interdependence, support, and identity (Peregoy & Boyle, 2013).

Teachers can do much to model positive attitudes toward the students' primary language. A teacher–family conference may be advisable if a student continues to show poor attitudes toward the first or second language or the school. (Chapter 10 offers a range of strategies for involving the family in schooling.)

Psychological Factors: Cognitive

The cognitive perspective helps educators understand language learners as people who are active processors of information. Language is used in school in expanded ways: to create meaning from print, to encode ideas into print, to analyze and compare information, and to respond to classroom discussion. All of these activities involve cognitive factors. Students learn in many different ways using a variety of strategies and styles. This section addresses students' cognitive and learning styles.

Cognitive Style. A cognitive style refers to "consistent and rather enduring tendencies or preferences within an individual" (Brown, 2007, p. 119). Tharp (1989b) suggested two cognitive styles that have relevance for classrooms: visual/verbal and holistic/ analytic. For students who learn by observing and doing rather than through verbal instructions, schools may be mystifying until they catch on to a different cognitive style. Similarly, students with more holistic thought processes learn by seeing the "big picture."

Adapted Instruction

Teaching to Diverse Learning Styles

Although in the typical classroom it is not possible to tailor instruction precisely to meet individuals' needs, some modifications can be made that take learning styles into account.

- Students who are dependent may benefit from encouragement to become more independent learners; the teacher may offer a choice between two learning activities, for example, or reduce the number of times a student has to ask the teacher for help.

- Students who are highly competitive may be provided activities and assignments that encourage collaboration and interdependent learning.

- Students who show little tolerance for frustration can be given a range of tasks on the same skill or concept that slowly increases in complexity, with the student gradually gaining skill and confidence.

Learning Styles. Many researchers have documented differences in the manner in which learners approach the learning task. These preferences help instructors anticipate the different needs and perspectives of students. Once learning styles have been identified, instructors can use the information to plan and to modify certain aspects of courses and assignments. Hruska-Riechmann and Grasha (1982) offer six learning styles: competitive versus cooperative, dependent versus independent, and participant versus avoidant. For Sonbuchner (1991), learning styles refer to information-processing styles and work environment preferences. Table 1.1 lists learning style variables that have been divided into four categories—cognitive, affective, incentive, and physiological—according to Keefe (1987).

Table 1.2 provides several learning style websites that feature learning style information, diagnostic checklists, and ideas for adapted instruction. The teacher who builds variety into instruction and helps learners to understand their own styles can enhance students' achievement.

Adapted Instruction

Accommodating Students' Psychological Factors

To adjust for individual psychological factors, teachers can provide verbal reassurances to timid students, alternative learning activities to address multiple intelligences, explicit opportunities to help students express their strong abilities, and additional mediation for students who need to achieve despite a possible weak ability in a specific area.

Table 1.1   Variables That Constitute Learning Style Differences

Cognitive	Affective	Incentive	Physiological
• Field independent/field dependent • Scanning (broad attention) v. focusing (narrow) • Conceptual/analytical v. perceptual/concrete • Task constricted (easily distracted) v. task flexible (capable of controlled concentration) • Reflective v. impulsive • Leveling (tendency to lump new experiences with previous ones) v. sharpening (ability to distinguish small differences) • High cognitive complexity (multidimensional discrimination, accepting of diversity and conflict) v. low cognitive complexity (tendency to reduce conflicting information to a minimum)	• Need for structure • Curiosity • Persistence • Level of anxiety • Frustration tolerance	• Locus of control (internal: seeing oneself as responsible for own behavior; or external: attributing circumstances to luck, chance, or other people) • Risk taking v. caution • Competition v. cooperation • Level of achievement motivation (high or low) • Reaction to external reinforcement (does or does not need rewards and punishment) • Social motivation arising from family, school, and ethnic background (high or low) • Personal interests (hobbies, academic preferences)	• Gender-related differences (typically, males are more visual–spatial and aggressive, females more verbal and tuned to fine-motor control) • Personal nutrition (healthy v. poor eating habits) • Health • Time-of-day preferences (morning, afternoon, evening, night) • Sleeping and waking habits • Need for mobility • Need for and response to varying levels of light, sound, and temperature

Source: Based on Keefe (1987).

Table 1.2   Websites That Feature Learning Style Information and Diagnostic Inventories

Website	Source	Content
www.engr.ncsu.edu/learningstyles/ilsweb.html	North Carolina State University	Users can take a learning styles questionnaire with 44 items to self-assess.
www.usd.edu/trio/tut/ts/style.html	University of San Diego	Learn about learning styles (auditory, visual, and kinesthetic); identify your own learning style.
http://ttc.coe.uga.edu/surveys/LearningStyleInv.html	University of Georgia	Are you visual, tactile, or auditory? Find out!

Sociocultural Factors That Influence Instruction

Language learning occurs within social and cultural contexts. A part of the sense of mastery and enjoyment in a language is acting appropriately and understanding cultural norms. Learners adapt patterns of behavior in a new language and culture based on experiences from their own culture. Thus, sociocultural factors—how people interact with one another and how they carry out their daily business—play a large role in second-language acquisition.

If, as many believe, prolonged exposure to English is sufficient for mastery, then why do so many students fail to achieve the proficiency in English necessary for academic success? Some clues to this perplexity can be found beyond the language itself, in the sociocultural context. Do the students feel that their language and culture are accepted and validated by the school? A well-meaning teacher, with the most up-to-date pedagogy, may still fail to foster achievement if students are socially and culturally uncomfortable with, resistant to, or alienated from schooling.

As students learn a second language, their success is dependent on sociocultural factors. These factors are explored here with a view toward helping teachers facilitate student learning by bridging the culture and language gaps.

Family Acculturation and the Use of First and Second Languages

Acculturation is the process of adapting to a new culture. English learners in the United States, by the mere fact of living in this country and participating in schools, learn a second culture as well as a second language. How the acculturation proceeds depends on factors beyond language itself and beyond the individual learner's motivation, capabilities, and style—it usually is a familywide phenomenon.

In studying students' differential school performance, Ogbu (1978) drew a distinction between various types of immigrant groups. Castelike minorities are those minority groups that were originally incorporated into society against their will and have been systematically exploited and depreciated over generations through slavery or colonization. Castelike minorities traditionally work at the lowest paying and most undesirable jobs, and they suffer from a job ceiling they cannot rise above regardless of talent, motivation, or achievement. Thus, academic success is not always seen as helpful or even desirable for members of these groups.

On the other hand, *immigrant minorities* who are relatively free of a history of depreciation, such as immigrants to the United States from El Salvador, Guatemala, and Nicaragua, believe that the United States is a land of opportunity. These immigrants do not view education as irrelevant or exploitative but rather as an important investment. Therefore, the internalized attitudes about the value of school success for family members may influence the individual student.

Adapted Instruction

Learning about the Family

- If possible, visit the student's home to observe the family's degree of acculturation.
- Note the family's media consumption:
  What television shows does the family watch, in which language?
  Do family members read books, magazines, or newspapers, and in which languages?

A family's use of L1 and L2 is also influenced by the relative status of the primary language in the eyes of the dominant culture. In modern U.S. culture, the social value and prestige of speaking a second language varies with socioeconomic position; it also varies as to the second language that is spoken.

Many middle-class parents believe that learning a second language benefits their children personally and socially and will later benefit them professionally. In fact, it is characteristic of the elite group in the United States who are involved in scholarly work, diplomacy, foreign trade, or travel to desire to be fully competent in two languages. However, the languages that parents wish their children to study are often not those spoken by recently arrived immigrants (Dicker, 1992). This suggests that a certain bias exists in being bilingual—that being competent in a "foreign language" is valuable, whereas knowing an immigrant language is a hurdle to be overcome.

There are many ways in which a second-class status is communicated to speakers of other languages, and because language attitudes usually operate at an inconspicuous level, school personnel and teachers are not always aware of the attitudes they hold. For example, the interlanguage of English learners—the language they use as they learn English—may be considered a dialect of English. Students learning English express themselves in many different dialects, depending on the language they hear in their homes and communities. These forms of English vary in the pronunciation of words, the selection of vocabulary that is used, and the way that words are arranged in sentences.

Some teachers only accept Standard English, the English found in textbooks. They may view nonstandard forms as less logical, less precise, or less elegant; sometimes they may even stigmatized these forms as corrupt or debased. Worse, they may view those who speak nonstandard English as less intelligent or less gifted linguistically. Research has shown that incorporating nonstandard language use in the classroom is often a helpful bridge to the learning of Standard English. When students feel that they are accepted and are confident of their language skills, they are more likely to want to acquire a second language (Siegel, 1999).

If teachers devalue the accent, syntax, or other speech characteristics of students as they learn English, English learners receive the message that their dialect is not accepted. If teachers use dialect to evaluate students' potential or use proficiency in Standard English to predict school achievement, it is possible that the teacher's own attitude toward the students' dialects—either positive or negative—has more to do with students' cognitive and academic achievement than does the dialect.

Adapted Instruction

Recognizing Biases towards Non-Standard English

- Recognize areas in which there may be differences in language use and in which those differences might create friction because the minority group's use may be deemed "inferior" by the majority.

- Be honest about your own biases, recognizing that you communicate these biases whether or not you are aware of them.

- Model correct usage without overt correction, and the student in time will self-correct—if the student chooses Standard English as the appropriate sociolinguistic choice for that context.

Family Values and School Values

As student populations in U.S. schools become increasingly diversified both linguistically and culturally, teachers and students have come to recognize the important role that attitudes and values play in school success. Not only the individual's attitudes as described above, but also the family's values and attitudes toward schooling, influence a child's school success.

Example of Concept *Family Values*

Amol is a third-grade student whose parents were born in India. As the only son in a male-dominant culture, he has internalized a strong sense of commitment to becoming a heart surgeon. His approach to classwork is painstaking. Often he is the last to finish an assignment during class. The teacher's main frustration with Amol is that he cannot quickly complete his work. However, when talking with Amol's family, the teacher notes that his parents seem pleased with his perfectionism and not at all concerned with his speed at tasks. In this respect, home and school values differ.

In this example, the teacher epitomizes a mainstream U.S. value: speed and efficiency in learning. Teachers may describe students of other cultures as being lackadaisical and uncaring about learning, when in fact they may be operating within a different time frame and value system.

Other values held by teachers and embodied in classroom procedures have to do with task orientation. The typical U.S. classroom is a place of work in which students are expected to conform to a schedule, keep busy, maintain order, avoid wasting time, conform to authority, and achieve academically in order to attain personal worth. Working alone is also valued in school, and children may spend a great deal of time in activities that do not allow them to interact verbally with other people or to move physically around the room.

Children need to find within the structure and content of their schooling those behaviors and perspectives that permit them to switch between home and school cultural behaviors and values without inner conflict or crises of identity (Pérez & Torres-Guzmán, 2002). Teachers need to feel comfortable with the values and behaviors of their students' cultures in order to develop a flexible cultural repertoire within the context of teaching. The implementation of a rich and flexible cultural repertoire is the strategy that can allow cultures to mix constructively and promote achievement.

The danger of excluding the students' culture(s) from the classroom is that cultural identity, if not included, may become oppositional. Ogbu and Matute-Bianchi (1986) described how oppositional identity in a distinctly Mexican American frame of reference influenced the performance of Mexican American children. They attributed achievement difficulties on the part of some Mexican American children to a distrust of academic effort. When schools were segregated and offered inferior education to this community, a general mistrust of schools caused a difficulty in accepting, internalizing, and following school rules of behavior for achievement. This element of resistance or opposition is not always overt but often takes the form of mental withdrawal, high absenteeism, or reluctance to do classwork.

Adapted Instruction

Accommodating Students' Cultures

Dalle and Young (2003) suggest that teachers check with families to see if family cultures have any "taboos" that would make students uncomfortable performing certain activities; discuss with family members the support available for homework, and arrange for after-class supervision if needed; and explain key concepts using ideas that are familiar from the students' perspective.

Institutional Support for Language-Minority Students

Educators may view a student's ability to speak a home language other than English as an advantage or as a liability toward school success. Those who blame bilingual students for failing in school often operate from the mistaken beliefs that students and/or their parents are uninterested in education; that students who are raised as native speakers of another language are handicapped in learning because they have not acquired sufficient English; or that cultural differences between the ways children learn at home or among their peers and the ways they are expected to learn at school interfere with school learning.

In fact, schools often operate in ways that advantage certain children and disadvantage others, causing distinct outcomes that align with social and political forces in the larger cultural context. Institutional support for the primary language and students who speak it is a prime factor in school success for these students.

Some social theorists see the culture of the school as maintaining the poor in a permanent underclass and as legitimizing inequality (Giroux, 1983). In other words, schooling is used to reaffirm class boundaries. This creates an educational class system in which minority students—or any students who are not successful in the classroom—emerge from their schooling to occupy the same social status as their parents.

Example of Concept

The Way Schools Use Language to Perpetuate Social Class Inequality

Consider this account from Erickson of a fourth-grade class that was electing student council representatives.

> Mrs. Lark called for nominations. Mary, a monolingual English-speaking European American student, nominated herself. Mrs. Lark accepted Mary's self-nomination and wrote her name on the board. Rogelio, a Spanish-speaking Mexican American child with limited English proficiency, nominated Pedro. Mrs. Lark reminded the class that the representative must be "outspoken." Rogelio again said "Pedro." Mrs. Lark announced to the class again that the representative must be "a good outspoken citizen." Pedro turned red and stared at the floor. Mrs. Lark embarrassed Rogelio into withdrawing the nomination. No other Mexican American child was nominated, and Mary won the election. Pedro and Rogelio were unusually quiet for the rest of the school day.

Source: Adapted from Erickson (1977, p. 59).

Incidents like the one in Mrs. Lark's classroom are generally unintentional on the teacher's part. A beginning step in helping all students feel fully integrated into the class and the learning environment is for teachers to become sensitive to their own cultural and linguistic predispositions.

Nieto and Bode (2008) identified numerous structures within schools that affect English learners: tracking, testing, the curriculum, pedagogy, the school's physical structure and disciplinary policies, the limited roles of both students and teachers, and limited parent and community involvement.

Tracking. The practice of placing students in groups of matched abilities, despite its superficial advantages, in reality often labels and groups children for years and allows them little or no opportunity to change groups. Secondary school personnel who place English learners in low tracks or in nonacademic ELD classes preclude those students from any opportunity for higher-track, precollege work. In contrast, a supportive school environment offers equal education opportunity to all students, regardless of their language background.

Testing. Students who respond poorly on standardized tests are often given "basic skills" in a remedial curriculum that is essentially the same as the one in which they were not experiencing success. A supportive school is one that offers testing adaptations for English learners as permitted by law; for example, academic testing in the primary language, extended time for test taking, and fully trained testing administrators.

Curriculum Design. Only a small fraction of knowledge is codified into textbooks and teachers' guides, and this is rarely the knowledge that English learners bring from their communities (see Loewen, 1995). In addition, the curriculum may be systematically watered down for the "benefit" of children in language-minority communities through the mistaken idea that such students cannot absorb the core curriculum. A supportive environment is one that maintains high standards while offering a curriculum that is challenging and meaningful.

Pedagogy. The way students are taught is often tedious and uninteresting, particularly for students who have been given a basic skills curriculum in a lower-track classroom. The pressure to "cover" a curriculum may exclude learning in depth and frustrate teachers and students alike. Pedagogy that is supportive fully involves students—teachers make every effort to present understandable instruction that engages students at high levels of cognitive stimulation.

The Physical Structure of the School. Architecture also affects the educational environment. Many inner-city schools are built like fortresses to forestall vandalism and theft. Rich suburban school districts, by contrast, may provide more space, more supplies, and campuslike schools for their educationally advantaged students. Supportive schooling is observable—facilities are humane, well cared for, and materially advantaged.

Example of Concept   *A School Culture That Disconnects, Bores, and Controls—for Teachers and Students Alike*

Order predominated at the traditional high school that Wells (1996) studied. Control trumped creativity. Teachers were not encouraged to voice their educational philosophies or innovate. Instruction was driven by textbooks, with few opportunities for students to write. Reading became an exercise in searching for answers to chapter questions or worksheet blanks. Little inquiry, exploration, or reflection was asked of students. Pope (2002) came to a similar conclusion. Students, for the most part, experienced little genuine engagement. They did schoolwork because they had to—there was little evidence of curiosity or interest. If this is the case for the average middle-class high school, conditions can only be worse in inner-city schools, where the majority of immigrant students are educated.

Disciplinary Policies. Certain students may be punished more often than others, particularly those who wear high-profile clothing, have high physical activity levels, or tend to hold an attitude of resistance toward schooling. Rather than defining students' predilections as deviant or disruptive, teachers can channel these interactions into cooperative groups that allow children to express themselves and learn at the same time, thus supporting rich cultural and linguistic expression.

The School Culture. The most powerful regularities about school are not found in the formalities such as course offerings and schedules. They are found in the school culture—such unspoken elements as the respect shown by students for academic endeavor, the openness that the teachers show when the principal drops in to observe instruction, and the welcome parents feel when they take an active role in the school. In its 1996 report *What Matters Most: Teaching and America's Future*, the National Commission on Teaching and America's Future argued that without a formal overhaul of school culture in America, students cannot learn well. This is a warning that applies especially to the aspects of school culture that promote success for English learners.

The Limited Role of Students. Students may be excluded from taking an active part in their own schooling, and alienation and passive frustration may result. However, in addition to language barriers, cultural differences may preclude some students from participating in ways that the mainstream culture rewards. The accompanying Example of Concept illustrates the ways in which the limited role of students is disempowering.

The Limited Role of Teachers. Teachers of CLD students may be excluded from decision making just as students are disenfranchised. This may lead teachers to have negative feelings toward their students. A supportive environment for CLD students is supportive of their teachers as well.

Example of Concept *The Limited Role of Students*

Natisha has not said a word to any of her teachers since the beginning of school. It's not that she was a "bad" student; she turned in assignments and made Bs. She certainly didn't cause her teachers trouble. Therefore Mr. Williams, her high-school counselor, was somewhat surprised to hear she was dropping out of school.

Natisha described her school experiences as coming to school, listening to teachers, and going home. School was boring and not connected to her real life. Nothing she was learning in school could help her get a job. She knew from more than ten years of listening to teachers and reading textbooks that her chances of becoming a news anchorwoman or even a teacher were about the same as winning the lottery.

School had helped silence Natisha. Classes provided no meaningful experience for her. The content may have been important to the teachers, but she could find no relationship to her own world.

Source: Adapted from Gollnick & Chinn (2006, p. 355).

Limited Family and Community Involvement. Inner-city schools with large populations of English learners may exclude families from participation. Parents may find it difficult to attend meetings, may be only symbolically involved in the governance of the school, or may feel a sense of mismatch with the culture of the school just as their children do. In circumstances like these, school personnel, in consultation with community and parent representatives, can begin to ameliorate such perceptions by talking with one another and developing means of communication and interaction appropriate for both parent and school communities (see Chapter 10).

Academic Risk Factors. Stressful events and conditions during school years create risk factors for academic success. Major obstacles that students face include attending a poorly funded inner-city school or coming from a low-income home in which English is not the primary language. Many students report having their academic capabilities questioned by school personnel: teachers who have low expectations or guidance counselors who advise against attending college or scheduling Advanced Placement (AP) courses. Even when students are placed in AP or honors courses, they are often made to feel as outsiders (Pérez, 2012).

Resilience in the Face of Risk Factors. Personal characteristics can provide protective factors that mitigate risk. Being socially competent plays an important role, as do problem-solving skills, a sense of personal autonomy, and a vision of purpose and positive future (Bernard, 1995). Good communication skills, a sense of responsibility, positive self-concept, optimism, achievement orientation, and a belief in self-help are factors that can be resources in times of stress. Resilient children have more internal and external resources to draw upon when times get tough (Luthar & Zelazo, 2003). These resources are strengthened by still other academically useful traits: forging an academic identity, being competitive, showing tenacity and determination, feeling an obligation to be a role model, and feeling obligated toward one's family (Pérez, 2012).

Coupled with parental support, these internal factors help children to overcome an environment that puts them at risk for school failure.

Academic Engagement. Several distinct school contextual factors encourage students to succeed academically. Being identified early in school as gifted is a huge "plus" toward a student's success, because this designation opens doors to academic enrichment and acceleration opportunities. Academic awards such as prizes for spelling bee competitions, "student of the month" certificates, character awards, achievement awards, and perfect attendance certificates serve as concrete evidence of recognition—especially in elementary and middle schools when students are solidifying their academic identities. Later, in high school, scholarships, sports recognitions, and leadership awards recognized merit and helped students to sustain high academic goals (Pérez, 2012).

Long-Term English Learners. Large numbers of English learners in California (and in other states) are close to the age at which they should be able to graduate from high school but still have not been redesignated. They are not yet considered English proficient—they are the so-called long-term English learners, those who have been in United States schools for more than six years without reaching sufficient English proficiency to be reclassified (Olsen, 2010). They are in the majority (59 percent) of secondary school English learners.

Olsen (2010) describes their history as characterized by their

> receiving no language development program at all; being given elementary school curricula and materials that weren't designed to meet English learner needs; enrollment in weak language development program models and poorly implemented English Learner programs; histories of inconsistent programs; provision of narrowed curricula and only partial access to the full curriculum; social segregation and linguistic isolation; and, cycles of transnational moves. (p. 2)

Often these "long-term" learners have high-functioning social language yet show grave weaknesses in academic language, reading, and writing skills. Worse, many have developed "habits of non-engagement, learned passivity and invisibility in school" (Olsen, 2010, p. 3). Because of their lack of progress, they may be placed into mainstream classes for which they are underprepared, be placed with beginning English learners, be taught by largely unprepared teachers, be precluded from participation in electives, be over-referred and inadequately served in intervention and support classes, and suffer limited access to core or college preparatory curricula.

Recommendations for modifying instruction to address these concerns include providing a specialized English Language Development program that is combined with explicit language and literacy development across the curriculum and taught by teachers skilled in adapting instruction to sustain high-support instructional techniques; placing these students in heterogeneous and rigorous grade-level content classes (including honors, A–G) mixed with English-proficient students; providing heritage language classes (in an articulated sequence through Advanced Placement levels); using a master schedule designed for flexibility and movement as students progress; using systems for monitoring progress and triggering support; and instituting a school wide focus on study skills, among other components.

A supportive classroom environment for CLD students is less effective if the environment or practices of the school are discriminatory. Chapter 11 offers ways in which teachers can exercise influence within the school and society at large to support the right of CLD students to receive an effective education.

Sociocultural Support for L1 in the Classroom Environment

Various sociocultural factors influence the support that is offered for the primary language and its speakers in the classroom. Teaching and learning in mainstream classrooms are often organized with social structures that deny the ways in which students are most likely to learn. Many students may benefit from the opportunity to interact with peers as they learn, speaking their primary language if necessary to exchange information.

Cooperative learning has positive results in the education of CLD students. Positive race relations among students and socialization toward pro-social values and behaviors are potential outcomes of a cooperative-learning environment. Students may gain psychological support from one another as they acquire English, and this support can help the students work as a group with the teacher to achieve a workable sociocultural compromise between the use of L1 and L2 in the classroom.

Adapted Instruction

Supporting the Primary Language

- Feature the primary language(s) of students on bulletin boards throughout the school and within the classroom.
- Showcase primary-language skills in written and oral reports.
- Involve primary-language speakers as guests, volunteers, and instructional assistants.

This chapter introduced the English learner and highlighted a variety of factors that a teacher must consider to design and deliver effective instruction. Some of these factors lie within the student, and others are factors in society at large that affect the individual, the family, and the school. The teacher as an intercultural, interlinguistic educator learns everything possible about the background of the students and marshals every available kind of support to advance the education of English learners.

LEARNING MORE

Further Reading

Carolyn Nelson (2004), in the article "Reclaiming Teacher Preparation for Success in High-Needs Schools," describes her first year of teaching in an inner-city school in Rochester, New York. This article offers a memorable glimpse at her daily challenges in a school comprised largely of Puerto Rican and African-American students. She details the strengths of the elementary teacher education curriculum at San José State in the context of preparing teachers as problem-solving intellectuals, a point of view that imparts a balance to the "prescriptive, curriculum-in-a-box" approaches to teaching.

Web Search

The U.S. Census Bureau's website "Minority Links" (online at http://www.census.gov /newsroom/minority_links/minority_links.html) features demographic information on special populations (Hispanic/Latino, Asian, Native Hawaiian and other Pacific Islander, and American Indian/Alaska Native) that includes demographics by regional, state, and local areas.

Exploration

Find out about the number of English learners in your local school district by visiting a local school district office, or look it up in the demographics section of the State Department of Education website in your state. Visit a school in a neighborhood that serves CLD students, or visit your neighborhood school and ask if there are English learners being served. If there are local teachers who specialize in the education of English learners, ask them about professional development opportunities in that field.

Experiment

Give a fifteen-word list in a foreign language to three different individuals: a primary school student (age 6–11), a middle school student (age 12–14), and an adult (age 18 or older). Let them study the words for five minutes and then ask them to recall the list. Compare the success of these learners. Ask them what strategy they used to complete the memory task. Which learner had more success? Which learner had more strategies?

MyEducationLab™

Culture and Self-Esteem

This video discusses that it is important for English-language learners to retain their self-esteem. Often they are made to feel inferior to students from different cultures. Teaching culture should go both ways.

To access the video, go to MyEducationLab (www.myeducationlab.com), choose the Díaz-Rico text, and log in to MyEducationLab for English Language Learners. Select the topic Diversity, and watch the video entitled "Culture and Self-Esteem."

Answer the following questions:

1. How would you define "self-efficacy"? What role does the teacher play in fostering this?

2. What are the possible consequences of teaching without concern for an individual's native culture?

3. What specific teaching strategies should a teacher include to ensure that all students are made to feel valued?

2

Learning about Language Structure

Language is dynamic—and young people are usually on the cutting edge of language change.

© Andy Dean Photography/Shutterstock

When I'm Fifteen

When I'm fifteen . . .
I want to be a moon fixer—
The pieces that fall off
To glue them back on.
And I'll be a tree pushermover

'Cause they lean over too far.
I want to kill bugs
And put flies on them,
And catch cats and
Put them back in their houses.

Sebastien G-E, age 4
Trilingual: Hungarian, English, French

Language—what it can do for us! It allows us to express hopes and dreams, as this young boy has done in his chat with a friend. It takes us beyond the here and now. It connects one individual to another. It communicates the heights of joy and the depths of despair. Language belongs to everyone, from the preschooler to the professor. Almost all aspects of a person's life are touched by language: Everyone speaks and everyone listens. People argue about language, sometimes quite passionately and eloquently. Language is universal, and yet each language has evolved to meet the experiences, needs, and desires of that language's community.

Understanding language structure and use builds teachers' confidence and provides them with essential tools to help their students learn (see figure on page 1). One of the fascinating facts about language is that speakers learn their first language without understanding how language "works." Thus, native speakers can converse fluently but may not be able to explain a sound pattern, a grammatical point, or the use of a certain expression to get their needs met. To them, that is "just the way it is."

This chapter explores these various aspects of language and provides examples and suggestions to help English-language-development (ELD) teachers pinpoint student needs and provide appropriate instruction. Such knowledge also helps teachers recognize the richness and variety of students' emerging language.

Language Universals

At last count, 7,358 languages are spoken in today's world (SIL International, 2009). Although not all of these have been intensely studied, linguists have carried out enough investigations over the centuries to posit some universal facts about language.

Language Is Dynamic

Languages change over time. Vocabulary changes are the most obvious: Words disappear, such as *tang* and *swik*. Words expand their meanings, such as *chip* and *mouse*. New words appear, such as *visitability* and *cyberbalkanization*. But languages change in many ways, not just in semantic meaning. Pronunciation (phonology) changes. We recognize that pronunciation in English has altered over time because the spelling of some words is archaic: We no longer pronounce the *k* in know or the *w* in write; at one time, the vowel sounds in *tie*, *sky*, and *high* did not rhyme. Even common words such as *tomato* and *park* are pronounced differently depending on which part of the country the speaker is from, indicating that part of the dynamics of language comes from dialectical differences.

Morphological (word form) changes have occurred in English, such as the gradual elimination of declension endings in nouns and verbs. Only the change in form of the third person ("he goes") remains in the declension of present-tense verbs, and only the plural shift remains in the inflection of nouns. Syntactically, as the inflections dropped off nouns, word order became fixed. Pragmatically, the fusing of the English second person into the single form *you* avoided many of the status distinctions still preserved in European languages.

Teachers who respect the dynamic nature of language can take delight in learners' approximations of English rather than be annoyed by constructions that can be considered mistakes. When a student writes, "When school was out he fell in love with a young girl, July" (meaning "Julie"), rather than correcting the misspelling, a teacher can consider that "July" may be a better way to spell the name of a summer love!

Language Is Complex

Without question, using language is one of the most complex of human activities. The wide range of concepts, both concrete and abstract, that language can convey—and the fact that this ability is the norm for human beings rather than the exception— combines with its dynamic quality to provide the human race with a powerful and flexible psychological tool.

No languages are "primitive." All languages are equally complex, capable of expressing a wide range of ideas, and expandable to include new words for new concepts.

Language is arbitrary. The relationships between the sounds and the meanings of spoken languages and between gestures and meanings of sign languages are, for the most part, not caused by any natural or necessary reason (such as reflecting a sound, like "buzz" for the sound that bees make when they fly). There is no inherent reason to call an object "table" or "mesa" or "danh t." Those just happen to be the sounds that English, Spanish, and Vietnamese speakers use.

Language comes easily to human beings. Every normal child, born anywhere in the world, of any racial, geographical, social, or economic heritage, is capable of learning any language to which he or she is exposed.

Language is open-ended. Speakers of a language are capable of producing and comprehending an infinite set of sentences. As we will see later, these facts help teachers recognize that their learners are proficient language users who can and will produce novel and complex sentences and thoughts in their own and their developing languages.

All Languages Have Structure

All human languages use a finite set of sounds (or gestures) that are combined to form meaningful elements or words, which themselves form an infinite set of possible sentences. Every spoken language also uses discrete sound segments, such as /p/, /n/, or /a/, and has a class of vowels and a class of consonants.

All grammars contain rules for the formation of words and sentences of a similar kind, and similar grammatical categories (for example, noun, verb) are found in all languages. Every language has a way of referring to past time; the ability to negate; and the ability to form questions, issue commands, and so on.

Teachers who are familiar with the structure of language can use this knowledge to design learning activities that build the language of English learners in a systematic way. Linguistic knowledge—not only about English but also about the possibilities inherent in languages that differ from English—helps teachers to view the language world of the English learner with insight and empathy.

Phonology: The Sound Patterns of Language

Phonology is the study of the system or pattern of speech sounds. Native speakers know intuitively the patterns of their mother tongue and when given a list of nonsense words can recognize which are possible pronunciations in their language.

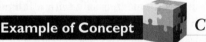

Example of Concept   *Could It Be English?*

Which of the following are *possible* English words and which would be *impossible* because they do not fit the English sound system?

dschang	borogrove	jëfandikoo
nde	takkies	

Phonemes

Phonemes are the sounds that make up a language. They are the distinctive units that "make a difference" when sounds form words. For example, in English the initial consonant sounds /t/ and /d/ are the only difference between the words *tip* and *dip* and are thus phonemes. The number of phonemes in a language ranges between twenty and fifty; English has a high average count, from thirty-four to forty-five, depending on the dialect.

Each language has permissible ways in which phonemes can be combined. These are called *phonemic* sequences. In English, /spr/ as in spring, /nd/ as in *handle*, and /kt/ as in talked are phonemic sequences. Languages also have permissible places for these sequences: initial (at the beginning of a word), medial (between initial and final position), and final (at the end of a word), or in a combination of these positions. English, for example, uses /sp/ in all three positions—*speak, respect, grasp*—but uses /tr/ in only two—*trial, metro*. Spanish, on the other hand, uses the sequence /sp/ medially—*español*—but never initially. This would explain why, in speaking English, native-Spanish speakers may say "espeak." Not all of the permissible sequences are used in every pattern. For example, English has /cr/ and /br/ as initial consonant clusters. *Craft* is a word but—at present—*braft* is not, although it would be phonologically permissible. *Nkaft*, on the other hand, is not permissible because /nk/ is not an initial cluster in English.

Phonemes can be described in terms of their characteristic point of articulation (tip, front, or back of the tongue), the manner of articulation (the way the airstream is obstructed), and whether the vocal cords vibrate or not (voiced and voiceless sounds). Not all languages distinguish between voiced and voiceless sounds. Arabic speakers may say "barking lot" instead of "parking lot" because to them /p/ and /b/ are not distinguishable.

Although learners may be able to articulate all the phonemes in their native language, they do not necessarily have phonemic awareness—such knowledge as what is a sound unit, how many phonemes there are in a given word, and how one phoneme may change the sound of an adjacent one.

Pitch

Besides the actual formation of sounds, other sound qualities are important in speech. Pitch, the vibration of the vocal chords, is important in distinguishing meaning within a sentence: "Eva is going," as a statement, is said with a falling pitch, but when it is used as a question, the pitch rises at the end. This use of pitch to modify the sentence meaning is called *intonation*. Languages that use the pitch of individual syllables to contrast meanings are called *tone languages*. Pitch, whether at the word level or at the sentence level, is one of the phonological components of a language that plays an important role in determining meaning.

Stress

Stress, the increase in vocal activity, also modifies the meaning of words. Speakers of English as a second language must learn to properly stress syllables in a word or words in a sentence, because in American English, syllables and words are not said with equal stress: particular syllables and words are emphasized with a higher pitch, a louder volume, and/or a longer vowel.

There are some rules to follow when learning what to stress. For example, in compound words, the first syllable is stressed: *checkbook*, *take-out*, *cell phone*. When saying proper nouns, the rule is opposite: the last word in a phrase is stressed: Statue of Liberty, Golden Gate Bridge, President Clinton. A similar rule is followed for abbreviations: the last initial is emphasized: Ph.D., IBM, HBO. With homonyms, the first syllable is accented for nouns, the second for verbs: Project/project, record/record (Wilner & Feinstein-Whitaker, 2008).

One aspect of English pronunciation that is often difficult for English learners is the fact that English speakers not only reduce the vowels in unaccented syllables to the schwa sound, but also de-emphasize unimportant words in a sentence, creating a strong contrast that highlights the focus of meaning. Contractions—shortened forms of pronoun–auxiliary verb combinations—are one form of de-emphasis, and reductions are another ("n" for *and*; "'e" for *he*; "'er" for *her*). These elements may require focused listening training, especially because pronouns carry important contextual information, without which a listener may become confused (Gilbert, 2006).

Correct pronunciation is one of the most difficult features of learning a second language. Teachers who overemphasize correct pronunciation when learners are in the early stages of learning English may hinder the innovative spirit of risk taking that is preferable when a learner is trying to achieve fluency. Instead, teaching intonation through fun activities such as chants and songs brings enjoyment to language learning.

Native speakers are seldom if ever explicitly taught the phonological rules of their language, yet they know them. Phonological knowledge is acquired as a learner listens to and begins to produce speech. The same is true in a second language. A learner routinely exposed to a specific dialect or accent in English views it as the target language.

The Sound System as Written Language

Spelling in English has long been difficult, but some anomalies persist for a reason. Related words with similar spellings may have contrasting phonemes, such as *medical* and *medicine* (the *c* is pronounced as *k* in one and as *s* in the other). Silent letters are not always better eliminated; for example, *g* in *sign* is silent, but it remains as a holdover from its relative, the *g* that is pronounced in *signify*. People may complain that homonyms should be spelled the same, but the visual distinction serves a purpose to clarify meanings when written. Moreover, even if they were spelled the same, some homonyms would still diverge in some dialects (the words *are* and *our* are homonyms only in certain dialects). Therefore the current spelling system, while inconsistent, is not always illogical (Freeman & Freeman, 2004).

No language has a writing system in which letters exactly represent the corresponding sounds. One letter may have two sounds, and a sound may be written more than one way. Linguists use phonemic transcription to represent sounds in a consistent way, using slash marks to indicate phonemes (for example, /m/ for the first phoneme in *make*). For even more precise rendering, linguists use a phonetic transcription, employing brackets. For example, some people pronounce *which* and *witch* alike, using the phoneme /w/. Others distinguish these words using a [w^h] sound for *which*.

> **Did You Know?** Linguists use the International Phonetics Alphabet (http://en.wikipedia.org/wiki/International_Phonetic_Alphabet) to describe phonemes precisely. Student dictionaries also have phonetic conventions that are specific to that book.

Morphology: The Words of Language

Morphology is the study of the meaning units in a language. Many people believe that individual words constitute these basic meaning units. However, many words can be broken down into smaller segments—morphemes—that still retain meaning.

Morphemes

Morphemes are the basic building blocks of meaning. *Abolitionists* is an English word composed of four morphemes: *aboli* + *tion* + *ist* + *s* (root + noun-forming suffix

+ noun-forming suffix + plural marker). Morphemes can be represented by a single sound, such as /a/ (as a morpheme, this means "without" as in *amoral* or *asexual*); a syllable, such as the noun-forming suffix *-ment* in *amendment*; or two or more syllables, such as in *tiger* or *artichoke*. Two different morphemes may have the same sound, such as the /er/ as in *dancer* ("one who dances") and the /er/ in *fancier* (the comparative form of *fancy*). A morpheme may also have alternate phonetic forms: The regular plural *-s* can be pronounced either /z/ (*bags*), /s/ (*cats*), or /iz/ (*bushes*).

Morphemes are of different types and serve different purposes. *Free morphemes* can stand alone (*envelop, the, through*), whereas *bound morphemes* occur only in conjunction with others (*-ing, dis-, -ceive*). Most bound morphemes occur as *affixes*. (The others are bound roots.) Affixes at the beginning of words are *prefixes* (*un-* in the word *unafraid*); those added at the end are *suffixes* (*-able* in the word *believable*); and *infixes* are morphemes that are inserted into other morphemes (*-zu-* in the German word *anzufangen*, "to begin").

Part of the power and flexibility of English is the ease with which families of words can be understood by knowing the rules for forming nouns from verbs and so forth—for example, knowing that the suffix *-ism* means "a doctrine, system, or philosophy" and *-ist* means "one who follows a doctrine, system, or philosophy." This predictability can make it easier for students to learn to infer words from context rather than to rely on rote memorization.

Example of Concept *Working with Morphemes*

At the beginning of the science unit, Mrs. Pierdant selected several roots from a general list (*astro, bio, geo, hydr, luna, photo, phys, terr*) along with a representative word. She then had students look for and make a list of words with those roots from various chapters in the science text. Next she gave the students a list of prefixes and affixes and asked each team to generate five to ten new words with their definitions. Students played various guess-the-meaning games with the new words. Interest in science increased after these activities.

Word-Formation Processes

English has historically been a language that has welcomed new words—either borrowing them from other languages or coining new ones from existing words. Studying processes of word formation heightens students' interest in vocabulary building.

Example of Concept *Creating New Words*

Product names often use existing morphemes combined in ways to create a new word that fits within the English sound system and evokes a positive image for the product. For example, "Aleve" connotes "alleviate," as in making a headache better.

Clipping. Clipping is a process of shortening words, such as *prof* for *professor* or the slangy *teach* for *teacher*. Learning two words for one gives students a sense that they are mastering both colloquial and academic speech.

Acronyms. In English, *acronyms* are plentiful, and many are already familiar to students—UN, CIA, and NASA, for example. A growing list of acronyms helps students increase their vocabulary of both the words forming the acronyms and the acronyms themselves. Who can resist knowing that *scuba* is a *self-contained underwater breathing apparatus?*

Computer Shorthand. Acronyms are also used to text or type using a computer or cell phone. Examples include BRB (be right back), CYL (catch you later), CYT (see you tomorrow), IMHO (in my humble opinion), LMK (let me know), NM (never mind), ROFL (rolling on the floor laughing), and WTH (what the heck). For a glossary of chat room abbreviations, go to www.petrospec-technologies.com/Herkommer /chatword.htm.

Blends. Words formed from parts of two words are called blends—for example, *smog* from *smoke* + *fog*, *brunch* from *breakfast* + *lunch*, and *blog* from *web* + *log*. The prefixes *e-* and *i-* have combined to form many new words and concepts over recent decades (e.g., *e-commerce* and *iTunes*). Students can become word detectives and discover new blends through shopping (Walmart?) or advertisements, or add to their enjoyment of learning English by finding new words and creating their own. The study of morphology adds fun to learning English as well as word power.

Syntax: The Sentence Patterns of Language

Syntax refers to the structure of sentences and the rules that govern the formation of a sentence. Sentences are composed of words that follow patterns, but sentence meaning is more than the sum of the meaning of the words. Sentence A, "The teacher asked the students to sit down," has the same words as sentence B, "The students asked the teacher to sit down," but not the same meaning.

All native speakers of a language can distinguish syntactically correct from syntactically incorrect combinations of words. This syntactic knowledge in the native language is not taught in school but is constructed as native speakers acquire their language as children. This internal knowledge allows speakers to recognize the sentence "'Twas brillig and the slithy toves did gyre and gimble in the wabes" in Lewis Carroll's poem "Jabberwocky" as syntactically correct English, even though the words are nonsense.

Fortunately, speakers of a language who have this knowledge of correct and incorrect sentences can, in fact, understand sentences that are not perfectly formed. Sentences that contain minor syntactic errors, such as the preschool student's poem cited at the beginning of this chapter, are still comprehensible.

Adapted Instruction

English Syntax and Mandarin Speakers

English learners with Mandarin as a mother tongue may need additional teacher assistance with the following aspects of English:

- Verb tense: *I see him yesterday.* (In Mandarin, the adverb signals the tense, not the verb, and the verb form is not changed to mark tense; so in English changing the verb form may prove to be difficult for the learner.)

- Subject–verb agreement: *He see me.* (In Mandarin, verbs do not change form to create subject–verb agreement.)

- Word order: *I at home ate.* (In Mandarin, prepositional phrases come before the verb—the rules governing the flexibility in adverb-phrase placement in English are difficult for many learners.)

- Plurals: *They give me 3 dollar.* (In Mandarin, like English, the marker indicates number, but in English the noun form changes as well.)

Whereas syntax refers to the internally constructed rules that make sentences, *grammar* looks at whether a sentence conforms to a standard. An important distinction, therefore, is the one between standard and colloquial usage. Many colloquial usages are acceptable sentence patterns in English, even though their usage is not standard—for example, "I ain't got no pencil" is acceptable English syntax. It is not, however, standard usage. Through example and in lessons, teachers who are promoting the standard dialect need to be aware that students' developing competence will not always conform to that standard and that students will also learn colloquial expressions they will not always use in the appropriate context (see the Appropriate Language section later in this chapter).

Adapted Instruction

Teaching Grammar

Grammar need not be a difficult or boring subject. Grammar rules for forming verb tenses in English, for example, are easy to learn; only about fifty commonly used verbs are irregular, and the rules for irregular verbs have their own consistency (see Jesness, 2004). Parts of speech are used in a regular way. Teachers who take the time to become proficient in discussing the rules of grammar are much more effective teachers of English to speakers of other languages. There are many amusing ways to teach grammar, like asking absurd questions ("Do you sleep in the doghouse?") to help students use negative sentences ("No, I don't.").

Example of Concept *Colloquial versus Standard Usage*

As Mrs. Ralfe hears students using new colloquial phrases, she has them write them on the left half of a poster hanging in the room. At the end of the day, she and the students discuss the phrases and how to say them in a more standard English. The students then write the standard phrase on the right side of the poster.

Semantics: The Meanings of Language

Semantics is the study of meanings of individual words and of larger units such as phrases and sentences. Speakers of a language have learned the "agreed-upon" meanings of words and phrases in their language and are not free to change meanings of words at will, which would result in no communication at all (Fromkin, Rodman, and Hyams, 2009).

Some words carry a high degree of stability and conformity in the ways they are used (*kick* as a verb, for example, must involve the foot—"He kicked me with his hand" is not semantically correct). Other words carry multiple meanings (e.g., *break*), ambiguous meanings (*bank*, as in "They're at the bank"), or debatable meanings (*marriage*, for example, for many people can refer only to heterosexual alliances, and to use it for nonheterosexual contexts is not only unacceptable but inflammatory to them). For second-language acquisition, the process of translating already-recognized meaning from one language to the next is only part of the challenge.

Another challenge is that the English language is extraordinarily rich in synonyms. One estimate of English vocabulary places the number at over three million words. Fortunately, only about 200,000 words are in common use, and an educated person uses about 2,000 in a week (Wilton, 2003). The challenge when learning this vast vocabulary is to distinguish denotations, connotations, and other shades of meaning.

Adapted Instruction

Denotations and Connotations

- With students, generate a list of eight to ten thematically linked words, such as colors.
- Have students define each word using objects, drawings, or basic definitions (denotation).
- Elicit or provide connotative (the implied, emotional) meanings of the words, for example: *red* = irritated or angry.
- During their independent reading, have students be alert to the connotative use of the words. Add representative sentences to the chart.

About two-thirds of English words did not originate in English, but are borrowed from around the world. English has borrowed words for beasts (*aardvark*, from Afrikaans, *zebra* from Bantu), for food and drink (*coffee* from Arabic, *pretzel* from German, *paprika* from Hungarian), or clothes (*khaki* from Hindi), for dances (*tango* from Ibibio, *hula* from Hawai'ian), spiritual ideas (*messiah* from Hebrew), vices (*cigar* from Maya), politics (*caucus* from Iroquois, *fascist* from Italian), and for miscellaneous ideas (*berserk* from Norse, *sleazy* from Latvian, *kowtow* from Mandarin). Visit www.krysstal.com/borrow.html to find other examples. Our world would be impoverished without these loanwords to discuss spice, samba, and the martial arts!

Adapted Instruction

Borrowed Words

Making charts of English words that English learners use in their first language and words English has borrowed from the students' native languages increases everyone's vocabulary and often generates interesting discussions about food, clothing, cultural artifacts, and the ever-expanding world of technology.

Speakers of a language must also make semantic shifts when writing. It may be understandable when a speaker uses the colloquial "And then she goes . . ." to mean "she says," but in academic English, one must make a semantic shift toward formality, using synonyms such as "she declared," "she remarked," and "she admitted." A teacher who encourages this type of semantic expansion helps students acquire semantic flexibility.

Example of Concept   *Learning Synonyms*

Each week, Mrs. Arias selects five to eight groups of synonyms from a list (Kress, 1993). During time spent at a language center, pairs of students choose two groups to study. They look up the words and write definitions, write a story incorporating the words (five) in each group, or develop games and quizzes for their classmates to play. At the end of the week, students report on their learning.

Semantics also includes word meanings that have become overused and trite. A list of clichés to avoid in the near future: proactive, utilized, closure, über, basically, whatever, touch base, absolutely, and no problem (*Los Angeles Times*, 2008, p. M2).

So what does it mean to "know" a word? The meaning of words comes partially from the stored meaning and partially from the meaning derived from context. In addition, knowing a word includes the ability to pronounce the word correctly, to use the word grammatically in a sentence, and to know which morphemes are appropriately connected with the word. This knowledge is acquired as the brain absorbs and interacts with the meaning in context. For English learners, acquiring new vocabulary in semantically related groups helps them make connections and retain important concepts.

Pragmatics: The Influence of Context

Pragmatics is the study of communication in context. It includes three major communication skills. The first is the ability to use language for different functions—greeting, informing, demanding, promising, requesting, and so on. The second is the ability to appropriately adapt or change language according to the listener or situation—talking differently to a friend than to a principal, or talking differently in a classroom than on a playground. The third ability is to follow rules for conversations and narrative—knowing how to tell a story, give a book report, or recount events of the day. Because these pragmatic ways of using speech vary depending on language and culture (Maciejewski, 2003), teachers who understand these differences can help learners to adjust their pragmatics to those that "work" when speaking English.

Language Functions

Halliday (1978) distinguished seven different functions for language: *instrumental* (getting needs met); *regulatory* (controlling others' behavior); *informative* (communicating information); *interactional* (establishing social relationships); *personal* (expressing individuality); *heuristic* (investigating and acquiring knowledge); and *imaginative* (expressing fantasy). Providing English learners with opportunities to engage in the various functions is critical for them to develop a full pragmatic range in English.

Adapted Instruction

Promoting Language Functions

- *Instrumental:* Analyze advertising and propaganda so that students learn how people use language to get what they want.
- *Regulatory:* Allow students to be in charge of small and large groups.
- *Informative:* Have students keep records of events over periods of time, review their records, and draw conclusions; for example, keeping records of classroom pets, weather patterns, or building constructions.
- *Interactional:* Have students work together to plan field trips, social events, and classroom and school projects.
- *Personal:* Encourage students to share thoughts and opinions.
- *Heuristic:* In projects, ask questions that no one, including the teacher, knows the answer to.
- *Imaginative:* Encourage "play" with language—the sounds of words and the images they convey.

Source: Adapted from Pinnell (1985).

Appropriate Language

To speak appropriately, the speaker must take into account the gender, status, age, and cultural background of the listener. The term *speech register* is often used to denote the varieties of language that take these factors into consideration. For example, in the classroom in which the teacher's assistant is an older woman who shares the language and culture of the children, students may converse with her in a manner similar to the interactions with their own mothers, whereas their discourse with the teacher could reflect usage reserved for more formal situations. A reverse of these registers would be inappropriate.

Example of Concept   *Learning to Be Appropriate*

In preparation for a drama unit, Mrs. Morley has her students develop short conversations that might occur with different people in different situations, such as selling ice cream to a child, a teenager, a working adult, and a retiree. Pairs of students perform their conversations and the class critiques the appropriateness of the language. Students develop a feel for appropriate expressions, tones, and stances before working on plays and skits.

Conversational Rules

Numerous aspects of conversation carry unexamined rules. Conversations generally follow a script. There are procedures for turn taking, for introducing and maintaining topics, and for clarifying misunderstandings.

Classroom Interacting Patterns. Classroom procedures have patterns, and one of the important tasks of kindergarten and first-grade teachers is to teach children how to initiate and respond appropriately in the school setting. Confusion and possibly a sense of alienation can arise for English learners who are used to the school patterns in their own countries and find a different one in U.S. schools. It may take time—and explicit coaching—for students to learn the set of behaviors appropriate for a U.S. school context.

Turn Taking. Speakers of a language have internalized the rules of when to speak, when to remain silent, how long to speak, how long to remain silent, how to give up "the floor," how to enter into a conversation, and so on. Linguistic devices such as intonation, pausing, and phrasing are used to signal an exchange of turns. Some groups of people wait for a clear pause before beginning their turn to speak, whereas others start while the speaker is winding down. It is often this difference in when to take the floor that causes feelings of unease and sometimes hostility. A speaker may constantly feel that he is being interrupted or pushed in a conversation or, conversely, that he has to keep talking because his partner does not join in when appropriate.

Topic Focus and Relevance. These elements involve the ability of conversationalists to explore and maintain one another's interest in topics that are introduced, the context of the conversation, the genre of the interchange (storytelling, excuse making), and the relationship between the speakers.

Conversational Repair. This involves techniques for clearing up misunderstandings and maintaining conversation. For example, a listener confused by the speaker's use of the pronoun *she* might ask, "Do you mean Sally's aunt or her cousin?" With English learners, the alert teacher will notice quizzical looks rather than specific conversational interactions that signal lack of understanding.

Classroom Discourse. Although classroom discourse patterns vary greatly across cultures, they also show some remarkable similarities. For example, research on U.S. classrooms shows that teachers talk about 70 percent of the time, and when they talk, about 60 percent of the time they ask questions that students are expected to answer. Often these questions are *display questions* that ask students to answer quickly with information that has been memorized. Typically, students are given less than one second to respond (Andrews, 2001).

Many students have difficulty learning the classroom discourse patterns of another culture:

> I had difficulty with the opinion in the class where peoples in groups discuss about subject. I was surrounded by Americans with whom I couldn't follow their tempo of discussion half of the time. I have difficulty to listen and speak, but also with the way they handle the group. I felt uncomfortable because sometimes they believe their opinion strongly. I had been very serious about the whole subject but I was afraid I would say something wrong. I had the idea but not the words. (Barna, 2007, p. 68)

Nonverbal Communication

A complex nonverbal system accompanies, complements, or takes the place of the verbal. "An elaborate and secret code that is written nowhere, known by none, and understood by all" is Edward Sapir's definition of nonverbal behavior (quoted in Miller, 1985). This nonverbal system involves sending and receiving messages through gesture, facial expression, eye contact, posture, and tone of voice. Because this nonverbal system accounts for a large part of the emotional message given and received, awareness of its various aspects helps teachers to recognize students' nonverbal messages.

Body Language

Body language, the way one holds and positions oneself, is one way teachers communicate their authority in the classroom. Standing in front of the room, they become the focus of attention. In turn, students' body language communicates that they are paying attention (eyes up front and hands folded is the standard way teachers expect attentive students to act). Students who look engaged are often seen as more successful academically.

In a parent conference, for example, cultural differences in body language may impede communication. Parents may need to be formally ushered into the classroom and not merely waved in with a flick of the hand. Parents from a culture that offers elaborate respect for the teacher may become uncomfortable if the teacher slouches, moves his or her chair too intimately toward the parent, or otherwise compromises the formal nature of the interchange.

Gestures

Gestures—expressive motions or actions made with hands, arms, head, or even the whole body—are culturally based signs that are often misunderstood. Gestures are commonly used to convey "come here," "good-bye," "yes," "no," and "I don't know." In European American culture, for example, "come here" is signaled by holding the hand vertically, palm facing the body, and moving the index finger rapidly back and forth. In other cultures, it is signaled by holding the hand in a more horizontal position, palm facing down, and moving the fingers rapidly back and forth. "Yes" is generally signaled by a nod of the head, but in some places a shake of the head means "yes." This can be particularly unnerving for teachers if they constantly interpret the students' head shakes as rejection rather than affirmation.

Example of Concept   *Teaching Gestures*

Preteach and demonstrate the twelve gestures that accompany the phrases below. Form groups in circles of four or five. Give each a set of twenty-four cards (two each of the twelve gestures). A student from each group picks a card and acts out the gesture on the card. The other group members must try to guess the expression that goes with the card. When someone has guessed correctly, the turn passes to the next person in the circle. The first group to get through all the cards wins the game.

1. Please come over here.
2. Don't worry!
3. Psst! Over here!
4. I'm hoping!
5. Good work!
6. I'm cold!
7. Don't tell!
8. I'm bored . . .

Source: Based on Saslow & Ascher (2006).

Facial Expressions

Through the use of eyebrows, eyes, cheeks, nose, lips, tongue, and chin, people nonverbally signal any number of emotions, opinions, and moods. Smiles and winks, tongue thrusts, and chin jutting can have different meanings depending on the context within a culture as well as across cultures. Americans, for example, are sometimes perceived by others as being emotionally superficial because of the amount of smiling they do, even to strangers. In some cultures, smiles are reserved for close friends and family.

Eye Contact

Eye contact is another communication device that is highly variable and frequently misunderstood. Both insufficient and excessive eye contact create feelings of unease, yet it is so subject to individual variation that there are no hard-and-fast rules to describe it. Generally, children in European American culture are taught not to stare but are expected to look people in the eye when addressing them. In some cultures, however, children learn that the correct way to listen is to avoid direct eye contact with the speaker. In the following dialogue, the teacher incorrectly interprets Sylvia's downcast eyes as an admission of guilt because, in the teacher's culture, eye avoidance signals culpability.

> **Teacher:** Sylvia and Amanda, I want to hear what happened on the playground.
> **Amanda:** (looks at teacher) Sylvia hit me with the jump rope.
> **Teacher:** (turning to Sylvia) Sylvia, did you hit her?
> **Sylvia:** (looking at her feet) No.
> **Teacher:** Look at me, Sylvia. Am I going to have to take the jump rope away?
> **Sylvia:** (continuing to look down) No.

By being aware that eye contact norms vary, teachers can begin to move beyond feelings of mistrust and open up lines of communication. If a student's culture mandates that a young person not look an adult in the eye when directly addressed, the teacher may need to explain to the student that in English the rules of address call for different behavior.

Communicative Distance

People maintain distance between themselves and others, an invisible wall or "bubble" that defines a person's personal space. Violating a person's space norm can be interpreted as aggressive behavior. In the United States, an accidental bumping of another person requires an "excuse me" or "pardon me." In Arab countries, such inadvertent contact does not violate the individual's space and requires no verbal apology.

Adapted Instruction

Learning about Communicative Distance

- *Interviews.* Students interview others and ask questions such as "What distance is too close for a friend? For a family member?" "At what distance do you stand to an adult, a teacher, or a clerk?"
- *Observations.* Students observe people, videos, pictures, and television and compare these people's distance behavior in relation to the situation, culture, sex of participants, and so forth.

Source: Adapted from Arias (1996).

Conceptions of Time

In the mainstream culture of the United States, individuals' understanding of time may be at odds with that of students of other cultures. For speakers of English, time is handled as if it were a material. English expressions include "saving time," "spending time," and "wasting time." Time is considered to be a commodity, and those who misuse this commodity earn disapproval.

With an awareness of mainstream U.S. conceptions of time, teachers become more understanding of students and their families whose time values differ from their own, and are willing to make allowances for such differences. In oral discourse, some students may need more time to express themselves, not because of language shortcomings per se, but because the timing of oral discourse is slower in their culture.

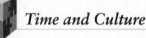

Example of Concept   *Time and Culture*

Parents who were raised in cultures with radically different concepts of time may not be punctual to the minute for parent conferences. One group of teachers allowed for this by not scheduling specific individual conference times. Instead, they designated blocks of three hours when they would be available for conferences, and parents arrived when they could.

Language allows speakers a means for rich and dynamic expression. By knowing about language and its various properties and components, teachers are in a position to promote English-language development while welcoming students' primary languages as an alternative vehicle for self-expression. Languages have universal features; so, regardless of the language of the student, teachers are assured that by having successfully acquired one language, students will also be successful in a second (or third or fourth). Understanding the basics of language helps to make language learning a meaningful, purposeful, and shared endeavor.

LEARNING MORE

Thinking It Over

What do people need to know to talk to one another? List as many rules as you can that you think must be followed by people who are interacting in face-to-face conversations. How do children learn these rules? (Adapted from Farrell, 2006)

Web Search

To learn more about the subsystems of language, Dr. R. Beard provides short, amusing, enlightening essays.

- How to Pronounce "Ghoti" . . . and Why (www.facstaff.bucknell.edu/rbeard/phono.html)
- There Are No Such Things as Words (www.facstaff.bucknell.edu/rbeard/words.html)

- You Have to Pay Your Syntax (www.facstaff.bucknell.edu/rbeard/syntax.html)
- Can Colorless Green Ideas Sleep Furiously? (www.facstaff.bucknell.edu/rbeard /semantic.html)

Exploration

Go through the checkout line at a grocery store. Pay attention to the verbal and nonverbal elements of the checkout procedure. Record as much as possible of the procedure. Repeat this procedure, observe others going through the same procedure, or engage in the exploration with several colleagues. Look for patterns. What signals the beginning? What words are exchanged? What topics of conversation are permissible? How does the interaction terminate? Once you've discovered the script for the checkout, begin to pay attention to the scripts in your classroom.

Try It in the Classroom

Engage students in an activity to determine personal comfort in distance. Have students stand in two opposing lines. At a signal, have one line move one step toward the other. Repeat, alternating the line that moves until a student says, "Stop." Mark that distance. Continue until all students have said "Stop." Discuss the implications of the various distances. The activity can also be done sitting.

MyEducationLab™

An ESL Vocabulary Lesson

In this video, the teacher demonstrates a vocabulary lesson in which she first pronounces each word, has the children pronounce each word, and then asks students to make vocabulary cards of the words for study. Next, she gives a definition of each word, sometimes has children act out a word, and describes each word in ways that will help the children know them. Finally, they write their own sentences with the words and play games with the words to build fluency.

To access the video, go to MyEducationLab (www.myeducationlab.com), choose the Díaz-Rico text, and log in to MyEducationLab for English Language Learners. Select the topic Vocabulary, and watch the video entitled "An ESL Vocabulary Lesson."

Answer the following questions:

1. How could these words be taught differently?

2. Would this lesson be very different for older students who are beginners in English-language development? Intermediate in English-language development? How?

3. What difference does it make in long-term retention if vocabulary words are presented with or without an accompanying context?

3

Learning about Second-Language Acquisition

Students develop communicative competence as they use language to interact with one another.

A few months ago in class a student approached me; she was distressed about her lack of friends at work. She was a young Korean woman who had gotten a job in Los Angeles in the art department of a small film company. She was almost completely fluent in English and that's why she was frustrated. Somehow, her ability to speak the language was not enough to create friendships with her peers. Consequently, she felt lonely and isolated.

I asked her for an example of where she thought things fell apart with her language. She said that every Monday when she would come to work someone would ask her, "How was your weekend, what did you do?" She would respond, "I went to shop, I bought a dress. . . . I went out to a nice restaurant with my friend. . . . I saw a movie on TV. . . ."

I explained to her that when people ask those questions, they are more interested in connecting than actually hearing a list of activities. She then said, "How does one connect? What part of the language am I not using?"

This got me thinking. Language is more than vocabulary and grammatical structure. It's more than simply knowing all the verb tenses or idiomatic expressions. It's more than communicating facts. Language that really engages people includes facial expressions, physical gestures, pauses, hesitations, intonation, cadence, inflection, and high and low tonal sounds. Language can sound robotic—like my young student who was listing her activities as if reciting a laundry list—or it can be expressive and alive with color, meaning, excitement, and emotion.

Deirdre Higgins (2011)

Almost 5 million students in the United States face the daily challenge of attending school in a new language—English. By knowing about language acquisition and use, teachers (particularly those who are monolingual) can come to recognize and use communication strategies that help break down barriers.

As an introduction to the study of language teaching and learning, this chapter presents an overview of historical and contemporary theories that will help the teacher place issues of English-language learning within an orienting framework.

Historical Theories of Language Teaching and Learning

Humans have been describing and analyzing language for more than 2,300 years. As early as the fourth century BC, Greek philosophers were debating the nature of language. In about the second century BC, Dionysius Thrax identified eight different word classes. His book *The Art of Grammar* became a model for both Greek and Latin grammars. Latin was the model for grammar throughout the Middle Ages. When grammarians finally began writing grammars for vernacular languages, they generally copied the Latin grammars, using the same terminology and the same word classes. Unfortunately, Latin was not an appropriate model for all languages, but the model persisted nonetheless.

Grammar-Translation Methodology

Throughout the Middle Ages and even until the earliest years of the twentieth century, the educated classes in Europe used the method by which Latin grammar was taught as a model for learning language: drilling on vocabulary, verb tenses, and parts of speech. Teachers were expected to have a thorough knowledge of grammar rules.

This grammar-translation method of instruction is still widely used throughout the world in settings in which the main goal of instruction is reading and grammar knowledge of the second language. Students are rewarded for precisely defined goals such as memorizing word lists or correct translation.

The strengths of this methodology are twofold. First, desirable results are clearly defined, and success can be precisely correlated to the amount of effort expended. Second, the curriculum can be carefully structured and controlled.

Drawbacks are that students have little choice in what they learn, little contact with actual speakers of the language they are acquiring, almost no actual use of the language in a social context, and little stimulation of curiosity, playfulness, and exploration—aspects of learning that are intrinsic to the nature of the mind. In contrast, current second-language teaching, especially in the elementary school, features extensive social interaction and active language use among learners (see Takahashi, Austin, & Morimoto, 2000).

Structural Linguistics

In the eighteenth and nineteenth centuries, scholars began to notice similarities among languages. Studying written documents of earlier forms of languages, they traced the origins of words and sounds, attempted to show that languages had undergone changes over time, and traced historical relationships among various languages. Linguists developed a method for identifying the sound units of languages, for analyzing the ways that morphemes form words and words form sentences.

This *descriptive* linguistics led to the comparison of languages for the purpose of teaching. Knowledge of the grammar and sound structure of one language was believed to transfer to a second language so that the second language could be explained in terms of the first.

However, this contrastive analysis—with its premise that the more similar two languages, the easier a speaker of the first would learn the second—proved to be an unworkable predictor of learning ease or difficulty in a second language. (See Gass & Selinker [2001] for a discussion of contrastive analysis.) For example, Chinese and English are comparatively different in many aspects (writing system, tonal system, word structure, verb tense system, etc.), but these differences do not exactly predict what difficulties a particular learner might experience. Therefore, descriptive linguistics and contrastive analysis are largely ineffectual in second-language learning.

Behaviorism

Although behaviorism is not strictly a linguistic theory, its vast influence on learning theory has affected second-language teaching. Behaviorists claim that the mind is a "blank slate"; a learner must be filled with content during the course of teaching (see Skinner, 1957). Strict principles of timing, repetition, and reward led to classroom methodology that incorporated extensive drill and practice of language components, from sounds to complex sentences. Three aspects of behaviorism are still used in contemporary language teaching: audiolingualism, direct teaching/mastery learning, and total physical response (TPR). The latter is explained in Chapter 4.

Audiolingualism. The audiolingual method of language learning is based on behavioral principles. Oral practice is believed to be the primary means to language learning. Teachers provide oral pattern drills that are based on specific grammatical forms;

for example, a complete lesson can be centered on a tag question ("It's cold today, *isn't it?*"). The goal for the learner is to learn new habits of speech, including correct pronunciation, in the second language. Students develop correct language behavior by repetitious training, often using technology such as tape recordings in language laboratories. The role of the teacher is to direct and control students' behavior, provide a model, and reinforce correct responses.

Direct Teaching and Mastery Learning. Direct teaching and mastery learning are both forms of behaviorist instruction, and their widespread use in classrooms of English learners with reading programs such as Open Court and Direct Instruction demonstrates that behaviorism is still widely practiced. Direct teaching incorporates explicit instructional objectives for students and promotes the learning of facts, sequenced steps, or rules. The instructor maximizes learning time by using carefully scripted lessons. Students are regularly tested over the material that is covered and receive immediate remediation if performance lags.

Mastery learning resembles direct teaching. In both methods, the course of study is divided into small units with specific objectives. In mastery learning, rather than learning in strict unison, students progress at their own rates and demonstrate mastery of each unit before proceeding to the next. Mastery learning provides immediate feedback and reinforcement of performance. In the best use of mastery learning, students are gradually taught how to self-monitor, regulate, and reward their own actions.

Advantages and Disadvantages of Behavioral Methods for Second-Language Teaching. The strength of the audiolingual method is its focus on correct pronunciation. An advantage of direct teaching and mastery learning is the focus on the subskills of language, including word recognition and low-level comprehension skills, and the focus on immediate remediation when these skills are weak.

A weakness of audiolingual pedagogy is that it limits exposure to the target culture and fails to emphasize self-motivated language acquisition; it also places pressure on learners to perform accurately under classroom or laboratory conditions instead of equipping learners with language that would enable them to communicate spontaneously with native speakers.

Example of Concept

Communicating with Language Learned by Audiolingual Instruction

In 2000 I spent a week in Beijing. Unfortunately, due to a busy schedule, before departing to the People's Republic of China I had no opportunity to review the Chinese-language materials I still have from my graduate years at the University of Pittsburgh, a training that had consisted in part of long hours in a language laboratory repeating phrases in Mandarin. During the second taxi trip across Beijing, I gathered up my courage to speak Mandarin. I strung together every word I could remember and—not sounding too bad, at least to myself!—I asked the driver if he thought it would rain.

That one sentence was my downfall! In return for my one sentence, I was treated to a twenty-minute treatise on local weather conditions—I guess—I could understand so little of it! When I asked the question, my adequate pronunciation—a result of audiolingual instruction—must have sounded like I knew what I was saying, but my comprehension certainly did not keep pace with my accent!

The weakest part of direct teaching is that students are seldom asked to set their own goals in learning or pursue their own interests (as they might do in a literature-based program that encouraged free choice in reading), and they have little time to explore language creatively. Balancing the strengths and weaknesses of behavioral-based pedagogy, one might conclude that these teaching approaches have a distinct, yet limited, role in instruction.

Instead of behavioral teaching of language, Cummins is an advocate of "critical literacy" as an essential component of educational reform to promote achievement for Latino/Latina students. According to Cummins, students who achieve only "functional literacy" often fail to develop a sense of empowerment through acquisition of cultural and critical literacy and cannot successfully challenge the "status quo" in which their culture and language is relegated to a second-class status.

Cummins (2010) also distinguishes between coercive and collaborative relations of power. "Coercive relations of power refer to the exercise of power by a dominant group (or individual) to the detriment of a subordinated group (or individual)" (2010, n.p.).

Cummins (2010) goes on to state,

> Collaborative relations of power. . . . can be *generated* in interpersonal and intergroup relations. . . . In other words, participants in the relationship are *empowered* through their collaboration such that each is more affirmed in her or his identity and has a greater sense of efficacy to effect change in her or his life or social situation. Collaborative relations of power create *empowerment*; *transformative pedagogy* refers to interactions between educators and students that foster the collaborative relations. (n.p.)

Learning Strategies and CALLA

The term *strategy* denotes both general approaches and specific actions taken to learn. Learning strategies can be divided into *indirect* and *direct*.

Indirect Strategies. Indirect strategies tend to originate at a level of unconscious or automated performance and may or may not enter consciousness during operation. As an example of an indirect strategy, suppose a given person has a preference for learning by listening, rather than reading. The person probably did not consciously acquire this preference. Once the person becomes aware that listening is a preferred means of input, though, that person has a choice whether to maintain that as a preference or try to modify that by, for example, consciously trying to read more.

Language-use strategies are indirect strategies for communicating an idea when the learner cannot produce a precise linguistic form. Cohen (1996) defined four language-use strategies: *rehearsal, retrieval, communication,* and *cover.*

- Rehearsal is used to memorize a correct language form.
- Retrieval is used to retrieve a word or phrase from memory.
- Communication indicates the attempts to convey meaning when the correct form is not available.
- Cover strategies are used to create the impression that the learner is in control when, in fact, there are gaps in proficiency; for example, a speaker may fail to remember a word and must use gestures or a synonym to compensate.

Other communication strategies include avoiding sounds, structures, or topics that are beyond current proficiency; memorizing stock phrases to rely on when all else fails; asking a conversant for help or pausing to consult a dictionary; and falling back on the primary language for help in communication. The last strategy, often called *code switching,* has been studied extensively because it permeates a learner's progression in a second language. Code switching—the alternating use of two languages on the word, phrase, clause, or sentence level—has been found to serve a variety of purposes, not just as a strategy to help when expressions in the second language are lacking.

Baker (2001) lists ten purposes for code switching: (1) to emphasize a point, (2) because a word is unknown in one of the languages, (3) for ease and efficiency of expression, (4) as a repetition to clarify, (5) to express group identity and status and/ or to be accepted by a group, (6) to quote someone, (7) to interject in a conversation, (8) to exclude someone, (9) to cross social or ethnic boundaries, and (10) to ease tension in a conversation. Code switching thus serves a variety of intentions beyond the mere linguistic. It has important power and social ramifications.

According to Buell (2004), "Code-switching is a key marker of social identities, relations, and context. When a speaker uses or changes a code, she is signaling who she is, how she relates to listeners or readers, how she understands the context and what communication tools are available to her" (pp. 99, 100). Students' writing and other discourse practices are apt to be complex, multilayered, and sometimes contradictory. Understanding students in the full splendor of their code-switching and use of dialect, peer-influenced, or idio-syncratic language is part of the joy of teaching.

Example of Concept *Code Switching*

Jennifer Seitz, a third-grade teacher, uses Alicia's primary language, Spanish, as a way to help Alicia learn English. A recent Spanish-speaking immigrant to the United States, Alicia has acquired whole phrases or words in English from a fellow student and intersperses these when speaking Spanish to gain access to her peer group. On the playground, she has been heard to repeat in Spanish something just said in English, perhaps to clarify what was said or to identify with two groups. She often uses English when learning concepts in the classroom, but uses Spanish when she is discussing the concept with another student or when the conversation involves a personal matter. The content of the instruction and the interpersonal link between speakers seem to be the main factors in her language choice.

Although language purists look down on language mixing, a more fruitful approach is letting children learn in whatever manner they feel most comfortable, so that anxiety about language will not interfere with concept acquisition. In fact, a teacher who learns words and expressions in the students' home language is able to use the students' language to express solidarity and share personal feelings when appropriate.

Direct Strategies. In contrast to indirect strategies, direct strategies tend to originate at a level of conscious performance and may or may not become unconscious, or automated, during operation. A person may be taught a strategy, try it, reflect upon

Ways for Teachers to Facilitate Indirect Strategies

- Familiarize language learners with language-use strategies so they can recognize them when they occur.
- Practice with students a set of formulaic expressions to cover most interactions so that they feel comfortable in routine language use.
- Recognize that in a bilingual context, code-switching is common and relieves anxiety; too much code-switching, however, may interfere with second-language use.

its success, and eventually decide to add it to the ongoing repertoire of behaviors. Literacy and oracy strategies are treated in Chapter 4.

Cognitive Academic Language Learning Approach (CALLA). The three kinds of direct strategies that are discussed here (*cognitive, metacognitive,* and *social-affective*), are incorporated into Chamot and O'Malley's Cognitive Academic Language Learning Approach (CALLA). This approach was designed for English learners at the advanced-beginning and intermediate levels.

The CALLA model includes the development of academic language skills and explicit instruction in learning strategies for both content and language acquisition. Academic language skills include all four language modes in daily content lessons, as well as cognitive functions important for the specific curricular areas, such as analyzing, evaluating, justifying, and persuading; gathering, analyzing, and interpreting data; and explaining, inferring, predicting, and communicating results.

Metacognitive strategies are *planning strategies* that help students learn how to organize themselves for a learning task; *monitoring strategies* that help students to check their comprehension in listening and reading and their production while speaking and writing; and *performance evaluation strategies* that teach students how to assess their own performance on a task, using learning logs or other reflective tools to keep track of their progress.

Social-affective strategies teach how to elicit needed clarification, how to work cooperatively with peers in problem solving, and how to use mental techniques or self-talk to reduce anxiety and increase a sense of personal competency. Students might ask for clarification, explanation, or feedback about their language use. This supports learning by helping the learner to make use of the social environment when learning tasks.

Teaching Strategically. What can educators hope to accomplish by the use of strategy-based instruction? It can raise students' awareness of strategy preferences, reinforce systematic strategy use among learners, and help learners to understand the effectiveness of different kinds of strategies.

How does the instructor train learners to use a variety of learning strategies? Students can use checklists, interviews, think-aloud procedures, learning journals, or self-report surveys to become familiar with the overall schema of strategies. In directed-strategy training, the learner acquires and practices one or two strategies, matched to specific tasks.

Cognitive strategies also include teaching study skills and enhancement of cognitive functions by the use of specific psychological tools, including schema building, scaffolding, use of alternative information representations, such as graphic organizers, and fostering critical and creative thinking. Brain-compatible learning is addressed in a separate section.

Schema Building. A schema (plural: schemata) is a unit of understanding that can be used to store knowledge in long-term memory. Students use existing schemata when they recognize a connection between what they know and the learning experience. If students have little prior knowledge about the topic at hand, teachers will need to build schemata by providing new experiences that arouse interest and attention to a topic. These may include field trips, guest speakers, films and movies, experiments, classroom discovery centers, computer simulations, and so on to help students link what they already know with these new experiences.

Scaffolding. During scaffolding, the teacher helps to focus the learner's attention on relevant parts of the task by asking key questions that help to give children the opportunity to think and talk about the task and by dividing the task into smaller, manageable subcomponents and sensitively withdrawing assistance when it is no longer required. By using scaffolding techniques, teachers can help students build schemata.

Adapted Instruction

Helping Students Develop a Personal Set of Learning Strategies

Teachers can help students to get to know their own learning strategies and help them to acquire a more flexible repertoire. Students can:

- Describe how they came up with an answer, solution, or process.
- Listen to one another's explanations and acquire alternative ways to solve problem.
- Persevere with resilience when they try a new strategy that does not come easily.
- Seek out diverse strategies.

Source: Based on Gregory & Kuzmich (2005).

Information-Processing Theories of Learning

For information-processing theorists, the mind functions similar to a computer: It processes information by recognizing input, storing it, retrieving it when needed, and generating responses. The sensory register (input/recognition), short-term memory (information encoding), and long-term memory (storage) work together during learning.

During information processing, *perception* takes in stimuli—either as images or sound patterns—and selects input for further processing. Meaning is constructed by combining objective reality with existing prior knowledge. However, the mind can pay attention to only one demanding task at a time. Teachers can help students to manage their attention.

Adapted Instruction

Enhancing Perception of Information

Teachers can assist the first phase of students' information processing in the following ways:

- Stating the purpose of a lesson to help students focus on how the material will be useful or important to them.
- Arousing curiosity by asking questions such as, "What would happen if . . .".
- Asking students to touch, smell, or taste to shift sensory channels during a lesson.
- Using movements, gestures, and voice inflection (speaking softly and then more emphatically) or writing with colored pens or chalk.

The next phase, short-term memory (STM) (also called working memory) retains patterns of images or sounds for about 20 to 30 seconds, unless it is kept activated by rehearsing or repetition). Individuals differ in the ability to retain information in STM.

Long-term memory (LTM) is the permanent store of knowledge, encoded either as visual images, or verbal units, or both. To move information into LTM requires time and effort, but once it is securely stored, it can remain there permanently. Teaching memory-enhancement strategies can help students store and retrieve information from LTM.

Parallel/distributed models of information processing describe learning as a simultaneous adjustment of a net of neural connections in the brain. These models view learning as the acquisition and strengthening of brain patters. In contrast, Ratey (2001) uses a metaphor of the brain as an ecosystem—with perception, function, consciousness, and identity alternately taking precedence, depending on task and predilection. His view—that function and consciousness are semi-separate theaters of operation—is an interesting way to look at the use of language: a human skill that often involves simultaneous conscious and unconscious performance.

Emotional intelligence (EI) is a construct proposed by Salovey and Mayer (1990) and popularized by Goleman (1998). According to Goleman, emotional intelligence is "the capacity for recognizing our own feelings and those of others, for motivating ourselves, and for managing emotions well in ourselves and in our relationships" (p. 317).

EI consists of five competencies: self-awareness, self-regulation, motivation, social skills, and empathy. Empathy is a foundation for social skills and includes understanding others, having a service orientation, developing the skills of others, leveraging diversity, and being politically aware (Goleman, 1998, p. 137). Whereas some may argue that identifying the importance of the emotional aspect of life is not new, especially in education, it is useful to have the term "EI" as a shorthand for discussing competencies that need to be encouraged in educating English learners.

Emotional scaffolding is a term that Fredericks-Malone and Gadbois (2005/2006) use to mean the following: "... when a teacher designs a lesson plan, activity, or approach to a subject that incorporates the students' personal lives, including ethnicity, socioeconomic group, history, and culture" (p. 21). Emotional engagement, in addition to intellectual engagement, is key to higher academic performance. Teachers' powers of observation and experience are invaluable tools to discovering what aspects of the students' lives—what topics they gravitate to in their personal lives—will spur self-motivation.

Brain-Compatible Learning

A basic question concerning second-language acquisition is, "What is the role of the brain in learning language?" Neurolinguists attempt to explain the connection between language function and neuroanatomy and to identify, if possible, the areas

Adapted Instruction

Using Principles of Brain-Based Learning in Oral Presentations

Before a Presentation
- Have students lower anxiety by taking a few deep breaths, visualizing success, and repeating positive self-talk phrases (brain-based principle 2: Learning engages the entire physiology).

- Remind students to review the structure of the information, especially how the parts of the presentation fit together (brain-based principle 6: The brain processes parts and wholes simultaneously).

During the Presentation
- The speaker concentrates on the task while staying tuned to the needs of the audience (brain-based principle 7: Learning involves both focused attention and peripheral perception).

- Tenseness that is redefined as "eustress" ("good stress") supplies energy for learning rather than inhibits performance (brain-based principle 11: Learning is enhanced by challenge and inhibited by threat).

After the Presentation
- Students evaluate their accomplishment, ask for feedback and tune in to the reactions of others, identify problem areas, and make a plan for improvement (brain-based principle 10: Learning occurs best when facts and skills are embedded in natural, spatial memory—including the memory of positive performance).

of the brain responsible for language functioning. Recent studies have looked at the role of emotions and visual and gestural processing in second-language acquisition, tracing the brain processing not only of verbal language but also of nonverbal input such as gestures, facial expressions, and intonation (Paradis, 2005; Schumann, 1994).

Several contemporary educators have specialized in developing learning methods that take into consideration brain processing. According to research (Caine & Caine, 1994; Hart, 1975, 1983), learning is the brain's primary function. Many parts of the brain process reality simultaneously, using thoughts, emotions, imagination, and the senses to interact with the environment. This rich reaction can be tapped to facilitate language acquisition (see Table 3.1). For further information about brain-based learning, see *Brain/Mind Learning Principles in Action: The Fieldbook for Making Connections, Teaching, and the Human Brain* by Caine, Caine, McClintic,

Table 3.1   Principles and Implications for Brain-Based Instruction

Principle	Implications for Instruction
1. The brain can perform multiple processes simultaneously.	Learning experiences can be multimodal. As students perform experiments, develop a play from the text of a story, or take on complex projects, many facets of the brain are involved.
2. Learning engages the entire physiology.	Stress management, nutrition, exercise, relaxation, and natural rhythms and timing should be taken into consideration during teaching and learning.
3. The search for meaning is innate.	Language-learning activities should involve a focus on meaning; language should be learned in the context of interesting activities.
4. The brain is designed to perceive and generate patterns.	Information is presented in a way that allows brains to extract patterns and create meaning rather than react passively.
5. Emotions are crucial to memory.	Instruction should support the students' backgrounds and languages. Interaction should be marked by mutual respect and acceptance.
6. The brain processes parts and wholes simultaneously.	Language skills, such as vocabulary and grammar, are best learned in authentic language environments (solving a problem, debating an issue, exploring) in which parts (specific language skills) are learned together with wholes (problems to be solved).
7. Learning involves both focused attention and peripheral perception.	Music, art, and other rich environmental stimuli can enhance and influence the natural acquisition of language.
8. Learning always involves conscious and unconscious processes.	Students need opportunities to review what they learn consciously so they can reflect, take charge, and develop personal meaning.
9. There are at least two types of memory: spatial memory and rote learning systems.	Teaching techniques that focus on the memorization of language bits—words and grammar points—use the rote learning system. Teaching that actively involves the learner in novel experiences taps into the spatial system.
10. Learning occurs best when facts and skills are embedded in natural, spatial memory.	Discrete language skills can be learned when they are embedded in real-life activities (demonstrations, field trips, performances, stories).
11. Learning is enhanced by challenge and inhibited by threat.	Learners are taken from the point where they are at present to the next level of competence through a balance of support and challenge.
12. Each brain is unique.	Teaching should be multifaceted. English learners can express developing understanding through visual, tactile, emotional, and auditory means.

and Klimek (2004); Jensen's *Teaching with the Brain in Mind* (1998); Lyons and Clay's *Teaching Struggling Readers: How to Use Brain-Based Research to Maximize Learning* (2003); and Smilkstein's *We're Born to Learn* (2002).

To summarize these alternative views of brain functioning during learning, the brain is stimulated to input and store information. The brain contains a basic set of neurons that interconnect to remember and respond to the environment. Various kinds of mental processing are used, depending on the best response to the immediate challenge. Emotions are an important part of learning, and constitute a kind of intelligence that can be learned.

Current Theories of Language Development

Starting in the mid-twentieth century, several important new theories have shaped current understanding of language acquisition and development. In 1959, Noam Chomsky claimed that language is not learned solely through a process of memorizing and repeating, but that the mind contains an active language processor, the language acquisition device (LAD), that generates rules through the unconscious acquisition of grammar.

In 1961, Hymes directed attention toward the idea of communicative competence: that the *use* of language in the social setting is important in language performance. Halliday (1975) elaborated on the role of social relations in language by stating that the social structure is an essential element in linguistic interaction. Current theories of language have thus moved away from the merely linguistic components of a language to the more inclusive realm of language in use—which includes its social, political, and psychological domains.

Current language teaching is being shaped by several important ideas. First, the shift toward a cognitive paradigm means that *learning* has taken precedence over *teaching*. What the student learns is the important outcome of the teaching–learning process, not what the teacher teaches. Second, learning is maximized when it matches the processes that take place naturally within the brain. Third, thematic integration across content areas unifies the language processes of reading, writing, speaking, listening, thinking, and acting. Thus, current perspectives on second-language learning align with brain-compatible instruction that emphasizes higher-order thinking skills.

Cognitive Approaches to Language Learning

Cognitive psychology has gradually emerged as the dominant approach to learning, including the learning of a second language. Building on the developmental work of Piaget with children, Chomsky's focus on innate language processing, and the application of information processing models to human thinking, the cognitive approach has given rise to studies in transformational grammar (and a similar approach, Krashen's monitor model); Cummins's theories of bilingualism and cognition; learning strategies research, including the Cognitive Academic Language Learning Approach (CALLA);

information-processing theories of learning; brain-compatible learning; neurolinguistic research; and constructivist learning. These will be examined in turn.

Transformational Grammar

Following Chomsky's lead, transformational grammarians envision language as a set of rules that human beings unconsciously know and use. They believe that the mind has the capacity to internalize and construct language rules. The goal of transformational grammar is to understand and describe these internalized rules. In the early 1970s, some grammar texts included the use of transformational grammar to explain language structures, but this never became a popular approach to teaching grammar.

Krashen's Monitor Model

Krashen (1981, 1982) theorized that people acquire second-language structures in a predictable order only if they obtain comprehensible input, and if their anxiety is low enough to allow input into their minds. Krashen's theory included five hypotheses: the *monitor hypothesis*, the *acquisition-learning hypothesis*, the *natural order hypothesis*, the *input hypothesis*, and the *affective filter hypothesis*.

The *monitor* is an error-detecting mechanism; it scans an utterance for accuracy and edits—that is, confirms or repairs—the utterance either before or after attempted communication. However, the monitor cannot always be used. In a situation involving rapid verbal exchange, an individual may have little time to be concerned with correctness.

Krashen defined *acquisition* and *learning* as two separate processes in the mastering of a second language. Learning is formal knowledge about the rules of a language. Acquisition, on the other hand, is an unconscious process that occurs when language is used for real communication. Acquirers gain a "feel" for the correctness of their own utterances as their internal monitor is gradually adjusted. Students produce some language unself-consciously and need rules and help for others. Thus, when children chat with one another as they work in cooperative groups, they are learning not only content (science, social studies) but also the English language.

Krashen formulated the hypothesis that there appears to be a *natural order* of acquisition of English morphemes. The order is slightly different for second-language learners from the first-language order, but there are similarities. Children acquire correct usage of grammatical structures in their second language (L2) gradually, as do children acquiring a first language (L1).

The *input* hypothesis claims that language is acquired in an "amazingly simple way—when we understand messages" (Krashen, 1985, p. vii). Language must contain what Krashen calls "comprehensible" input. Comprehensible input has generally been assumed to contain predictable elements: shorter sentences; more intelligible, well-formed utterances; less subordination; and more restricted vocabulary and range of topics with a focus on communication.

Adapted Instruction

Differentiated Questions for Comprehensible Input in Science Lesson on "Signs of the Seasons"

Questions to Ask

Beginning: What season has the hottest weather?"

Early Intermediate: "What season do you like better, summer or fall? What is one thing you like about each?"

Intermediate: "What season comes after the one we're in? What are signs to look for that the season is changing?"

Advanced: "What changes do we make in our lives during the hottest season? How do our bodies adapt to the heat?"

The *affective filter* hypothesis addresses emotional variables, including anxiety, motivation, and self-confidence. Most teachers understand that a nonthreatening and encouraging environment promotes learning, and that it is important to increase the enjoyment of learning, raise self-esteem, and blend self-awareness with an increase in proficiency as students learn English.

Cummins's Theories of Bilingualism and Cognition

Jim Cummins's work falls within the cognitive approach to language. Cummins's research has furthered the belief that being bilingual is a cognitive advantage and that knowledge of the first language provides a firm foundation for second-language acquisition.

Separate or Common Underlying Proficiency. Some critics of bilingual education have argued that proficiency in English is separate from proficiency in a primary language and that content and skills learned through the primary language do not transfer to English—a notion that Cummins (1981b) has termed *separate underlying proficiency (SUP)*. In contrast, Cummins asserted that cognition and language fundamentals, once learned in the primary language, form a basis for subsequent learning in any language. This position assumes a *common underlying proficiency (CUP)*, the belief that a second language and the primary language have a shared foundation, and that competence in the primary language provides the basis for competence in the second language.

For example, children learning to read and write in Korean develop concepts about print and the role of literacy that make learning to read and think in English easier, despite the fact that these languages do not share a similar writing system. Students do not have to relearn in a second language the essentials of schooling: how to communicate, how to think critically, and how to read and write.

Basic Interpersonal Communication Skills and Cognitive Academic Language Proficiency. Cummins (1979, 1980) posited two different yet related language skills: basic interpersonal communication skills (BICS) and cognitive academic language proficiency (CALP). BICS involve those language skills and functions that allow students to communicate in everyday social contexts that are similar to those of the home, as they perform classroom chores, chat with peers, or consume instructional media as they do television shows at home. Cummins called BICS *context embedded* because participants can provide feedback to one another, and the situation itself provides cues that further understanding.

In contrast, CALP is the language needed to perform school tasks successfully. Such tasks generally are more abstract and decontextualized. Students must rely primarily on language to attain meaning. Cummins (1984) called CALP *context-reduced* communication because there are few concrete cues to aid in comprehension. CALP provides the human brain with necessary tools to systematically categorize, compare, analyze, and accommodate new experiences, a cognitive toolbox—the in-depth knowledge that characterizes the well-educated individual in a complex modern society.

During the elementary school years, and then even more so throughout middle and high school, students who may appear to be fluent enough in English to survive in an all-English classroom may in fact have significant gaps in the development of academic aspects of English. Conversational skills have been found to approach nativelike levels within two years of exposure to English, but five or more years may be required for minority students to match native speakers in CALP (Collier, 1987; Cummins, 1981a; Hakuta, Butler, & Witt, 2000).

Example of Concept   *Teaching Students to Use CALP*

A look at an elementary classroom shows the integrated work that takes place across these CALP areas.

Mrs. Gómez found in her second-grade transitional bilingual class that although the students were fairly fluent English conversationalists they were performing poorly in academic tasks. Students seemed to understand English when pictures and other visual clues were present. However, when she gave instructions or briefly reviewed concepts, the students appeared lost. She realized that students needed lessons that eased them along the continuum from their interpersonal language usage to the more abstract academic requirements.

When Linda and several of her classmates were jumping rope during recess, Mrs. Gómez wrote down many of the patterned chants the girls were reciting. She transferred these to wall charts and read and recited them with the children. Next she introduced poems with more extensive vocabulary on wall charts, supplementing the charts with tapes that children could listen to in learning centers. The instructions for these centers featured patterned language similar to that already encountered in the rhymes. Gradually Mrs. Gómez was able to record more complex and abstract instructions in the learning centers. This progression and integration of activities helped the children to move along the continuum from BICS to CALP.

The complexity of CALP can be captured by examination of the five Cs: communication, conceptualization, critical thinking, context, and culture (see Table 3.2). Many of the skills that are a part of CALP are refinements of BICS, whereas others are more exclusively school centered.

Table 3.2 Components of Cognitive Academic Language Proficiency (CALP)

Component	Explanation
Communication	Reading: Increases speed; uses context cues to guess vocabulary meaning; masters a variety of genres in fiction (poetry, short story) and nonfiction (encyclopedias, magazines, Internet sources) to "read the world" (interprets comics, print advertising, road signs).
	Listening: Follows verbal instructions; interprets nuances of intonation (e.g., in cases of teacher disciplinary warnings); solicits, and profits from, help of peers.
	Speaking: Gives oral presentations, answers correctly in class, and reads aloud smoothly.
	Writing: Uses conventions such as spelling, punctuation, and report formats.
Conceptualization	Concepts become abstract and are expressed in longer words with more general meaning (rain becomes *precipitation*).
	Concepts fit into larger theories (*precipitation* cycle).
	Concepts fit into hierarchies (rain → precipitation cycle → weather systems → climate).
	Concepts are finely differentiated from similar concepts (sleet from *hail*, typhoons from *hurricanes*).
	Conceptual relations become important (opposites, subsets, causality, correlation).
Critical thinking	Uses graphic organizers to represent the structure of thought (comparison charts, Venn diagrams, timelines, "spider" charts).
	Uses textual structures (outlines, paragraphing, titles, main idea).
	Uses symbolic representation (math operators [<, >, +, =]; proofreading marks, grade indications [10/20 points, etc.]).
	Reads between the lines (inference).
	Employs many other kinds of critical thinking.
	Plans activities, monitors progress, evaluates results, employs self-knowledge (metacognition).
	Increases variety and efficiency in use of learning strategies.
Context	Nonverbal: Uses appropriate gestures (and is able to refrain from inappropriate ones); interprets nonverbal signs accurately.
	Formality: Behaves formally when required to do so.
	Participation structures: Fits in smoothly to classroom and schoolwide groups and procedures.
Culture	Draws on experience in mainstream culture (background knowledge).
	Moves smoothly between home and school.
	Deploys primary-language resources when required.

Neurolinguistic Research about Brain Function

What mechanisms help the brain to store words during learning? Does being bilingual enhance brain function? Is the left side of the brain really the language side? Do people who read languages written from left to right (like English) think differently from people who read languages written from right to left (like Hebrew and Arabic)? What about if a language is written using some other kind of symbols, like Chinese or Japanese?

Neurolinguists use techniques like functional magnetic resonance imaging (fMRI) to picture the brain's tissues and functions. Evidence shows that listening, understanding, talking, and reading each involve activities in certain parts of the brain, mostly in the left hemisphere of the brain, regardless of what language serves as input. In contrast, areas in the right side are essential for communicating effectively and for understanding the point of what people are saying.

Human brains are not all organized in the same way. Everybody's brain is different in terms of size, structure, and function, as well as the effects of experience and aging. Among cognitive skills, however, language stands apart as one of the most complex of all human mental abilities. Using the wealth of information about language learning stemming from neurolinguistic research is a key challenge for teachers in the years ahead.

Constructivist Learning

Constructivism is an offshoot of the cognitivist tradition, in which teachers help students to take responsibility for constructing their own knowledge within complex and challenging learning environments. Students and teachers share responsibility for the knowledge construction process, collaborating on the goals of instruction and the planning needed for learning to take place. Instructional objectives are tailored to the needs and levels of students, with a wide range of learning materials provided for enrichment, remediation, and student self-pacing.

Key elements of constructivist learning are particularly relevant to learning in multicultural classrooms: students are supported in their autonomy and initiative, student responses shape lesson content and instructional strategies, and the focus is on students' concept understanding rather than rote memorization. Students discuss, ask questions, give explanations to one another, and present ideas and solve problems together. A constructivist learning environment is of vital importance in students' ability to address global issues and understanding and orient themselves to its challenges (Brown & Kysilka, 2002).

At the middle and high school levels, students use research resources featuring various types of information representation such as printed text, oral interviews, visual images, charts, and graphs. Project-based learning, for example, is a constructivist technique in which teams of students pool resources and expertise while solving problems that are, one would hope, both comprehensible and compelling. This is particularly relevant to such technology-enhanced projects such as web quests. Constructivism requires the teacher to be a learner as well; complex environments that include computer-assisted learning require that learning be continuous.

Communicative Competence

Language is a form of communication that occurs in social interaction. It is used for a purpose, such as persuading, commanding, and establishing social relationships. Knowing a language is no longer seen as merely knowing grammatical forms. Instead, the competent speaker is recognized as one who knows when, where, and how to use language appropriately.

Communicative competence is the aspect of language users' competence, or knowledge of the language, that enables them to "convey and interpret messages and to negotiate meanings interpersonally within specific contexts" (Brown, 2007, p. 219). Canale (1983) identified four components of communicative competence: grammatical competence, sociolinguistic competence, discourse competence, and strategic competence. Each of these is discussed in the following paragraphs.

Grammatical Competence. Some level of grammar is required when learning vocabulary, word formation and meaning, sentence formation, pronunciation, and spelling. This type of competence focuses on the skills and knowledge necessary to speak and write accurately, and becomes increasingly important to the English learner in more advanced stages of proficiency.

Sociolinguistic Competence. To communicate well, one must know how to produce and understand language in different sociolinguistic contexts, taking into consideration such factors as the status of participants, the purposes of the interaction, and the norms or conventions of interaction. One of the tasks of teachers is to help learners use both appropriate forms and appropriate meanings when interacting in the classroom.

Discourse Competence. In both speaking and writing, the learner needs to combine and connect utterances (spoken) and sentences (written) into a meaningful whole. A speaker may be both grammatically correct and appropriate socially but lack coherence or relevance to the topic at hand. Such a disconnected utterance shows a lack of discourse competence.

Strategic Competence. A speaker may use strategic competence in order to compensate for breakdowns in communication (as when a speaker forgets or does not know a term and is forced to paraphrase or gesture to get the idea across) and to enhance the effectiveness of communication (as when a speaker raises or lowers the voice for effect).

Teachers can specifically plan to increase students' skills in discourse and sociolinguistic and strategic competence by building experiences into the curriculum that involve students in solving problems, exploring areas of interest, and designing projects. Students carry over knowledge of how to communicate from experiences in their first language. This knowledge can be tapped as they develop specific forms and usage in English.

Even in communicative language teaching, not every classroom activity needs to be "authentic"—or as close as possible to a real-life situation. Students learning English still may need to memorize dialogues and vocabulary words, drill on pronunciation, engage in choral repetition, and copy dictation. These are like warmups that runners need for training before running a "real" race. These "chunks" of drill or practice are later applied to the English needed for communicative interaction (Zamach, 2009).

Example of Concept   *Developing Communicative Competence*

In a high-school economics class, Mr. Godfried often demonstrated consumer economics to the students by having them role-play. In the fifth-period class, several students were recent immigrants who had been placed in this class as a graduation requirement despite their limited English. Mr. Godfried's job became more complicated than in the past; now he had to teach not only economics but also basic communication skills in English. The process of opening a checking account was not difficult for Takeo, a Japanese student, who had had a checking account as a student in Japan. But Vasalli,

an immigrant from Byelorussia, found the task mystifying. He had had limited experience with consumerism in general and no experience with the concept of a checking account. What he did have, however, was a general knowledge of how to interact with an official. Through the role-plays, Mr. Godfried was able to help the students use their background knowledge to conduct appropriate verbal interactions in the banking situation and use their communication experience to expand their content knowledge.

The Social Context for Language Learning

Learning a language is not strictly a communicative endeavor; it includes social and cultural interaction. The Russian psychologist Lev Vygotsky emphasized the role played by social interaction in the development of language and thought. According to Vygotsky (1978), teaching must be matched in some manner with the student's developmental level, taking into consideration the student's "zone of proximal development." Vygotsky defines this zone as "the distance between the actual developmental level as determined by independent problem solving and the level of potential development . . . under adult guidance or in collaboration with more capable peers" (p. 86).

Vygotsky's theory of cognitive development was sociocultural: He believed that teachers must understand the historical and cultural contexts of each child's background in order to understand how that person's mind has developed. He also emphasized the important role that language plays in human development—we internalize the language we learn in our social context, and this language is the basis of our mental "toolkit." Children hear others talking, and as they take in this language they use it to create their own understanding.

The Vygotskian approach has often been called "social constructivist" because learners use their language to help one another make sense of the world. A social-constructivist view is that social interaction is key to learning. As Gillen stated, "children make sense of symbolic practices . . . through their presence in communities. People create and interpret meanings together . . . children learn how to dance or how to draw, partly through watching others, partly through responses that others make to their own efforts, and partly through the special individually motivated capabilities they bring to the activity in question" (2003, p. 13).

A social constructivist way of teaching uses social interaction to help students find personal meaning in what they learn. As Powell and Kalina state,

> Learning English can be overwhelming and intimidating for ESOL students, but it can also be enjoyable when enhanced by social interaction in a supportive classroom. . . . The words that are put together to express personal meaning become more authentic and include total application of the culture. (2009, p. 36)

Using peer conversation as a means of enriching a student's exposure to language maximizes the opportunity for a student to hear and enjoy English. Mixing more-skilled with less-skilled speakers supplies more advanced language models to English learners. Thus, the context of instruction plays as critical a role in language development as does the actual language exchanged.

The teacher who is aware of the social uses of language provides a classroom environment in which students engage in communicative pair or group tasks. These can include practicing a readers' theater with other students in order to perform for their class or school, developing interview questions in order to survey local opinion on a timely topic, and planning an exhibition of art or written work to which to invite parents or other students.

Just as important as providing ample opportunity for students to interact within an information-rich environment is the assurance that such interaction takes place between language equals. Placing equal value on the primary language and its speakers creates a classroom in which there is no unfair privilege for native-English speakers.

Discourse Theory

Discourse theorists have analyzed conversation to understand how meaning is negotiated. According to them, face-to-face interaction is a key to second-language acquisition. By holding conversations (discourse), non-native speakers attend to the various features in the input they obtain. Through their own speech output, they affect both the quantity and the quality of the language they receive. The more learners converse, the more opportunity they have to initiate and expand topics, signal comprehension breakdowns, and try out new formulas and expressions.

In constructing discourse, second-language learners use four kinds of knowledge: knowledge about the second language, competence in their native language, ability to use the functions of language, and their general world knowledge. The language they produce is an *interlanguage*, an intermediate system that they create as they attempt to achieve nativelike competence (Selinker, 1972, 1991). Through a variety of discourse opportunities, learners sort out the ways language is used and gradually achieve proficiency.

Understanding how discourse is used during instruction and modifying classroom discourse to encourage participation by English learners is a large part of specially designed academic instruction in English (SDAIE; see Chapter 5) and also culturally compatible teaching (see Chapter 9).

Encouraging Native-Speaker/Non-Native-Speaker Interaction

- Students can interview others briefly on topics such as "My favorite sport" or "My favorite tool." The responses from the interviews can be tallied and form the basis for subsequent class discussion.
- English learners can also interact with native-English speakers during school hours through cross-age or peer interactions.

Semiotics

Not all second-language acquisition depends on verbal language. Semiotics is a discipline that studies the ways in which humans use signs to make meaning. According to semiotic theory, there are three kinds of signs: symbols, icons, and indexes. *Symbols* are signs for which there is an arbitrary relationship between the object and its sign; the word *table*, for example, is arbitrarily linked to the object "table." Icons are signs that resemble what they stand for, such as a drawing of a table. *Indexes* are signs that indicate a fact or condition; for instance, thunderclouds indicate rain.

Signs are organized into systems of objects and behaviors. Thus, the way chairs are arranged in a classroom and the manner in which students are expected to respond to the teacher are both signs that signal meaning. Signs—and the meanings they carry—vary across cultures and languages, adding richness to the study of second language that words alone seldom express fully.

Semiotics provides a perspective for examining human development through the interplay of multiple meaning systems. As students learn English, wise teachers provide and accept various ways through which students demonstrate their knowledge.

Using Semiotics to Acquire a Second Language

- Students can view themselves, other students, teachers, the community, and culturally authentic materials (phone books, voicemail messages, advertising brochures, music videos, etc.) to examine ways that meaning is communicated using both verbal and nonverbal messages.
- Students can engage in a variety of cross-media activities—produce music, create collages, and write poems, journal entries, or advertising slogans—to display their identities, values, or ideas.
- Students can "people-watch" using semiotics to read nonverbal messages sent by dress styles, posture, demeanor, and so forth as a way to increase their interactions with one another at all levels of language proficiency.

Source: Based on Díaz-Rico and Dullien (2004).

Semiotics has become increasingly important within the last decade as visual information, rather than primarily text, has become increasingly available and salient in the lives of students. Sophisticated computer art, animation, and graphics programs available through the Internet have opened up a language of two-dimensional shape and color that supplements, if not replaces, text as a source of information and experience for many young people. To learn more about this field, see Chandler (2007), Kress and Van Leeuwen (1995), Martin and Ringham (2006), Scollon and Scollon (2003).

Theories of second-language learning provide the rationale and framework for the daily activities of instruction. Teachers who are aware of the basic principles of contemporary language acquisition and learning are better equipped to plan instruction and explain their practices to peers, parents, students, and administrators.

Although the teacher's role is valuable as students learn a second language, the actual language learned is the responsibility of the learner. Research on cognitive processes shows that learners construct and internalize language-using rules during problem solving or authentic communication. The shift from *what the teacher does* to *what learners do in social interaction* is a characteristic of contemporary thinking about learning in general and language acquisition specifically and has wide implications for teaching English learners.

LEARNING MORE

Further Reading

Excellent general background reading on discourse and context is Mercer's *Words and Minds* (2000), which traces the codevelopment of language and thinking. Mercer gives many examples of how people use discourse to shape events, such as arguing, persuading, laying the ground rules for conversation, and even giving and receiving a bribe. The discussion of the role of the teacher in fostering communicative talk in the classroom is broadly applicable across many levels of schooling.

Web Search

The site www.thereading.people.org/docs/open_court.pdf gives the rationale for teaching reading through a structured program based on systematic and explicit scaffolding of skills. In contrast, the Heinemann website (online at www.heinemann.com) offers reading materials such as Pransky's *Beneath the Surface: The Hidden Realities of Teaching Culturally and Linguistically Diverse Young Learners, K–6* (2008) that present a child-centered view of the reading process. Use these two sources to contrast top-down and bottom-up reading practices and their related underlying theories of learning.

Exploration

Visit several local ELD teachers to investigate the second-language-learning theories underlying their classroom practice. Ask what they know about Krashen's monitor theory, or such terms as *comprehensible input* and *affective filter*. Ask if they recognize the terms *basic interpersonal communication skills* (BICS) and *cognitive academic learning proficiency* (CALP). If not, ask what techniques they use to make instruction understandable to their English learners, and if they believe that lowering anxiety (the affective filter) increases learning.

Experiment

Ask a friend to learn ten words in a foreign language (you supply). If the friend agrees, see how long it takes him or her to memorize the words to your satisfaction. Next, ask the same friend if he or she would have learned the words faster for a reward. If so, what reward would have been sufficient? Does your friend think the reward would have increased the speed of learning? Why or why not?

MyEducationLab™

Peers Provide Scaffolding for Language Learning

In this video, two English-language learners in a multilingual classroom participate in a peer/buddy reading activity guided by their teacher. With their teacher's help, the older student reads to the younger student. Both of the students are Hmong, but the older student is much more proficient in English than the younger student, who only speaks in Hmong on the video. As you watch the video, observe the children's interaction with the book and with each other. Try to identify portions of the video that illustrate how this interaction has a positive effect on each student's ability to respond to the text. Also think about what theory of cognitive development is being applied.

To access the video, go to MyEducationLab (www.myeducationlab.com), choose the Díaz-Rico text, and log in to MyEducationLab for English Language Learners. Select the topic Comprehensible Input, and watch the video entitled "Peers Provide Scaffolding for Language Learning."

Answer the following questions:

1. How might the peer interaction in this video provide examples of the following teaching and learning principles in action?
   - Active engagement
   - Cultural relevance
   - Collaboration
   - Comprehensible input
   - Prior knowledge

2. Not all children are "born teachers." How can the classroom teacher assist peer tutors to assist others?

3. How does the classroom teacher monitor the situation to assess the effectiveness of peer tutoring?

Instruction

Oracy and Literacy for English-Language Development, Content-Area Instruction, and Bilingual Education

Part Two examines methods for enhancing listening, speaking, reading, and writing skills in English for English learners (Chapter 4); models of schooling for academic development in the content areas of social studies, literature, mathematics, science, visual/performing arts, and physical instruction (Chapter 5); and various models of bilingual education that serve students with varying degrees of support for heritage-language proficiency (Chapter 6). The accompanying figure highlights Part Two of the theoretical model presented in the introduction.

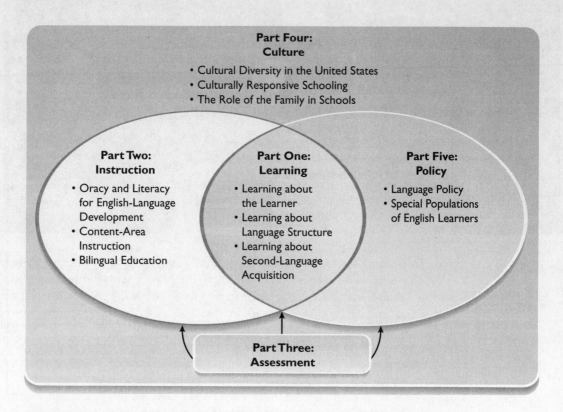

Theoretical Model for CLAD Instruction: Oracy and Literacy for English-Language Development, Content-Area Instruction, and Bilingual Education

4

Oracy and Literacy for English-Language Development

Se Lyun Lee and Ozan Alpan, prospective English teachers, plan a collaborative class project.

© Lynne Diaz-Rico

I am equally proficient and bilingual in both English and Turkish. Neither is my second or foreign language. Obviously I can't remember, but I'm certain the minute I was born I started hearing both English and Turkish (I assume the doctor said, in Turkish, "It's a boy!"). In the US, my father was the only person I spoke Turkish with. However, each summer my family and I would go to Turkey where I had informal exposure. I started taking private Turkish lessons at the age of eleven. Yet, my real formal exposure began at the age of twelve when I moved to Turkey and continued my studies there. My multilingualism is a result of my natural multilingual environment as well as deliberate practices by my parents. Simply put, I learned English because I was born and raised in the US and English was the language I needed to communicate with everyone (with the exception of my father who only spoke Turkish with me), and I learned Turkish because my parents are Turkish and

I lived, studied, and worked in Turkey. So my English literacy started in America, and continued in Turkey. My biliteracy did not come easily. My parents pushed me, and I had to work hard to attain it.

Ozan Alpan (2013)

Developing proficiency in English is a multifaceted task. Not only must students read and write at a level that supports advanced academic success, but they must also use their skills of *listening* and *speaking* to gain information and demonstrate their knowledge. A fifth necessary skill is the ability to *think* both critically and creatively. The teacher's role is to integrate these separate, but interrelated, skills in a unified curriculum that moves students from beginning to advanced proficiency in classroom English.

In this chapter, we first discuss English-language development standards that help teachers organize and develop their programs. Next, we explore the four language modalities and provide suggestions for specific lessons and activities that foster English-language oracy and literacy development. Because of the pervasiveness of technology in today's world, a separate section on oracy, literacy, and technology provides information and activities to integrate technology with literacy instruction.

Critical Literacy

Second-language acquisition is intimately joined to issues of cultural identity and social differences. Classroom activities are never neutral: Some help to develop students' oracy and literacy skills that can enhance their social and cultural prospects in life. Conversely, in some activities students are passive, simply marking time until the day is done. At worst, some classwork leads to students acquiring a sense of frustration and inadequacy in school. Teachers who are dedicated to helping students overcome poverty, gender discrimination, racism, and social class oppression link literacy activities to efforts that address these social inequities (Auerbach, 1993).

Acquiring English is more than learning to read, speak, and write: It is a social practice, a social currency. English skills are part of the capital needed to overcome the unequal and limited access to education and other resources. These limitations too often lead to social and economic marginalization.

Some educators and researchers take a social justice perspective: that critical literacy can help learners "make sense of what they are learning by grounding it in the context of their daily lives and reflecting on their individual experiences, with an eye toward social action" (Corley, 2003, p. 1). Freire and Macedo (1987) emphasize that critical literacy gives learners the tools and language to critique ideas, information, and patterns of privilege that link literacy, socioeconomic contexts, and opportunity.

In the following sections, you will read about state and national efforts to improve accountability for English learners by holding educators to the goal of achieving a high standard of education for all students. Yet the real accountability rests in the heart of each teacher: What have I taught today that will give learners the language skills needed to forge a successful educational and social future?

English-Language Development Standards

To provide educators with directions and strategies to assist English learners, the international professional organization Teachers of English to Speakers of Other Languages developed a standards document (TESOL, 1997) to draw attention to English learners' needs. This document served as a complement to other standards documents and specified the language competencies that English learners need in order to become fully fluent in English. In 2006, TESOL published its revised standards that expanded the scope and breadth of the 1997 standards. The former ESL standards were consolidated (Standard 1) and four new standards address the language of the core curriculum areas (Standards 2–5). Information on this document is available at the TESOL website, www.tesol.org.

Numerous states have also produced documents to assist teachers working with English learners. California, for example, has prepared *English-Language Development Standards* (California Department of Education [CDE], 2012) to ensure that English learners develop proficiency in both the English language and the concepts and skills contained in the English-Language Arts (ELA) Content Standards (CDE, 1998a). Because California's English-Language Development standards were designed with the same categories as the English-Language Arts standards for mainstream students, teachers are able to identify "big ideas" in both sets of standards (such as "Follows directions") so that in a tightly focused lesson, English learners and English-only students are learning the same core skills. ELD Standards to match the Common Core are now under development.

State English-Language Development Standards

Florida adopted the *Reading/Language Arts Standards with English Language Proficiency Standards* in 2007 as part of its Sunshine State Standards. Texas adopted English Language Proficiency Standards (ELPS) in 2007 to replace the English as a Second Language Texas Essential Knowledge and Skills (ESL TEKS) beginning in the 2008–2009 school year (online at www.tea.state.tx.us/curriculum/biling/elps .html). In New York, the *Teaching of Language Arts to Limited English Proficient/ English Language Learners: Learning Standards for English as a Second Language* document (www.emsc.nysed.gov/biling/resource/esl/standards.html) was adopted to serve as the foundation for ESL curriculum, instruction, and assessment in grades PreK–12, and to serve as the framework for the New York State ESL Achievement Test (NYSESLAT), which is administered annually to all English learners in New York.

The importance of these standards documents is that teachers now can work with English learners through a developmental framework, recognizing that students cannot be forced to produce beyond their proficiency level, but knowing that students are expected to attain certain levels of competency commensurate with their proficiency.

Integrating Language Skills

Instead of teaching reading apart from writing, listening, and speaking, educators now recommend that these skills be combined smoothly into instruction that develops language skills in a unified way. For example, students tell stories as the teacher writes them down for later reading aloud (Language Experience Approach); students listen to stories and then retell them or write a new ending; and students write poems and then read them aloud. This reinforces one skill using another, allowing vocabulary words to be seen, heard, and spoken, and language to convert from receptive (listening and reading) to productive (speaking and writing) and vice versa.

Example of Concept   *"Play-full" Integrated Language Skills*

As a parent volunteer, I was part of an exciting example of integrated language arts when my son was in the third grade. The teacher, myself, and another parent volunteer noticed one English learner in the class who seemed to have fallen behind the rest of the students. In addition, she was not acquiring vocabulary as rapidly as necessary to keep up with the class. Furthermore, she had become socially withdrawn and was having a difficult time interacting with the other students. We debated whether we should take her aside to work separately on her word knowledge (pull-out ESL). Instead, we decided to try using an integrated language-arts approach: sponsoring a class play.

The purpose was two-fold; working in groups she would have no alternative but to socialize with the other students and at the same time she would work on her vocabulary skills as well as her reading and writing.

Working in small groups, the students chose fairy-tale characters and wrote small scenes that would later join together as a script. For example, the students would draw the characters using crayons and markers and then with the help of the aides they would write a description.

It was really an episodic play—a string of dramatic moments—but students talked with one another to design their scenes, listened to one another as they read aloud what they had written, drafted dialogue in five-minute chunks, and then acted out their plots in daily rehearsals.

During this small-group time, the other parent volunteer and I rotated among the different groups and prompted where necessary, "What more can you tell me about your scene?" "Who will say this line? "What happens next?" Although both parent volunteers were bilingual in English and Spanish, the students' discussion ranged across languages. Often, a long exchange occurred in the primary language as the students sorted out ideas, clarified their interpretations, and then drafted their written work. A lot of discussion went on during this group work. There were often three- and four-way conversations with questions and discussion going back and forth in various episodes of code-switching between languages.

From their initial ideas, the children elaborated on the dialogue and actions in their mini-scenes. The editing evolved as a part of group discussion as students prepared their scene for presentation. As part of the process of creativity, story ideas ebbed and flowed. As language consultants, we parent volunteers addressed the specific language needs (spelling, word choice, sometimes translation) of the small groups in the context of the students' writing.

Each child chose a part that he or she wanted to play. There were several princesses; but in the various scenes, each princess, like each wicked witch or fairy, had an enjoyable part. Those who did not wish to act could help to draw and color the poster (playbill) for the play.

When it was time for one princess (our shy English learner) to perform, she blossomed as she wore a gauzy dress and delivered her lines. The ogre wore a fake beard and carried a huge plastic bat. There was not much scenery, because the classroom opened onto a small patio that functioned as the stage. The bushes and trees became the scenery. The main focus was on the students. At the end of the play, the class applauded and cheered and the actors beamed with pride.

The actors were not necessarily the students that were the most proficient in English. But they had an unforgettable experience using their language skills to the fullest.

So what began as a way to increase fluency and vocabulary acquisition in one English learner turned into an entertaining way for all children in the class to develop integrated language skills . . . and it has become one of my most treasured memories of my son's school years. . . .

—Micaela Martínez (2013)

English learners, like native speakers of English, do not necessarily demonstrate a balance in language acquisition and ability. Some prolific speakers lag behind in reading, whereas some capable readers are shy about speaking, and so forth. The integrated skills approach supports those language skills that may be underdeveloped, while allowing students with strong skills in other areas to shine.

Listening

Although listening has been classified along with reading as a "receptive" skill, it is by no means a passive act. Listeners draw on their store of background knowledge and their expectation of the message to be conveyed as they actively work at understanding conversational elements.

The role of the teacher is to set up situations in which students feel a sense of purpose and can engage in real communication. In this way, students can develop a personal agenda—their own purposes and goals—for listening, and the English they acquire is most useful in their daily lives. Although the current emphasis is on communicating for authentic purposes, activities are discussed under the categories of listening to repeat, listening to understand, and listening for communication.

Listening to Repeat

A common listening strategy is *minimal pair* pattern practice, in which students are asked to listen to and repeat simple phrases that differ by only one phoneme—for example: "It is a ship/It is a sheep"; "He is barking/He is parking." Little attention,

Adapted Instruction

Listening for Sounds

- Use poems, nursery rhymes, and songs to introduce words that differ by only one phoneme.
- Ask students to orally fill in the blanks at the end of lines, demonstrating their knowledge of the sound and the word within the context.
- Read aloud wordplay books, alliterative books, and books with tongue twisters.

however, is paid to meaning. Current methods encourage students to listen to minimal pairs within meaningful contexts. Not only do these activities help students to hear the language, but the work with sounds also provides opportunities for preliterate students to develop phonemic awareness, "the insight that every spoken word is made up of a sequence of phonemes" (CDE, 1999, p. 278) and considered by many to be a prerequisite for learning to read.

Students also need to listen attentively to longer sections of discourse to hear sentence intonation patterns. Jazz chants provide rhythmic presentations of natural language in a meaningful context: "The rhythm, stress, and intonation pattern of the chant should be an *exact* replica of what the student would hear from a native speaker in natural conversation" (Graham, 1992, p. 3).

Example of Concept   *Sentence Intonation*

Mr. Pang used "Late Again" (Graham, 1978) not only to help students with intonation in short phrases but also as a means to get them ready to leave for the day. After learning the chant, students brainstormed words like *backpack, homework,* and *pencil case* to substitute for *keys, socks,* and *shoes* in the original chant. Mr. Pang would start the chant, "Are you ready?" and students would respond as they gathered their things and lined up at the door.

Listening to Understand

Students perform tasks such as writing the correct response or selecting the correct answer to demonstrate comprehension (Morley, 2001). To be successful, they must listen carefully. Typical classroom tasks are listening to an audiotape and completing true/false exercises based on the content, listening to a prerecorded speech and circling vocabulary items on a list as they appear in the text, and listening to a lecture and completing an outline of the notes.

Listening objectives in language tasks can vary from simply identifying words or facts, to comprehending details, or getting the main idea. Listeners can respond by choosing from two alternatives, taking notes, transferring what has been heard to a chart, answering questions, making a summary, discussing, or acting out what was heard.

Total Physical Response. Total physical response (TPR) is based on the association between language and body movement and can be an engaging, lively addition to classroom techniques. In studying and observing children learning their first language, Asher (1982) noted three elements that he made the basis for his approach:

1. Listening, and hence understanding, precedes speaking.
2. Understanding is developed through moving the body.
3. Speaking is never forced.

In TPR, students respond to an oral command that is simultaneously being modeled. For example, the teacher says, "Stand" while standing up, and "Sit" while sitting down, and students follow along. The instructor repeats the commands followed by the appropriate action until students perform without hesitation. The instructor then begins to delay his or her own action to allow students the opportunity to respond and thus demonstrate understanding. Eventually, the students, first as a whole group and then as individuals, act on the instructor's voice command alone. Novel commands are given that combine previously learned commands in a new way. For example, if the students were familiar with "Run" and "Walk to the chair," they might be given "Run to the chair." Students continue to respond in a nonverbal manner until they feel comfortable issuing their own commands.

Reading and writing are also introduced through commands. The instructor may write "Stand" on the board and gesture to the students to perform the action. After practice with the written form in class, students can be given lists of familiar commands that they can then manipulate in their own fashion. The concrete, hands-on methodology recommended by Asher is associated with early stages of second-language learning and is recommended by Krashen and Terrell (1983) for promoting comprehension in a low-anxiety environment. (For TPR used in storytelling, see Ray and Seely [1998].)

When students listen for understanding they can demonstrate comprehension in several ways. They can act out what they heard, they can point to parts of a chart or picture to indicate comprehension, they can draw a picture of what they have heard, or they can consult a partner and together construct a verbal response to questions.

Example of Concept *Orienting Students to Classroom Procedures*

Ms. Knight reviews her classroom procedures and selects five that she wants students to learn the first week; for example, "Take out your reading book"; "Look at the directions on the board." She says and models the behavior. The students mimic her first as a whole group and then in table groups. By having all students participate, Ms. Knight allows her English learners to become confident members of the class without singling them out.

Listening is a complex activity. Brown (2006) offers the following tips for improving listening comprehension:

- Draw upon—or build up—students' schemata before listening so that what they hear will make sense.
- Make sure students have a clear purpose for listening: Will the emphasis be on the main idea, details, or making inferences?
- Place a listening task in a real-world context so students are learning information that they can use outside of class.
- Listening is more likely to lead to comprehension when followed by speaking tasks that feature topics that students find interesting to discuss.

Listening for Communication

Current language-teaching methods emphasize the interactional aspects of language and recognize the importance of the listener's construction of meaning. During the initial "silent period," learners actively listen, segmenting the sound stream, absorbing intonation patterns, and becoming comfortable in the second-language environment. They demonstrate comprehension through nonverbal means. With this methodology, academic subjects can be included even in the early stages of language acquisition.

Adapted Instruction

Preparing for a Speaker

Before the Talk
- Discuss the topic of an upcoming talk (by a guest speaker, cross-age, or grade-level peer).
- Brainstorm questions and comments the students might like to make.

During the Talk
- Ask students to listen for answers to their questions.
- Record the talk.

After the Talk
- With the recording at a listening center, have students listen again, making note of ideas they want to share in the class follow-up activities. The recording also serves as a mediator when students have varying recollections of a particular point. The students can listen carefully to the tape in order to reconcile their points of view.

Listening, far from merely being a receptive skill, can be successfully combined with other language modes as part of an integrated approach to English acquisition. Table 4.1 provides listening comprehension activities within each of the three categories discussed.

A favorite activity to develop speaking and listening skills is Information Gap. In this activity, two students have copies of the same materials, but they sit with a manila folder held vertically between them. One describes a picture, and the other identifies which one is the subject of the description. In the same manner, one student can be seated to watch a movie segment in order to describe it to another student whose back is turned. The one listening must summarize the action after the description, and then both can watch the segment again together. This activity is easily adapted for various levels of language proficiency.

Table 4.1 Activities for Listening Comprehension

Repetition	Understanding	Communication

To hear sound patterns:
  Rhyming poems
  Songs
  Couplets
  Tongue twisters
  Jingles
  Alliterative poems and books
To listen to sentences:
  Jazz chants
  Dialogues
  Skits
	Listening to answer factual questions orally or in writing:
	  Dialogues
	  Talks
	  Lectures
	  Arguments
	Listening to make notes:
	  Support an argument
	  Persuade
		Playing games:
		  Twenty Questions
		  Pictionary
		  Password
		  Simon Says
		  Mother May I?
		Interviews
		Conversation starters
		Cooperative problem-solving activities:
		  Riddles
		  Logic puzzles
		  Brainteasers

Speaking

Speaking involves a number of complex skills and strategies. Spoken discourse involves not only stringing words together in proper grammatical sequence but also organizing those strings into coherent wholes. This produces an oral text, one that has an inherent form, meaning, purpose, and function.

Spoken discourse can be informal, such as conversations between friends, or formal, such as lectures or presentations. Informal conversations are interactive; speaker and listener share common knowledge and support one another with nonverbal cues. In a formal presentation, the listener is less able to interact with the speaker to negotiate meaning. Part of the role of the teacher is to help students understand and produce discourse not only for the purpose of basic interpersonal communication (informal) but also for the comprehension and production of cognitive/academic language (formal).

Situations for Spoken Discourse

Students need opportunities to talk in natural interactional contexts and for a variety of purposes: to establish and maintain social relationships; to express reactions; to give and seek information; to solve problems, discuss ideas, or teach and learn a skill; to entertain or play with language; or to display achievement. In addition, students learn needed discourse skills by interacting with different conversational partners: other students, the teacher, other adults at school, cross-age peers, classroom visitors, and so on. Beginning language learners may need basic survival language:

- Can they give their name, address, and telephone number?
- Can they say their parents' names?

- Can they ask for help politely, using "please" and "thank you"?
- Can they understand simple classroom procedures, such as how to ask to use the bathroom?
- Can they name several classmates?

Schools should be environments that challenge students to use language to meet the social, emotional, and cognitive demands of their lives in and out of school. The following three principles (Dudley-Marling & Searle, 1991) help teachers set up such environments:

1. *Consider the emotional setting.* Teachers set up a climate of trust and respect by encouraging students to respect the language of their peers, by listening respectfully when students speak, and by working with students to establish classroom rules of respect and support.

2. *Create a physical setting for talk.* Classrooms need to be arranged so that students have flexibility in working and interacting. Some desks can be replaced with round or rectangular tables; other desks can be arranged in clusters.

3. *Group students for instruction.* Students need frequent opportunities to talk. Flexible grouping allows students to work with a variety of classmates; cross-age tutors provide one-on-one time with an older student; and aides, parent volunteers, and volunteer "grandparents" can lead small-group discussions.

Some educators argue that English learners do not need a separate block of time to develop oral language because students in structured English immersion and other nonbilingual programs are immersed in English throughout the day. Saunders, Foorman, and Carlson, in a 2006 study, looked at 1,400 native-Spanish-speaking students in thirty-four schools across California and Texas to study whether the English learners received a separate block of oral English preparation and, if so, what this entailed and what achievement data these programs generated. The researchers found that 58 percent of classrooms had a separate ELD block of time, dedicated largely to listening-comprehension tasks. Less than 6 percent of such class time was devoted to vocabulary or grammar in English, although the achievement data showed some students had higher word identification scores after spending time in dedicated ELD instruction. The authors advised more attention to "academic" English during such instruction.

Improving Oral Proficiency

English learners must have a comprehensible control of the English sound system. Pronunciation involves the correct *articulation* of the individual sounds (phonemes) of English as well as the proper *stress* and *pitch* within syllables, words, and phrases. Longer stretches of speech require correct *intonation* patterns (see Chapter 2).

The goal of teaching English pronunciation is not necessarily to make second-language speakers sound like native speakers of English. The teacher's role is to create

Example of Concept | *Chant and Dance Syllable Work*

Artist, guitarist, and literacy coach Eduardo García has a novel way of introducing fifth-grade English learners to syllables using the African-based rhythms of Latin America. Students each wear flash cards around their necks with one syllable of a long word. They sit in a circle. The coach-as-drummer sits in the center, and calls out a syllable: "o." Everyone chants "o." The student wearing the *o* dances to the center, soon to be joined by the "per," "a," and "tion." Soon everyone chants "operation" and they all sit down. Next come the syllables of the word *recommendation*, then *cooperation* until a roomful of words has been danced into memory. (García, 2004, p. 49)

a nonthreatening environment that stimulates and interests students enough that they participate actively in producing speech. Finders and Hynds (2007) point out that a strong focus on correctness may stifle students' enthusiasm and creativity—the emphasis should be on "progress, not perfection" (p. 97).

In other cases, however, teachers may want to intervene actively. Clarification checks may be interjected politely when communication is impaired. Correction or completion by the teacher may be given after the teacher has allowed ample "wait time." Students' attempts to produce English may be enhanced if they are taught strategies that help them to overcome anxiety and are given opportunities to speak in the context of reading and other content activities.

Table 4.2 organizes representative oral activities into the three categories ranging from tightly structured (on the left) to freely constructed (on the right).

Adapted Instruction

Acquiring the Oracy Strategy—"Self-Talk for Speaking"

As a warm-up, ask students if they talk to themselves as they prepare to do something new. Elicit positive and negative examples. Tell students they will practice positive *self-talk* as they prepare for and carry out speaking tasks in English. Next, model self-talk when making a telephone call.

Then, hand out a worksheet with several blank lines, with the heading, "When I prepare for a presentation, I can tell myself _____" (students will fill in the blanks with several self-selected phrases).

For homework, students should prepare and rehearse a one-minute presentation using self-talk. They give the presentation the next day, and then report which phrases they found most helpful before and during delivery.

Source: Chamot, Barnhardt, El-Dinary, and Robbins (1999, pp. 231–232).

Table 4.2 Formats for Oral Practice in the ELD Classroom

Guided Practice	Communicative Practice	Free Conversation
Formulaic exchanges:	Simulations	Discussion groups
Greetings	Guessing games	Debates
Congratulations	Group puzzles	Panel discussions
Apologies	Rank-order problems	Group picture story
Leave-taking	Values continuum	Socializing
Dialogues	Categories of preference:	Storytelling/retelling
Mini-conversations	Opinion polls	Discussions of:
Role-plays	Survey taking	Films
Skits	Interviews	Shared experiences
Oral descriptions	Brainstorming	Literature
Strip stories	News reports	
Oral games	Research reports	
	Storytelling	

Example of Concept   *Cued Story Retelling*

Beginning language learners can use pictures from the stories they read to cue story retellings. To prepare them for retelling, each student is given a set of pictures. As the story is read aloud, each student holds up a relevant picture. After the story is read, students mix up their pictures and then arrange them in order of events, telling the story as they go (Malinka, 2006).

Vocabulary Development

According to educational researchers, native-English speakers typically know at least 5,000 to 7,000 English words before kindergarten—a huge vocabulary, as anyone who has struggled to learn a second language knows. English-language learners must close that initial gap, but also keep pace with the native speakers as they steadily expand their vocabulary mastery.

The vocabulary of academic language goes well beyond that used in most social conversations. Through structured talk about academically relevant content students learn the words needed to engage in class discussions and to comprehend what they read in various subjects. Beyond intermediate states of English acquisition, they must acquire new words independently. Moras (2001) suggested several strategies: guided discovery (how to guess word meanings), contextual guesswork (how to use cues such as parts of speech to guess the function of a word in a sentence), and dictionary use (looking up a word's definition, pronunciation, grammar, and usage). Lastly, dictionaries such as the *Oxford Collocations Dictionary* can give suggestions and restrictions on a word's use.

Example of Concept *Discussion about Vocabulary*

Group discussions can also take place about new words. Tinker Sachs and Ho (2007) described Ms. Wu's vocabulary-building lesson, in which small groups grappled with the definitions, synonyms, and antonyms for new words they acquired during an exercise in which they classified books into genres such as classics, humor, drama, and autobiography. After small-group discussion, Ms. Wu invited one member of each group to teach the whole class about a new word that the group acquired.

Vocabulary instruction is multifaceted. Students need a variety of strategies to gain meaning from context, including ways to guess what part of speech a word is, to look for embedded definitions in which the following text explains the meaning, and to find theme-related clues in the surrounding text. Students can learn to distinguish connotative from denotative meanings of words, so they can acquire the emotions and nuances that accompany new words as they are learned. They can identify words with multiple meanings to avoid confusion (Newman, 2006).

Students can learn new vocabulary words in a variety of ways:

- Say it aloud and clap the syllables.
- Add it to a Pictionary game file and play once a day.
- Work with an older child ("vocabulary buddy") and look it up together.
- Once a week "borrow" another teacher for a class interview about the word meanings.
- Look up the word online.
- Use a bilingual dictionary to draw upon L1 knowledge.

Example of Concept *Vocabulary through Visualization*

Especially when faced with a new language, many learners rely on visuals for understanding, such as textbook illustrations, gestures, photos, drawings, and charts. Zemach (2007) encourages students to illustrate new vocabulary words with sketches, and then to quiz one another with their homemade flash cards. Instead of making an outline to brainstorm for an essay, she encourages students to use mind maps. These visuals reduce the stress of all-verbal learning.

Reading

Literacy instruction is a crucial aspect of K–12 schooling in the United States. For decades, educators have debated the best way to help children learn to read and read to learn. Recent research has revealed a dismal literacy level for students who are classified as "formerly English learners"—only 20 percent scored at the proficient or advanced levels of the reading portion of the 2005 NCES testing (Calderón, 2007). However, a complicating factor that is sometimes not considered by monolingual reading researchers is the varying background experiences that English learners bring to the reading task. California TESOL (CATESOL, 1998) provided the following five classifications for English learners that help teachers to understand the varying backgrounds of English learners.

1. Young learners [K–3] whose beginning literacy instruction is in their primary language
2. Young learners [K–3] acquiring initial literacy in English because they do not have access to primary-language reading instruction
3. Older learners with grade-level primary-language literacy, who are beginning to develop literacy in English
4. Older learners with limited formal schooling in their home country
5. Older learners with inconsistent school history, with limited development of either the primary language or English (p. 1)

Even when teachers use this classification to understand that English learners' literacy backgrounds differ widely, standards documents such as the one for California (CDE, 2012) are written with the expectation that teachers can raise English learners quickly to the literacy levels of monolingual English speakers. The document specifically states that the ELD standards "are designed to move all students, regardless of their instructional program, into the mainstream English-language arts curriculum" (p. 2).

What, then, characterizes literacy instruction for English learners? Evidence from research in second-language acquisition indicates that the natural developmental processes that children undergo in learning their first language (oral and written) also occur in second-language acquisition (oral and written). For reading, these processes

Adapted Instruction

Characteristics of Classrooms That Support English Learners' Literacy Development

- Activities are meaningful to students and are often jointly negotiated with the teacher.
- Instruction is cognitively demanding yet is scaffolded—that is, temporarily supported—to ensure student success.
- Learning is organized into topics and themes so that students can build on previous learning.
- Students work collaboratively and grouping is flexible.
- Students are immersed in a print-rich environment so that they have constant opportunities to interact with the written word.

Source: Hamayan (1994) and Peregoy and Boyle (2013).

include using knowledge of *sound–symbol relationships* (graphophonics), *word order and grammar* (syntax), and *meaning* (semantics) to predict and confirm meaning, and using background knowledge about the text's topic and structure along with linguistic knowledge and reading strategies to make an interpretation (Peregoy & Boyle, 2013).

Several important issues for teachers working with reading and English learners are discussed here. These include transferring literacy from first to second languages, students without literacy in their first or second language, and phonics for English learners. These discussions are followed by explanations of specific strategies that support English learners' literacy development.

Transferring Literacy from First to Second Languages

Many English learners already have basic understandings of the reading/writing process that they can transfer to a second language. One of the most important of these is the concept that print carries meaning. Others involve directionality, sequencing, and visual discrimination—concepts about print that kindergarten and first-grade teachers work with in teaching students to read.

In classrooms where English learners are already literate in their first language, they transfer that knowledge to reading and writing in English. (See Snow, Burns, and Griffin [1998] for a review of research findings supporting transfer.) Table 4.3 lists concepts that transfer from the first language to the second.

However, even though learners may be literate in their first language, they are still English learners and as such need support to develop their English proficiency and to have the background information necessary to read and produce English texts. Teachers' tasks are more difficult if students are not literate in their first language.

Table 4.3 Literacy Skills That Transfer from the First Language to the Second

Concepts and Skills Shown to Transfer from First-Language Literacy to Second-Language Literacy	

• Print has meaning
• Reading and writing are used for various purposes
• Concepts about print
  Book-orientation concepts (how to hold a book, how to turn pages)
  Directionality (in English, left to right, and top to bottom)
  Letters (letter names, lowercase, uppercase)
  Words (composed of letters, spaces mark boundaries)
	• Knowledge of text structure
	• Use of semantic and syntactic knowledge
	• Use of cues to predict meaning
	• Reading strategies (hypothesizing, constructing meaning, etc.)
	• Confidence in self as reader

Students without Literacy in First or Second Languages

Preschoolers without a knowledge of print, older students without previous school-ing, and the partially literate who may have acquired some decoding skills in their primary language but whose overall level of literacy does not provide them useful access to print—these groups need special treatment. Appropriate programs for these learners adhere to three important principles of literacy instruction:

1. Literacy is introduced in a meaningful way.
2. The link between oral language and print is made as naturally as possible.
3. Students have the opportunity to enjoy reading and writing.

Example of Concept   *A Reading Program for Nonliterates*

In a five-year study of English learners in New York City schools, the Center for Applied Linguistics identified a group they called "students with interrupted formal education" (SIFE)—immigrant students who may have had only a few years of schooling in their country of origin. Educators devised an intervention program entitled Reading Instructional Goals for Older Readers (RIGOR), taught by ESL dual-language educators, tutors, or reading specialists. Levels I and 2 feature decoding and comprehension tools using high-interest narratives with phonetically regular vocabulary words (Calderon, 2007).

Seven instructional procedures have proved successful in leading students to literacy in their second language (Hamayan, 1994). (Although these strategies are especially important for preliterate second-language learners, they are also helpful for English learners in general, even those who are literate in their first language.)

Environmental Print. The classroom is saturated with meaningful environmental print. Students see labels, announcements, names, and signs with as many contextual clues as possible. Labels can be bilingual or trilingual, thus incorporating students' native languages into their beginning literacy experiences.

Meaning-Based. Literacy activities move from the "known" to the "unknown." They revolve around content of interest to the learners. One way of starting with the known is to base literacy activities on the learners' oral language (see LEA later in this chapter).

A Silent Period in Reading. Literacy is allowed to emerge naturally. Students go through a silent period in reading, often mouthing words while the teacher reads aloud. Dialogue journals are a means of allowing language to emerge in a natural, developmental way.

Low-Anxiety Environment. Effective literacy environments are free of anxiety. Learners' attempts at reading and writing are greeted with enthusiasm. When they see their efforts are rewarded, students feel encouraged to continue.

Motivating Activities. Activities stimulate thinking and have value beyond that of a classroom exercise. Learners sense the intrinsic worth of reading when it leads to a dramatic presentation or sharing with a buddy.

Integration of Structure and Function. Students' attention is focused on specific structures and forms of written language within the context of meaningful activities. Their own oral-language stories, dialogue journals, and so on provide the basis for specific instruction.

Integration of Content and Literacy. Content-area instruction is integrated with literacy. Vocabulary, grammatical structures, and language functions needed in academic areas are incorporated into literacy activities.

Table 4.4 provides examples of materials and reading and writing activities that have been found to support English learners.

Balanced Literacy Instruction for English Learners

Meaning-Centered Approaches. Researchers looking at children learning to read in naturalistic settings noticed that they actively seek meaning. They work to make sense of text. They combine text clues with their own prior knowledge to construct meanings. The theory called *whole language* arose from the idea that meaning plays

Table 4.4 Materials and Activities to Support English Learners' Literacy Development

Materials	Activities with a Reading Focus	Activities with a Writing Focus
Literature, literature, and more literature	Read-aloud	Dialogue journals
Big books, pattern books	Readers' theater	Buddy journals
Wordless picture books	Storytelling	Writing workshop
Ads, posters, pamphlets, brochures	Shared reading	Response groups
Songbooks	Oral reading activities:	Peer editing groups
Poetry, rhymes, riddles, tongue twisters	Choral reading	Author's chair
Journals, diaries	Buddy reading	Classroom/school newspaper
Magazines	Repeated reading	Literature response journals
Comic books	Independent reading	Content-area journals
How-to books	Language Experience Approach (LEA)	Developing scripts for readers' theater
Dictionaries, encyclopedias		Language Experience Approach (LEA)
		Pattern poems

a central role in learning, and that language modes (speaking, listening, reading, writing) interact and are interdependent. Whole language, a philosophy of reading instruction, complemented many of the findings of studies in first- and second-language acquisition.

Meaning-centered systems of language acquisition (also called *top-down* systems—see Vacca, Vacca, Gove, Burkey, Lenhart & McKeon, 2011) support the view that learners are generating hypotheses from and actively constructing interpretations about the input they receive, be it oral or written. Language is social in that it occurs within a community of users who attach agreed-upon meaning to their experiences, and explore the multiple functions of literacy, reading, and writing to satisfy their own needs and goals.

Bottom-Up Approaches. Advocates of *bottom-up* approaches are concerned that learners connect the individual sounds of language with its written form as soon as possible, leading to the ability to decode whole words. Once words are identified, meaning will take care of itself. Instruction in decoding the sound–symbol relationship includes a set of rules for sounding out words.

To present the learner with easily decodable text, basal reading materials with controlled vocabulary are used to present simplified language, and teachers are encouraged to "preteach" vocabulary words that appear in reading passages. The emphasis is on skills for identifying words and sentence patterns, rather than on strategies for creating meaning from text.

Research and observation of children learning to read indicates that in fact readers use both top-down strategies and bottom-up skills as they read. Current reading instruction now favors a balanced approach (see Tompkins, 2009, particularly Chapter 1, for further discussion; also see Fitzgerald, 1999).

Teachers who use a "balanced literacy" approach employ a variety of components to help students become better readers and writers:

- Shared reading: The teacher reads an enlarged text aloud as students read along; students use various strategies when they encounter difficulty.
- Read aloud: The teacher reads a text while students listen; the teacher models thinking aloud about how to interpret the information.
- Reading workshop: Students work independently, with partners, or in a small group; the teacher gives mini-lessons to teach reading strategies.
- Shared writing: The teacher composes texts with students, modeling the thought process by thinking aloud.
- Interactive writing: Students and teacher write a text together; the teacher helps students build up structure and meaning.
- Writing workshop: Students work independently, with partners, or in a small group; the teacher gives mini-lessons to teach writing strategies.
- Word study, which might include phonemic awareness, phonics, and/or spelling. (Mermelstein, 2006)

Phonics. The alphabetic principle is the idea that the sounds of spoken words correspond to written words in systematic ways. Phonics instruction teaches readers sound–letter correspondences in order to recognize words. Quick recognition of words is the basis for fluent reading, which in turn is the basis for comprehension—the real goal of reading.

In "part-to-whole" phonics, the focus is on learning to match sounds with letters, which in English is a process with many exceptions to the rules. The beginning reader must recognize which combinations of letters are associated with specific sounds, and then blend these sounds in the proper sequence to create meaningful words. The beginning writer must work in reverse, to produce letters that correspond to the sound of the words to be written. Using "decodable" text with a minimal number of exceptions to phonics rules assists this process.

In an embedded phonics approach, students are guided to make discoveries about phonics rules by the use of familiar texts. "Hands-on" letter manipulations with magnetic letters or letter tiles involves students in taking words apart and reassembling them to induce the word-making process. Computer games can be used interactively in this process, with the discovery of correct sound-letter combinations rewarded by computer recognition and rewards. The goal is to provide what Villaume and Brabham (2003, p. 478) called "varied, flexible, and responsive" phonics instruction.

Phonics for English Learners. Cummins (2003) reviewed and synthesized research on teaching reading both to native- and non-native-English speakers. He found that almost all studies agree that the following type of instruction leads to success in decoding skills and reading comprehension: Students must be immersed in a literature-rich environment, and they must develop phonemic awareness, letter knowledge, and concepts about print while instruction is focused on actual reading.

Phonics instruction alone gradually leads to students' losing interest in reading. They must "catch afire"—learn to love literature—from teachers who are excited about reading, who share the books they love and who interest students on an individual basis in selected stories and non-fictional resources.

Phonemic Awareness. When children learn language, they acquire phonological awareness as they separate the oral sound stream they encounter into syllables and words. Literacy development builds on this ability, helping young readers connect sounds to written symbols (Burns, Griffin, & Snow, 1999). Phonemic awareness is the ability to use the sound–symbol connection to separate sentences into words and words into syllables in order to hear, identify, and manipulate the individual phonemes within spoken words (Block & Israel, 2005). Phonemic awareness tasks are used to help students to hear and isolate individual phonemes (see Table 4.5).

Explicit Phonics Instruction. Educational regulators have insisted that "explicit" phonics instruction is the key to higher reading scores; by this they seem to mean

Table 4.5 Tasks for Teaching Phonemic Awareness

Task	Sample Activity
Rhyming	Recognize or produce rhymes.
Word-to-word matching	Which of three words does not begin or end the same as the others?
Sound-to-word matching	Is this sound found in this word? (Is there an /m/ in *man?*)
Initial (or final) sounds	The child gives the first (or last) sound in the spoken word (Give the last sound in *dish*).
Segmentation	The child identifies each sound heard in a word by putting the correct letter in a separate box (number of boxes available for letters matches number of phonemes in the word).
Blending	Given a sequence of phonemes, the child blends them to form a word.
Reading words in isolation	The learner is given a set of words to read, perhaps having the same phonics principle.
Reading words in stories	The learner applies phonics knowledge to achieve comprehension of words in context.
Writing words: dictation	The learner practices writing words that are given in spoken form.
Writing words: using invented spelling	The learner writes without achieving perfect spelling in a transitional focus on fluency over accuracy.

Source: Based on Stahl, Duffy-Hester, and Stahl (1998).

clearly expressed instructions that teachers should follow to ensure that students understand and use the alphabetic principle when they read. Many districts require teachers to follow scripted reading lessons, as if adhering to the letter of a teaching routine is in itself sufficient to create effective readers. But as Villaume and Brabham (2003) pointed out, "Scripts cannot capture the interactive and dynamic conversations expert teachers have with their students about the ways that words work" (p. 479).

> **Did You Know?** The principal concern that teachers may have in developing word recognition skills in English is the students' tendency to be too good at transferring their word-unlocking strategies from Spanish to English. "Because the techniques have served them well in Spanish, the students may become very successful at *calling words.* This apparent prosperity must be monitored thoughtfully to ensure that students are obtaining meaning from the English words they have recognized" (Thonis, 2005, p. 108).

Frustrations with Phonics. Since the National Reading Panel stated in 2000 that phonics produces significant benefits as a part of reading instruction, the federal government has been influencing school districts to adopt programs with a strong phonics component. The rules of English phonics are complex, and not easy for children to learn. Research has shown that children who rely on phonics read slowly, paying more attention to the form of the word than its meaning. As a consequence, they are easily bored with reading. Uribe (2008) summarizes educators' frustrations with phonics-based instruction:

> [T]he most frustrating in all this is that many educators now think of phonics as a substitute for reading and devote more class time to sound and spelling correspondences than to literary experiences. And that is unfair. Phonics is a tool that students can use to help understand a text in some situations, but what really makes the difference is reading itself, the social event that takes place between reader and book. This, not phonics, nurtures students' positive attitudes to books and reading. To say that phonics is an essential element in the reading process is outrageous. And the consequences for our students and for our society in the long run will be incalculable. (p. 37)

One elementary teacher, using the phonics-based program Success for All, identified the following problems in using the program with his English learners: Reading (decoding) is separated from comprehension; emphasis is on sound and sound-blend identification to the detriment of coherent, logical reading material; specially written stories focus on targeted sounds and do not include commonly occurring English words and natural language use; and unnatural, awkward syntax contradicts English learners' growing knowledge of spoken English and/or reinforces use of problematic language (Lee, 2000).

Approaches to Teaching Reading

Reading is an essential skill. Children who do not learn to read in elementary school enter secondary education as severe underachievers and are at risk for dropping out. How can teachers encourage English learners to acquire skills that will result in academic achievement and an enjoyment of reading?

Standards-Based Reading Instruction. New reading materials in the marketplace reflect the current insistence on standards-based instruction, with explicit references to standards on each page. *High Points* from Hampton-Brown (Schifini, Short, & Tinajero, 2002) is a typical ELD series, complete with teaching tips designed to facilitate comprehensible input, decodable small books, learning strategies for enhancing cognitive academic language, ways to increase reading fluency, writing support for students with non-Roman alphabets, and cultural tips. Texts are now under development that are aligned with Common Core Standards.

Emergent Literacy. When children—or adolescents or adults, for that matter—are first learning to read, they are in the stage of *emergent literacy*; their reading and writing behaviors precede and develop into conventional literacy. Emergent literacy involves a combination of components. Emergent readers must learn to:

- Draw upon their prior knowledge of the world to connect the printed word with its meaning; for example, most preschool children connect a red octagonal sign at a street corner with the meaning "stop."
- Use phonemic awareness to understand that sounds correspond to symbols.

- Recognize a set of sight words that are frequently used in English but may not be phonetically predictable ("the" is not "ta-ha-ay").
- Acquire reading behaviors, such as handling books, using a library, and reading for enjoyment.
- Participate in a culture of reading, sharing their pleasure in reading with others and working in the company of others to acquire meaning from books.

Most learners read and write because they see others doing it—reading directions, newspapers, or road signs for information; or notes they have written to themselves to jog their memory; or novels, just to pass the time. However, many English learners do not see their families reading or writing, even in their home language. It is important, then, that the classroom as a community be a place in which reading is an everyday, enjoyable feature. This socializes students into a culture of literacy. By creating shared contexts, modeling language and literacy behaviors such as reading and writing, encouraging peer interactions, relating to students' cultural backgrounds, and according high status to students' first languages, teachers can successfully develop language and literacy skills in multilingual classrooms.

The Basics of Learning to Read. Within the social context of shared enjoyment among a group of readers, there are four important facets of learning to read: skill with print, decoding text, utilizing prior knowledge, and comprehension.

Skill with print involves understanding that a printed text contains words which carry meaning, and that printed words correspond to spoken language. Words, not pictures, are read. Learners note that language is divided into words which can be written down, with spaces in between; letters make words and words make sentences; sentences begin with capital letters and end with punctuation; a book is read from front to back, and reading goes left to right and top to bottom; a book has a title, an author, and sometimes an illustrator. In a *print-rich environment*, children see print wherever they turn—on bulletin boards, calendars, book displays, labels on objects in several languages, shopping lists at play centers, and so forth.

In *decoding text*, as in a sentence with an unknown word, various readers use distinct strategies. One type of reader uses *semantic knowledge*. If a sentence reads, "Joey pushed open the door of the haunted . . ." a reader might guess that the next word is not *hose*, because its meaning would not make sense. Another type of reader might use *syntactic knowledge* on the sentence "Joey drives a small . . ." to reject the word *care* as the wrong choice for that part of the sentence. Still a third type of reader might use *orthographic shape* in the sentence "Joey drove a load of trees to the paper mill," knowing that the words *pap* and *paperwork* look wrong. A single reader might use these three types of meaning making equally often, or one might detect a preference for one type of decoding. Interventions would be designed accordingly (Newman, 1985).

Utilizing students' *prior knowledge* helps to forge connections between what they already know and what the curriculum presents. Assessing students' background knowledge before instruction helps teachers to ascertain if it is necessary to include activities that build schemata. This is true for both rural and urban children; while their own environments may be rich in stimuli, schooling offers the opportunity for a greatly expanded knowledge of the world. Reading that speaks to their lived experience must be balanced with reading that opens up entirely new possibilities.

| Example of Concept | *Building Students' Schemata* |

Educators have long known that prior knowledge of a subject can improve a child's performance not only in reading, but also on tests. New York State English and math exams include several questions about livestock, crops, and other aspects to rural life to which students at the Harlem Success Academy have little point of reference. So each fall, students take a "field study" trip to the Queens County Farm Museum to pet cows, learn where wool comes from, and hoist pumpkins into the air.

"They are good at reciting and remembering things," said Abigail Johnson, a teacher at Harlem Success Academy 3, "but they can't make the connection unless you show it to them" (Hernández, 2009 p. A25).

The key to meaning is reading *comprehension*. Readers generally form some initial hypothesis about the content or main idea of a book or a reading passage, based on their expectations, title, first sentence, previous knowledge of genre, or other clues. Reading further, the reader modifies the initial prediction. Getting the gist of a passage is the most important concept a reader can develop, because getting the main idea makes further reading more purposeful, facilitates recall, and helps to make sense of the supporting details.

Adapted Instruction

Sticky Notes for Reading Comprehension

One sixth-grade teacher models aloud to students the process of thinking aloud about the type of connections made during reading—such guidance as details linked to main ideas (MI), connections made to world knowledge (W) or personal experience (ME), and connections made to causal knowledge (C) drawn from other parts of the text.

After the teacher models this process, students use sticky notes to code texts as they read with these codes (Dewitz & Dewitz, 2003).

The Three-Stage Reading Process. Activities prior to reading prepare students to get "into" the reading. Other strategies help students read "through" the material, and, finally, follow-up activities help students organize and retain their understanding "beyond" the act of reading. Actually, in a classroom in which literacy is socially constructed, reading is more complex—students are moving into, through, and beyond their own reading on an individual basis as they dip into some books, pick up and discard others, or "surf" the Internet. Therefore "into–through–beyond" activities represent reading for an entire topic.

"Into" activities generate interest. Two such activities are brainstorming and KWL (What do I *know*? What do I *want* to learn? What have I *learned*?). Asking "What do I know?" allows students to place new knowledge in the context of their own episodic memories and existing concepts. The students list everything they know about a topic. They then tell the teacher what they would like to learn. A chart is maintained for the duration of the unit and students refer to it from time to time to talk about what they have learned. Starting each topic or unit with KWL actively engages students in reviewing their own experiences relevant to the topic.

"Through" activities help students as they work with the text. Teachers find reading aloud a useful strategy that gives the students an opportunity to hear a proficient reader, to get a sense of the format and story line, and to listen to the teacher "think aloud" about the reading. To help students develop a sense of inflection, pronunciation, rhythm, and stress, a commercial tape recording of a work of literature can be obtained for listening and review, or adult volunteers may be willing to make a recording. Various activities can be used for students to perform the actual reading. Table 4.6 offers a variety of reading methods for in-class use.

"Beyond" activities are designed to extend students' appreciation of literature, usually in another medium, such as poems, book reviews, letters to authors or to pen pals, cued retelling, or mock television shows. This encourages students to read for a purpose. *Story mapping* is a way for students to use a graphic organizer to summarize the plot. Younger students can work with four boxes (*Who? Wants? But? So?*) to fill in their knowledge of what happens in the story. Older students can use the terms *Characters, Intent, Opposition*, and *Resolution*. Using this device, students can follow the story grammar, or progression of events in the plot.

Table 4.6   In-Class Reading Methods for English Learners

Method	Description
Page and paragraph	Teacher or fluent reader reads a page, then an English learner reads a paragraph, then group discusses what has been read.
Equal portions	Students work in pairs, and each reads aloud the same amount of text.
Silent with support	Students read silently in pairs, and can ask each other for help with a difficult word or phrase.
Choral reading	A passage is divided into sections, and different members of the audience read various sections.
Radio reading	One student reads while others close their books and listen. After reading, the reader can question each student about what was read.
Repeated reading	Students read silently a book that has been read aloud, or independently re-read books of their choice.
Interactive read-aloud	Students can join in on repetitious parts or take parts of a dialogue.
Echo reading	For rhythmic text, students echo or repeat lines.
Nonprint media support	Students can follow along with a taped version of the book.

Source: Hadaway, Vardell, and Young (2002).

Example of Concept   *Daily Reading Interventions*

Based on observations during the previous school year of those children who had made unexpected progress in reading skills, Mrs. Hedberg, the ELD teacher, and Mrs. Greaver-Pohzehl, the second-grade homeroom teacher, devised a new program. The program included additional opportunities for practice and fluency through the use of volunteers and a take-home reading program.

In the classroom, the students received daily directed, guided reading instruction with one of the teachers during which they were introduced to new texts, participated in oral discussion, and completed activities to build comprehension. Parent volunteers, trained to provide appropriate prompts for struggling readers, provided additional daily opportunities for children to reread texts for fluency, to practice spelling words, and to develop phonemic awareness

through games and activities. Fifth-grade buddies also came daily for a period of twenty minutes to play phonics-based games and reread familiar texts. Each child received a tape recorder and checked out books and tapes to read or listen to at home with a parent. In addition, they took home fluency-reading bags with a reading log.

Although the program did not always run smoothly (bags and tapes left at home, for example), by the end of the year, every child in the program made progress—all of them advanced at least two reading divisions on the district's literacy scale; developed a greater range of reading and writing skills; developed a stronger, more fluent voice while reading; and showed positive attitudes toward reading and writing (Greaver & Hedberg, 2001).

Strategies for English Learners' Literacy Instruction

An explanation of all the literacy strategies appropriate for English learners is beyond the scope of this book. However, certain strategies that encompass the main principles for suitable instruction with English learners are explained here. These include the Language Experience Approach (LEA), a strategy particularly helpful for nonliterate students, self-monitoring, forming visual images; literature-based reading, and a postreading strategy that invites active student participation.

Language Experience Approach. A language-development activity that encourages students to respond to events in their own words is the Language Experience Approach (LEA). As a student tells a story or relates an event, the teacher writes it down and reads it back so that students can eventually read the text for themselves. Because the students are providing their own phrases and sentences, they find the text relevant and interesting and generally have little trouble reading it. The importance of LEA in developing the language of English learners cannot be overemphasized. Its advantages include the following:

- LEA connects students to their own experiences and activities by having them express themselves orally.
- It reinforces the notion that sounds can be transcribed into specific symbols and that those symbols can then be used to re-create the ideas expressed.
- It provides texts for specific lessons on vocabulary, grammar, writing conventions, structure, and more.

Example of Concept *Using Activity Centers after Reading*

Sixth-grade teacher Quito Reitan used LEA after his students read *Pharaoh: Life and Afterlife of a God* (David Kennett) to help reinforce key concepts. He explains what students do as a follow-up to their reading:

> After finishing the lesson on the ancient Egypt, I had my class reinforce key ideas by rotating through 12 different activity centers. Each center was organized by a set of instructions contained in laminated colored folders. The first center, "Preserving," showed how to mimic the action of Egyptians' *natron*, the chemical used in mummification, by carefully burying a fresh flower in fine sand inside a cardboard box. A scientific data sheet asked the student to state a hypothesis and explain the procedure used; each day for two weeks students uncovered the flowers to note the drying process.
>
> In a second center, "Pyramid Pattern," students cut out and folded paper to construct a pyramid. In "Three Crowns of Egypt," they can cut and fold paper to make the pharaoh's headdress. In "Drawing Egyptian Style" students can copy the profile portraits seen on tomb walls, including copying the distinctive dress styles of the men and women. In "Papyrus Scrolls" students can use parchment (baking) paper to copy hieroglyphs, and in the "Hieroglypic Code Wheel" center, each student creates a code wheel from two circles that connect the roman alphabet with hieroglyphs. The "Nile" center offers the opportunity to construct a "fact book" about the world's longest river, and in the "Map of Egypt" center, students color a map and label important geographic features. In yet another center, students solve math problems using Egyptian numerals. A poetry center provides a template for a cinquain based on an Egyptian theme as the subject.

Self-Monitoring. Sentence-by-Sentence Self-Monitoring (SSSM; Buettner, 2002) helps students to chunk texts into small units. The teacher selects a section of text, and the student counts the sentences. The student reads the text silently, and when ready, reads aloud. The teacher notes miscues, and sometimes reads back the sentence exactly as the student read it, asking, "Does that make sense?" or "Is that what we see in the picture?" The reading process becomes like coaching, a conversation about the meaning of the text and the strategy that the reader is using. A score sheet may be used to help students track their own progress and strategies.

Forming Visual Images. Even though visual images bombard students through the Internet, films, and television, students may not have the capacity to form their own visual images as they read. Many struggling readers focus solely on decoding words; without forming images of the plot or content, and do not achieve comprehension. Research on visual imagery indicates that students may need to be prompted repeatedly as they read to produce mental images ("television in the mind"). To facilitate this process, students may learn to sketch illustrations as they read, draw upon pictures in the text to assist comprehension, or even go back and forth between a movie and the associated work of literature to learn to work interactively with images (Hibbing & Rankin-Erickson, 2003).

Literature-Based Reading. More and more teachers are using literature as the core of their reading program. For an overview of the use of literature in a children's reading program, see Tunnell and Jacobs (2000). A literature-based approach to reading uses *controlled readers* (literature-based basal reader is tailored for the target reading level), text sets (thematically related books, such as books on sports and hobbies, or sets of multicultural readers on the Cinderella theme), *core books* (those specifically featured in a statewide adoption list for all classrooms to use), and *thematic units* (literature as integrated content with science, social studies, and art/music/performing arts) to provide reading experiences that are rich in meaning and interest for students.

Multicultural literature helps students to see life from a variety of points of view, to compare cultures on different aspects of life, and to see their own culture represented in the curriculum. *Multicultural Voices in Contemporary Literature* (Day, 1994) presents thirty-nine authors and illustrators from twenty different cultures. A follow-up book, *Latina and Latino Voices in Literature for Children and Teenagers* (Day, 1997) has biographies of thirty-eight authors with synopses of their work, as well as anextensive list of resources for books in English on Latino themes. Day (2003) is a follow-up extending the Latina and Latino theme.

As students become better readers, they begin to read their own *self-selected books*. As they read independently, they are encouraged to use familiar techniques for comprehension: making mental images, surveying a book and making predictions, and monitoring their reading to make sure they understand. Students keep a simple reading log of the books they finish. Several sources are available that suggest age-level *appropriate reading material*. Public libraries have detailed reference books that list thousands of children's books, including the Caldecott and Newbery Medal books. *Book conferences* with the teacher, if there is time, allow students to benefit from the teacher's direct guidance.

Picturebooks are becoming increasingly popular, with growing recognition that text and visual elements can separately contribute to increased literary enjoyment and comprehension. The postmodern picturebook (Wolfenbarger & Sipe, 2007) moves the reader into a nonlinear pattern, often including elements that are satirical, self-referential, or anticonventional. *The Stinky Cheese Man* (Scieszka & Smith, 1992) is the epitome of such a genre, a tale in which the clever protagonist avoids being eaten because he steps outside the text and uses its features to trick and trap his assailant. These texts delight readers because they simultaneously employ and undermine accepted conventions, provoking meta-literary insights into fiction and nonfiction.

To summarize Stahl, Duffy-Hester, and Stahl (1998), an effective reading program in the early grades might entail direct instruction in decoding using easily decodable texts, including some contrived texts that sound interesting and authentic (*not* "Dan takes Fran to the prom in the fog"). Authentic literature may be chosen for repetition of a taught pattern. Children's comprehension growth can be aided by the teacher's reading aloud. Children practice their knowledge of sound–symbol correspondence as they use temporary spelling when writing, using these experiments to hypothesize about the sounds they hear and refine their developing phonemic awareness. These efforts are augmented by an extensive program of choice reading.

Example of Concept · *New Literacy Genres*

Many young adults are fond of comic books and graphic novels, comparatively new forms of literature. Stephanie Craig, a young *manga* lover, relates what she enjoys about the Japanese genre: "I can buy either *shoujou* (girls') *manga*, featuring fantasy, action, and adventure, or *shouman* (boys') *manga*, in which romance will not play as large a role in the plot." She goes on to explain *manga* has many of the same archetypes (warriors, heroes, sages, magicians, creators, innocent fools, etc.) that are in young adult Western literature, but characters in *manga* are not as black and white (evil versus good) as in Western literature, but instead are interesting shades of gray. She also likes ways in which the serial form of the novels furthers the plots (Nilsen & Donelson, 2009, pp. 178–179).

Literacy Communities. When teachers encourage English learners to enjoy reading, the classroom becomes its own literacy community. Books are exchanged and so are the ideas they contain. Students write books, and everyone is an audience for each other's literacy. The enthusiasm is contagious.

Example of Concept · *Literacy Communities*

When does a classroom practice cease to become a strategy and instead become a movement and a way of life for students? Fisher (2005) describes two Participatory Literacy Communities (PLCs) that use spoken word poetry to promote purposeful, meaningful literacy. Teachers in these settings work to liberate language and to help students seize control of words as they co-construct their learning community. When reading and writing are partnered with speaking and "doing," students take literacy and oracy to new levels of engagement.

The Three-Tier Model of Instruction

Some English learners can meet or exceed expectations for reading performance while instructed using a repertoire of English-language-development strategies, including special designed academic instruction in English literature (SDAIE, see Chapter 5). Other English learners, for a variety of reasons, may need additional mediation if they are at risk of falling behind in reading skills or comprehension. A more focused kind of teaching may be necessary if screening, progress monitoring, and diagnostic testing document that a students needs more help. Strategic supplemental intervention is a Tier II level of instruction for those students who are below grade level (Honig, Diamond, & Gutlohn, 2008), and at Tier III, students receive intensive intervention who are at risk of failing.

Tier I: Core Reading Program. In the general education classroom, students receive English-language arts (ELA) or English-language-development instruction using strategies aligned with the ELA and/or ELD standards. Differentiated instruction targets students who may be at various levels of second-language acquisition as measured by the CELDT or other English-learner placement test.

Tier II: Strategic Supplemental Intervention. In small groups or individually, students not making adequate progress in Tier I instruction are supported with specific, targeted teaching so they can eventually be successful in the general education setting. They may be given additional instruction time; repeated opportunities for practice; and more frequent monitoring in such skills as phonics, reading fluency and comprehension, and vocabulary development. In this way, reading problems are treated before the student becomes frustrated with repeated failure.

Tier III: Intensive Intervention. Individual attention or very small homogenous group work, combined with additional periods of intensive instruction, may be necessary for students who have not progressed in reading skills and are at risk for school failure. Placement in Tier III instruction is based on results of reading assessment that determines if customized and sustained attention is required. This approach may be needed until the student makes enough gains to return to a less intensive setting.

Response to Intervention (RTI). The three-tiered model of instruction has also been called response to intervention (RTI). This model provides additional support for students who do not meet grade-level expectations, based on continuous progress monitoring. For English learners, this allows many opportunities for learning before drastic steps are taken, such as referral to special education.

When students do not like to read, schooling becomes a cycle of failure—poor reading habits exacerbate poor academic work, leading in turn to the dislike to read. Minority students reported to Zanger (1994) that their literacy was adversely affected by their feelings of low status in high school, with classroom experiences and curriculum that alienated them from the teacher and from other students, and with their home language and cultures not included in a respectful and meaningful way. Literacy is fostered by inclusionary, multicultural learning environments in which English learners feel accepted, productive, and successful.

Writing

Writing is more than just an exercise for the teacher to assign and critique. It is an opportunity for students to link with the social and cultural heritage of the United States and to begin communicating effectively across cultures. At the heart of the classroom writing task is its relation to the real world. Through writing, students perform a purposeful social action, an action that takes them beyond a mere school assignment. Communicating with one another—with others outside the classroom, with home and family, with presidents and corporate officers, with city officials and nursing home residents—establishes real discourse and helps students to convey information that is real and necessary. This is the essence of writing as a communicative task.

After careful study of students learning to write in their second language, Fitzgerald and Amendum (2007) drew the following conclusions:

- For preschool and primary-grade English learners, features of ESL writing may develop in ways that are similar to certain features of early writing development in native-English speakers (such as phases of developmental spelling).
- For primary- and intermediate-grade students, knowledge and skills in writing (such as concepts about print) can transfer between their first and second language.
- For intermediate-grade and secondary-level students, some composing processes resemble those used by native-English speakers (such as prewriting and planning strategies).

Based on these findings, Fitzgerald and Amendum (2007) suggest that writing techniques used for native-English speakers be adapted for English learners, taking into consideration the length of time it takes to master the syntax, semantics, and sociocultural features of a second language. They promote an adaptation of the Language Experience Approach they call Daily News, in which students dictate their ideas about current events to a scribe who uses chart paper. They also suggest the use of dialogue journals and the writing of structured persuasive essays as ways for students to benefit by sharing authentic purposes for writing and employing a limited set of well-rehearsed genres.

Texts and Contexts

Children learning to write create *texts*; within the classroom these texts are part of the school *context*. Discourse experts are now able to use tools of analysis to deconstruct the more complex levels of children's writings in ways never before thought possible. Instead of seeing childish jumbles of words and pictures, analysts can note the development of concepts about signs and messages, embedded references to other texts and contexts (intertextuality and intercontextuality); mixtures of genres and voices, developing forms of visual and verbal syntax, and hybrid representations of information the children have received at home, from mass media, and from schooling. According to Kamberelis and de la Luna (2004):

> Because children have only nascent control over the tools and strategies for graphically representing their messages, their writing may actually be shorthand for richer, longer, and more complex messages than meets the eye. . . . Therefore, [we] need to find ways to make visible the sometimes invisible richness, complexity, and variability that are often embodied in children's texts. (p. 242)
>
> Writing contexts are not simply containers in which actions, practices, and activities occur. Instead, they are dynamic streams of overlapping and integrated discourses, spaces, sociocultural practices, and power relations. . . . (p. 243)

The child brain as it manifests itself in writing is a creative and meaning-seeking organ as is the adult brain, even though its surface manifestation may seem to lack sophistication. Drawing forth this depth and complexity from students requires teaching that is subtle, evocative, and capable of understanding the myriad symbol systems that may be combined within the seemingly primitive expressions of children.

A sociocultural approach to writing holds that individuals engage in literacy for specific purposes, in specific contexts, and as participants in specific communities. Writers learn from one another as they take part in the larger community.

Thus the texts and contexts of children's writing are far deeper than first imagined. The texts and contexts of English learners' writing mirror this complexity.

The Writing Process

Writing as a process has become increasingly accepted as an alternative to the "product" view of writing. It changes the way students compose, provides situations in which language can be used in a meaningful way, and emphasizes the *act* of writing rather than the result. The process approach is particularly important for English learners who are developing their oral language skills at the same time as their written skills, because it involves more interaction, planning, and reworking. Students are not moving from topic to topic quickly, but instead have an opportunity to work with a topic (and therefore vocabulary and structures) over a sustained period.

The three general stages—*prewriting*, *writing*, and *editing*—allow students to organize, develop, and refine concepts and ideas in ways that the product approach to writing does not. For example, during prewriting, students are involved in oral-language experiences that develop their need and desire to write. These activities may include talking about and listening to shared experiences, reading literature, brainstorming, or creating role-plays or other fantasy activities.

Example of Concept	*Brainstorming*

The students gather at the front of the room and brainstorm the topic—butterflies. Mrs. Dowling writes their ideas on the board. A student says, "I have my first sentence" and tells the class how she will start her writing. Mrs. Dowling dismisses the student so she can begin writing. When only a few children remain, Mrs. Dowling rereads the list and helps each decide how he or she will start.

During the writing stage, students write quickly to capture ideas, doing the best they can in spelling, vocabulary, and syntax without a concern for accuracy. They then rewrite and redraft as necessary, again working with other students and/or the teacher to share, discuss, expand, and clarify their ideas.

Example of Concept *Drafts*

Each Tuesday morning, cross-age tutors and parent volunteers (many of whom share the primary language of their group of students) work with Mrs. Dowling's students on their drafts. They listen and comment but know that the actual writing needs to be done by the child.

In the final stages, editing and publishing, students are helped to fix up their mechanics of usage and spelling, particularly when their writing is going to be shared in a formal way. By using the writing process, students have generated writing that is satisfying in its ability to capture and share ideas—the essence of writing for the purpose of communication. If, however, the writing is published or publicly shared, students also achieve the pride of authorship. Ways of publishing may vary: a play performed, a story bound into a book for circulation in the class library, a poem read aloud, an essay posted on a bulletin board, a video made of a student reading aloud, a class newspaper circulated to the community.

Example of Concept *Publishing*

At the "bookmaking" center, Mrs. Dowling provides samples of book types (circle, small, folded, accordion, pop-up). Students choose which story they wish to "publish," decide which type of book will best show off the story, and copy their edited draft. Three times a year they write invitations to family members to come to their "publishing party." They read their books and then enjoy snacks and drinks with their proud families.

The Six Traits Approach

The "six traits" approach to writing has become popular due to the wealth of associated materials available from Great Source publishers. The six traits are as follows: *ideas*, the content for writing; *organization*, the way the content is structured; *voice*, the effectiveness of personal experience or authentic flavor of writing; *word choice*, using powerful vocabulary well adapted to the purpose of the writing; *sentence fluency*, employing direct, well-structured sentences that are varied in form, logical, and well connected; and *conventions*, appropriate punctuation, capitalization, citations, and other rules of usage (Spandel & Hicks, 2006). A good writer adapts each of these components to genre, audience, and purpose.

Writing in the Age of the Internet

Writing in a Web 2.0 environment requires a change in assumptions and procedures from writing in the past. According to Knobel and Lankshear (2006), a different approach is needed, one that "inevitably involves networks, collaboration, and shared visions of how knowledge is made and distributed differently in digital space" (p. 80). In other words, digital writing is not just writing using technology instead of paper and pencil, but rather is about designs of meaning that may use aural, spatial, and gestural modalities, as well as visual.

Example of Concept *Using Student Blogs*

Student blogs are web pages that can feature essays, thoughts, analyses, experiences of daily life, interesting links, book reviews, jokes, or other forms of content. They can also include pictures, photos, audio podcasts, and videos. Most allow readers to post written comments, making blogs a kind of social software. Classes can have a single shared blog to which everyone enters content. Learners can be asked to post to their blogs at least once or twice a week. PBWorks is a common blog site that is easy for teachers to set up and for learners to use. Dudeney and Hockly (2007) provide a useful "owner's guide" to teaching English with technology.

Writing Poetry

Ingrid Wendt uses poetry writing as a motivator for learning English. In her class, students can write in their first language and then translate their work into English. She uses poems as models that speak of shared dreams, fears, hopes, and values from many ethnicities and cultures. "Whatever the student's age or ability level in English or Spanish, I find that writing poetry is an empowering experience," she says. "Students discover that poetry can come from real-life experience, and when they wrote poetry, words become tools for them to share their own experience. There is a reason for them to read and write these words" (Harris, 2006).

Adapted Instruction

Poetry Slam

What is required to hold a poetry slam? An uninhibited master of ceremonies; numbered "tickets" on which students write their name and the name of their poem, which make it easier for the master of ceremonies to introduce the next performer; simple refreshments to add to the "coffee house" atmosphere; two sets of judges' score cards, wielded by student volunteers seated on opposite sides of the room; and small prizes such as pencils and erasers for the "winning" poets (Nilsen & Donelson, 2009).

Error Correction and Grammar in Oracy and Literacy Instruction

Teachers do need to focus on form. English learners cannot be expected to merely absorb the language as they listen to teachers and interact with peers in learning groups. However, for English learners, indiscriminate error correction and decontextualized grammatical practice do not appear to enhance language acquisition. Instead, teachers need to provide both formal and informal language-learning opportunities in meaningful contexts (Dutro & Moran, 2003).

Treatment of Errors

In any endeavor, errors are inevitable, and language learning is certainly no exception. People generally accept errors (or do not even notice them) when children are learning their first language, but teachers expend much energy correcting errors when students are learning a second language. The learner's age and level of fluency determine how a teacher should deal with language errors.

In the early stages of language learning, fluency is more important than accuracy. Thus, the teacher, instead of monitoring and correcting, should converse in and model appropriate language. When a student says, "My pencil broken," the teacher's response is, "Go ahead and sharpen it." In this interchange, language has furthered meaning despite the imperfection of syntax. Error correction is not necessary. The teacher focuses on the student's message and provides correction only when the meaning is not clear.

Younger children in particular appear to learn more when teachers focus on meaning rather than form. Older students and those with more English proficiency need and can benefit from feedback on recurring errors. The teacher can observe systematic errors in the class and discuss them with the class, or provide mini-lessons with small groups who display the same error. By observing systematic errors, the teacher will recognize that random errors do not need to be corrected.

Teaching Spelling

Spelling errors jeopardize academic success because misspelling is one of the most noticeable kinds of error. Learning to spell should not be confused with vocabulary acquisition in content areas (e.g., distinguishing *desperate* versus *disparate* is a vocabulary issue that is best learned through rich context). Although it is useful to spell newly acquired words correctly, the emphasis in vocabulary belongs on acquiring the meaning for the purposes of expanding input vocabulary.

Even though computer word-processing programs have built-in spellcheck functions, learning to spell correctly functions as the mark of an educated person. Of course, training in spelling should be accompanied by training in handwriting—no one can tell if a word is misspelled if it is illegible!

A good spelling curriculum focuses on the few and powerful spelling rules that cover 95 percent of words that students use in writing, such as learning when to double final consonants, how to form plurals, and how to distinguish commonly confused words (*your/you're*). More difficult to acquire spelling distinctions (e.g., *-ence* versus *-ance,* or *-able* versus *-ible*) should be flagged, "Always look it up!"). (See Crosby & Emery, 1994.)

POINT   COUNTERPOINT

Should Cursive Be Taught in Schools?

The new Common Core Standards for English do not require instruction in cursive writing. Should schools abandon teaching students to write in longhand?

POINT: Legible handwriting is an important communication skill. Legible penmanship remains an important universal tool; not everyone has the capacity to communicate through a keyboard. The steady improvement that comes when students practice handwriting promotes self-esteem and pride. Without learning to write cursively, students cannot read cursive writing, making it impossible for them to access important historical documents like the *Declaration of Independence* (Avery, 2012).

COUNTERPOINT: Cursive is unnecessary. Calligraphy is passé—the world has moved beyond the physical art of writing. In the age of iPads, cell phones, and computers, it is more important to teach keyboarding and texting skills. Students do not need to spend long hours practicing cursive letterforms; they can write just as fast, and usually more legibly, when they print. Students who become historians can learn to read cursive writing if they need to look at source documents (Ellis, 2012).

Implications for Teaching
Perhaps parents can take on this assignment of teaching cursive writing at home. If parents say they want more "challenges" for their child, practicing beautiful handwriting might just fill the bill!

Treatment of Grammar

Historically, grammar has been seen as the organizational framework for language and as such has been used as the organizational framework for language teaching. In many classrooms, second-language instruction has been based on learning the correct use of such items as the verb *to be*, the present tense, definite articles, subject–verb agreement, and so forth. Linguists dispute the value of such a structured approach for the attainment of grammatical competence. The effective language teacher, therefore, organizes instruction around meaningful concepts—themes, topics, areas of student interest—and deals with grammar only as the need arises.

How can teachers help English learners to improve their grammar? McVey (2007) offers several suggestions. Teachers can encourage self-correction by showing students how to use the grammar-checking feature on computer word-processing programs, by focusing on students' using correctly the grammar structures that they are already using in their writing, and by targeting for correction only those grammar errors that interfere with the communication of meaning.

Overall, the use of correct grammar is not an end in itself, but is a means toward achieving writing that is fluid, compelling, and deeply meaningful. The study of language structure should be used to explore what makes language fascinating and enjoyable.

Oracy, Literacy, and Technology

The digital revolution is changing the way people spend their free time—playing video and computer games, chatting on the Internet, conducting business transactions, and much more. Language classrooms can be similarly transformed with the capabilities now available through multimedia computing, the Internet, and the World Wide Web. Computer-assisted language learning (CALL) has the potential for extending learning beyond the four walls of the classroom to include the whole world.

Computer-Assisted Language Learning/ Computer-Mediated Communication

Computer-assisted instruction has long been available for classrooms. *Computer-assisted language learning* (CALL) applied to English learning has moved beyond skill drills into more innovative applications. *Computer-mediated communication* (CMC) is a term that describes the role of computers in facilitating virtual communication by people. Both CALL and CMC have proved useful in the education of English learners.

Learning has been transformed through multimedia computing and the Internet—the digital revolution. Lesson plans, quizzes, chat rooms, and bulletin boards are available that allow learners to sample English idioms, prepare for standardized tests, or connect with English learners around the world. Desktop and laptop computers, tablets, cell phones and mobile devices, and the Internet have had a huge impact on the accessibility of learning. E-mail is used to deliver course content and facilitate online discussions; information of all kinds is readily accessible; and learners can post to bulletin boards and download materials at their leisure (Ryan, 2008).

Personalized Learning

What counts as literacy achievement? Brass (2008) describes one at-risk student's involvement in an after-school literacy program called the Technology and Literacy Project. A Latino teenager, Horatio received poor grades on school-based measures of literacy achievement, yet he created complex digital movie text on a digital movie-composing platform, using his local knowledge and out-of-school literacy practices in a sophisticated way. How is school literacy, with its negative labeling of his skills, serving Horatio?

The World Wide Web delivers authentic texts, images, streaming audio and video recordings, video and sound clips, virtual reality worlds, and dynamic, interactive presentations. Students can listen to live radio stations from around the world or hear prerecorded broadcasts of music, news, sports, and weather. Search engines help students find a wealth of material for classroom, group, or individual research topics.

Current classroom computer use will undergo even more rapid change in the near future as broadband power becomes available to mobile personal devices. Commonly known as "third generation" (3G), this means that vast amounts of multimedia content will be accessible through handheld devices, including television programs, movies, videoconferencing, and music. Next will come 4G, in which data rates are expected to be 100 times faster than 3G. As the delivery platform of broadband content and functionality shifts from computer to personal devices, learning will be unlike anything humans have yet experienced (March, 2007, p. 213).

CALL Impacts Literacy Instruction. Literacy practices are changing in the twenty-first century under the influence of Web-based technologies. Penrod (2008) calls this "Literacy 2.0" in contrast to Literacy 1.0, the traditional reading and writing based on the innovations introduced by Gutenberg's printing press. Literacy 2.0 is more than academic literacy—it is on-demand and flexible, with multiple modalities of input. This literacy extends beyond the school walls to involve its users in social networking sites, blogs, podcasts, wikis, and Moodles, and provokes teachers to design instruction that addresses a spectrum of literacies. According to Penrod (2008, p. 52), such literacy has created "a cultural and technological wave" in which learners demand "immersive educational experiences that are socially rich and information-ally engaging." These multimodal literacies are extending the reach of the human mind and creativity.

One of the major innovations at the end of the twentieth century was the use of hypertext in digital media. By clicking on active links in a web page, a reader can jump between texts or text segments in a nonlinear way. Information is interactive—connections are set up through a database of sources and links. Because texts are intertextually linked, documents become "multidimensional and dynamic" (Yates, 1996, p. 122).

However, this means that current notions of reading comprehension may have to change to accommodate technology. A web page—typically nonlinear, interactive, often in multimedia format—may have multiple forms of hypertext links; for example, leading to word definitions, parallel topics, linked activities, or e-mail. In addition to new kinds of text comprehension, users of web-based text need the ability to navigate cyberspace, avoid distracting commercial messages, and stay focused on a topic despite a myriad of textual distractions (Coiro, 2003). Reading on the Internet produces the need for guidance in the use of complex communication tools.

Reading software that leverages the most current advances in media design and culturally and kid-sensitive iconography, combined with rigorous research-based content, has the capacity to create "flow," the feeling of energized and enjoyable focus in an activity. Using technology, literacy opportunities built around solid reading content can maintain "flow" while increasing the learner's fluency, comprehension, and language skills (Quinn, 2007, p. 26).

A host of programs are available that provide reading intervention for struggling English learners. Zeiler (2007) described several of these. One web-based learning system, Let's Go Learn, combines online diagnostic assessment with differentiated instruction so educators can assess, provide individualized intervention, and then monitor and track the growth in a student's reading ability. This is typical of computer-assisted reading systems.

However, the world of the future may be "postliterate." Futurist William Crossman sees this as a positive development for human evolution. Using voice in/voice out (VIVO) technology, computers will "allow the world's millions of functionally illiterate people to access information via the Internet and the Web without having to learn to read and write. They will become as skillfully literate in the information technology of their generation as we are in ours" (Labbe, 2007).

CALL Supports Strategic Learning. Computers have become an integral part of classroom activities. For example, word processing supports the writing process by allowing students to electronically organize, draft, revise, edit, and publish their work. Students can develop oral skills by using authoring software to create professional-looking oral presentations, developing English skills as they learn content.

Researchers have found that students' attitudes toward writing improve when they use word processing programs (Bitter & Pierson, 2004); students are motivated to produce longer writing, and find revision easier. Students who use word processing enjoy reading their own writing aloud, are more likely to return to their writing for revision, and more willing to exchange feedback about their writing with peers when working on a computer screen.

Both software programs and online resources are used in classrooms to help students achieve their language-learning goals. Software programs include traditional drill-and-practice programs that focus on vocabulary or grammar; tutorials; games; simulations that present students with real-life situations in the language and culture they are learning; and productivity tools (word processing, databases, spreadsheets, graphics, desktop publishing, and presentation-authoring programs). Material from encyclopedias and *National Geographic* is available on CD-ROMs and online.

Example of Concept · *WebQuests*

WebQuests are a popular form of Internet-based instruction because teachers can use the *WebQuest .org* template to adapt to their own lessons. Ideally, WebQuests involve students using the Internet to carry out inquiry-based tasks in which students pose interesting, open-ended questions. Such questions spark true learning: They require students to think for themselves, and to analyze, synthesize, and evaluate the information they find on the Web (Cunningham & Billingsley, 2006).

CALL and CMC Increase Communicative Abilities. The Internet connects students with other parts of the world, with speakers of English, and with rich sources of information. E-mail, bulletin boards, online chat rooms, and social networking sites make such interaction available both spontaneously in real time (synchronously) and asynchronously (students can take their time to draft responses). A new kind of English (English as a lingua franca) is emerging as non-native speakers of English converse with one another, with syntactic differences from Standard English—not to mention the influences of cyberspeak on English (CYL on this).

Example of Concept · *Students' Digital Online Activity*

Digital games and online activities are stimulating students' linguistic creativity in ways that were unavailable in the past—and often outshine the input students receive from language activities in school. Research on the online activities of a community of Korean American teenagers in the U.S. Midwest who had grown up partly in the United States and partly in Korea found that their instant messaging and web postings to other members of their local peer group contained copious mixing of English and Korean and frequent references to school culture, music, and other forms of popular culture in both Korea and the United States (Yi, 2009).

Adapted Instruction

The Interactive Whiteboard

Linked to a computer or electronic tablet and beamed on the wall with a data projector, the interactive white board (IWB) can be manipulated with the teacher's pen, or images can be dragged from place to place on the screen by students passing the tablet from person to person. Video, CD audio, pictures, interactive exercises, and access to the Internet can be displayed, and teachers can mark up these images directly on the screen. Research shows this tool can positively affect learners' motivation and attention levels—but there is, as yet, no evidence that it improves test scores (Dudeney & Hockly, 2007).

CALL Supports Learner Autonomy. The computer is a powerful learning tool that requires the teacher's input to organize, plan, and monitor. Egbert and Hanson-Smith (2007) found that computer technology can provide students with the means to control their own learning, to construct meaning, and to evaluate and monitor their own performance.

However, the computer should not be viewed as something students use without benefit of teacher guidance. Hanson-Smith (1997) described three levels of CALL implementation in the classroom, noting the teacher's role in each. At a modest level, language-learning software can provide a passive listening experience as students click on a word or sentence to hear it repeatedly, look up a meaning, analyze grammar, view a related picture or video clip, and/or read a related text. The teacher monitors students' progress, encouraging, instructing, and modeling as appropriate. At a higher level, students can research current events, historical and cultural topics, business matters, art or literature, weather or geography—any topic of interest to them consonant with the learning goals of the class. Again, the teacher's role is crucial in maximizing the use of computer tools.

CALL Enhances Creativity. English learners in well-equipped schools are already experiencing ways in which computers afford creative learning, whether through digital storytelling, student-created PowerPoint projects, or student-made podcasts and webcasts. Rennebohm Franz uses a classroom website to publish students' writing (www.psd267.wednet.edu/~kfranz/index.htm).

Students in schools across the United States are using multimedia computer tools for video and film production, using Quicktime and other digital video production techniques to add sound effects, animation, and other presentation enhancements to create unique works. Bitter and Legacy (2007) have included a host of classroom-friendly multimedia production tools, both software and hardware. English learners should have access to these tools on a par with other learners.

Personalized Learning

Paula uses the Internet in her sheltered high-school American History class to research current events for her weekly "news" assignment, as well as to find information for her PowerPoint talk on Robert E. Lee. She uses SDAIE-classroom-adapted American history software that enables her to click on a word or sentence to hear it repeatedly, look up the meaning, see a related picture or video clip, and/or read a related text. Her teacher and peers provide help as needed.

 Example of Concept *Digital Storytelling*

"A digital story is a 2- to 5-minute movie-like production that learners create using one of several readily available software programs" (Rance-Roney, 2008, p. 29). Each student writes and records a short script and adds digital images such as text, pictures, drawings, and photographs, as well as music. Creating a digital story engages the learners' skills in reading, writing, and speaking, as well as stimulates the flow of creative juices. Rance-Roney adds, "I have found the process of putting together the story is not linear; students continue to revise the script, edit images, change the music, and re-record their voice, giving them the opportunity to practice language more and more at each stage" (p. 29).

Such digital stories can be used to promote critical multicultural education (McShay, 2010). If students are encouraged to explore and analyze each other's stories, they can broaden their perspectives, creating new opportunities for them to acquire more complex points of view on the experiences, problems, and themes that they and their classmates share. Self-reflection is the cornerstone of such digital stories.

Generating and examining personally meaningful questions can affect the way students think about their own identities in the face of societal discourses about poverty, hate crimes, gender, interracial dating, and other issues that roil daily life.

CALL Brings Together a Classroom Learning Community. Internet technologies have been developed that support a community of learning in the classroom. Holding e-mail discussions by means of a listserv or group e-mail list automates the process of broadcasting one posting to an entire group. Listservs can also distribute electronic journals, e-magazines, or newsletters. A teacher can "prime" the list by asking thoughtful questions, recommending useful resources, or by requiring students post a minimum number of messages or responses. (Mills, 2006).

Teachers have found creative ways to use the Internet to develop collaborative projects between classrooms (Karchmer-Klein, 2007). Susan Silverman (www.kids-learn.org) and Marci McGowan (www.mrsmcgowan.com) have used the Internet to open the classroom window and invite in the world.

Computers can also be the subject of debates and conversations in class as a means of improving students' oral proficiency. Teske and Marcy (2007) offer speaking topics that engage students in lively discussions about the world of cybernetics.

Unfortunately, computer use also has the potential to undermine a sense of community. Willard (2007) relates interesting insights into the minds of cyberbullies and the rationalizations they use to justify their actions. Understanding this reasoning may help teachers to combat such behaviors.

Technological Literacy. The education of English learners must involve more than CALL—students also need a broader technological literacy. Hansen (2000) defined technological literacy as "a personal ability to adopt, adapt, or invent proper technological tools in an information society to positively affect his or her life, community, and environment" (p. 31). As people recognize its importance, technological literacy will become a growing field. English learners will need in-depth computer skills for the workplace of the future.

One problem inherent in the use of technology in education is the "digital divide" in terms of race, culture, and economics. If access to digital information or the ability to use technology separates students across geographic, ethnic, language, financial, disability, gender, or political barriers, then technology becomes problematic. The U.S. Department of Education has found that 41 percent of African American and Latino students use a computer at home, compared with 77 percent of European American students; 31 percent of students from families with a total income less than $20,000 use computers, whereas 89 percent of students from families earning more than $75,000 per year are using computers (Ryan, 2008).

Moreover, schools with predominantly minority enrollments are more likely to use technology for drill, practice, and test taking. Thus, race, culture, and economics act as dividers in students' acquisition of computer skills at school (Cavanaugh, 2006). In contrast, computers can be used in more exciting ways, to model weather systems, to visualize molecular science, and to map complex ideas and concepts (Jonassen, 2006). English learners who use computers in boring ways are not well served by the digital revolution. Teachers in CLAD classrooms need to advocate for their own continual training in CALL and CMC in order to ensure that English learners are at the cutting edge of technology-enhanced learning.

Learning Online

The proliferation of interactive technology tools, including blogs, wikis, mobile devices, and friendship networks, has extended the possibilities of learning at a distance. Certainly, the advantages of anywhere/anytime learning and the convenience of being able to learn from home outweigh the challenges. Despite the use of chat rooms, SMS and video-conferencing sessions, and Skype to promote synchronous interaction, distance study can still be an "isolating and lonely way to learn" (Nunan, 2012, p. ix).

Building communities of learners who can work together as teams, with a high level of communication and cooperation among learners, is a key part of online virtual learning. "The new computing includes consideration of relationships, collaborations and partnerships, which encourage finding win-win deals in which both sides benefit" (Schneidermann, 2003, p. 135). In this case, the "both sides" that benefit are both teachers and students...that is, many students. According to Allen and Seaman (2010), in 2011, more than 6 million students studied online, with 1 million having been added between 2009 and 2010. The effort to train teachers for English learners worldwide is one of the foremost uses of online learning in contemporary education (England, 2012).

Upcoming Technologies

How can today's technologies motivate students to engage in learning English? Table 4.7 suggests possible classroom uses.

Table 4.7   Some ELD Uses for New Technologies

Technology	Possible Classroom Applications
Social networking	Teachers can use educational social networking sites whose content can be managed and made available only to invitees, and yet allows students to chat, post blog entries, and interact.
Microblogging and Twitter	Teachers can ask students to store and analyze the language sent on "tweets"; teachers can receive updates on areas of ELD teaching technology.
Gaming	Students can write about the problem solving, characters, tip sites, and other literacy practices needed to master various games.
Wiki	Group input sites that allow entries, edits, and publication from multiple authors can be used to host class books and other writings, as well as group digital stories, photos, and links.

Source: Wilber, 2010.

Using Social Media

Digital technologies—for the most part laptops, but increasingly, mobile phones and social media—are used by the majority of the 2,462 Advanced Placement (AP) and National Writing Project (NWP) middle school and high school teachers polled in a recent survey. Over 92 percent of these teachers say the Internet has had a major impact on their ability to access educational resources for the classroom. Students and teachers alike use tablet computers (43 percent) and e-readers (45 percent). Many classrooms also feature interactive online learning activities (wikis, online discussions, and online editing using collaborative tools such as GoogleDocs). The teachers also reported that 79 percent of students access assignments online, and 76 percent submit assignments online; 73 percent use their mobile phones to complete assignments, whether in the classroom or at home.

There seems to be a growing "digital divide"—although the AP and NWP teachers reported that a majority of students can access these computer tools in the classroom, only 18 percent can do so at home. (Purcell, Heaps, Buchanan, & Friedrich, 2013)

The ELD classroom is a complex environment. The classroom teacher orchestrates a wide variety of language-acquisition activities, involving students whose English-language abilities vary greatly. Standards documents provide teachers with frameworks within which they can design their language-development program and maintain the momentum their learners need to progress through the grades. Often, oracy and literacy instruction is integrated so that students can benefit from repeated exposure to themes, concepts, language, and vocabulary.

Teachers of English learners have a wide array of strategies available to them as they help students develop oracy and literacy skills. With the current emphasis on "every child a reader," teachers are under pressure to help all students attain grade-level competencies. Teachers invariably face the complication of mixed levels of student ability—in any single class they may have students who are literate in their first language, students who may have decoding skills only in that language, and/or students who have no literacy in either their first or their second language. Fortunately, various strategies have proved helpful for diverse learners, including activities that integrate oracy, literacy, and technology. Although classrooms with English learners are complex, they are also joyful places where teachers see students making daily progress.

LEARNING MORE

Further Reading

Reading, Writing, and Learning in ESL (Peregoy & Boyle, 2013) is an indispensable resource for K–12 teachers of English learners. It orients the reader to English learners, explores second-language acquisition, discusses oracy and literacy for English learners, and provides practical strategies for developing these skills.

Web Search

Children's Theatre/Creative Drama (www.childdrama.com) features resources for drama teachers in elementary and secondary schools, and for producers of theater for young audiences. The website contains a wealth of ideas for scenes and plays that can be used as a framework for reinforcing language skills or just for having fun.

Exploration

Choose one of your English learners to observe. Note the student's use of English in different contexts (class, playground, arrival/departure from school, lunchtime). Write down specific examples of the student's language. Sit down with the student to find out about his or her prior literacy experience in both L1 and L2. What instruction has he or she had? In which language? What variety of materials? What computer experiences? What literacy experiences are available in the home?

Collaboration

Based on your findings about your student, design a lesson addressing one or more of his or her needs. If possible, engage a colleague in the same exploration and experiment so you can discuss your findings, lessons, and results together. What specifically did you learn by working with the student? How will what you learn change your teaching? What are the next steps?

MyEducationLab™

Additional Sentences

This clip shows a teacher working with several students to sharpen their language skills. The teacher has her entire class work together to form sentences to create a story. She then asks each student to be responsible for writing part of the story on chart paper.

To access the video, go to MyEducationLab (www.myeducationlab.com), choose the Díaz-Rico text, and log in to MyEducationLab for English Language Learners. Select the topic Speaking, and watch the video entitled "Additional Sentences."

Answer the following questions:

1. How does the teacher in the clip include all of her students in the writing process? Why is this essential to the development of language skills for this group of students? How do the students learn from each other in this situation?

2. In the clip, the teacher is able to teach language skills by
   A. having students read alone.
   B. having students read aloud, write the story together, and format their sentences together as a class.
   C. creating the story for her class to write.
   D. assigning the story to be written for homework.

3. How does the teacher include all students in the group? Is there individual accountability for each student's speaking level?

5

Content-Area Instruction

Science activities incorporate English-language-learning opportunities.

© AVAVA/Shutterstock

At my school we are now doing a schoolwide intervention program: SMART GOALS: specific, measurable, attainable, relevant, time-bound goals. This year the history department is targeting reading comprehension, focusing on the understanding of primary sources. We meet monthly to go over our past data to remediate learning gaps, and at the end of each cycle we assess to see if our intervention worked. I think SMART GOALS will benefit my English learners because the lessons we create will be scaffolded and geared towards meeting their learning needs.

Many of our English learners do not meet the reclassification requirements in the four essential domains of listening, speaking, reading and writing due to their lack of middle-class English language ability. They cannot understand the language used in the texts . . . they just get lost, and then they lose interest. They just stop caring about learning.

Agnim Rosas, middle-school history teacher (2013)

Educators in schools, school districts, and state and federal agencies are working to develop programs and lessons to educate the growing number of second-language students in the nation's schools. Fortunately, programs that include sheltered instruction address this specific need.

Sheltered instruction is an approach used in multilinguistic content classrooms to provide language support to students while they are learning academic subjects, rather than expecting them to "sink or swim" in a content class designed for native-English speakers. Sheltered instruction may take place either in mainstream classes made up of native-English speakers mixed with non-native-English speakers of intermediate proficiency, or in classes consisting solely of non-native speakers who operate at similar English proficiency levels (Echevarria, Vogt, & Short, 2012).

Sheltered instruction is, ideally, one component in a program for English learners that includes ELD classes for beginning students, primary-language instruction in content areas so students continue at grade level as they learn English, and content-based ESL classes.

Sheltered English, or as it is often called, specially designed academic instruction in English (SDAIE), combines second-language-acquisition principles with those elements of quality teaching that make a lesson understandable to students. Such instruction enables them to improve listening, speaking, reading, and writing through the study of an academic subject. A SDAIE (pronounced "sah-die") classroom has content objectives identical to those of a mainstream classroom in the same subject but, in addition, includes language and learning-strategy objectives. Instruction is modified for greater comprehensibility. Augmenting mainstream content instruction with SDAIE techniques is the subject of this chapter.

Principles of Specially Designed Academic Instruction in English (SDAIE)

English learners can succeed in content-area classes taught in English. Basically, SDAIE addresses the following needs of English learners, (1) to learn grade-appropriate content, (2) to master English vocabulary and grammar, (3) to learn "academic" English (i.e., the semantic and syntactic ways that English is used in content subjects), and (4) to develop strategies for learning how to learn.

To accomplish these goals, SDAIE teachers provide a context for instruction that is rich in opportunities for hands-on learning and student interaction. Teachers devote particular attention to communication strategies. By altering the means of presenting material to make it more accessible and understandable, the teacher maintains a challenging academic program without watering down or overly simplifying the curriculum

SDAIE teachers have knowledge of second-language acquisition and instructional techniques for second-language learners. In mainstream elementary and content classrooms, English is an invisible medium. In SDAIE classrooms, English is developed along with content knowledge.

It is sometimes helpful to understand a concept by defining what it is *not*. The following statements put SDAIE into perspective by stating what it is *not*:

- SDAIE is *not* submersion into English-medium classrooms—that is, placing students in mainstream classes in which the teacher makes *no* modifications to accommodate English learners.
- SDAIE is *not* a substitute for primary-language instruction. Even in a sheltered classroom, students still are entitled to, and need support in, their primary language for both content and literacy development.
- SDAIE is *not* a watered-down curriculum. The classroom teacher continues to be responsible for providing all students with appropriate grade-level content learning objectives.

A Model for SDAIE

The model for SDAIE provides a frame for discussing appropriate instruction in sheltered classes (see Figure 5.1). This model uses four critical components—*content, connections, comprehensibility,* and *interaction*—as a guiding framework. Discussion and observation revealed that the teacher's attitude played such a critical part in the success of the class that it needed to be explicitly incorporated into the model. *Teacher attitude* is a fifth component.

In addition to the model, an observation form (Figure 5.2) provides more explicit elements and strategies within each component. It allows teachers to focus on, observe, and incorporate SDAIE elements into their lessons. Teachers find they do not use every aspect of the model in every lesson, but by working within the overall frame they are more assured of providing appropriate learning opportunities for their English learners. In the following sections, each of the five SDAIE components is explained and illustrated.

Figure 5.1 A Model of the Components of Successful SDAIE Instruction

Teacher Attitude The teacher is open and willing to learn from students	
Content Lessons include subject, language, and learning-strategy objectives. Material is selected, adapted, and organized with language learners in mind.	**Connections** Curriculum is connected to students' background and experiences.

Comprehensibility
Lessons include explicit strategies that aid understanding:
    Contextualization
    Modeling
    Teacher speech adjustment
    Frequent comprehension checks through strategies and appropriate questioning
Repetition and paraphrase
	Interaction
	Students have frequent opportunities to:
	    Talk about lesson content
	    Clarify concepts in their home language
	    Re-present learning through a variety of ways

Figure 5.2 Specially Designed Academic Instruction in English (SDAIE) Observation Form

Date: _____ Duration of observation: _____		Subject: _____ Number of students: _____
SDAIE Component	✓	**Evidence (describe with specific evidence the components observed)**

CONTENT
 Content objective
 Language objective
 Learning-strategy objective
 Materials and text
    Clear and meaningful
    Support objectives		

CONNECTIONS
 Bridging1
    Concepts/skills linked to student experiences
 Bridging2
    Examples used/elicited from students' lives
 Schema building
    New learning linked to old through scaffolding strategies
    (webs, semantic maps, visual organizers, etc.)		

COMPREHENSIBILITY
 Contextualization
    Use of pictures, maps, graphs, charts, models, diagrams,
     gestures, labels, and dramatizations to illustrate
     concept clearly
    Appeal to variety of learning styles
 Modeling
    Demonstration of skill or concept to be learned
 Speech adjustment
    Slower rate
    Clear enunciation
    Controlled use of idioms
 Comprehension checks
 Teacher and student strategies
    Appropriate questioning
    Recitation and paraphrase		

INTERACTION
 Opportunities for students to talk about lesson content
    Teacher to student
    Student to teacher
    Student to student
    Student to content
    Student to self
 Clarification of concepts in L1
    Primary-language material
    Student interaction
 Re-presentation of understanding
    Students transform knowledge through illustration,
     dramatization, song creation, dance, story rewriting,
     critical thinking		

Teacher Attitude

Previous chapters have mentioned affective aspects of learning and classroom environments that foster meaningful language acquisition, but they did not specifically address the role of the teacher's attitude. Good teachers find delight and satisfaction in working with all learners, particularly English learners.

Three aspects characterize a successful attitude in working with second-language learners:

1. Teachers believe that all students can learn. They do not assume that because a student does not speak English he or she is incapable of learning.
2. Teachers recognize that all students have language. Students have successfully learned their home languages and have understandings and skills that transfer to their second language.
3. Teachers recognize that a person's self-concept is involved in his or her own language and that at times students need to use that language.

In SDAIE classrooms, it is not only the students who are learning. Successful teachers themselves are open, not only *willing* to learn but also *expecting* to learn. Teachers using SDAIE reflect on their teaching using videotapes of themselves, peer observation, reflective journals, informal discussions with colleagues, and summative notations on lesson plans. They also set aside a quiet time for contemplation about the effectiveness of their teaching.

A popular form of SDAIE employs the Sheltered Instruction Observation Protocol (SIOP) model. Lesson plans in science using SIOP can be found in Short, Vogt, and Echevarría (2011). SIOP plans for mathematics are found in Echevarría, Vogt, and Short (2010).

Example of Concept   *A Positive Environment*

An ELD teacher observed and interviewed her colleagues at her school. She discovered that accomplished teachers set up effective learning environments for the English learners. They understood the needs of their culturally and linguistically diverse students and created an atmosphere in the classroom that helped newly arrived students integrate into the life of the school. For example, they encouraged friendships by asking a classmate to sit with the English learner at lunch. They provided appropriate instruction for their English learners and applauded their successes. This environment helped relieve much of the newcomers' anxiety (Haynes, 2004).

Content

Teaching SDAIE-modified academic content involves the careful planning of content, language, and learning-strategy objectives and the selecting, modifying, and organizing of materials and text that support those objectives. A lesson with a clear objective focuses the instruction and guides the teacher to select those learning activities that accomplish the goal. Once objectives are clearly stated, the teacher selects material that will help students achieve those objectives.

What are the benefits of lesson planning? For evaluation purposes, a good plan can be used as a checklist to see what has been accomplished. With a good plan in place, teachers can focus on students rather than worrying what should come next. Finally, a thorough plan helps teachers to evaluate material needs in advance as well as to estimate the duration of the activity.

Content Objectives. Planning begins by the teacher's first specifying learning goals and competencies students must develop. Standards documents that spell out what students should know and be able to do are available to provide an overview of the goals. Curricular programs follow the goals put forth in the documents. The teacher divides these overall goals for the year into units. These units are further divided into specific lessons. Each lesson contains the essential content-area objectives.

In developing their sequence of content objectives, teachers should keep two important questions in mind: (1) Have I reviewed the objectives for the year and organized them for thematic flow? and (2) Have I considered the sequence of objectives and rearranged them, if necessary, putting more concrete concepts before more abstract ones (i.e., those that can be taught with hands-on materials, visuals, and demonstrations before those that are difficult to demonstrate or that require more oral and/or written skills)?

Language Objectives. Each content area has specific language demands. Language objectives take these into account. The teacher considers the various tasks that language users must be able to perform in the different content areas (e.g., describing in a literature lesson, classifying in a science lesson, justifying in a mathematics lesson, etc.). A language objective takes into account not only vocabulary but also the language functions and discourse of the discipline.

In reviewing the language objectives, a teacher can keep the following questions in mind:

- What is the concept focus of the unit and what are the key concepts students must master?
- What are the structures and discourse of the discipline and how can these be included in the language objectives?
- Are all four language modes included—listening, speaking, reading, writing?

Learning-Strategy Objectives. Learning strategies help students learn *how* to learn. These include cognitive strategies (critical thinking, using graphic organizers); social-affective strategies (learning to work cooperatively, appreciating art); and metacognitive strategies (planning, self-monitoring, and self-evaluating).

Figure 5.3 Liberty: Content, Language, and Learning-Strategy Objectives

Social Studies. Students will ...

Examine the contributions of the New England, middle, and southern colonies in the American Revolution

Choose a famous figure to profile the role he or she played in the Revolutionary War

Language. Students will ...

Gather information by reading biographical sources

Write a brief dialogue, inventing a conversation the famous figure might have had pertaining to revolutionary activities

Learning Strategies. Students will ...

Apply basic reading comprehension strategies to find relevant information (skimming, scanning, previewing text)

Take notes to record important information

Source: Based on Majors (n.d.).

Figure 5.3 shows how content, language, and learning strategies can be used in a high-school social studies lesson on liberty. The objectives align with national and state standards.

Materials and Texts. A critical aspect of any lesson is the proper selection and use of materials. Textbooks have become a central tool in many classrooms, but they often need to be supplemented by other materials. The SDAIE teacher must select and modify text materials to best accommodate the needs of English learners.

Because texts can be problematic for English learners, teachers need to include specific objectives (either language or learning strategy) that teach students how to read and study academic discourse. Students need to understand the structure of a text as well as the actual content. Teachers teach students how to preview or "walk through" a text by noting the structure of the assigned chapter(s), including the main headings, subheadings, specialized words in bold or italic, maps, graphs, and pictures that are included to assist comprehension.

Teachers should also familiarize students with the difference in the style and structure of texts of the particular discipline. Content texts are more information-rich than stories, have specialized organizing principles that may be discipline specific, and use abstract and specialized vocabulary. The language may feature complex sentence structures and reference may be made to background knowledge characteristic of that discipline.

Selecting materials involves an initial choice of whether the teacher wishes to have one primary content source or a package of content-related materials (chapters from various texts, magazine and newspaper articles, encyclopedia entries, literary selections, Internet sources, software programs, etc.). Regardless of what is chosen, the teacher must consider two main criteria: Are the content objectives for the lesson adequately presented by the material? Is the material comprehensible to English learners? The following list enumerates additional items to consider when selecting materials:

- Is the information accurate, up-to-date, and thorough?
- Are the tasks required of students appropriate to the discipline?
- Is the text clearly organized, with print and layout features that assist students' comprehension?
- Does the text appeal to a variety of learning styles?
- Is the language of the text straightforward, without complex syntactic patterns, idioms, or excessive jargon?
- Is new content vocabulary clearly defined within the text or in a glossary?
- Are diagrams, graphs, and charts clearly labeled? Do they complement and clarify the text?
- Will most of the students have prior experience with the content, or will much time be necessary for schema building? (Allan & Miller, 2005)

Content area teachers must also consider the use of primary-language resources, such as dictionaries, books, software programs, and Internet sites, as well as people resources, such as cross-age tutors, parents, and community volunteers, in helping students to understand concepts.

 Example of Concept   *Primary Language Support*

One teacher organized a schoolwide Translation and Bridging Committee of students in grades 2 through 6 that prepared notes for parents and programs for school assemblies in Tagalog and Spanish. This gave students a sense of pride in the contributions their native-language skills made to the school (Echevarria & Graves, 2007).

Modifying materials may be necessary to help English learners comprehend connected discourse. Some learners may need special textual material, such as excerpts taken from textbooks or chapters from the readings that have been modified. Rewriting text selections requires a sizable time investment, however, so one of the following alternative approaches may be preferable:

- Supply an advance organizer for the text that highlights the key topics and concepts in outline form, as focus questions, or in the form of concept maps.
- Change the modality from written to oral. By reading aloud, the teacher can also model the process of posing questions while reading to show prediction strategies used when working with text.
- Record selected passages for students to listen to as they read along in the text. Podcast the passages for students to access from home.
- Develop a study guide for the text. For each reading section create ten sentences that reflect the main ideas, then turn each sentence into a question or selectively omit key words that students must supply.

- Ask students to work in groups so they can share their notes and help one another complete missing parts or correct misunderstood concepts.

Example of Concept · *Using Multiple Sources*

Materials for the social studies theme "acculturation" may include primary documents, personal histories, and literature. Students who research specific concepts related to acculturation—such as immigration assimilation, culture shock, job opportunities, or naturalization—may find that each document features a unique voice. A government document presents a formal, official point of view, whereas a personal or family story conveys the subject from a different perspective. In addition, numerous pieces of literature, such as Eve Bunting's *How Many Days to America?* (1991) or Laurence Yep's *Dragonwings* (1975), offer yet other points of view.

Connections

Students engage in learning when they recognize a connection between what they know and the learning experience. This can be accomplished in several ways: *bridging*—linking concepts and skills to student experiences (bridging1) or eliciting/using examples from students' lives (bridging2)—and *schema building*—using scaffolding strategies to link new learning to old.

Bridging1: Developing Experiences. SDAIE teachers help students develop new schemata for the concepts to be learned by providing new experiences that arouse interest in and attention to a topic. These experiences may include field trips, guest speakers, films and movies, experiments, classroom discovery centers, music and songs, poetry and other literature, computer simulations, and so on. To deepen these experiences, the teacher can guide the students to talk and write about them, associating what they already knew with these new experiences.

Example of Concept · *Experiences That Focus Instruction*

The firsthand experiences of a field trip piqued the interest of Dorothy Taylor's students in Virginia history and prepared them for the colonial unit she had planned (Taylor, 2000, pp. 53–55).

In the fall, all of the fourth-grade classes in the school went on a field trip to Jamestown, Virginia. The children returned from their trip eager to talk about what they had learned. The field trip and students' enthusiasm were a perfect introduction to the social studies unit on the hardships faced by the Jamestown colonists. The students shared with each other what they knew about Jamestown and colonial America and added to their knowledge and vocabulary by reading and watching a video.

Bridging2: Linking from Students' Lives. Prior knowledge of a topic may be tapped to determine the extent of students' existing concepts and understandings. Many students may have relevant experiences to share. Tapping prior knowledge allows them to place new knowledge in the context of their own episodic memories rather than storing new information solely as unrelated concepts. Teachers may use brainstorming, K-W-L charts (see Chapter 4), or peer interviews to elicit information from students and assess the extent of students' understanding.

Schema Building. If they have little prior knowledge about the topic at hand, students will need more instructional support to construct a framework of concepts that shows the relationships of old and new learning.

Graphic organizers help students order their thoughts by presenting ideas visually. Semantic mapping and webs are ways of presenting concepts to show their relationships. After a brainstorming session, the teacher and students could organize their ideas into a semantic map, with the main idea in the center of the chalkboard and associated or connected ideas as branches from the main idea. Figure 5.4 shows the results of a brainstorming session after second-grade students had heard *Cloudy with a Chance of Meatballs* (Barrett, 1978). They brainstormed on the questions "What junk food can you think of?" and "What is in junk food that our bodies don't need?"

Figure 5.4 Semantic Web Created While Brainstorming "Junk Food" after Reading *Cloudy with a Chance of Meatballs*

Comprehensibility

A key factor in learning is being able to understand. Through all phases of a lesson, the teacher ensures that students have plenty of clues to understanding. This is one of the aspects of SDAIE that makes it different from mainstream instruction. Teachers increase the comprehensibility of lessons in four ways: *contextualization, modeling, speech adjustment,* and *comprehension checks.*

Contextualization. The verbal presentation of a lesson is supplemented by the use of manipulatives, realia, media, and visual backup as teachers write key words and concepts on the chalkboard or butcher paper and use graphs, pictures, maps, and other

Example of Concept *Supplementing the Verbal Presentation*

In a biology class, when teaching about flowers, the teacher refers students to the explanation in the text (paragraph form), a diagram of a flower in the text (graphic form), a wall chart with a different flower (pictorial form), a text glossary entry (dictionary form), and actual flowers that students can examine. Through these numerous media, the concepts "petal," "stamen," "pistil," and "sepal" are understood and provide a basis for future study about life-forms.

Table 5.1 Media, Realia, Manipulatives, and Human Resources to Contextualize Lessons

Object Resources		Human Resources
Picture files	Science equipment	Cooperative groups
Maps and globes	Manipulatives:	Pairs
Charts and posters	M&Ms	Cross-age tutors
Printed material:	Buttons	Heterogeneous groups
Illustrated books	Cuisinaire rods	Community resource people
Pamphlets	Tongue depressors	School resource people
News articles	Gummy bears	Parents
Catalogs	Costumes	Pen pals (adult and child)
Magazines	Computer software	Keypals
Puzzles	Internet	

physical props to communicate. By presenting concepts numerous times through various means and in a rich environment of visual, auditory (e.g., software programs and websites that offer sounds and experiences), and kinesthetic (drama and skits, "gallery" walks) experiences, lessons also appeal to students' different learning styles.

Table 5.1 provides a list of both object and human resources that can help contextualize classroom content.

Example of Concept   *Resources for English-Language Development*

Jasper Elementary is one of four schools in the Waterloo (Iowa) Community School District that is designated to offer services to ELD students. Because the ELD students are integrated into mainstream classes, each teacher must find resources to help the students in his or her classroom. One fourth/fifth-grade teacher makes use of the Minnesota Migrant Resource Center, a repository of hands-on materials that can be borrowed. These include objects and pictures for bulletin boards and centers, song lyrics, worksheets, books, and other materials. The staff of the center is trained to help teachers match materials to student needs (Milambiling, 2002).

Verbal Markers. In addition to contextualizing the content of a lesson, teachers of English learners must also make accessible the organization and management procedures in the classroom. During the lesson, verbal markers provide structure so that students can understand what is expected of them. Markers for key points, such as *now, note this, for instance,* or *in conclusion,* cue students to material that is especially important. Terms such as *first, second,* and *last* clearly mark the steps of a sequence. To help with directions, teachers can determine the ten most frequently used verbal markers and provide mini-TPR-type lessons to help students learn them.

Modeling. Demonstrating new concepts can involve hands-on, show-and-tell explanations in which students follow a careful sequence of steps to understand a process.

The teacher ensures that the demonstration illustrates the concept clearly and that there is a one-to-one correspondence between the teacher's words and the demonstration.

Speech Adjustment. Teachers in SDAIE classrooms modify their speech to accommodate the various proficiency levels of their students. One way they do this is by monitoring their own language usage and reducing the amount of their talking in the classroom. This provides more opportunities for students to talk both with the teacher and among themselves.

By slowing their delivery and articulating clearly, teachers allow English learners greater opportunity to separate words and process the language. Teacher speech modification exists at all linguistic levels: phonological (using precise pronunciation); syntactic (less subordination; shorter sentences that follow subject-verb-object format); semantic (more concrete, basic vocabulary); pragmatic (more frequent and longer pauses, exaggerated stress and intonation); and discourse (self-repetition, slower rate).

As students become more proficient in English, teachers again adjust their speech, this time increasing speed and complexity. Ultimately, English learners will need to function in an all-English-medium classroom.

Comprehension Checks. Teachers use strategies to continually monitor students' listening and reading comprehension. During formal presentations, they use devices such as asking students to put their thumbs up or down, to paraphrase to another student, or to dramatize, write, or graph their understanding. Depending on student response, teachers may need to rephrase questions and information if the students do not initially understand.

When asking questions, the teacher can consider a linguistic hierarchy of question types. For students in the "silent period" of language acquisition, a question requiring a nonverbal response—a head movement, pointing, manipulating materials—will elicit an appropriate and satisfactory answer. Once students are beginning to speak, either/or questions provide the necessary terms, and the students need merely to choose the correct word or phrase to demonstrate understanding: "Is the water evaporating or condensing?"; "Did explorers come to the Americas from Europe or Asia?" Once students are more comfortable in producing language, *wh-* questions are appropriate: "What is happening to the water?"; "Which countries sent explorers to the Americas?"; "What was the purpose of their exploration?"

In addition to using comprehension strategies, teachers may also need to teach students how to verbalize their understanding. Teachers may need to find ways in which English learners can voice their need for clarification, such as accepting questions that are written on index cards (Díaz-Rico, 2013).

An important part of providing a comprehensible learning environment for students is the teacher's use of the same type of direction throughout various lessons. For example, an elementary teacher might say, "Today we are going to continue our work on . . ."; "Who can show me their work from yesterday?" These sentences can be repeated throughout the day to introduce lessons so that students know what to expect and how to proceed.

Adapted Instruction

Strategies for Comprehensibility

- Use sentence structures that expand the students' output by supplying needed phrases and vocabulary.
- Use gestures to convey instructions.
- Concentrate on understanding and communicating rather than on error correction.
- Provide alternative grouping procedures so that students can share their understanding with one another and with the teacher.
- Maintain regular classroom procedures and routines.

Interaction

The organization of discourse is important for language acquisition in content classes. Teacher-fronted classrooms are dominated by teacher talk. The teacher takes the central role in controlling the flow of information, and students compete for the teacher's attention and for permission to speak. However, the learner has a role in negotiating, managing, even manipulating conversations to receive more comprehensible input. Instead of English learners being dependent on their ability to understand the teacher's explanations and directions, classrooms that feature flexible grouping patterns permit students to have greater access to the flow of information.

The teacher orchestrates tasks so that students use language in academic ways. Students are placed in different groups for different activities. For example, when learning new and difficult concepts, English learners who speak the same language are placed together so that they can use their native language, whereas students of varying language backgrounds and abilities are grouped for tasks that require application of key concepts and skills. Teachers themselves work with small groups to achieve specific instructional objectives.

Student Opportunities to Talk. In planning for interaction in the SDAIE lesson, the teacher considers opportunities for students to talk about key concepts, expects that students may clarify the concepts in their primary language, and allows a variety of means through which students can demonstrate their understanding. Students engage in a variety of opportunities to explore, express, debate, chat, and laugh, with numerous conversational partners. Interaction patterns include teacher to student, student to teacher, student to student, student to content, and student to self. Cooperative learning activities, both formally and informally structured, allow English learners to work with one another in a noncompetitive, equal opportunity environment.

Probably one of the most powerful strategies teachers can use to ensure both content and language development in an interactional setting is the Instructional Conversation (IC). The lessons in this discussion-based strategy focus on an idea or concept that has educational value as well as meaning and relevance for students.

The teacher encourages expression of students' own ideas, builds on students' experiences and ideas, and guides them to increasingly sophisticated levels of understanding. The following summarizes the use of the IC in the classroom.

Adapted Instruction

The Instructional Conversation

1. Conversations take place in a circle of about 8 chairs. The teacher is fully present as a participant, so a classroom assistant is required to manage the non-participating other students in the classroom.
2. A clear academic goal guides the conversation with students, such as a follow-up discussion about a work of literature that students have been reading.
3. The conversation has a clear instructional focus, targeting the deep ideas and meanings of the work of literature.
4. The teacher is the conversational manager, but not the main talker—students should be talking at least 80 percent of the time.
5. All discussion turns are self-selected. The teacher previews and reviews techniques of "how to get a turn," such as making eye contact with the current speaker, leaning forward, and being ready with a comment when there is a conversational lull.
6. The teacher uses questioning, restating, praising, encouraging, and so forth to promote students' learning through conversation.

Clarification of Concepts in the Primary Language. In SDAIE classrooms, students are afforded opportunities to learn and clarify concepts in their own language. Research continues to show that when students are able to use their first language, they make more academic gains in both content and language than if they are prohibited from using it (Collier, 1995).

Re-Presentation of Knowledge. After students have had the opportunity to learn new material in a meaningful way, they can transform that knowledge through other means, such as illustrating, dramatizing, creating songs, dancing, and rewriting stories. By re-presenting information in another form, students must review what they know and think about how to organize and explain their knowledge in the new format. By sharing their discoveries in a variety of ways—in learning centers; through dramatic, visual, or oral presentations; by staging readers' theater; by developing slide, video, or computer-based audiovisual shows; through maps and graphs—they also use their developing language skills in a more formal setting.

Re-presentation of knowledge is also an important means for teachers to assess student learning and to pinpoint areas for reteaching, expansion, and/or modification. In this manner, assessment becomes a part of the learning cycle instead of something divorced from classroom practices.

Example of Concept   *Re-Presenting Knowledge*

In one fifth-grade class, the students produced a news program with a U.S. Civil War setting. The program included the show's anchors; reporters in the field interviewing generals, soldiers, and citizens; a weather report; and reports on sports, economics, and political conditions. There were even commercial breaks.

The students engaged in much research in order to be historically accurate, but enthusiasm was high as they shared their knowledge in a format they knew and understood. In addition, students were able to work in the area of their particular interest.

When a unit of instruction is completed, it is time to evaluate its success. The teacher should reflect on and record (Gibbons, 2006):

- What evidence is there that students have learned the lesson objectives, including the language and content?
- Did the students have adequate access to resources?
- Did the students express interest in the lesson? Were they actively involved?
- Were the lesson activities matched well to students' level and prior knowledge?
- Was the instruction effective, both on the part of the main teacher and the aides and/or volunteers?

SDAIE offers English learners an important intermediate step between content instruction in the primary language, an environment in which they may not advance in English skills, and a "sink-or-swim" immersion, in which they may not learn key content-related concepts. Although standards-based instruction emphasizes the acquisition of content, SDAIE requires additional lesson objectives that foster English-language acquisition. This supplementary focus on language development is the key that unlocks the core curriculum for English learners.

In summary, among the principles and practices recommended for SDAIE are the following:

1. Both content and language should be taught in the same lesson.
   - Content objectives are drawn from school district or statewide content standards, and English-language-development objectives are drawn from ELD standards at the level of the individual student's assessed proficiency
   - Vocabulary words drawn from the content are specifically taught, combined with academic terms that are used often within and across specific disciplines (such as *summarize, compare, contrast*)
2. The instructional focus is on comprehensibility for the learner
   - Multimodal input and output (reading, discussing, and looking at drawing, maps, charts, etc.) allow for variety in learning styles
   - Students' prior knowledge is the starting point for each lesson; if students lack specific prior knowledge, the lesson plan creates schemata
3. Both the language of the text and the teacher are modified for to increase students' content comprehension

- Focus is placed on ways to make complex or sophisticated language understandable
- The teacher speaks clearly, using gestures if necessary, without significantly altering the natural flow of speech

4. Teachers instruct students on specific learning strategies.
   - Direct strategies are used to gain knowledge of content, English-language development, thinking skills, and cooperative groupwork techniques
5. Formative and summative assessment monitors achievement in content knowledge and English proficiency

Content-Area Application

Each content area has standards that guide curriculum development. Applying the standards for English learners has been a thorny issue. The No Child Left Behind legislation (2002) states that English learners will develop high levels of academic proficiency in English and meet the same challenging state academic standards as do their native-English-speaking peers. How do they have access to the same challenging content as their peers? How do they meet the standards? While native-English-speaking students are learning content, English learners have the dual task of learning content *and* language, sometimes in sheltered classes, but more frequently in mainstream ones (McKeon, 1994).

Explanatory Models for Academic Disciplines

Beyond the use of visuals, manipulatives, and other types of modified instruction, students need to acquire explanatory models for each discipline. These are typical ways that practitioners use to make sense of the world, to use patterns of ideas to solve problems.

According to Duran, Dugan, and Weffer (1997), more successful students are those who are socialized into specific ways to think about the academic subjects they are studying. It is not enough to use the language of a scholar; one must also acquire a specific worldview and orientation toward particular kinds of knowledge. This way of thinking is an integral part of modified instruction.

Social Studies

According to the social studies standards document *National Curriculum Standards for Social Studies: A Framework for Teaching, Learning, and Assessment*. The primary purpose of social studies is to help young people develop the ability to make informed and reasoned decisions for the public good as citizens of a culturally diverse, democratic society in an interdependent world (National Council for the Social Studies [NCSS], 2010; Herczog, 2010). This purpose represents a tall order for teachers working with English learners who may have limited background with the social studies program in U.S. schools. However, by implementing certain strategies on a regular basis, teachers have found that their English learners are able to achieve the goals outlined in the social studies standards documents.

Content: Flexible, Thematic Curricula. A recent trend in many public schools has been to organize instruction around broad themes. Students learn social studies by researching, reading, and experimenting to answer real-world questions that they have posed themselves. The question-driven or problem-posing format forces a reconceptualization of the curriculum away from a narrow focus on subject areas to broader concepts that connect to significant ideas and issues (Freeman & Freeman, 1998). For English learners, this reconceptualization allows for more interactive engagement with a number of other speakers, for continuous concept development, and for an expanding base of vocabulary and language structures that can be used in a variety of contexts.

Example of Concept *Using Multiple Resources for Depth of Content*

Students studying a fifth-grade unit on Settlement of the West can examine the legal issues involved in the Treaty of Guadalupe-Hidalgo, compare the various cultures that came into contact in the Southwest, delve into the history of land grant titles, and pursue many more issues of interest. Through filmstrips, films, videos, computer simulations, literature, nonfiction texts, and oral discussions, students develop conceptual knowledge. Such a unit incorporates history, geography, sociology, economics, values, information-seeking skills, group participation, and perhaps dramatic skills as students act out the signing of treaties and other cultural events.

Connections: Linking to Prior Knowledge. By starting each class with an activity that actively engages students in reviewing their own experiences relevant to the topic, the teacher not only gains valuable insights that can help in teaching, but he or she also gives students an opportunity to see how their experiences fit into the realm of the social studies.

Using an oral history approach, for example, actively involves students in gathering information from their families and communities. Furthermore, not only do students learn that history is composed of their own and their family's stories, but also, by delving into their own backgrounds, they may learn about complex issues, such as religious persecution, tyranny of autocratic rulers, and the rights and responsibilities of self-governance. Through such oral history projects, students are engaging in many of the historical thinking skills outlined in the U.S. history standards (e.g., reading historical narratives, describing the past through the perspectives of those who were there, and preparing a historical analysis and interpretation) (Anstrom, Steeves, & DiCerbo, 1999).

Example of Concept *History with a Hip-Hop Beat*

"Gandhi, the freedom fighta!" is an unconventional phrase for a sixth-grade history class. Scott Sayre, a teacher at Jackson Elementary School in Los Angeles who is also an amateur musician, called on friends in the music-recording industry to help students record a rap song. Students continued their research on civil rights by recording a complete album featuring eight to ten songs. Twelve-year-old Cristela Gomez liked this novel approach. "I'm really shy," she says. "It helps me get rid of the shyness" (Green, 2007, p. B3).

Comprehensibility: Contextualizing Instruction. Specific strategies can increase the ability of English learners to understand content and to experience history "come alive." A timeline can be used to place important events in chronological sequence. A population graph can show the effect of events on people, and maps can place significant events in their geographical locale. Pictures from a variety of sources can bring past events to life. Pictures, charts, and diagrams help students identify main concepts.

Adapted Instruction

Using Social Media to Teach History/Social Studies

- Students take on the role of a famous person in history to send class members tweets about daily life or historical events.
- Using Skype, students link with local experts to discuss events in the area.
- On Twitter, students can follow feeds from their representative; senator; the President of the United States; local, regional, or national news sources.

Interaction: Cooperative Learning. Social studies topics in particular have been difficult for English learners because the topics are generally abstract, cognitively complex, and highly language dependent. Cooperative learning can be used to structure the classroom so that English learners have increased opportunities to verify their comprehension by receiving explanations from their peers and sharing prior knowledge. In this way, students are involved in their own learning and teachers can rely less on lectures and worksheets.

Adapted Instruction

Cooperative Learning Structures

- *Three-step interview.* One student interviews another and then the two reverse roles. They share with each other what they have learned.
- *Roundtable.* In a small group, the first student writes a contribution and then passes the paper to the next student. Each contributes in turn. The group discusses their findings. (This procedure can be done orally.)
- *Think-pair-share.* After the teacher asks a question, students think of a response. Students use the interview technique to share answers.
- *Solve-pair-share.* The teacher poses a problem and students work on solutions individually. Students explain their various solutions in interview or roundtable procedures.
- *Numbered heads.* Each team member has a number. The teacher asks a question. The teams put their heads together to find the answer and make sure everyone knows it. The teacher calls a number and the student with that number in each team raises his or her hand.
- *Jigsaw.* Each student is in a home team and an expert team. Expert teams work together on specific material different from other expert teams. Students return to their home team and share what they have learned.

Re-Presenting Knowledge: Linking Instruction to Assessment. Many of the tasks, projects, and role-plays that students are engaged in to learn content can be further used in assessment. Such authentic tasks provide a richer means of assessing students who are still struggling with the language than the traditional paper-and-pencil tests.

Example of Concept   *Re-Presenting Knowledge*

The culminating activity for the Holocaust unit in Kathy Reckendorf and Wilma Ortiz's class was the creation of a quilt based on the *Diary of Anne Frank*. The class was separated into teams and each team created one quilt square based on their depiction of a theme or message that they felt was the most relevant in the book. The teams referred to the text

and wrote one or two lines or phrases that captured their attention. They sketched these ideas and selected the one that they agreed represented the theme and message they had identified. The students then displayed their quilt in the school cafeteria (Reckendorf & Ortiz, 2000).

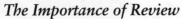

Adapted Instruction

The Importance of Review

Schedule time for review at the end of each lesson; point out key concepts and vocabulary while making connections to lesson objectives and state standards. This is essential, because English learners may concentrate so intently on processing language during instruction that they forget the importance of the information (Friend & Bursuck, 2006, p. 320).

Literature

Of the twelve standards in the *Standards for the English Language Arts* (National Council of Teachers of English [NCTE] & International Reading Association [IRA], 1996, online at www.ncte.org/standards/ncte-ira), two provide support for English learners: Standard 9, "Students develop an understanding of and respect for diversity in language use, patterns, and dialects across cultures, ethnic groups, geographic regions, and social roles"; and Standard 10, "Students whose first language is not English make use of their first language to develop competency in the English language arts and to develop understanding of content across the curriculum." In addition, Standard 1 calls for wide reading, including texts about the cultures of the United States and the world.

Content: Material Selection. An appropriate selection of genre may be one way to help English learners develop their conceptual and linguistic schemata. The literature curriculum can be a planned sequence that begins with familiar structures of folktales and myths and uses these as a bridge to more complex works of literature. Students can move from these folktales and myths to selected short stories by authors of many cultural backgrounds, then to portions of a longer work, and then to entire works.

Students who read books that interest them are more motivated to read. A study of sixth-grade students' reading preferences found that most preferred books with scary stories, comics, and content about popular culture, sports, cars and trucks, and animals (Worthy, Moorman, & Turner, 1999). The features of the text make a motivational difference. Frey and Fisher (2007) described common features of various text genres: Chapter books are largely text-only, whereas graphic novels are based on pictures, with text used largely for dialogue—these are often recommended to jump-start reading for the reluctant adolescent.

Example of Concept — *A Variety of Materials*

William Pruitt (2000, pp. 33–49) describes how his students benefit from studying different versions of a folktale:

> One of the goals of the story unit is for students to examine how the same story may differ as it appears in different perspectives, media, and cultures, and compare and contrast these forms. Over the course of the 2-week unit, we read and compare and contrast an original (translated) version of "Beauty and the Beast," a poem entitled "Beauty and the Beast," and three video versions of the story. Once students have gained experience with this folktale and understand the pattern of activities, we move to other texts that have film adaptations, for example, *Tuck Everlasting* (Babbitt, 1976) or *To Kill a Mockingbird* (Lee, 1960).

Connections and Comprehensibility: *Into, Through,* **and** *Beyond.* "Into" activities activate students' prior knowledge. Once students are ready for the text, they can make predictions about the story. Some teachers put these predictions into short-term "time capsules" that can be opened and analyzed once the text has been read. Students can discuss what happened later in the book to confirm or disprove their original predictions.

Adapted Instruction

Ways "into" Literature

- *Anticipation/reaction guides.* A short list of statements provokes students to agree or disagree.
- *Pictures, art, movies.* Visual means build a feeling for the setting.
- *Physical objects.* Items relating to the reading selection allow students to identify and discuss.
- *Experiences.* Field trips can interest students in the topic.

"Through" activities help students as they work with the text. Teachers find reading aloud a useful strategy that gives the students an opportunity to hear a proficient reader, to get a sense of the format and story line, and to listen to the teacher "think aloud" about the reading. In the think-aloud, teachers can model how they monitor a sequence of events, identify foreshadowing and flashback, visualize a setting, analyze character and motive, comprehend mood and theme, and recognize irony and symbols.

Ways "through" Literature

- *Character review.* Specific students become a character and provide background for other students' questions throughout the reading.

- *Image/theme development.* Charts, graphs, pictures, and symbols can trace the development of images, ideas, and themes.

- *Read-along tapes.* Tapes encourage slower readers, allow absent students to catch up, and provide auditory input for students who learn through that modality.

- *Visual summaries.* Groups of students create chapter reviews, character analyses, or problem–solutions on overhead transparencies.

"Beyond" activities are designed to extend the students' appreciation of literature. These can be analytical, creative, or communicative and use language in an integrative manner to deepen comprehension and spur thoughtful reactions.

Using Social Media to Teach Literature

Students create a Facebook page for a literacy character, listing likes and dislikes as the voice of the character. They then link the content to peers and the teacher (http://mrfeatherstone .blogspot.com/2009/04/unit-project-facebook-character.html).

Interaction: Literature Response Groups. To help develop a community of readers and assist students in understanding the richness of the literacy experience, teachers engage them in literature response groups. After having read a piece of literature, the teacher and a small group meet to discuss the piece. Each student is given an opportunity to express ideas about the story before a general discussion begins. The teacher listens and, after each student has had a turn, opens the discussion with a thought-provoking question. As points are made, the teacher guides the students to deeper understandings by, for example, asking them to support their point with words from the text and asking what words or devices the author used to invoke a mood, establish a setting, describe a character, move the plot along, and so on.

Interaction: Maintaining the First Language. Teachers can use several strategies that support students' first language within the context of the classroom program. Aides and tutors can assist in explaining difficult passages and helping students summarize their understanding. Native-language books, magazines, films, and other materials relating to the topic or theme of the lesson can support and augment students' learning. Students can also keep reading logs or journals in their native language.

Example of Concept *Primary-Language Poetry*

Judith Casey (2004) encourages students to share their native language with their classmates during a poetry activity. When Ms. Casey invites students to bring in and read aloud a poem in their L1, someone always shouts out, "But we won't be able to understand them!" But she tells them that everyone can enjoy the sounds and rhythms of the various languages. On Poetry Day, the atmosphere of the class is charged. No one knows exactly what to expect but the students are excited. Amazingly, hearing each other read in their L1 lets the students see each other in a new light. The class is forever changed as students recognize the value, contributions, and abilities of their classmates.

Mathematics

The National Council of Teachers of Mathematics' (NCTM) standards document, *Principles and Standards for School Mathematics* (NCTM, 2000), provides six principles: equity, curriculum, teaching, learning, assessment, and technology. Those specifically relevant for English learners (although they are never directly addressed) include equity (high expectations and strong support for all students), teaching (challenging and supporting students to learn mathematics well), and learning (actively building new knowledge from experience and prior knowledge to learn mathematics with understanding). For non-native speakers of English, specially designed activities and teaching strategies must be incorporated into the mathematics program in order for them to have the opportunity to develop their mathematics potential.

Example of Concept *Teaching to a Standard*

To fulfill the National Council of Teachers of Mathematics (2000) standard "Using Nonstandard Measures," students in the "Inchworms" unit (grades K–2) read *Inch by Inch* by Leo Lionni. The teacher set up a center in which students could use paper inchworms to measure various parts of colorful paper birds. This "nonstandard measure" helped the children to understand that units of measure are not necessarily only those on a ruler (Beeghly & Prudhoe, 2002).

The Language of Mathematics. Instead of being "language neutral," mathematics does in fact pose numerous problems for English learners. These difficulties lie in four major areas: vocabulary skills, syntax, semantics, and discourse features.

Vocabulary in mathematics includes words of a technical nature such as *denominator, quotient,* and *coefficient,* and words such as *rational, column,* and *table* have a meaning different from everyday usage. Often, two or more mathematical concepts combine to form a different concept: for example, *least common multiple* and *negative exponent*. The same mathematical operation can be signaled with a variety of mathematics terms: *add, and, plus, sum, combine,* and *increased by* all represent addition. Moreover, special symbols are used to stand for vocabulary terms (Dale & Cuevas, 1992).

Example of Concept   *Specialized Vocabulary*

Many words in mathematics are special uses of words with common meanings outside of math. Base is a word also used in baseball; a teacher can explain that just as it is a place to rest between plays, it can mean a surface upon which an object rests. A *yard* is a grassy area around a house, but can also be a unit for measuring this area. Developing a list of content words for each year's math instruction and explicitly teaching these words helps students to gain math literacy (Adams, 2003).

Syntax problems arise because of the complexity of the language of mathematics. Students may not recognize that a concept is made up of the relationship between two words (e.g., *greater than, less than, as much as, the same as*). Complex structures such as "Twenty is five times a certain number. What is the number?" can confuse students. In addition, students often do not understand the use of the passive voice: "Nine is divided by three," "Thirty is represented by one-half of sixty" (Carrasquillo & Rodríguez, 2002).

Semantic problems occur when students are required to make inferences from natural language to the language of mathematics. For example, in the problem "Five times a number is two more than ten times the number," students must recognize that "a number" and "the number" refer to the same quantity.

Discourse features that are unlike natural language characterize the texts used in mathematics. The tendency to interrupt for the inclusion of formulae may be confusing to the reader of mathematics textbooks. Such texts require a reading rate adjustment because they must be read more slowly and require multiple readings.

Adapted Instruction

The Mathematical Language Requirements of Common Core

The set of Common Core standards grouped under "Comprehension and Collaboration" state that students in K–12 schools will be expected to interact with one another using listening and speaking at relatively high levels of sophistication. At the high school level, students are expected to carry out intellectual conversations independently of teacher support and supervision. They are expected to critique and query one another—behaviors seldom seen even in college classes!

These listening and speaking expectations have not yet been applied to mathematics classes, but contemporary math teaching is following a path of increased use of language, expecting students to use journal entries and other kinds of writing to write about their math knowledge. This places an increased stress on English learners, as they are expected to learn math verbally as well as numerically, in a second language.

Content: Learning Strategies. Metacognitive strategies are especially important during math instruction. Students who can monitor their own thinking while reading a math textbook are likely to discover for themselves when they need to reread, summarize, question, or clarify what they are reading (Unrau, 2008). Mathematics textbooks have a predictable lesson structure, consisting of the following sequence: preview concept set; present concept one, give example of concept one, demonstrate sample problem using concept one; present concept two, give example of concept two, demonstrate sample problem using concept two, and so on; then a problem set utilizing concepts in order of presentation, then a final problem set ranging in difficulty from those using simple algorithms to those requiring more advanced application of concepts, including bonus problems. At any point in this sequence, a student can reread, attempt problems, check for understanding, and review. Monitoring this process for comprehension is a skill that each math student can learn and use to increase success.

Connections: Using Students' Experiences. Teachers can find out from their students what activities they engage in after school and then capitalize on those for mathematics instruction. For example, those students who participate in sports can learn to calculate their batting average, points per game, race times, average speed, and so on. Older students with after-school jobs can use their pay stubs to figure the percentages of their various withholding categories (Anstrom & DiCerbo, 1999). Younger students may be able to assist their parents with shopping by helping to keep purchases within the budget and determine the best-priced item. They can also help calculate the tax that will be added to the total.

Comprehensibility: Modeling Technology and Other Tools. Many English learners are unfamiliar with the basic tools associated with mathematics (rulers, protractors, calculators, etc.). After demonstrating each, teachers can provide students with real-life opportunities to use them. For example, students are told that the classroom needs to be recarpeted. They first have to estimate the area, then check their estimates with the actual tools (using both standard and metric measuring instruments, as they will not know which system the carpet company uses). Computer programs can also be used to provide estimates and calculations.

Comprehensibility: Differentiated Instruction. Teachers should vary the classroom instructional routine, design tasks that appeal to students' various intellectual gifts, and allow students some choice in the types of learning in which they engage.

In *Mathematics Teaching Today,* NCTM makes this clear: "Students may use the Internet to research and collect data, use interactive geometry software to conduct investigations, or use graphing calculators to translate among different mathematical representations. . . . [T]eachers should use various arrangements and tools flexible to pursue their goals" (NCTM, 2007, p. 41).

Interaction: Working in Groups. Strategies for reading math texts and for supplementing students' math with language instruction involve more student interaction and small-group work. Students need to be encouraged to think aloud about mathematics and to talk with one another about the processes involved. In this way, they use language as a tool for tackling mathematics concepts. Working in groups, students can discuss with one another the activities they engage in at math centers or stations in various parts of the classroom. This gives them an opportunity to try out ideas and learn various mathematical strategies from their peers.

Re-Presenting Knowledge: Alternative Assessment. Alternative assessment requires students to perform tasks similar to those used to teach and learn the material. In mathematics, tasks such as asking students to develop a series of graphs based on student characteristics, to run a school store, or to pretend playing the stock market (Anstrom, 1999a) keep students actively engaged in mathematics while allowing the teacher to assess their understanding.

Adapted Instruction

Alternative Means of Demonstrating Math Knowledge

- Students play "Who is X?" They create mini-mystery stories with a missing fact that can be found from combining given facts.
- Students interview friends and neighbors to find "X and Y Facts": ("How many tables are in your house? How many are square? How many are round?")
- Students can illustrate story problems in their math books using stick figures.

In response to teachers' requests for materials that would help students of nonmainstream cultures acquire the knowledge, skills, and most importantly, dispositions to succeed in mathematics, NCTM published a series of books called *Changing the Face of Mathematics,* with separate volumes addressing adapted mathematics education for African Americans, Asian Americans and Pacific Islanders, Latinos, and multiculturalism and gender equity. For example, in the book targeted to help educators interest Native American students in mathematics (Hankes & Fast, 2002), an article describes a Rug Task designed for Navajo students that challenges them to connect the mathematic concepts of symmetry and area to the skill of weaving a rug.

PROFILE OF AN EDUCATOR:

Despite Poverty, Students Pass Advanced Math

Basil Lee teaches trigonometry at Benjamin Banneker High School in College Park, Georgia. Lee left a job as a factory manager in 1991 to work as a teacher for one-third of his previous salary. Banneker High School had not made adequate yearly progress (AYP) on No Child Left Behind measures. Students in Mr. Lee's class were poor; 63 percent of students in the school receive free or reduced-rate lunch. Sixteen-year-old Lucie Kamga took Lee's advanced algebra and trigonometry class last year. "He really cares about whether we learn or not," she says. (Copeland, 2008, p. 9D).

Science

The *National Science Education Standards* (National Research Council, 1996) emphasize inquiry as the means for students to become scientifically literate. Inquiry is described as

> multifaceted activity that involves making observations; posing questions; examining books and other sources of information to see what is already known; planning investigations; reviewing what is already known in light of experimental evidence; using tools to gather, analyze, and interpret data; proposing answers, explanations, and predictions; and communicating the results. Inquiry requires identification of assumptions, use of critical and logical thinking, and consideration of alternative explanations. (p. 23)

Working in inquiry classrooms with English learners can be challenging but extremely rewarding for teachers who recognize the connections between inquiry and SDAIE and who organize learning activities to maximize their students' experiences. Teachers need to recognize that as English learners construct science knowledge, they have linguistic and cultural demands placed on them over and above those placed on native-English-speaking students.

Example of Concept   *Scaffolded Science*

Hammond (2006) defines scaffolding as "specific help that enable[s] students to engage in tasks and develop understandings that they could not do on their own" (p. 152). At the end of scaffolded instruction, students should be able to transfer their understanding and skills to new tasks with a sense of independence as learners. Instead of simplifying the curriculum, a key idea is to provide high levels of systematic support.

Hammond teaches science in a cycle, beginning with hands-on experiments and discussion, followed by students' reading and reflecting in a structured cooperative-learning format; they then make charts of key information and use these charts to write about what they have learned. This cycle distributes the responsibility for learning among peer groups in a carefully structured way.

In a paragraph about instruction for English learners, the addendum to the standards document, *Inquiry and the National Science Education Standards* (Olson & Loucks-Horsley, 2000), notes that "learner-centered environments in which teachers build new learning on the knowledge, skills, attitudes, and beliefs that students bring to the classroom, are critical to science learning of English language learners" (p. 122).

The following sections present the language of science and the problems it can pose for students. Specific strategies that need to be incorporated to facilitate English learners' science learning are then provided.

The Language of Science. The four major language areas (vocabulary, syntax, semantics, and discourse features) detailed in the section on mathematics are also relevant for science. Students not only have to learn scientific definitions of some common words they may already know (e.g., *energy, sense, work*) but they must also learn complex syntactic structures, which include passive voice, multiple embeddings, and long noun phrases (Chamot & O'Malley, 1994).

Furthermore, English learners need to understand the structure of scientific text. A number of types of text structures are common in science content materials. The *cause–effect* structure links reasons with results or actions with their consequences. The *compare–contrast* structure examines the similarities and differences between concepts. The *time–order* structure shows a sequential relationship over the passage of time (Pérez & Torres-Guzmán, 2002). To assist in their comprehension, students can receive special training in following written instructions for procedures or experiments and can be shown ways to organize their recognition of science vocabulary.

Example of Concept   *Using Digital Texts in Science*

Digital texts offer the potential of revolutionizing teaching and learning in science. They can contain interactive, model-based simulations that promote deep and powerful inquiry. Using digital tools such as probes, sensors, and real-time data analysis, students can visualize the unseen and conduct experiments that would otherwise be impossible. They can create virtual experiments, altering the values of variables and immediately seeing results graphed.

In the Cumulative Learning through Embedded Assessment Results (CLEAR) project at the University of California, Berkeley, students can work in a virtual greenhouse; tinker with molecules; modify logic gates to explore transistors; or change the sunlight on a simulated mountain slope to see how light, atmosphere, and the earth interact (see www.concord.org/fall2009/lessons) to launch the experiments (Dorsey, 2009).

Adapted Instruction

Developing Scientific Language

• Provide appropriate contexts for new vocabulary, syntactic structures, and discourse patterns. Isolated lists or exercises do not appear to facilitate language acquisition.

- Engage students in hands-on activities in which they discuss concepts in a genuine communicative context.

- Promote activities in which students actively debate with one another about the truth of a hypothesis or the meaning of data gathered.

Source: Adapted from Carrasquillo and Rodríguez (2002).

Content: Common Themes. Organizing instruction around broad themes—such as the nature of matter, the pollution and purification of water, or the impact of drugs on the physiology and behavior of living organisms—puts science in a comprehensible context that can have relevance to students' lives. Such contextualizing increases the probability that students will continue to want to learn science on their own; extends the time a single topic is studied, thus allowing more time for understanding and reflection as well as repetition of key English words and phrases; and reduces the tendency toward superficial treatment of subjects.

In planning around themes, teachers often prepare a choice of projects for students to complete to strengthen their comprehension of difficult science material. Each project is tied to a central objective. For example, if students are to understand the basic properties of a cell, the list of projects might include drawing and labeling a cell diagram, preparing an oral report on the structure and function of a cell, or summarizing the current research on cloning.

Connections: Keeping a Science Notebook. Writing is one way students can connect with science. The science notebook is more than a place where students record data they collect, facts they learn, or procedures they conduct. "It is also a record of students' questions, predictions, claims linked to evidence, conclusions, and reflections— all structured by an investigation leading to an understanding of "big ideas" (not factoids) in science. A science notebook is a central place where language, data, and experience work together to form meaning for the student" (Klentschy, 2005, p. 24).

Example of Concept   *Science Vocabulary through Music and Drama*

Students in the second grade experienced the water cycle in guided imagery as they listened to Tchaikovsky's "Waltz of the Snowflakes" from the *Nutcracker Suite.* They began as a water drop, turned into vapor, condensed, and fell to ground as a snowflake. Later, students created a "sound sculpture," making different sounds for each stage of the cycle. These activities motivated a deeper interest in the science they learned as they tried to embody abstract concepts: accumulation, evaporation, and precipitation (Jacobs, Goldberg, & Bennett, 2004, pp. 93–94).

Comprehensibility: Modeling. If the teacher feels the need to lecture, a helpful strategy for English learners is to videorecord the lesson. Students should be encouraged to listen to the lecture, concentrating on understanding and writing down only questions or parts of the lecture they do not understand. Later, the recording is played and the teacher and several students take notes on the board. The teacher can model the type of outline that emphasizes the main ideas and clearly indicates supporting details. The students use whatever strategies are comfortable for them, including use of their native language. After a few minutes, the recording is stopped and the notes compared. The discussion then highlights various note-taking strategies and provides new strategies for everyone involved. This activity can be used on a periodic basis to determine students' ability to comprehend lectures and take effective notes.

Interaction: Talking about Lesson Content. Scientific investigation provides a natural setting for students to talk about science concepts. Discovery learning, problem posing and solving, experiments, and hypotheses testing all give students numerous opportunities to interact with various members of the class, with the teacher, and potentially with experts.

Example of Concept   *Talking in Science*

Debbie Zacarian described the way in which students interact with one another during a science unit about the solar system. During the first week of the solar system unit, the names of the planets were tossed into a hat. Each of nine pairs of native-English-speaking and English-learning students selected one planet and developed a poster session about their planet based on resources in the school library. After each pair presented their planet, the teacher combined pairs into small groups. Each group was to create a tenth planet based on what they had learned during the paired experience. Each group engaged in a lively discussion developing ideas about their tenth planet. After a short lesson on papier-mâché making, each group created a papier-mâché model of their planet and presented it to the class. This activity extended the amount of social and academic interactions and understandings about the content.

The Visual and Performing Arts

The visual and performing arts are often used as a medium for English learners to illustrate their understandings of concepts in other disciplines. Ideas that were originally presented in linguistic form can be translated into the artistic medium so that students can demonstrate their comprehension. However, arts lessons in themselves help students develop language skills. The *Visual and Performing Arts Standards* (CDE, 2004) provide specific objectives and sample tasks for each of the five strands: artistic perception; creative expression; historical and cultural context; aesthetic valuing; and connections, relations, applications (p. 3).

Teachers knowledgeable about SDAIE techniques can organize instruction so that it meets the content objective while addressing the needs of English learners. For example, English learners in any of the primary grades would be able to participate in the following, learning not only artistic principles but also vocabulary. For the theater objective "Replicate the sound and movement of objects, animals, and people," the following is a sample task: "After a walk around the school during which students have observed the movement of natural objects, they pantomime the actions of such objects as leaves, branches, clouds, and the animals they saw" (CDE, 1998b, p. 81). For creative expression (music), third graders need to sing or play, with increasing accuracy, a varied repertoire of music, alone and with others (CDE, 1998b, p. 58). Obviously, songs from their own cultures can be included in this repertoire. English learners can find their culture valued as well by the objective in historical and cultural context (dance): "Learn and perform dances from their own and other cultures. After viewing a dance performed by a visiting dancer and being assisted in learning some movements to the dance, students perform the movements in unison" (p. 11). SDAIE techniques have been used successfully to introduce students to art concepts.

Physical Education

The *Physical Education Framework for California Public Schools* (2009) is typical of state frameworks. It presents five "overarching" standards addressing motor skills and movement patterns; knowledge of movement concepts, principles, and strategies for physical activities; physical fitness assessment and maintenance; knowledge of physical fitness concepts, principles, and strategies; and knowledge of psychological and sociological concepts, principles, and strategies that apply to the learning and performance of physical activity.

These standards are part of a standards-based instructional design process that uses evidence-based learning. The framework specifically links physical activity to cognitive functioning, emphasizing the strong link between physical fitness and academic performance (see California Department of Education, 2005). A section of the *Framework* includes the use of instruments such as pedometers, accelerometers, and electronic blood pressure measuring devices, and another section describes possibilities for instructional software and web resources for teaching physical education. An appendix addresses adapted physical education for students requiring individualized or independent study, as well as for students with disabilities. The *Framework* also includes a list of possible careers in physical education.

Section 7 of the *Framework* (Universal Access) contains a wealth of differentiation strategies for physical education instruction. Diversity is addressed in various ways: how to avoid stereotyping and marginalizing students, including those with body types that differ from the norm; how to promote gender equity; and how to accommodate cultural and religious practices. The *Framework* provides suggestions on adapting instruction for English learners, prescribing a set of best practices involving linguistic modifications (clear enunciation, avoidance of idioms, and use of cognates when possible), alternative forms of information presentation, cooperative learning, use of manipulatives and contextual cues, and evocation of prior knowledge before instruction—all well-known SDAIE strategies. The *Framework* also discusses ways to involve families and communities.

Physical education is more than activity—it is "a discipline that encourages the thoughtful development of body and mind" (Unrau, 2008, p. 379). Experts in the field emphasize the connection between language and physical education, including the acquisition of a vocabulary that includes physiology (names of muscles), rules of sports, and so on. Students can be encouraged to develop their own philosophies and plans for personal recreation, discuss healthy attitudes toward athletic participation, and debate the dangers of extreme risks. In this way, the PE class is focused on the development of the whole student and the acquisition of lifelong dispositions and habits (Griffin & Morgan, 1998).

Additionally, physical education activities can be carefully structured to motivate students' cooperation and sense of group cohesiveness. This is particularly important in a class in which English learners of various cultures are together.

Example of Concept   *Modeling and Working Together*

According to Debbie Zacarian, a physical education teacher helped an English learner by modeling and placing the student with carefully selected peers. When Tien attended his first PE class in the United States, he was not sure what to do. Fortunately, his teacher used many physical movements to model the desired activities, enabling Tien to follow along and imitate the movements. When the teacher separated the class into teams, he carefully placed Tien with two students who modeled the volleyball activity. Tien continued to participate because he was able to see what he needed to do to be successful in class.

Instructional Needs beyond the Classroom

To be successful in their academic courses, English learners often need assistance from organizations and volunteers outside of the classroom. This assistance can come from academic summer programs, additional instructional services such as after-school programs and peer tutoring, and Dial-a-Teacher for homework help in English and in the primary language. Support in the affective domain may include special home visits by released-time teachers, counselors, or outreach workers and informal counseling by teachers.

Example of Concept   *Meeting Instructional Needs beyond the Classroom*

Escalante and Dirmann (1990) profiled the Garfield High School calculus course in which Escalante achieved outstanding success in preparing Hispanic students to pass the Advanced Placement (AP) calculus examination. Escalante was the organizer of a broad effort to promote student success. In his classroom, he set the parameters: He made achievement a game for the students, the "opponent" being the Educational Testing Service's examination; he coached students to hold up under the pressure of the contest and work hard to win; and he held students accountable for attendance and productivity. But beyond this work in the classroom was community support.

Community individuals and organizations donated copiers, computers, transportation, and souvenirs such as special caps and team jackets. Parents helped Escalante emphasize proper conduct, respect, and value for education. Past graduates served as models of achievement, giving pep talks to students and hosting visits to high-tech labs. The support from these other individuals combined to give students more help and encouragement than could be provided by the classroom teacher alone. The results were dramatized in the feature film *Stand and Deliver*.

Escalante's successful AP calculus program at Garfield High School involved much more than excellent classroom instruction. It is not surprising that the five key features of SDAIE were incorporated in his teaching: *content* and *language* teaching, the latter through an extensive attention to specific mathematics vocabulary; *connections* between the math curriculum and the students' lives and development of appropriate schema when background was lacking; *comprehensibility* through use of realia and visual support for instruction and modification of teacher talk; *interaction* with one another through cooperative learning; and *teacher attitude,* a positive coaching approach that conveyed high expectations. This is the instructional enhancement that opens the door to success for English learners.

LEARNING MORE

Further Reading

Making Content Comprehensible for English Language Learners (Echevarria et al., 2012) presents the sheltered instruction observation protocol (SIOP) model, a tool for observing and quantifying a teacher's implementation of quality sheltered instruction.

Web Search

Visit the website of the professional organization of the content field that interests you the most. Search under "English learners" to find what standards, criteria, lessons, and advice are provided.

Exploration

Using the SDAIE model observation form, elicit from a number of teachers specific activities, approaches, and methods they use. If possible, observe the teachers and together discuss the lessons and their results for English learners.

Discussion

You firmly believe in the use of cooperative learning and seat your students in tables of four in your classroom. Students with special education Individualized Educational Plans (IEPs) who are mainstreamed, some of whom are English learners, are mixed with other students, including other English learners. However, parents of some students have contacted you to express concerns that their students are more occupied teaching others than learning new things (Brahier, 2009). What arguments can you use to continue your practice of heterogeneous grouping?

MyEducationLab™

Literature for a Range of Learners Part 2

Roberta Sejnost discusses how to use both fiction and nonfiction in all three steps of the reading process. A teacher talks about how she chooses articles to use with her students. Her class discusses an article and practices finding the main idea.

To access the video, go to MyEducationLab (www.myeducationlab.com), choose the Díaz-Rico text, and log in to MyEducationLab for English Language Learners. Select the topic Content Area Reading and Writing, and watch the video entitled "Literature for a Range of Learners Part 2."

Answer the following questions:

1. How does the teacher accommodate the needs of learners who might not be able to benefit from a grade-level reading text?

2. Where does the teacher look for resources to match the thematic content of a unit?

3. What steps does the teacher use to help students find the main idea?

6

Theories and Methods of Bilingual Education

Dual-language immersion bilingual education employs two languages for academic purposes.

© Blend Images/SuperStock

When we hear the child speak, we see only what is above the surface of the water, the water lily itself. But the roots of the mother tongue lie deep beneath the surface, in the more or less unconsciously acquired connotative and non-verbal meanings. When the child learns a foreign language, that language easily becomes . . . a splendid water lily on the surface which superficially may look just as beautiful as the water lily of the mother tongue. . . . But it is often the case that for a very long time the second language is a water lily more or less floating on the surface without roots.

If at this stage we allow ourselves to be deceived by the beautiful water lily of the foreign language into thinking that the child knows this language . . . well enough to be able to be educated through it . . . the development of the flower of the mother tongue may easily be interrupted. If education in a foreign language poses a threat to the development of the mother tongue, or leads to its neglect,

147

then the roots of the mother tongue will not be sufficiently nourished or they may gradually be cut off altogether. . . . [A] situation may gradually develop in which the child will only have two surface flowers, two languages, neither of which she commands in the way a monolingual would command her mother tongue. . . . And if the roots have been cut off, nothing permanent can grow any more.

Tove Skutnabb-Kangas (1981, pp. 52–53)

Bilingual education has existed in the United States since the colonial period, but over the more than two centuries of U.S. history it has been alternately embraced and rejected. The immigrant languages and cultures in North America have enriched the lives of the people in American communities, yet periodic waves of language restrictionism have virtually eradicated the capacity of most U.S. citizens to speak a foreign or second language, even those who are born into families with a heritage language other than English. For English learners, English-only schooling has often brought difficulties, cultural suppression, and discrimination even as English has been touted as the key to patriotism and success.

In many parts of the world, people are not considered well educated unless they are schooled in multiple languages. Many young people in the United States enter school fluent in a primary language other than English, a proficiency that can function as a resource. Programs that assist students to sustain fluency and develop academic competence in their heritage language offer bilingual education in its best sense. Exemplary bilingual education programs are explicitly bicultural as well so that students' natural cultures as well as their heritage languages can be fostered.

Despite the argument—and the evidence—that bilingual education helps students whose home language is not English to succeed in school, bilingual education continues to be an area of contention. Figure 6.1 presents ten common misconceptions about bilingual education.

The challenge to any English-language-development program is to cherish and preserve the rich cultural and linguistic heritage of the students as they acquire English. One means of preserving and supplementing the home languages of our nation's children is through bilingual instruction (see figure on page 69).

In this chapter, three important areas of bilingual education are discussed: (1) the foundations of bilingual education, bilingual education's legal evolution, issues related to educating students in two languages, and the role of teachers, students, parents, and the community; (2) various organizational models currently used in the United States; and (3) instructional strategies.

Foundations of Bilingual Education

Progress in bilingual education in the United States has taken place on three fronts: cultural, legislative, and judicial. Culturally, the people of the United States have seemed to accept bilingualism when it has been economically useful and to reject

Figure 6-1   Common Misconceptions about Bilingual Education

Misconception	Fact
Children learning English are retained too long in bilingual classrooms, at the expense of English acquisition.	Well-designed bilingual programs present knowledge and skills in the native language that transfer to English, as well as actually teaching English. Therefore, time spent in primary-language instruction does not detract from learning English. English-only approaches and quick-exit bilingual programs interrupt cognitive growth at a crucial stage, with negative effects on achievement.
Language-minority parents do not support bilingual education because they feel it is more important for their children to learn English than to maintain the native language.	Research has shown that students' native language can be maintained and developed at no cost to English. When polled on the principles underlying bilingual education—for example, that developing literacy in the primary language facilitates literacy development in English or that bilingualism offers cognitive and career-related advantages—a majority of parents are strongly in favor of maintenance bilingual programs (Krashen, 1996).
Bilingual teachers are being hired in preference to teachers of English to speakers of other languages (ESL) or teachers of English as a new language (ENL).	According to the U.S. Department of Education (2012), twenty-one states indicated teachers needed for ESOL or ENL, versus seven states indicating openings for bilingual education teachers.
Bilingual education means instruction mainly in students' native languages, with little instruction in English.	The vast majority of U.S. bilingual education programs promote an early exit to mainstream English-language classrooms, whereas only a tiny fraction of programs are designed to maintain the native tongues of students.
Bilingual education is more costly than English-language instruction.	All programs serving LEP students—regardless of the language of instruction—require additional staff training, instructional materials, and administration. So they all cost a little more than regular programs for native-English speakers.
Disproportionate dropout rates for Hispanic students demonstrate the failure of bilingual education.	Bilingual programs touch only a small minority of Hispanic children. Other factors, such as recent arrival in the United States, family poverty, limited English proficiency, low academic achievement, and being retained in grade, place Hispanic students at much greater risk.
Having to learn in two languages is confusing for the brain.	Part of the metalinguistic advantage of the bilingual brain is enhanced operation of the executive control system, part of the prefrontal cortex that controls conscious attention, choice, and other high-level functions. As the brain switches back and forth between two or more languages (Bialystok, 2009; Kroll & Tokowitz, 2005), the brain is strengthened, eventually even developing enhanced abilities to focus, prioritize, and multi-task. In fact, after the first three or four years of second-language instruction, students outperform their monolingual peers in enhanced pattern recognition, problem solving, divergent thinking, creativity, critical thinking, performance on standardized tests (not only verbal, but also mathematical), and task focus, and demonstrate enhanced understanding of the contextual use of language (Porter, 2010).

it when immigrants were seen as a threat. In periods when the economic fortunes of the United States were booming, European immigrants were welcome and their languages were not forbidden. (Immigrants of color, however, faced linguistic and cultural barriers as they strove for assimilation.)

In times of recession, war, or national threat, immigrants, cultures, and languages were restricted or forbidden. Periodically throughout history, English has been proposed as the national language. Although the United States has no official language, twenty-three states have passed laws proclaiming English as official (Crawford, 2003).

Because the states reserve the right to dictate educational policy, bilingual education has depended on the vagaries of state law. When the U.S. Congress enacted legislation to begin Title VII of the Elementary and Secondary Education Act, federal funding became available for bilingual education programs. Almost simultaneously, the courts began to rule that students deprived of bilingual education must receive compensatory services. Together, the historical precedents, federal legislative initiatives, and judicial fiats combined to establish bilingual education in the United States. However, it has been left to the individual states to implement such programs, and this has at times caused conflict.

Historical Development of Bilingual Education

Early Bilingualism. At the time of the nation's founding, a wide variety of languages could be heard in the American colonies, including Dutch, French, German, and numerous Native American languages. In 1664 at least eighteen colonial languages were spoken on Manhattan Island. The Continental Congress published many official documents in German and French as well as in English. German schools were operating as early as 1694 in Philadelphia, and by 1900 more than 4 percent of the United States' elementary school population was receiving instruction either partially or exclusively in German. In 1847, Louisiana authorized instruction in French, English, or both on the request of parents. The Territory of New Mexico authorized Spanish–English bilingual education in 1850 (Crawford, 1999).

Language Restrictionism. Although there were several such pockets of acceptance for bilingual education, other areas of the country effectively restricted or even attempted to eradicate immigrant and minority languages. Under an 1828 treaty, the U.S. government recognized the language rights of the Cherokee tribe. Eventually, the Cherokees established a twenty-one-school educational system that used the Cherokee syllabary to achieve a 90 percent literacy rate in the native language. In 1879, however, the federal government forced the Native American children to attend off-reservation, English-only schools where they were punished for using their native language. In the East, as large numbers of Jews, Italians, and Slavs immigrated, descendants of the English settlers began to harbor resentment against these newcomers. New waves of Mexican and Asian immigration in the West brought renewed fear of non-English influences. Public and private schools in the new U.S. territories of the Philippines and Puerto Rico were forced to use English as the language of instruction (Crawford, 1999).

During World War I, various states criminalized the use of German in all areas of public life (Cartagena, 1991). Subsequently, fifteen states legislated English as the basic language of instruction. This repressive policy continued in World War II, when Japanese-language schools were closed. Until the late 1960s, "Spanish detention"—being kept after school for using Spanish—remained a formal punishment in the Rio Grande Valley of Texas, where using a language other than English as a medium of public instruction was a crime (Crawford, 1999).

Assimilationism. Although the U.S. Supreme Court, in the *Meyer v. Nebraska* case (1923), extended the protection of the Constitution to everyday speech and prohibited coercive language restriction on the part of the states, the "frenzy of Americanization" (Crawford, 1999) had fundamentally changed public attitudes toward learning in other languages. European immigrant groups felt strong pressures to assimilate, and bilingual instruction by the late 1930s was virtually eradicated throughout the United States.

After World War II, writers began to speak of language-minority children as being "culturally deprived" and "linguistically disabled." The cultural deprivation theory rejected genetic explanations for low school achievement for English learners and pointed to such environmental factors as inadequate English-language skills, lower-class values, and parental failure to stress educational attainment. On the basis of their performance on IQ tests administered in English, a disproportionate number of English learners ended up in special classes for the educationally handicapped.

The Rebirth of Bilingual Education. Bilingual education was reborn in the early 1960s in Dade County, Florida, as Cuban immigrants, fleeing the 1959 revolution, requested bilingual schooling for their children. The first program at the Coral Way Elementary School was open to both English and Spanish speakers. The objective was fluency and literacy in both languages. Subsequent evaluations of this bilingual program showed success both for English-speaking students in English and Spanish-speaking students in Spanish and English. Hakuta (1986) reported that by 1974 there were 3,683 students in bilingual programs in the elementary schools nationwide and approximately 2,000 in the secondary schools.

The focus of bilingual education on dual-language immersion and developmental bilingualism that had been featured in the Dade County bilingual programs was altered when the federal government passed the Bilingual Education Act of 1968 (Title VII, an amendment to the 1965 Elementary and Secondary Education Act). This act was explicitly compensatory. Children who were unable to speak English were considered to be educationally disadvantaged, and bilingual education was to provide the resources to compensate for the "handicap" of not speaking English.

Thus, from its outset, federal aid to bilingual education was seen as a "remedial" program rather than an innovative approach to language instruction (Wiese & García, 1998). The focus shifted again in 1989, when developmental bilingual programs were expanded. Maintaining and developing the native language of students became an important goal for bilingual education.

The English-as-Official-Language Movement. In the early 1980s, during a period of concern about new immigration, a movement arose to seek the establishment of English as the nation's official language, including repeal of laws mandating multilingual ballots and voting materials, restriction of bilingual funding to short-term transition programs, and universal enforcement of the English language and civics requirement for naturalization (Cartagena, 1991).

Emergence of a New Nativism. Many U.S. communities are feeling the pressure not only of increased immigration but also of immigration from underdeveloped nations. (See Chapter 1 for demographic trends.) Since the mid-1980s, language loyalties have become a subtle means of reframing racial politics, and bilingual education has become an integral part of the issue. Bilingual education is a subject that is bound up with individual and group identity, status, intellect, culture, and nationalism.

Maceri (2007) points out the difficulty some Americans have with the concept of dual-language use. Although 47 million residents of the United States speak a language other than English at home, according to figures of the U.S. Census, the presence of these languages is a problem for Americans who believe in the concept of one language, one country. The most serious concern is caused by the preponderance of Spanish, which some people see as challenging the supremacy of English. The presence of the Spanish language in banks, ATMs, hospitals, and even some government services may create the image that one does not have to learn English. Maceri notes:

> Although it's true that some services are available in Spanish, not speaking English means a very limited horizon and few opportunities. However, these days some third-generation Americans are beginning to [regret] having lost the language of their grandparents. . . . Now they try to correct it and study some of these languages in school as they try to recapture their roots. (p. 15)

Bilingualism in the Modern World. Many countries in today's world are officially bilingual, including Canada, Belgium, Finland, Cameroon, Peru, and Singapore. Official bilingualism, however, does not imply that all inhabitants of a country are bilingual; it simply means that more than one language may be used in government or education. But as the world becomes progressively smaller and more and more regions interact in economic, political, and cultural exchanges, bilingualism, and even multilingualism, has become a fact of daily life. In the global society, proficiency in more than one language is a highly desirable trait—what Cook (1999) called *multicompetent language use*.

Legal Evolution

The use of English and other languages in public life, particularly language use in the schools, has been affected by "cycles of liberalism and intolerance" (Trueba, 1989) in which conflicting beliefs and policies about language have influenced legislation and judicial actions. Together, Congress and the state and federal courts have supported bilingual education through a combination of federal mandates and legal protections for the rights of non-English-speaking students.

Federal Law and Judicial Decisions. Since the initial legislation in 1968, there have been six reauthorizations of the Bilingual Education Act (1974, 1978, 1984, 1988, 1994, and 2001). The 2001 reauthorization was contained within the No Child Left Behind Act (2002). Numerous court cases have upheld or clarified the rights of English language learners.

Title VI of the Civil Rights Act (1964) set a minimum standard for the education of any student by prohibiting discrimination on the basis of race, color, or national origin in the operation of a federally assisted program (National Clearinghouse for English Language Acquisition [NCELA], 2002). The Title VI regulatory requirements have been interpreted to prohibit denial of equal access to education because of an English learner's limited proficiency in English (U.S. Office for Civil Rights, 1999).

The Bilingual Education Act of 1968 was the first federal law relating to bilingual education. It authorized $7.5 million to finance seventy-six projects serving 27,000 children. The purpose of these funds was to support education programs, train teachers and aides, develop and disseminate instructional materials, and encourage parental involvement.

The May 25 Memorandum from the U.S. Office for Civil Rights (1970) informed school districts with more than 5 percent national-origin minority children that the district had to offer some kind of special language instruction for students with a limited command of English, prohibited the assignment of students to classes for the handicapped on the basis of their English-language skills, prohibited placing such students in vocational tracks instead of teaching them English, and mandated that administrators communicate with parents in a language they can understand.

Serna v. Portales Municipal Schools (1972) was the first case in which the federal courts began to enforce Title VI of the Civil Rights Act. A federal judge ordered instruction in native language and culture as part of a desegregation plan.

Lau v. Nichols (1974) was a landmark case in which the U.S. Supreme Court ruled:

> There is no equality of treatment merely by providing students with the same facilities, textbooks, teachers and curriculum, for students who do not understand English are effectively foreclosed from any meaningful education.

Lau v. Nichols made illegal those educational practices that excluded children from effective education on the basis of language. By finding school districts in violation of a student's civil rights based on discriminatory *effect,* rather than on proof of discriminatory *intent,* it extended the protection afforded under the *Brown v. Board of Education* decision to language-minority students under Title VI of the 1964 Civil Rights Act.

Moreover, *Lau v. Nichols* assumed that private individuals—the Chinese-speaking students in San Francisco for whose benefit the lawsuit was put forward—could sue for discriminatory effect to ensure that the mandates of Title VI were met. This last assumption was subsequently overturned in *Alexander v. Sandoval* (2001), when the U.S. Supreme Court ruled that private individuals could sue successfully under Title VI only if discriminatory intent could be proved (see Moran, 2004).

To further define the civil rights of students, the Equal Education Opportunities Act (EEOA) of 1974 states the following:

> No state shall deny equal educational opportunities to an individual on account of his or her race, color, sex, or national origin by the failure of an educational agency to take appropriate action to overcome language barriers that impede equal participation by its students in its instructional programs.

The 1974 reauthorization of Title VII specifically linked equal educational opportunity to bilingual education. Bilingual education was defined as "instruction given in, and study of, English, and, to the extent necessary to allow a child to progress effectively through the educational system, the native language" (Bilingual Education Act, 1974, p. 2).

Other changes in the legislation included eliminating poverty as a requirement; mentioning Native-American children as an eligible population; providing for English-speaking children to enroll in bilingual education programs; and funding for programs for teacher training, technical assistance for program development, and development and dissemination of instructional materials (Bilingual Education Act, 1974).

The 1975 *Lau Remedies* were guidelines from the U.S. Commissioner of Education that told districts how to identify and evaluate children with limited English skills, what instructional treatments to use, when to transfer children to all-English classrooms, and what professional standards teachers need to meet (U.S. Office for Civil Rights, 1976).

Ríos v. Read (1977) was a federal court decision that a New York school district had violated the rights of English learners by providing a bilingual program that was based mainly on ESL and that included no cultural component (Crawford, 1999). Although no specific remedy was mandated, the U.S. Office for Civil Rights began to visit school districts with large numbers of English learners to ensure that districts met their responsibilities.

Between 1974 and subsequent reauthorizations, public opinion moved toward an assimilationist position, that public funds should be used for English-language acquisition and assimilation toward the mainstream (Crawford, 1999). The 1978 Title VII reauthorization added to the definition of bilingual education: Instruction in English should allow children to achieve competence in English and English-speaking students in bilingual programs were to help children with limited English proficiency to improve their English-language skills. Additionally, parents were included in program planning, and personnel in bilingual programs were to be proficient in the language of instruction and English (Wiese & García, 1998).

Castañeda v. Pickard (1981) tested the EEOA statute. The Fifth Circuit Court outlined three criteria for programs serving English learners. District programs must be (1) based on "sound educational theory," (2) "implemented effectively" through adequately trained personnel and sufficient resources, and (3) evaluated as effective in overcoming language barriers. Qualified bilingual teachers must be employed, and children are not to be placed on the basis of English-language achievement tests. The outcome of the *Idaho Migrant Council v. Board of Education* (1981) case was a mandate that state agencies are empowered to supervise the implementation of federal EEOA requirements at the local level.

Plyler v. Doe (1982) was a Supreme Court decision stating that under the Fourteenth Amendment a state cannot deny school enrollment to children of illegal immigrants (NCELA, 1996). *Keyes v. School District #1* (1983) established due process for remedies of EEOA matters.

The 1984 reauthorization of Title VII provided for two types of bilingual programming: transitional and developmental. Thus, for the first time, the goal of bilingual education was competence in two languages. However, limited funding was provided for these programs (NCELA, 2002).

Gómez v. Illinois State Board of Education (1987) was a court decision that gave state school boards the power to enforce state and federal compliance with EEOA regulations. Children must not sit in classrooms where they cannot understand instruction, and districts must properly serve students who are limited in English. In none of the rulings did the courts mandate a specific program format, but in all they clearly upheld the notion that children must have equal access to the curriculum.

The Title VII reauthorization of 1988 increased funding to state education agencies, placed a three-year limit on participation in transitional bilingual programs, and created fellowship programs for professional training (NCELA, 2002).

The Improving America's Schools Act (IASA; 1994) amended and reauthorized the Elementary and Secondary Education Act of 1965 within the framework of the Goals 2000: Educate America Act (1994). The comprehensive educational reforms called for in Goals 2000 entailed reconfiguration of Title VII programs, with new provisions for reinforcing professional development programs, increasing attention to language maintenance and foreign-language instruction, improving research and evaluation at state and local levels, supplying additional funds for immigrant education, and allowing participation of some private school students. IASA also modified eligibility requirements for services under Title I so that English learners became eligible for services under that program on the same basis as other students (U.S. Office for Civil Rights, 1999).

Title III of the most recent reauthorization of ESEA, the No Child Left Behind (NCLB) Act of 2001, provided funding for language instruction programs for limited-English-proficient and immigrant students, provided these students "meet the same challenging State academic content and student academic achievement standards as all children are expected to meet" (NCLB, Title III, Part A, Sec. 3102. Purposes [1]). However, the program has been criticized for its rigid adherence to standards without providing additional financial assistance to schools with large populations of English learners.

According to James Crawford, executive director of the National Association for Bilingual Education, the No Child Left Behind Act does little to address the most formidable obstacles to the achievement [of English learners]: resource inequities, critical shortages of teachers trained to serve ELLs, inadequate instructional materials, substandard school facilities, and poorly designed instructional programs. Meanwhile, its emphasis on short-term test results—backed up by punitive sanctions for schools—is narrowing the curriculum, encouraging excessive amounts of test preparation, undercutting best practices based on scientific research, demoralizing dedicated educators, and pressuring schools to abandon programs that have proven successful for ELLs over the long term. (Crawford, 2004a, pp. 2–3)

Instead of supporting bilingual instruction, NCLB heavily emphasizes English-language proficiency not only for students but also for teachers, who must be certified in written and oral English. The elimination of federal support for bilingual education represents the culmination of several decades of heated debate, among lawmakers and educators, as well as the general public. Arguments against bilingual education have often centered on the effectiveness of bilingual instruction in teaching English, with no attention given to the potential benefits of bilingualism or primary language use and maintenance (Peregoy & Boyle, 2013).

The online article *Federal Policy, Legislation, and Education Reform: The Promise and the Challenge for Language Minority Students* (Anstrom, 1996), provides a clear discussion of educational reform and the challenges faced by English learners, chiefly whether they will have access to the kind of curricula and instruction necessary for them to achieve the high standards stipulated by government mandates. In sum, the kinds of legislative support for bilingual education changed according to the social politics of each era. As Freeman (2004) reported,

> During the 1960s and 1970s, the dominant discourses emphasized tolerance, civil rights, and inclusion. Bilingual education was encouraged, but no particular model or program type was endorsed. During the 1980s, we saw increasing English-only activity across the country, and Title VII supported bilingual and/or English programs that emphasized a quick transition to English. In the 1990s, we saw competing discourses about linguistic and cultural diversity on the national level as well as increasing support for dual-language programs at school. (p. 25)

State Law. Although federal protections of the rights of English learners continue, many states are at present more concerned about achieving compliance with federal NCLB mandates than about safeguarding their requirements regarding bilingual education. Educational agencies operate under legislative provisions for limited-English-proficient-student instructional programs in each specific state; these provisions may specify ELD instructional programs, bilingual/dual-language instructional programs, or both.

In 1998, California, with a school enrollment of approximately 1.4 million limited- English-proficient children, passed Proposition 227, a measure rejecting bilingual education. The proposition stipulates that

> all children in California public schools shall be taught English by being taught in English. In particular, this shall require that all children be placed in English language classrooms. Children who are English learners shall be educated through sheltered

English immersion during a temporary transition period not normally intended to exceed one year. . . . Once English learners have acquired a good working knowledge of English, they shall be transferred to English language mainstream classrooms. (California State Code of Regulations [CSCR], 1998, Article 2, 305)

Article 3, Provision 310, of the CSCR provided parents with waiver possibilities if their children met criteria spelled out in the law: "Under such parental waiver conditions, children may be transferred to classes where they are taught English and other subjects through bilingual education techniques or other generally recognized educational methodologies permitted by law."

The *Florida Consent Decree* was an agreement signed in 1990 giving the U.S. District Court, Southern District of Florida, the power to enforce an agreement with the Florida State Board of Education (FSBE) regarding the identification and provision of services to students whose native language is other than English. This remains the most extensive set of state mandates for the education of English learners.

The *Decree* includes provision that the national origin data of all students must be collected and retained in school districts, who must also form Limited-English-Proficient committees to oversee the assessment, placement, and reclassification of English learners; school districts must provide equal education opportunities for academic advancement and language support to English learners (including provisos for enhancing crosscultural understanding and self-esteem); school districts must provide equal access to appropriate categorical programs LEP students; and teachers must have various levels of English-language-development endorsement. School districts' compliance must be monitored by the FSBE to see if student achievement is improved as a result of application of the implementation guidelines.

Unfortunately, laws such as this one often result in a lack of support for the education of English learners. Dismantling bilingual education and expecting children to learn English (along with academic subjects) in a single year flies in the face of contemporary research on language acquisition (see, in particular, Collier, 1995). After thirty-five years of legislation supporting the rights of English learners, it can only be assumed that such laws will be found to infringe on students' rights.

Educational Issues Involving Bilingual Education

What obligation does a community have toward newcomers—in particular, non-native, non-English-speaking children? When education is the only means of achieving social mobility for the children of immigrants, these young people must be given the tools necessary to participate in the community at large. When school dropout rates exceed 50 percent among minority populations, it seems evident that the schools are not providing an adequate avenue of advancement. Clearly, some English learners do succeed: Asian American students are overrepresented in college attendance, whereas Hispanics are underrepresented.

The success or failure of ethnic minority students has caused concern and has prompted various explanations for students' mixed performances. A *genetic inferiority* argument assumes that certain populations do not possess the appropriate genes for high intellectual performance. The *cultural deficit* explanation attributes lower academic achievement to deficiencies in the minority culture. The *cultural mismatch* perspective maintains that cultures vary and that some of the skills learned in one culture may transfer to a second but that other skills will be of little value or, worse, will interfere with assimilation to the new culture. The *contextual interaction* explanation posits that achievement is a function of the interaction between two cultures—that the values of each are not static, but adapt to each other when contact occurs.

In schools, three phenomena occur in which language-minority students are disproportionately represented: underachievement, dropping out, and overachievement. In response to the perception that some students underachieve or overachieve or drop out or are pushed out, schools have designed various mechanisms to help students succeed. Some of these have been successful, others problematic. A fourth phenomenon is the loss of heritage languages; in the case of the United States, particularly ominous is the extinction of Native American languages. This issue is addressed later in this chapter.

Underachievement. Several measures of achievement reveal discrepancies in the achievement of Whites in comparison with ethnic minorities. On the Scholastic Assessment Test in 2011, the average score for Whites on the Critical Reading subtest was 528, whereas those of three ethnic minority groups (Hispanic, Black, and American Indian) were between 44 and 100 points lower (Asian Americans scored 517). With the exception of Asian Americans (average score 595), all ethnic groups were lower than Whites (535) on the mean score of the mathematics subtest (College Board, 2011).

Ethnic minority groups, except for Asian Americans, attain lower levels of education. Hispanic Americans, for example, are particularly hard hit by the phenomenon of educational underachievement. By 2025, more than 28 percent of the youth ages eighteen to twenty-four will be Latino. Unless college graduation rates change, this will be an undereducated population. Of the 30.6 million youth enrolled in higher education in 2009, only 12.5 percent were Latino students, underrepresented in their percentage (18) in the demographic (compared to 14.2 for African Americans, who comprise 14.3 percent of the college-age population). Only 35 percent of Latino high-school graduates are enrolled in college, compared to 46 percent of Whites; 40 percent of these Latinos attend two-year institutions. Only 13 percent of Latinos have a college degree or higher, compared with 30 percent among Americans overall (Alonso-Zaldivar & Tompson, 2010). Half as many (1.9 percent) of Latinos compared to Whites (3.8 percent) pursue graduate degrees. Latinos make up only 4 percent of university faculty nationwide (Ponjuan, 2011). Low educational levels have resulted in poor subsequent incomes and a lower likelihood of high-prestige occupations.

It is unclear that underachievement is the real problem. Even ethnic minorities who achieve in school may not be able to attain positions of responsibility in society because of discrimination. It is equally unclear to what extent English proficiency—or lack of it—is linked to underachievement.

Segregation. Despite decades of desegregation laws in response to the U.S. Supreme Court's 1954 ruling in the *Brown v. Board of Education of Topeka* case that segregated schools furnish an inherently inferior education, sixty years later schools in the United States are still segregated. In 2005–2006, White students were the most likely to attend segregated (all-White schools); Latinos are second in segregation, with approximately 78 percent attending predominantly minority schools (from 50 to 100 percent minority). Third in this dubious distinction are African Americans, of whom 73 percent attend segregated schools.

In fact, more than 60 percent of Latino students living in western U.S. cities are enrolled in "hypersegregated" schools, in which 90 to 100 percent of students are nonwhite (Orfield & Frankenberg, 2008). Such segregation has negative consequences. Schools with high-minority populations are less likely to offer their students adequate facilities and materials, experienced and qualified teachers, and successful peers; Latinos in these schools are more likely to drop out (Rumberger & Palardy, 2005).

Latinos, like African Americans, tend to be segregated by race/ethnicity as well as by poverty. However, Latinos who are Spanish speakers are segregated by language, a third disadvantaging factor (Gándara, 2010). School policies that isolate English learners for some or part of the day have been shown to slow English mastery and stigmatize students (Suárez-Orozco, Suárez-Orozco, & Todorova, 2008; Rios-Aguilar, Canche-González, & Moll, 2010).

Dropping Out. There is a disparity in graduation and dropout rates among various ethnic groups in the United States.* An important marketplace repercussion of graduation and dropout statistics is the differential rate of employment of these two groups: Sixty-one percent of high-school dropouts are in the labor force versus 80 percent of graduates who were not in college (Kaufman, Alt, & Chapman, 2004).

In fact, recent data show that the school districts serving the nation's largest cities have shockingly high dropout rates; only 52 percent—about one half—of students in the principal school systems in America's fifty largest cities complete high school with a diploma. Using a measure called the cumulative promotion index, researchers estimated the likelihood that a ninth-grader would complete high school on time with a regular diploma. Four districts—Baltimore, Cleveland, Detroit, and Indianapolis—had less than 32 percent. Clearly, to be young and urban in the United States is to be educationally at risk. Limited-English-proficient students drop out of school at a rate five times as high (51 percent) as their English-speaking peers, citing lack of English language knowledge as the primary reason for leaving school early (Rahilly & Weinmann, 2007).

---

*A Harvard University report released March 23, 2005, claimed nearly half of the Latino and African American students who should have graduated from California high schools in 2002 failed to complete their education. The Harvard report said that current education policies—including those that require annual standardized testing of students—may exacerbate the dropout crisis by creating "unintended incentives for school officials to push out low-achieving students" (Helfand, 2005, p. A26).

Many English learners who are new immigrants to the United States are not prepared for the racism, anger, and suspicion they face. A persistent myth is that immigrants can achieve the "American dream" through hard work and determination. In reality, immigrants face barriers such as the need to work multiple low-paying jobs to provide for their families, lack of access to English classes, separation from their home culture, and ethnocentrism. One study reported that Latino students who dropped out of school did so because of discrimination: They felt they were "not part of the school or the classroom . . . being treated as if they were less worthy than other students" (Valdes, 2007, p. 31).

Noting the alarmingly high percentage of Hispanic dropouts, U.S. Secretary of Education Richard W. Riley in 1995 initiated a special project to study issues related to the problem. In its final report, *No More Excuses,* the Hispanic Dropout Project (1998) highlighted the continuing stereotypes, myths, and excuses that surround Hispanic American youth and their families:

> What we saw and what people told us confirmed what well-established research has also found: Popular stereotypes—which would place the blame for school dropout on Hispanic students, their families, and language background, and that would allow people to shrug their shoulders as if to say that that was an enormous, insoluble problem or one that would go away by itself—are just plain wrong. (p. 3)

The Hispanic Dropout Project found that teachers may make one of two choices that undermine minority students' school achievement: either to blame the students and their families for school failure or to excuse the students' poor performance, citing factors such as low socioeconomic status or lack of English proficiency (Lockwood, 2000). The three recommendations the report made for teachers are consistent with the principles, concepts, and strategies outlined in this text: (1) provide high-quality curriculum and instruction, methods and strategies provided in Part Two of this book; (2) become knowledgeable about students and their families, as discussed in Part Four of this book; and (3) receive high-quality professional development . . . an ongoing task for which this entire text can be an impetus. The online article *Transforming Education for Hispanic Youth: Exemplary Practices, Programs, and Schools* (Lockwood & Secada, 1999) provides more in-depth information about, and examples of, exemplary schools for Hispanic American youth.

Example of Concept   *Segregation and Dropping Out*

The predominantly Puerto Rican community in North Philadelphia is located in an economically depressed part of the city that is plagued by many of the problems of low-income urban neighborhoods across the United States. Latinos make up between 85 and 99 percent of the total student population in this community, and the Latino dropout rate is disproportionately high in the district. According to a Harvard University report that examined issues of racial justice in the United States, such segregation of Latinos in poorly performing schools in low-income neighborhoods is pervasive in cities in the Northeast (Harvard Civil Rights Project, online at www.civilrightsproject.harvard.edu /research/reseg03/resegregation03.php) (Freeman, 2004, p. 88).

Overachievement. An equally pernicious view ascribes exceptional achievement to a specific group, such as is the case for Asian Americans. The term *model minority* has been evoked for Asian Americans, connoting a supergroup whose members have succeeded in U.S. society despite a long history of racial oppression.

Example of Concept   *Seeing Beyond the Myth*

The model minority myth employs the notion that Asian Americans are "devoted, obedient to authority, smart, good in math and science, diligent, hard workers, cooperative, well-behaved, docile, college-bound, quiet, and opportunistic" (Chang & Au, 2007–2008, p. 15) and thus all headed to Ivy League universities. This bias negatively affects the Asian American community because it conveniently ignores the substantial role that class privilege plays in school success, and reflects poorly on other groups (African Americans and Latino) that racism holds back.

This stereotype plays out in at least two ways with equally damaging results. First, ascribing a "whiz kid" image to students can mask their individual needs and problems and lead the teacher to assume a student needs little or no help. This may ultimately lead to neglect, isolation, delinquency, or inadequate preparation for the labor market among these students (Feng, 1994). Second, by lumping all Asian Americans together into this stereotype, it ignores the different cultural, language, economic, and immigration status of the various groups and severely limits those most in need of help.

Among Southeast Asian students, the Khmer and the Lao have a grade point average (GPA) below that of White majority students, whereas Vietnamese, Chinese Vietnamese, Japanese, Korean, Chinese, and Hmong students are well above this GPA (Trueba, Cheng, & Ima, 1993).

Bias toward Asian Americans has also been found in college admissions. When voters in several states passed measures that ended affirmative action programs as a basis for college admissions, Asian American enrollment increased significantly, indicating that race-conscious admission policies actually had unfairly held Asian Americans to higher standards of performance to gain entrance to universities (Schmidt, 2008).

Adapted Instruction

Countering the Model Minority Myth

To avoid reenacting the model minority myth in the classroom,

- What is the general level of assimilation to mainstream American culture of the Asian/Pacific American student and his or her family? Does the family adhere to traditional customs and values, and do these include an emphasis on high academic achievement?

- Get to know the parents and family members of each student. What are their expectations for the student's future schooling or career success?

- Find out more about each Asian/Pacific American students in class. What language is spoken in the home? Is it English? Is the family bilingual? Is the home language, if used, a standard version of a national language or a dialect?

"Asian-American Children: What Teachers Should Know" (Feng, 1994) provides general information about Asian American students and a list of practices to help teachers become more knowledgeable about Asian cultures.

Placement. Educators have responded to these educational issues by developing special programs and procedures and by placing students in special classes.

Special education referrals and placements for culturally and linguistically different students have been disproportionate (Cummins, 1984; Rodríguez, Prieto, & Rueda, 1984). Explanations for this overreferral include the following: low level of acculturation, inadequate assessment, language problems, poor school progress, academic/cognitive difficulties, and special learning problems (Malavé, 1991). Biased assessment has resulted in negative evaluation of English learners, largely because intelligence testing has been derived from models of genetic deficiency, cultural deprivation, and other deficit models (Payan, 1984; Rueda, 1987). Chapter 12 provides a more in-depth discussion of the issues and challenges facing special education for English learners and their teachers.

Retention/promotion policies are not carried out with equity. Unfortunately, some students begin falling behind their expected grade levels almost immediately on entering school.

In 2007 The National Center for Education Statistics (NCES) reported the following:

> In 2003, some 17 percent of Black students had been retained, a higher percentage than that of White, Hispanic, or Asian/Pacific Islander students. The percentage of Hispanic students (11 percent) who had been retained was higher than the percentage of White students (8 percent) retained, while the percentage of Asian/Pacific Islander students (5 percent) was lower than that of Whites. (NCES, 2007)

Students who repeat at least one grade are more likely to drop out of school. On the other side of the coin, students are also differentially distributed in Advanced Placement courses, a type of "in-house" promotion. Table 6.1 illustrates this distribution.

Tracking offers very different types of instruction depending on students' placement in academic or general education courses. Tracking has been found to be a major contributor to the continuing gaps in achievement between minorities and European Americans (Oakes, 1985, 1992).

Several reform efforts have attempted to dismantle some of the tracking programs previously practiced in schools. These have included accelerated schools, cooperative learning, restructured schools, and "untracking." A particularly noteworthy high-school program is Advancement Via Individual Determination (AVID). This "untracking" program places low-achieving students (who are primarily from low-income and ethnic or language-minority backgrounds) in the same college-preparatory academic program as high-achieving students, who are primarily from middle- or upper-middle-income and "Anglo" backgrounds (Mehan, Hubbard, Lintz, & Villanueva, 1994).

Access for English Learners. Inclusion of English learners in mainstream classrooms is now the trend. In a study of "good educational practice for LEP [Limited English

Table 6.1   AP Exams Taken in U.S. Public Schools by the Class of 2011 (excluding data from ethnic category "Other")

	Number of Graduates	Percent of Total Graduates*	Percent of Test-Takers**	Average Score***	Percent Passing (Score = 3, 4, or 5)
Asian Pacific Islander	93,475	10.3	14.4	3.13	65.4
Black	81,215	9.0	7.2	2.02	22.5
Hispanic[†]	148,407	15.2	17.0	2.35	40.1
Native American	5,108	.5	.5	2.38	46.0
White	515,201	57.1	57.0	2.97	62.5
Total	903,630				

* Percentage of population of high-school graduates in 2011
** Percentage of total AP tests (2,720,084) taken by high-school graduates in 2011
*** Average score on AP tests taken by high-school graduates in 2011 = 2.8 (3, 4, 5 = earns academic credit)
[†] Includes Mexican/Mexican American, Puerto Rican, and Other Hispanic/Latino/Latin American

Source: Based on College Board (2012).

Proficient] students," researchers found numerous schools that have successfully been educating English learners to high standards (McLeod, 1996). In these schools, programs for English learners were an integral part of the whole school program, neither conceptually nor physically separate from the rest of the school.

> The exemplary schools have devised creative ways to both include LEP students centrally in the educational program and meet their needs for language instruction and modified curriculum. Programs for LEP students are so carefully crafted and intertwined with the school's other offerings that it is impossible in many cases to point to "the LEP program" and describe it apart from the general program. (p. 4)

School programs that recognize the rights and abilities of minority students and strive to reverse the discriminatory patterns of the society at large have proved more successful in helping these students through the schooling process (Cummins, 1984, 1989). *School Reform and Student Diversity: Exemplary Schooling for Language Minority Students* (McLeod, 1996) details features of exemplary schools, goals for ensuring access to high-quality teaching, ways to improve teaching and learning for EL students, and an appendix of the featured schools.

Organizational Models: What Works for Whom?

Bilingual education is an umbrella term used to refer to various types of programs and models. It is a term used in two ways: first, for education that promotes academic and linguistic development in two languages; and second, to denote programs that include students who speak languages other than English. In the first instance, bilingualism is being fostered; in the second, English learners are present but bilingualism is not a goal of the curriculum (Baker, 2001). Obviously, the school experience for language-minority students varies depending on the aim of the program in which students participate. The program can support and extend the home language and culture, or it can consider the students' language and culture irrelevant to schooling.

The term *bilingual education* rarely includes a discussion of foreign-language instruction for native-English-speaking students. Traditionally, this instruction has consisted of three to four years of high-school classes. In recent years, a limited number of school districts in the United States have begun programs of foreign language in the elementary school (FLES) in which students in K–6 classrooms receive one or more hours a week of instruction from a foreign-language specialist. Because this language is used neither as the language of academic instruction nor as a language of peer conversation, however, it is difficult for native-English-speaking students to achieve a high level of dual-language proficiency through FLES.

The bilingual education program models discussed in the following sections vary in the degree of support provided for the home language in the context of multicompetent language use (Cook, 1999). The most supportive is dual-language instruction that actively promotes bilingualism, biliteracy, and biculturalism for native-English-speaking students and language-minority students alike. The models reflect different goals—for example, remediation or enrichment—as well as the influence of federal, state, and local policies. In this discussion of bilingual programs, an ideal goal of instruction will be proposed: multicompetent language use not only for those students with a primary language other than English but also for native-English speakers.

Submersion

The default mode for educating English learners in U.S. classrooms is submersion—no provisions are made for the language and academic needs of English learners. Students receive instruction in English, with English monolingualism as the goal. The associated social difficulties experienced by English learners in a language-majority classroom are not addressed. Moreover, submersion programs do not utilize the language skills of English learners to enrich the schooling experience of native-English speakers. Research has shown that parents of students in submersion programs have been less involved in helping their children with homework than parents of students in bilingual programs (Ramírez, 1992). Expecting children to acquire English without help has long-term adverse consequences for school achievement.

In addition to being academically disabling, submersion denies students their rights under law:

> Submersion is not a legal option for schools with non-native-English speakers; however, oversight and enforcement are lax, and many smaller schools with low populations of NNS [non-native-speaking] students are simply unaware that they

are required to provide some sort of services to these students. Parents of these children, for cultural and other reasons, tend not to demand the services their children are entitled to; thus it is not uncommon to find submersion in U.S. public schools. (Roberts, 1995, pp. 80–81)

A meta-analysis of program effectiveness for English learners found that bilingual or English-Plus rather than English-only or English-immersion approaches to curriculum and instruction help students to succeed academically (Rolstad, Mahoney, & Glass, 2005).

The Teaching of English-Language Development (ELD)

Before describing the various models of bilingual education, it is useful to survey the programs that teach English-language development (ELD). English instruction is delivered in a variety of ways, and studies have shown varying degrees of student success depending on the program model (Thomas & Collier, 1997). However, if ELD is the only component, then the program is not a bilingual program.

In few of the ELD models is the primary language of the students explicitly acknowledged or used—ELD teachers are seldom required to be fluent in the primary languages of the students. Individual teachers may have second-language competencies with which to support students on an individual basis, but this is not part of the program design.

Pull-Out ELD. English learners leave their home classroom and receive instruction in vocabulary, grammar, oral language, and spelling for separate half-hour- to one-hour-per-day classes with a trained ELD teacher. Such instruction rarely is integrated with the regular classroom program; and, when they return to the home classroom, children usually are not instructed on curriculum they missed while they were gone. Of the various program models, ELD pull-out has been the most implemented (Thomas & Collier, 1997).

PROFILE OF AN EDUCATOR:

ELD Specialist

Cindy Wilcox is employed by Lincoln Intermediate Unit #12, a regional state-funded educational agency. She works at Mary B. Sharpe Elementary School in Chambersburg, Pennsylvania. Throughout the day, students are pulled from their classrooms to receive intensive ELD tutoring in small classes for forty-five to ninety minutes. Although most of her students speak Spanish as a first language, she also serves students from Pakistan, Haiti, and Indonesia. In the three-county service area, thirty-four languages are represented. Focusing largely on mastery-learning reading materials and vocabulary development, Cindy wishes she had more time to teach writing.

ELD Class Period. Students in the secondary school often have separate ELD classes that help them with their English skills. The effect of such segregation is that students may not receive rich academic instruction. Moreover, in some school districts, students who are placed in separate ELD classes at the high-school level often do not receive college-entrance-applicable credits for these classes—to be placed in an ELD class is to preclude the chance for college admission. Students should be placed in SDAIE-enhanced high-school English classes that bear college-entry credit value.

Content-Based ELD. Although content-based ELD classes are still separate and contain only English learners, students learn English through academic content in a curriculum organized around grade-level academic objectives (see Chapter 4). The most effective of these models is when the ELD teacher collaborates with content-area teachers and some team teaching occurs (Ovando & Collier, 1998).

Sheltered Instruction (SDAIE). As discussed in Chapter 5, sheltered instruction is provided by teachers who have both content background and knowledge of best practices in second-language acquisition. Lessons have content, language, and learning-strategy objectives. English learners and native-English speakers are often together in sheltered classrooms.

Transitional or Early-Exit Bilingual Education

The overriding goal of transitional bilingual education (TBE) programs is to mainstream students into English-only classrooms. In these programs, students receive initial instruction in most, if not all, content areas in their home language while they are being taught English. Most of these programs last only two to three years, long enough for students to achieve basic interpersonal communication skills (BICS) but, unfortunately, not long enough for children to build cognitive academic language proficiency (CALP) in either their native tongue or English. As a consequence, they may not be able to carry out cognitively demanding tasks in English and may be considered to be "subtractively bilingual."

There are numerous problems with a TBE program. It may be perceived as remedial compensatory education. The program rests on the common misconception that two or three years is sufficient time to learn a second language for schooling purposes (Ovando & Collier, 1998).

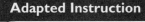

Adapted Instruction

Easing the Transition Phase

Transitioning from the bilingual to the mainstream classroom has always been problematic for students and teachers. One program developed to ease this transition includes the following components:

- *Challenge.* Students think, learn, and engage intellectually as they study novels and short stories in depth over an extended period (six to eight weeks).
- *Continuity.* Curriculum and instruction are connected as students move from the primary, to the middle, to the upper grades and from L1 to L2 language arts.

- *Connections*. Transition teachers build on students' existing knowledge, skills, and experiences and make explicit connections to the academic curriculum. They connect and build on the literature studies of the pretransition period: Themes studied in a Spanish-language story are revisited in an English-language story; strategies introduced during pretransition are continued to help students recognize commonalities of reading and writing in Spanish and in English.

- *Comprehensiveness*. The grades 2–5 program addresses both meaning and skills. Teachers teach directed lessons, facilitate group work, confer with individuals, and demonstrate strategies. Students have both assigned and pleasure reading, develop written projects and do dictation, participate in literary discussions, and receive formal grammar lessons. For further information about the program, see Saunders and Goldenberg (2001).

Maintenance or Developmental Bilingual Education

A maintenance bilingual education (MBE) program supports education and communication in the students' primary language as well as students' heritage and culture. The major assumption in such a program is that bilingualism is a valuable asset, not only for the individuals who are bilingual but also for society as a whole. Students in an MBE design are not quickly transitioned but are encouraged to be proficient in both English and their native tongue. Literacy in two languages is often an important goal (Roberts, 1995). These goals enhance self-concept and pride in the cultural background.

For the most part, maintenance/developmental programs have been implemented at the elementary level. Ideally, they are continued into the intermediate grades. Programs that offer continuing support for students' academic learning in their first language have also been called *late-exit* to distinguish them from the transitional *early-exit* programs (Ramírez, 1992).

A particularly compelling use of maintenance bilingual programs is in the education of Native Americans. The attempt to increase the number of speakers of Native American languages is sometimes called "restorative" bilingual education (see Grenoble and Whaley, 1998; Hinton and Hale, 2001).

Many American Indian languages are undergoing language revitalization. Of the 800 + Western hemisphere Amerindian languages, 500 are endangered or worse. In North America, even relatively "healthy" languages like Cherokee—spoken by 22,000 people—are threatened by low percentages of child speakers.

American Indian languages in the United States were deliberately destroyed as Indians were separated from their linguistic kin and resettled hundreds of miles away with individuals from other tribes who could not understand each other and as children were sent away to boarding schools. Many languages with few users have died entirely.

Simply leaving these languages alone will not cause their extinction trends to end. Languages can be revitalized by inspiring the younger generations to take an interest and pride in their ancestral languages and by providing the means for them to learn it. Navajo, for instance, was in steep decline until the 1940s, when its use by the Navajo Code Talkers in World War II caused its prestige to soar and numbers of users to increase steadily (Redish, 2001). Ironically, Indian casino gaming has furnished funds for tribes to sponsor language-revitalization classes, a hopeful trend toward language revitalization.

English-language development teachers can show support for indigenous languages by integrating local indigenous culture into English language learning—not only to educate learners about international cultures and geography throughout the world, but also so that students from indigenous cultures can recognize their own culture(s) in the curriculum. Barfield and Uzarski (2009) give multiple examples, two of which are incorporating the colors of Tibetan prayer flags into English teaching using environmental awareness as a theme and basing ESL lessons in North American classrooms on ideas and designs drawn from Native American star quilts. Despite the loss or future loss of an indigenous language, elements of culture such as storytelling, visual arts, beading, and cultural physical expressions can be preserved during English lessons.

Example of Concept *Navajo Language Revitalization*

The Navajo Nation extends across 25,000 square miles of the U.S. Southwest, with the largest number of speakers of its indigenous language—100,000—of any Native American group in the United States. Yet in 1993, a study of 3,300 Navajo kindergarteners found that fewer than one-third were reasonably fluent in Navajo.

When the Window Rock Unified School District began its Navajo immersion program in 1986, fewer than one-tenth of the preschoolers were deemed "reasonably competent" Navajo speakers; yet many were also identified as limited-English proficient. The initial curriculum featured developmental Navajo;

reading and writing—first in Navajo, then English; and math in both subjects. The program emphasized critical thinking, process writing, and cooperative learning. In addition, parents were required to spend time talking with their children in Navajo.

Successes of the program include fourth-grade Navajo immersion students' performing as well as nonimmersion students at the same school on local tests of English and well ahead on standardized tests of math. And what is more, they acquired Navajo as a heritage language without a cost to their English proficiency or their academic content (McCarty, 2005).

Example of Concept *A Typical Day in a Second-Grade Kaiapuni (the Hawaiian-Language Immersion Program) Classroom*

The Kaiapuni students lined up at 8:00 outside their classroom and began to *oli*—chant in Hawaiian—asking their teachers to allow them to enter their classrooms. The teachers chanted back, granting

permission and welcoming the children, and everyone sang *Hawai'i Pono'i*, the state song.

Once in the room, the children turned in their homework and sat on the floor for the daily morning routine. One child reviewed the month and day of the week, and charted the temperature and the phase of the moon. The children all counted the number of days left until the end of the year. Leialoha, the teacher, reviewed the agenda for the rest of the day. Students wrote a "morning letter" and collectively corrected the spelling and grammar.

During recess, students interacted with other Kaiapuni students and students from the English-language program. After recess, the class read for fifteen minutes (sustained silent reading) and then engaged in another language arts activity based on a book about how Native Alaskans made mittens. The students read the book in small groups and followed instructions written on the board about how to make their own mittens. After lunch was journal writing

time, followed by an art activity. Then students went outside for a music class with a resource teacher in preparation for an upcoming assembly. The school day ended at 2:30.

This description probably appears similar to classrooms in which English and not Hawaiian is the language of instruction. However, Kaiapuni is not just a Hawaiian translation of the English program. Hawaiian values, knowledge, and teaching methods are incorporated into classroom activities. For example, beginning the day with the oli reflects Hawaiian beliefs about social relationships and learning. Having students read about Native Alaskans reflects a curriculum that emphasizes indigenous peoples and their perspectives on life (Yamauchi & Wilhelm, 2001, p. 86).

Immersion Bilingual Education

Immersion bilingual education provides academic and language instruction in two languages, ideally from grades K through 12. The goal of immersion programs is for students to be proficient in both languages—to achieve *additive bilingualism*. The term has come from program models in Canada where middle-class, English-speaking children are instructed in French. In the United States, English-only submersion programs for English learners are sometimes mischaracterized as immersion.

Example of Concept

Distinguishing Features of the Inter-American Magnet School in Chicago

Inter-American Magnet School (IAMS) is dedicated to teaching and learning in two languages. From PreK through eighth grade, English-dominant, Spanish-dominant, and fully bilingual students learn and teach in their classrooms. IAMS is one of twenty-eight elementary magnet schools in Chicago. Students are selected to attend through a lottery system based solely on racial–ethic categories and gender. There are approximately 600 students: 70 percent Latino, 14.6 percent European American, 12.7 percent African American, and 1.9 percent Asian/Pacific Islander or Native American.

The school is the oldest dual-immersion school in the Midwest and the second oldest in the country. At all grade levels, English-dominant and Spanish-dominant students study together in the same classrooms. Teachers at the same grade level collaborate on designing thematic units, incorporating as much cooperative grouping as possible in activities to encourage peer assistance. However, despite its dedication to dual-language equality, for various reasons, English dominates in schoolwide competitions and few Spanish learners use Spanish for authentic communication. (Potowski, 2007)

Three features distinguish this immersion program: a model program, parent involvement, and studies of the Americas. IAMS is a model for other two-way bilingual immersion programs, and teachers model best practices for those just entering the teaching profession. Parents actively participate at various levels within the school as a whole and in individual classrooms. They take lead roles on school committees and they help develop schoolwide policies and effect positive change.

The Studies of the Americas program, which guides the school's entire social studies curriculum, represents and reflects the language and cultural diversity of the IAMS student body. By the end of sixth grade, students have studied the three predominant cultures of Latin America today: indigenous, Hispanic, and African. In addition, students take their new knowledge beyond the classroom. Many teachers are involved in social causes and encourage students to "connect classroom studies to the outside world and use Spanish and English to communicate for authentic purposes" (Urow & Sontag, 2001, p. 20).

This misconception has led to confusion. Canadian immersion is not, and never has been, a monolingual program, because both English and French are incorporated into the programs as subjects and as the medium of instruction (Lambert, 1984). In addition, the social context of French immersion is the upper-middle class in Quebec Province, where both English and French have a high language status for instructional purposes. In contrast, when English learners are submerged in mainstream English classes, instruction is not given in their home language, and they do not become biliterate and academically bilingual.

U.S. Enrichment Immersion. In the United States, a comparable social context to Canadian-style immersion is the exclusive private schools of the upper class, in which foreign languages are highly supported. This program model can be considered "enrichment immersion." Academic instruction may be delivered directly in a foreign language; and tutoring, travel abroad, and frequent, structured peer-language use (such as "French-only" dinners) are often an integral part of the program.

Example of Concept   *U.S. Enrichment Immersion*

The International School of Indiana (ISI) offers French and Spanish enrichment immersion programs in the heart of Indianapolis, a city with a two universities that attract scholars from around the world. Students with no prior experience in the target languages must enroll before grade 2 in order to benefit from the immersion opportunity (classes are 100 percent in the target language in the pre-elementary grades, 80 percent in grades 1–3, and 50 percent in grades 4–7).

The curriculum has an international content, with high standards—the French and Spanish curricula are imported from France and Spain respectively. Community support has been generous in the form of large grants from local foundations and corporations. Teachers are recruited for their language skills and well as their teaching abilities, are paid well, and work hard, using cross linguistic cooperation to offer innovative activities (Weber, 2001).

Dual or Two-Way Immersion. A two-way immersion (TWI) model enhances the status of the students' primary language by providing instruction in that language to English learners. This allows English learners to be in a position to help their English-speaking peers (see the Point/Counterpoints below and on page 172). As of 2012, there are 415 TWI programs in thirty-one states (plus the District of Columbia) (www.cal.org/twi/directory/index.html).

In the two-way immersion design, a high level of academic competence is achieved in two languages by both English learners and native-English speakers. Both groups of students participate in content-area instruction in the minority language as well as in English, although the two languages are not mixed. Both groups receive language instruction in both their native and the second language. This encourages English learners to develop their primary language and native-English-speaking students (e.g., Spanish-as-a-second-language [SSL] learners) to attain advanced levels of functional proficiency in the second language by performing academic tasks in that language.

POINT COUNTERPOINT

Does Dual Immersion Enhance English Learning?

Dual-immersion programs are designed to provide an enriched program of academic and language study in which students and teachers use both languages as the medium of communication for specific areas of the curriculum. But do immersion programs help English learners to develop English-language skills?

POINT: Dual Immersion Promotes English Learning Research has shown that students who enter school in the United States with limited or no proficiency in English make more progress in acquiring English and in developing academically if they receive schooling in their primary language as they are introduced to English as a second language (Cummins, 1981b; Ramírez, 1992; Thomas & Collier, 1997). Strong literacy skills in the primary language can be applied to the acquisition of English literacy. Dual-language immersion schools help English learners to develop their primary language fully while adding proficiency in English through enriched, challenging curricula. Students who act as language hosts—for example, Spanish-speaking children who serve as language models for native-English-speaking students in a dual-immersion program—gain self-esteem and increased cultural pride (Lindholm, 1992), leading to increased motivation to learn.

COUNTERPOINT: Dual Immersion Delays English Learning Some critics charge that dual-language immersion programs fail to teach English to English learners. Because programs teach content in the primary language, they do not emphasize communication in English, as do transitional bilingual programs. Amselle (1999) argued that "dual immersion programs are really nothing more than Spanish immersion, with Hispanic children used as teaching tools for English-speaking children" (p. 8). Experts concede that the greatest challenge in two-way bilingual programs is to "reduce the gap" between the language abilities of the two groups (English learners and native-English speakers acquiring the second language). This gap appears as content classes in English are modified (slowed down) for English learners to catch up, or as content delivery in the primary language is slowed for Spanish learners (SSLs). As Molina (2000) advised, "Without a watchful approach to the quality of two-way programs, schools will find themselves tragically exploiting the English learners they had hoped to help for the benefit of the language-majority students" (p. 12).

Implications for Teaching
Careful attention to a high-quality bilingual program in the context of primary-language maintenance and second-language acquisition is key.
Source: Veeder and Tramutt (2000).

POINT   COUNTERPOINT

Are Two-Way Immersion Programs the Best Model of Bilingual Education?

POINT: Two-Way Immersion Promotes Academic Achievement and Broad-Based Support for Bilingual Education. Two-way programs appeal to English-speaking parents who value bilingualism, offering peer models who are native speakers. Bilingual educators were initially attracted to this model, believing it offered more political support (Crawford, 2004b). Many educators believe it is a way to bridge the persistent achievement gap between English-speaking and language-minority students.

COUNTERPOINT: Two-Way Immersion Works Best with Economically Advantaged Students Who Are from Bilingual Homes. Studies have shown that, despite these programs, English learners still lag behind English-only students in achievement. For English learners who face challenges of poverty and parental illiteracy, two-way programs have not been shown to be superior to one-way developmental bilingual education (Crawford, 2004b).

Implications for Teaching

Like other school programs, two-way immersion programs vary in quality. Parental involvement is key to maintaining high standards.

Newcomer Centers

Newcomer programs offer recent immigrants an emotionally safe educational atmosphere that fosters rapid language learning, acculturation, and enhancement of self-esteem. Common goals for various newcomer program models include helping students acquire enough English to move into the regular language support program, developing students' academic skills, helping them gain an understanding of U.S. schools and educational expectations, and introducing students to their new communities. Programs may be organized as a school-within-a-school, as a separate program in its own location, or in district intake centers (Genesee, 1999; Short, 1998).

Programs vary in both length of day and length of time in program. Some are full-day, in which students have various content courses along with ELD, whereas others are half-day or after school. The majority of newcomers enroll for one year, although some may attend four years and others only one semester or one summer. Programs also distinguish themselves by whether they are primarily ELD or bilingual, and by the manner in which they exit students (Genesee, 1999; Short, 1998).

Newcomer centers should not be considered a substitute for bilingual education. Programs that offer only English, while disregarding instruction in content subjects, are not effective in the long run for three reasons. First, researchers have documented that learning a second language takes three to five years. A short-term program (three months, sixth months, or even a year) cannot create mastery. Second, students who do not receive content instruction suffer delayed or disrupted schooling. Finally, language—including content vocabulary—is best learned in the context of rich, meaningful academic instruction.

Example of Concept   *A Look at a Newcomers Center*

Newcomers High School in Queens, New York, offers recent-immigrant high-school students specialized preparation in English before making the transition to a regular high-school curriculum. Most of the 900 students are from China and Latin American countries, but they are also from countries such as Poland, Haiti, Tibet, Indonesia, India, and Bangladesh. Students spend half the day learning English, grouped according to their levels of English fluency. Beyond core academics, students enjoy classes in art, dance, music, and business. The library features books in thirty-five different languages as well as easy-to-read titles in English. After graduation, nearly 90 percent of graduates enroll in two- or four-year colleges. (H. S. 555, 2011)

Research Studies on Program Effectiveness

Bilingual education continues to be controversial, entangled as it is with societal conceptions and misconceptions, issues of power and status, and climates of acceptance and fear. Despite variables that might predict school failure (such as poverty, the school's location in an impoverished area, and low status of the language-minority group), Thomas and Collier (1997) found three key predictors of academic success. Those schools that incorporated all three predictors were "likely to graduate language-minority students who are very successful academically in high school and higher education" (p. 15).

The three predictors are as follows: (1) cognitively complex on-grade-level academic instruction through students' first language for as long as possible, combined with cognitively complex on-grade-level academic instruction through the second language (English) for part of the school day; (2) use of current approaches to teaching the academic curriculum through two languages, including discovery learning, cooperative learning, thematic units, activities that tap into the "multiple intelligences" (Gardner, 1983), and bridging techniques that draw on students' personal experiences; and (3) a transformed sociocultural context for English learners' schooling, with two-way bilingual classes frequently used to achieve this goal.

The task facing English learners is daunting. Consider that they need to acquire English and academic subjects while their native-English-speaking (NES) peers are learning academic subjects. Each school year the NES student sustains ten months of academic growth. If an English learner initially scores low on tests in English (say two or three years below grade level), he or she has to make fifteen months' progress (an academic year and a half) on the tests each year for five or six years to reach the average performance of an NES student. In studying the various program models for English learners, Thomas and Collier (1997) found that students who received on-grade-level academic work in their primary language were able to make these gains and, most important, sustain them.

Example of Concept   *One District's Experience with Long-Term English Learners*

Siloam Springs, Arkansas began its English as a second language program in 1996 when Hispanic families began to settle in that area, many finding jobs at the Tyson Foods processing plant. The ESL program varies; there is structured English immersion (SEI) at the elementary schools, with some pull-out ESL classes, and sheltered instruction begins at the middle school level (according to state law, Arkansas schools are not allowed to feature bilingual education programs). Currently, there are few immigrants; most of the ESL students (those who have been in the ESL program for 5 years or more) were born in the United States.

According to Leslie Moore, ESL program facilitator, "We have become better about identifying English learners and tracking their progress. Arkansas has implemented statewide criteria for redesignation, so we have started in the last three years to exit more EL students in the eighth grade. Long-term English learners are the challenge for us. Once they reach the stage where they have to learn a high level of academic content, they receive little support outside school." (Moore, 2013)

Instructional Strategies

Good classroom teaching must be a part of a bilingual classroom in the same way that good teaching is required in any classroom. The following sections focus on the use of two languages and exemplary means of classroom organization.

Language Management

If instruction is to be effective for children who potentially can function at a high level in two languages, the use of these languages must maximize cognitive and academic proficiency. Programs using two languages can separate them by time, personnel, subject, and manner of delivery. These strategies are particularly relevant to the two-way immersion context.

Time. Bilingual programs may devote a specific time to each language. In an "alternate use" model, languages are used on alternating days: Monday, primary language; Tuesday, English; Wednesday, primary language; and so on. In a "divided day" model, the morning may be devoted to the primary language and the afternoon to English. In both these models, academic instruction is occurring in both languages.

Example of Concept *Divided Day*

The two-way immersion program at Hueco Elementary School in El Paso, Texas, uses the 50–50 model for academic instruction. Fifty percent of daily instruction in grades K–6 is given in English and 50 percent in Spanish. Both Spanish-dominant and English-dominant students are in the same classes and serve as language models for one another during instruction in their dominant language (Calderón & Slavin, 2001).

Requiring that students use one language or the other in a dual-language environment is often frustrating for the teachers:

Ms. Torres was frustrated that students used English during their "Spanish" time. She tried posting signs demarking which language should be used, and when, but everyone ignored the signs. She did not require students from the other fifth grade to use

Spanish when they visited during Spanish time. In addition, the teacher often accepted public use of English without sanction during teacher-front lessons. Spanish-only was only successfully enforced by students who chastised each other during groupwork in classes where prizes were lost for not using Spanish. (Potowski, 2007, pp. 98–99)

Personnel. Languages can be separated by teacher. In a team-teaching situation, one teacher may speak in English, the other in the primary language. When working with an aide, the teacher will use English and the aide the primary language. A caution in using this latter design is the association of the minority language with school personnel who do not have fully credentialed teaching status.

Subject. Language can be organized by subject—primary language for mathematics, English for science. School personnel need to be cognizant of which subjects are taught in which language. Models in which the primary language is used only for language arts, music, and art, and English is used for science and mathematics, send a message about the status of the primary language.

Example of Concept   *Language Distribution by Subject*

In the two-way development bilingual program at the Valley Center Union School District in California, students study core subjects (language arts, math, science, and social studies) in their L1 as they gain fluency in their L2. In fourth grade, students transition to studying the core in their L2, and by fifth grade they are able to use either language for the district's grade-level curriculum (Richard-Amato, 2003).

Manner of Delivery. The novice bilingual teacher may say everything twice, first in English and then in the primary language. This *concurrent-translation* model is ineffective because students tune out when their subordinate language is spoken.

A better approach is *preview–review,* in which the introduction and summary are given in one language and the presentation in the other. When content-area materials are not available in the minority language, preview–review has been found to be particularly useful (Lessow-Hurley, 2009).

Example of Concept   *Preview–Review*

In a science lesson on measurement of temperatures, students receive an explanation in Korean of the general content of the upcoming lesson as well as the meaning of such English words as increase and decrease. After the lesson, delivered in English, students are divided into groups according to their dominant language and discuss what they have learned. This discussion allows the teacher to expand on concepts and correct misunderstandings (Ovando & Collier, 1998).

Primary-Language Use

In bilingual programs, the primary language can be used as the language of instruction in teaching students academic material, just as English is used for native-English-speaking students in mainstream programs. In addition to being a medium of instruction, the primary language is offered as an academic subject in its own right. Moreover, it can be used to help students in their acquisition of English.

Academic Learning. Primary-language instruction focuses on the development of the language itself (oral and literacy skills) through use of authentic written and oral literature and discourse as well as academic instruction. Once they have a well-developed conceptual base in their primary language, students can translate into English concepts and ideas that are firmly established rather than facing the far more difficult task of learning fundamental concepts in an unfamiliar language (Lessow-Hurley, 2009).

For example, hearing and reading familiar songs, poems, folktales, and stories in the native language exposes students to literary language and various genres. Once literacy is established in the native language, children can use these resources as they move into English.

Second-Language Acquisition. There are several educationally sound as well as logical and psychological reasons for the judicious use of the primary language in learning English (and vice versa). Certainly in bilingual settings, in which two language groups are working and learning together, a disciplined approach to the use of L1 can enhance and facilitate language learning. The Point/Counterpoint on page 177 outlines the reasons for and against the use of L1 in learning L2.

Code Switching

As students become more proficient in English, several factors help to determine which language they use. The primary factor is the students' free choice. They should be allowed to respond in whichever language is comfortable and appropriate for them. Teacher proficiency and material availability are other factors. In some cases, teachers may provide instruction in English while students, in their groups, talk and write in the home language. Code switching is accepted in this model, although students are expected to make final presentations, both oral and written, in whichever is the language of instruction.

Classroom Organization

Recent studies on school reform and education for English learners support the finding that students learn better when actively engaged in a nurturing environment that honors and respects their language and culture (McLeod, 1996; Nelson, 1996; Thomas & Collier, 1997). The active strategies and techniques outlined in Chapters 4 and 5 are equally valid for bilingual classrooms as for ELD and SDAIE classrooms, if not more so, as two groups of students are learning two different languages.

POINT COUNTERPOINT

What Should Be the Role of L1 in Learning L2?

Many of the teaching techniques used for English-language teaching in the twentieth century were developed for use in multilingual, often urban, classes in which learners do not share a sole primary language. In these classes, the use of L1 was not feasible or was strongly discouraged because of the belief that L1 would interfere with learning L2. However, in schools in the United States that feature a student population that shares an L1, this argument does not hold. What should be the role of L1 in learning L2?

POINT: L1 Is a Useful Tool in Learning English

- Many words—especially concrete nouns—are learned fastest when translated. Teaching a simple word such as *garlic* involves a great deal of description or use of a picture. (Does every teacher have a picture of garlic?)
- L1 is useful to highlight false cognates (*embarazada* is not *embarrassed*).
- L1 can be used to discuss grammar differences between languages (*English* does not use an article, as does *el ingles*) and abstract grammar ideas (how the rules of using the subjunctive differ in L1 and in English).
- Use of L1 lowers stress in learning L2.
- Most learners naturally use L1; rather than creating a new language store, they mentally map the L2 directly

on to the existing L1, drawing connections, contrasting ideas, and viewing the L2 through their L1.

COUNTERPOINT: L1 Is Not Useful in Teaching L2

- Overuse of L1 can cause dependency.
- Learners may misunderstand an exact translation of a word's many meanings, especially because English has multiple synonyms for words.
- Use of L1 can lead to a loss of useful language practice.
- Teachers who do not use English socially in class may communicate a low value for speaking and listening to English.
- Use of L1 may replace opportunities for listening and speaking practice in L2.

Implications for Teaching

Use of the L1 with beginners reduces anxiety, increases student–teacher rapport, and increases the effectiveness of instructional management. As students reach higher levels of proficiency in L2, less L1 may be used. Code switching may promote group solidarity and increase comprehension of more difficult topics.
Source: Based on Buckmaster (2000).

Curriculum that is organized around themes, that strives for depth of a topic rather than breadth, that is cross-disciplinary, and that has meaning to students and is relevant to their lives provides students with the opportunity to achieve academic success.

Cooperative Grouping. Cooperative grouping, in which English learners work cooperatively with native speakers of English or with one another, increases students' opportunities to hear and produce English and to negotiate meaning with others. Cohen's Complex Instruction (Cohen, Lotan, & Catanzarite, 1990) encourages equal access for all students in a cooperative group by assigning well-defined roles to each group member and ensuring that these roles rotate frequently. In addition to encouraging academic learning and language proficiency, cooperative learning helps children learn classroom conventions and rituals and become an active part of the culture of the classroom. To be most effective, grouping needs to be flexible and heterogeneous in language, gender, ability, and interest.

Example of Concept   *Cooperative Grouping*

A school in south Texas with a large number of migrant children implemented a cooperative grouping program for writing (Hayes, 1998). During their fifth-grade year, students were empowered to teach themselves—they talked and wrote about their lives outside the classroom and about what they were learning and the effect this learning had on their lives. Students were given choices and opportunities to express themselves using daily journals and class-made books. Writing conferences helped them evaluate their own writing and that of their classmates. A rich supply of stories and nonfiction books encouraged them to read.

Collaborative Teaching. When teachers have the opportunity to collaborate, they can share interests and experiences and build on one another's strengths for the benefit of their students. Dual-immersion teaching fosters collaboration between L1 and L2 teachers. ELD teaching often utilizes teaching assistants and paraprofessional resource people who provide support for English learners, acting as tutors, language informants, and small-group facilitators (Porter & Taylor, 2003).

Working with a paraprofessional can be a satisfying experience in what Villa, Thousand, and Nevin (2004) call "co-teaching." If the teacher and the instructional assistant are *team teaching,* they have equal, collaborative roles. Instruction is co-planned and divided so students can receive benefit from each teacher's strengths. In *complementary teaching,* the teacher and the aide each have equal, alternating duties, and each follows up or enhances the other's instruction. In a *parallel teaching* model, the paraprofessional and the teacher work with different groups of students in different sections of the classroom, each with separate duties. The most common model, however, is that of *supportive teaching,* with the teacher in the lead instructional role while the aide circulates among students to provide support in a subordinate role.

Adapted Instruction

Signs of Successful Co-teaching

Teachers who are paired with co-teachers (paraprofessionals, resource teachers, or other classroom helpers) have a sense of "give and take" with their teaching partner as they build a level of trust that is the foundation for a collaborative partnership. These are the signs of effective teamwork (Gately & Gately, 2001):

- Interpersonal communication is comfortable, with disagreements easily resolved.
- The physical arrangement of students, instructors, and materials is fluid, shared, and interspersed.
- Curricular planning is a mutual task, acknowledging the partners' distinct expertise.
- Co-teachers share in delivering and assessing instruction.

Working with Classroom Volunteers. Activities that a classroom volunteer can assist a teacher with include:

- Instructional review and practice for groups
  - Dictating spelling words
  - Listening to reading practice
  - Conducting drills on words, phrases, and flash cards
- Individual tutoring or assessment
  - Helping with written compositions
  - Helping children who were absent from class to make up work
  - Giving reinforcement to children new to the class
  - Supervising individual testing
  - Repeating a lesson for a child who needs extra help
  - Teaching a special enrichment skill
  - Recording primary-language stories
- Supervision of small-group activities
  - Helping students to publish a class newspaper
  - Supervising student research committees
  - Accompanying small groups to the library
- Other teacher assistance
  - Setting up learning centers
  - Working with projectors, recorders, listening posts
  - Serving as an interpreter for non-English-speaking children
  - Informing about local culture

Well-implemented bilingual education programs have been found to be successful in educating not only English learners but also native-English-speaking students. In a world that is constantly getting smaller, in which the majority of people are bilingual, it is incumbent on the United States to utilize the linguistic facilities of its citizens and to develop these resources to their maximum potential. This argument speaks to the international arena. Equally important is the education of these citizens for the nation itself. As Thomas and Collier (1997) so eloquently express:

> By reforming current school practices, all students will enjoy a better educated, more productive future, for the benefit of all American citizens who will live in the world of the next 15–25 years. It is in the self-interest of all citizens that the next adult generations be educated to meet the enormously increased educational demands of the fast-emerging society of the near future. (p. 13)

LEARNING MORE

Further Reading

Dual Language Instruction (Cloud, Genesee, & Hamayan, 2000) details ways to develop and sustain high-quality instruction in the context of dual-immersion education, what the authors call "enriched education." The book features interviews called "Voices from the Field," in which bilingual teachers share their experiences in dual-language education. One such vignette by Eun Mi Cho recounts her successes in teaching Korean to native-English speakers. She invites students to join the Korean Club, in which they play Korean traditional games. Students learn to make Korean crafts, sing Korean songs, read Korean literature, and meet Korean authors. They visit local Korean markets and cook traditional dishes. In this interesting and comfortable learning environment, students then begin to learn oral and written Korean.

Web Search

Use the Web to research the closest indigenous language in your area. Discuss with colleagues how you could show support for this language.

Exploration

Visit a grocery store in which products from other countries are sold. Find a packaged product for which the product information is given only in a foreign language that you do not speak or read—without translation into English. When these conditions are met, examine the product you have chosen. Is it an item that you might already know how to cook? Or is it totally unfamiliar? Is the product labeling or packaging in a familiar format, or is the information represented in a way that is totally unlike a similar label might look in English? What can you predict about the meaning of words based on your familiarity with the item or with the packaging? If you were teaching that language to native-English-speaking students, what part of the product or the label might be easiest to match with its English counterpart?

Looking at Classrooms

Visit a bilingual program at a local school. With permission, interview several language-minority students to ask if they would like to attend a program in which native-English-speaking students would learn their language while they learned English. See if they can explain what they believe might be the advantages and disadvantages of such a program.

MyEducationLab™

Family Literacy Program

A family literacy program has many benefits for families who speak English as a second language. In this video, parents visit the school regularly to participate in activities of their children's choosing.

To access the video, go to MyEducationLab (www.myeducationlab.com), choose the Díaz-Rico text, and log in to MyEducationLab for English Language Learners. Select the topic Programs for English Learners, and watch the video entitled "Family Literacy Program."

Answer the following questions:

1. Name three positive outcomes that occur when parents are involved in their child's education.

2. Why is it sometimes difficult to get parents who speak English as a second language, or not at all, to become involved in school activities? What can schools do to make these parents feel more welcome? And more specifically, what could you, as a teacher, do to involve parents more in your classroom?

Assessment

Assessment plays a key role in determining academic progress. Chapter 7 surveys the current emphasis on standards-based instruction and the various ways in which English learners are assessed and placed in appropriate instruction. The accompanying figure highlights Part Three of the theoretical model presented in the introduction. In the figure, one can see the key role assessment plays not only in instruction but also in learning about the learner, in the process of classroom instruction, and in the policy decisions that affect the organization and management of schooling.

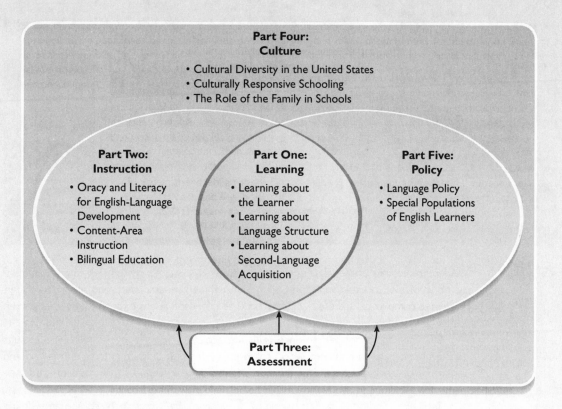

Theoretical Model for CLAD Assessment

7

Language and Content-Area Assessment

Peers can use scoring rubrics to give one another feedback before a final grade is recorded.

© OtnaYdur/Shutterstock

Students reveal their understanding most effectively when they are provided with complex, authentic opportunities to explain, interpret, apply, shift perspective, empathize, and self-assess. When applied to complex tasks, these "six facets" provide a conceptual lens through which teachers can better assess student understanding.

Student and school performance gains are achieved through regular reviews of results (achievement data and student work) followed by targeted adjustments to curriculum and instruction. Teachers become most effective when they seek feedback from students and their peers and use that feedback to adjust approaches to design and teaching.

Teachers, schools, and districts benefit by "working smarter" through the collaborative design, sharing, and peer review of units of study.

Grant Wiggins (2005)

Assessment is a process for determining the current level of a learner's performance or knowledge. The results of the assessment are then used to modify or improve the learner's performance or knowledge. Assessment informs educators about the strengths and needs of language learners so that students are properly placed and appropriately instructed. Assessment is also used to inform school authorities, parents, or other concerned parties of student progress. A final use of assessment is to compare student achievement against national goals and standards, which poses a significant problem for English learners.

Various evaluation methods have been used with English learners. Some are required by government programs and legal mandates, and others are a part of standard classroom practice. In the domain of reading instruction, for example, teachers use a variety of assessment tools, including informal reading inventories, literacy skills checklists, running records, miscue analysis, guided observations, and portfolio assessment (Consortium on Reading Excellence, 2008).

Aside from the usual concerns that such assessment practices be valid, reliable, and practical, teachers of English learners must be careful to ensure that tests are fair (free from cultural and linguistic bias) and normed for English learners—that is, that they do not unfairly measure English learners against a standard designed for native speakers of English. Furthermore, tests must advance students' understanding and abilities if they are to constitute a valid part of education. Tests should not be merely instruments of diagnosis for labeling, placing, and designing remediation.

Ideally, assessment provides information about students' abilities and enables teachers to use this information humanistically—that is, for the benefit of the student's academic and personal development. However, the use of testing to further second-language development is problematic. If testing is aligned with curricular goals that emphasize "correct" English rather than authentic communication, the learners may passively submit to acquiring a minimum level of achievement without intrinsic motivation. Testing must therefore be an integral part of a learning environment that encourages students to seek meaning and use a second language to fulfill academic and personal goals. In the model presented in the figure on page 183, assessment has an impact on instruction, learning, and policy, and is itself affected by culture.

Educational Standards and Standardized Assessment

The educational standards movement is an attempt on the part of educators and others to specify exactly what students are expected to learn in each content area and at each grade level (see Chapter 5). Assumptions that underlie this approach are straightforward. In order to achieve learning, teachers must first describe in detail what students are expected to accomplish, or perform; then propose the kind of evidence that will substantiate this performance; then design learning activities that

Table 7.1 Terms Associated with Common Core Standards

Common Core standards	The goals and expectations that are shared by those who design curriculum
College and career readiness	Providing evidence that students have literacy and problem-solving skills needed to succeed in higher education and in the workplace
Shared language and content expectations	Across various content domains and with diverse types of texts, students should be able to read complex texts and engage in academic discourse that offers rich explanation and argumentation
Meaningful assessment of English learners	Academic performance assessment that measures key concepts, capturing the breadth, depth, and complexity of receptive and productive language uses without undue linguistic complication
Benchmarks	Interim assessment that predicts outcomes and guides interventions

will accumulate the desired evidence. Thus, curricula are planned according to state content standards. Common Core standards (see p. 190) have been proposed for adoption by the states. Table 7.1 offers terms associated with Common Core.

Advantages of Standards-Based Instruction for English Learners

An advantage of establishing content and performance standards for English learners is that by using these standards, teachers can focus on what students need to know. Teachers can pursue an articulated sequence of instruction, integrating the teaching of English into increasingly sophisticated levels of language and meaningful discourse, fluent communication skills, and cognitive academic language proficiency.

The use of standards avoids what has been a too-frequent practice in the past: the use in ELD of materials and practices designed for younger students or for special education students (Walqui, 1999). Gándara (1997) reported vast discrepancies between the curricula offered to English speakers and to English learners. The use of standards can alter this practice. Moreover, surveys show that parents of all ethnic groups support standards and testing as a means to improve schools (Wadsworth & Remaley, 2007).

Why do standards matter? When learning is standardized, every student is expected to learn a specific, predetermined "amount" of knowledge, and that learning is measured by evidence of attainment of that knowledge. This protects students from being neglected, or from learning something that only one individual teacher believes is important. Such practices as giving students credit merely for occupying a seat in a class or giving a weak grade that is nevertheless sufficient for passing are no longer acceptable (Reeves, 2002).

Achievement Testing and No Child Left Behind

The federal No Child Left Behind Act of 2001 (NCLB, 2002) required that all students be "proficient" in reading and mathematics by the 2013–14 school year. All public school students in grades 3 through 8 must be tested annually, using state achievement tests. This group includes English learners, who must be assessed in a valid and reasonable manner that includes reasonable accommodations and, to the extent practicable, testing in the primary language. Those students who have completed thirty months of schooling must, however, be tested in English reading (special exemptions can be applied for on a case-by-case basis, and students living in Puerto Rico are automatically exempted). States must establish baseline proficiency goals to which yearly progress is compared (Gunning, 2005).

Although the noblest goal of assessment is to benefit the student, in the current climate of standards-driven instruction, the results of assessment are often used to assess the effectiveness of the teacher's instruction. This is called "high-stakes" assessment— and much is at stake: Under NCLB, schools that fail to make acceptable yearly progress (AYP) for two years in a row are subject to corrective action.

Example of Concept   *The TAKS Measure of Proficiency*

At the heart of NCLB is the call for all schoolchildren to become proficient in reading and mathematics by the year 2014—but each state is free to define and measure its own version of "proficiency." Texas uses the Texas Assessment of Knowledge and Skills (TAKS). Yet in a report published by the Fordham Institute (Cronin, Dahlin, Adkins, & Kingsbury, 2007), researchers found TAKS to be of below-average difficulty—in other words, a misleading indicator of proficiency. Using this measure, fewer of Texas's schools would be labeled "low-performing"—thus leading parents to believe a student was "proficient," even though the child scored below two-thirds of students in other states. Obviously, "standards" are relative (Julian, 2007).

NCLB insists that the status of English learners not be hidden among the averages, but specifically disaggregated. The rationale for testing is to promote accountability: to determine the level of English proficiency of students so appropriate services can be rendered, to ensure that English learners access the core curriculum, to identify individuals who are falling behind, and to report to parents what children have and have not accomplished (Rahilly & Weinmann, 2007).

Although NCLB mandated that states desiring federal funds require adequate yearly progress reporting for students with limited English proficiency (LEP), deep-seated structural flaws undermine the validity and reliability of the data that have been collected to date (Abedi, Hofstetter, & Lord, 2004). One problem is that the category of "English learner" is not defined in similar ways across states. Another issue is that in many states, the sparse population of English learners makes comparisons with mainstream populations statistically unreliable. The largest problem, however, is inherent in the logic of the category itself. When an English learner is redesignated, he or she is no longer a member of the subgroup, so the subgroup does not measure its most successful members. This makes it difficult to show that NCLB is indeed creating a success for English learners.

In 2012, more than thirty-eight states requested and eleven were granted waivers from the most strenuous requirements of No Child Left Behind, intending to spare schools that would be defined as "underperforming" and forced to hire tutors and pay students who wish to be bused elsewhere. The states requesting the waivers have argued that the 2014 student proficiency target is unrealistic and should be replaced (Leff, 2012). NCLB has been up for renewal since 2007, but the U.S. Congress has not acted to revise, extend, or replace it.

The aim of using standardized measures is to ensure that all students are held to the same level of performance. Yet the net result is often to penalize schools whose English learners do not score well on tests designed for native-English speakers. This poses a dilemma: On the one hand, high standards across schools do not permit school districts to lower academic standards for schools with high percentages of English learners. On the other hand, forcing students to undergo frustrating experiences of repeated testing in English when they are not ready can discourage students. Alternatively, testing students in their primary language is not effective if schools do not offer primary-language instruction.

Disadvantages of Standards-Based Instruction for English Learners

Although the overall goal is noble—devising a set of very broad standards for all students and measuring success according to a common set of criteria—the ongoing needs of English learners mandate that school districts remain flexible about the specific means for addressing standards and determining student achievement (Nelson-Barber, 1999). The heavy emphasis on high-stakes testing—and the attendant punitive consequences for schools with low test scores—places English learners at risk of failure (August, Hakuta, & Pompa, 1994). In fact, schools across the United States report low test scores for students who are linguistically "nonmainstream," including those who speak dialects of English at home that do not correspond to the academic English used in schools. Clearly, it is not the testing itself causing these low scores; the emphasis on testing, however, leaves little time for teachers to focus on teaching the academic subjects and the language that English learners need to acquire to perform well on high-stakes tests.

The high-stakes testing that drives the school-accountability movement has been shown to have important consequences for racial and ethnic minority students of low socioeconomic status. Valencia and Villareal (2003) predicted that Texas's requirement that all third-grade students take the Texas Assessment of Knowledge and Skills (TAKS) to be promoted would result in a 23 percent retention rate for English learners. Previous studies have shown that once retained, such students typically fall behind in their academic achievement and have a higher probability of dropping out of school.

The chief critique of standards-based school reform is that it treats the symptoms of school failure (poor achievement) rather than the cause (inferior schools). School failure is assigned to the individual rather than the systemic denial of equal educational opportunity by unequal school funding resulting in poor schools and lack of resources (Valencia & Villareal, 2003).

Standards work best when expectations are held constant for all groups of students at the same time that equal curricula and instruction are offered to all groups. This is not the case in most schools; students are tracked into classes of perceived high-, medium-, and low-instructional rigor. As Ryan (2008) pointed out, there is no quality education without equality in education.

Haycock (2001) has documented that students at risk of failure are more likely to have insufficient resources, less experienced teachers who are not prepared for the subjects they teach, and a watered-down curriculum, combined with low expectations for student achievement. This calls into question whether state standards and assessments can achieve educational equity.

Under NCLB, schooling is viewed as a market commodity: Schools whose students do not meet standards are perceived as "failing," and parents can obtain vouchers to take their children elsewhere. The burden, then, is on the family to find an alternative placement. Oakes and Lipton (2007) counter this rationale with the argument that every school should be given the funds to provide students with high-quality opportunities to learn, and families should not bear the burden of locating an alternative school.

The answer to this dilemma is for school districts to invest in high-level, late-exit primary-language instruction and allow students to be tested in their primary language. The catch is the NCLB provision that students must be tested in English reading after three years of schooling. This regulation pressures schools to begin English reading early. English learners, then, are assumed to attain grade-level expectations in English reading that are set for native-English speakers, resulting in pressure toward submersion—or, at best, early-exit transition bilingual education programs—as a preferred model.

Assessments under Common Core

By mid-2012, forty-five states and the District of Columbia adopted common content standards for grades K–12 in both English/language arts and math (Minnesota adopted only language arts), in an initiative led by the Council of Chief State School Officers (CCSSO) and the National Governors Association Center for Best Practices. The Common Core Standards were unveiled in 2010 and are now moving into the implementation phase. The goal is for states to ensure every student has access to a high-quality education. By adopting and implementing the Common Core Standards, states agree to make college- and career-readiness the salient objective of schooling; to assess students in such a way that the students most in need receive meaningful support and intervention; to provide timely, transparent data to guide instructional decisions; and to "foster innovation and continuous improvement throughout the system" (Council of Chief State School Officers [CCSSO], p. 3).

To participate in this initiative, states must agree to set up accountability systems that track student progress. The intention is to use "next-generation" assessments to determine the extent of student mastery of these standards. Most states are choosing to back assessments being developed by one of two nonprofit coalitions, the Smarter Balanced Assessment Consortium or the Partnership for Assessment of Readiness for College and Careers (PARCC), although some states have joined both coalitions. Assessments from both consortia will be administered using technology that employs new testing options such as simulations, video, and audio.

The main difference between the consortia is that the assessments created by Smarter Balanced will be adaptive—if a student answers correctly, the items become more difficult; or conversely, a wrong answer generates an easier next test item. Using adaptive assessment, two students in the same class could be taking tests over the same content using entirely different test items.

Delaware, Indiana, and Oregon (among other states that have adopted the new standards) are already employing online testing. Many states are assessing the school districts' existing digital tools to evaluate whether online testing based on common academic standards is feasible for all students by 2014–15.

Linking Assessment to Progress for English Learners

Aside from their performance on standardized tests, English learners' achievement in English is measured and directed by standards-based curricula. This is made possible by a linkage between standards, placement testing, instruction, and careful record keeping.

Placement tests that are directly linked to standards-based classroom instruction for English learners permit teachers to begin use of effective instructional practices as soon as students enter the classroom. Placement tests that align with standards, which in turn align with daily instruction, provide a seamless system that helps teachers to track students' continuous progress toward mainstream instruction. Each linkage—from standards to assessment to instruction and back to assessment—is explained in the following sections.

The English-Language Development (ELD) Framework

English-language development takes place in stages. Rather than using the four stages introduced in the Natural Approach (preproduction, early production, speech emergence, and intermediate fluency), the California English Language Development Standards (CDE, 2012) are divided into five stages: Beginning, Early Intermediate, Intermediate, Early Advanced, and Advanced. The ELD standards describe expected proficiency on the part of the English learner in each of six key domains of language (Listening and Speaking, Reading/Word Analysis, Reading Fluency and Systematic Vocabulary Development, Reading Comprehension, Reading Literary Response and Analysis, and Writing Strategies and Application). For example, in the domain of Listening and Speaking, expected language proficiency increases gradually from Beginning to Advanced levels. Table 7.2 depicts the expectations for each of the five levels. (California's Common-Core-compatible ELD standards are forthcoming.)

The ELD standards are incorporated into academic lessons as language objectives. For example, an English learner at the Beginning level is capable of

Table 7.2   Listening and Speaking Expectations in the California English-Language-Development Standards for English Learners at Five Levels

ELD Level	Expectations
Beginning (K–2)	• Begins to speak with a few words or sentences, using some English phonemes and rudimentary English grammatical phrases • Answers simple questions with one- or two-word responses • Responds to simple directions and questions using physical actions and other means of nonverbal communication • Independently uses common social greetings and simple repetitive phrases
Early Intermediate	• Begins to be understood when speaking, but may have some inconsistent use of Standard English grammatical forms and sounds• Asks/answers questions using phrases or simple sentences • Retells familiar stories and short conversations by using appropriate gestures, expressions, and illustrative objects • Orally communicates basic needs • Recites familiar rhymes, songs, and simple stories
Intermediate	• Asks/answers instructional questions using simple sentences • Listens attentively to stories/information and identifies key details and concepts using both verbal and nonverbal responses • Can be understood when speaking, using consistent Standard English forms and sounds; however, some rules may not be in evidence • Actively participates in social conversations with peers and adults on familiar topics by asking and answering questions and soliciting information • Retells stories and talks about school-related activities using expanded vocabulary, descriptive words, and paraphrasing

(continued)

Table 7.2 Continued

ELD Level	Expectations
Early Advanced	• Listens attentively to stories/information and orally identifies key details and concepts • Retells stories in greater detail including characters, setting, and plot • Is understood when speaking, using consistent Standard English forms, sounds, intonation, pitch, and modulation, but may have random errors • Actively participates and initiates more extended social conversations with peers and adults on unfamiliar topics by asking and answering questions, restating and soliciting information • Recognizes appropriate ways of speaking that vary based on purpose, audience, and subject matter • Asks and answers instructional questions with more extensive supporting elements
Advanced	• Listens attentively to stories/information on new topics and identifies both orally and in writing key details and concepts • Demonstrates understanding of idiomatic expressions by responding to and using them appropriately • Negotiates/initiates social conversations by questioning, restating, soliciting information, and paraphrasing • Consistently uses appropriate ways of speaking and writing that vary based on purpose, audience, and subject matter • Narrates and paraphrases events in greater detail, using more extended vocabulary

Source: Adapted from the California English-Language Arts Framework, online at www.cde.ca.gov/re/pn/fd/documents /englangdev-stnd.pdf.

the following: "Answer[ing] simple questions with one- or two-word responses." In order to advance to Early Intermediate, this student must become capable of "Ask[ing]/ answer[ing] instructional questions using simple sentences." Therefore, the Early Intermediate standard becomes an appropriate language objective not only for reading and language arts instruction but also for mathematics, social studies, or science.

If the lesson offers ample opportunity to develop this skill, and the teacher collects enough evidence (anecdotal/observational in the case of listening/speaking objectives) that the student has mastered it, the teacher may use this evidence to advance the learner to the next level using an ELD checklist or other tracking device. For example, Alhambra School District in Alhambra, California, uses the English Language Development Progress Profile, a folder with the ELD standards printed in checklist format, with spaces for yearly test scores (see Sasser, Naccarato, Corren, & Tran, 2002).

Linking Placement Tests to Language Development

Several states have developed or use commercially available language-development tests (Loop & Barron, 2002). California, for example, uses the California English Language Development Test (CELDT) to identify new students who are English learners in kindergarten through grade 12, determine their level of English proficiency, and assess their progress annually toward becoming fluent-English proficient (FEP). A student's score on the CELDT (see www.cde.ca.gov/ta/tg/el) corresponds to a student's skill level as defined in the California ELD standards.

The CELDT measures four language domains in grades 2–12: listening, speaking, reading, and writing (listening and speaking only in grades K–1). Students can score at five levels and are reclassified based on this score (plus their score on the state English language-arts test, teacher evaluation, and parent consultation). They are tested once upon entry (initial CELDT) to determine their status, and then annually (annual CELDT) to determine their progress (Linquanti, 2008).

When students attain a redesignation level on the CELDT and are transitioned into mainstream English classes, teachers use the California English-Language Arts (ELA) standards (CDE, 1998a) to create standards-based language arts lessons. Because the ELD and ELA standards are closely related, the expectation is that English learners will make a smooth transition from one set of standards to the other.

Linking Standards-Based Classroom Instruction to Assessment

In standards-based instruction, assessment is linked to instruction in two fundamental ways. First, instruction is designed with assessment in mind. The concern of the teacher is that instructional activities produce evidence that can be used to document student progress. Therefore, the assessment is embedded and authentic—the activities are designed in advance to be assessed.

Example of Concept   *Linking Standards, Instruction, and Assessment*

Mr. Phelan has two groups of third-grade English learners, twelve who are at the Early Advanced level and thirteen who are at the Advanced level. These levels share two similar ELD standards in the category Reading Comprehension: "Reads and uses basic text features such as title, table of contents, and chapter headings" (Early Advanced) and "Reads and uses basic text features such as title, table of contents, chapter headings, diagrams, and index" (Advanced). He prepares a treasure hunt assignment for the two groups. During their science class, the Early Advanced students answer questions from the science chapter that require them to list the source of the answer (title, table of contents, etc.) as well as the answer itself. The Advanced group has the same questions, as well as three bonus questions derived from the book's index and a chapter diagram. Mr. Phelan uses the results of the treasure hunt activity as evidence that both groups have met their corresponding ELD standards.

Second, assessment and instruction are linked through standardized testing. Because the classroom teacher does not know the test questions in advance, and because the tests sample the instructional content, there is no one-to-one match between instruction and assessment. Teachers can only hope that their efforts to meet the requirements of the standards-based curriculum produce high standardized test scores.

Purposes of Assessment

Assessment instruments can be used for a number of purposes: to make decisions about student placement, to make day-to-day instructional decisions such as when to provide a student with additional mediation, to make resource decisions such as allocation of instructional time or materials, and to measure student achievement against standards. Various types of tests are used for these purposes: *Proficiency tests, diagnostic* and *placement tests, achievement tests, student work samples, observations while students are working, performance-based tests,* and *competency tests.* Each will be discussed in turn.

Teachers who use assessment skillfully can choose which methods of assessment are most useful for classroom decision making; develop effective grading procedures; communicate assessment results to students, parents, and other educators; and recognize unethical, illegal, and otherwise inappropriate assessment methods and uses of assessment information (Ward & Murray-Ward, 1999).

Formative versus Summative Assessment

Before discussing types of tests, it is important to make one distinction. Not all assessment is end measurement (summative), used for final "sum-up" of student performance. Formative assessment is increasingly important as a way of providing an early measure of student performance so that corrective adjustment can be applied. Because many instructional activities are observable (such as guided, shared, and interactive reading), they can provide information about how well the student is doing. The teacher who monitors these activities and offers feedback can improve the quality of student work during the process of learning.

Example of Concept

Assessing Informational Writing under Common Core Standards

Beginning in upper elementary school (grades 4–6) and through middle and high school years, students submit informational writing—questions at the end of textbook chapters, summaries of reading, write-ups of laboratory experiments, science reports, and so forth. Although this writing is collected and graded, teachers do not usually demand craft in writing, as they do with the essays and creative writing that may be assigned in English classes.

The Common Core standards call for discipline-specific writing that is well-structured and features the use of careful detail and logic, including citations, quotes, and examples—after all, well-crafted expository text is required for college and career success. Clearly, in the later years of K–12 schooling students

must develop higher-order thinking under the tutelage of content instructors.

Increased use of formative assessment will be required, as teachers work with students to revise, rethink, and rewrite in the context of academic disciplines. Chemistry teachers will require increased clear and supple logic in explaining the outcomes of experiments. Mathematics teachers will assign project-based learning that must be proposed and reported by means of well-designed prose. Social studies teachers will expect succinct summaries of complex issues from original source documents. Content instructors will take corrective pencils in hand to deliver feedback that informs and improves writing. Thus the goal of Common Core Standards is assessment of writing across the curriculum.

Formative assessment takes place through five means: teacher questioning, offering feedback through grading, peer assessment, self-assessment, and the formative use of summative tests. Table 7.3 summarizes key points for using these types of formative assessment.

Table 7.4 compares attributes of formative and summative assessment.

Table 7.3   Types of Formative Assessment: Strengths and Challenges

Type of Formative Assessment	Strengths	Challenges
Teacher questioning	The teacher can gauge if a student understands by the quality of oral response	English learners may not have the proficiency to express fully what they understand
Feedback through grading	Rubrics can be used to guide assignments before submission as well as provide targeted feedback	Teachers who choose what items to assess are cautious not to overwhelm students with correction
Peer assessment	Peers learn from providing feedback	Peers may not provide adequate feedback
Self-assessment	Portfolios can archive first as well as final drafts so that students can track their own progress	Students vary in their abilities to be self-reflective, so self-assessment does not benefit all students equally
Formative use of summative assessment	A pretest can alert students about the format and requirements of a corresponding summative test	The corresponding summative test must provide parallel measure of the content to match the pretest

Table 7.4   Formative versus Summative Assessment

Attribute	Formative	Summative
Purpose(s)	Monitor the learning to provide feedback about the progress of the student in order to reteach if necessary	Apply a final grade to the progress of the student
Who assesses	Self, peer, or the teacher	Usually the teacher
When work is assessed	During the lesson	At the end of the lesson
Form of assessment	Teacher observation, self-check, peer assessment	Final test, or final grade of classwork/homework
How work is assessed	Monitoring includes checking on students while they are working, collecting work samples, or checking work against rubrics	Use of scoring criteria—points are assigned to each question
How grade is obtained	No grade given, or tentative grade is given to indicate progress	Points are assigned to each item, and grades are connected with different ranges of point totals

(continued)

Table 7.4 Continued

Attribute	Formative	Summative
Timing	During learning	After learning
How work is improved	Students may be given individual feedback, or class as a whole may be retaught; students may be grouped to be retaught portions that they have not mastered	The teacher may use results to rank or group students for subsequent teaching; results may inform next year's teaching—but it is too late to change current grades for current students
Who is informed by results	Teacher and students, in order to reteach what has not yet been learned	Teacher, students, administrators, and parents
Example	The teacher circulates, checking progress of worksheet completion	Fill-in-the-blanks Short-answer test Multiple-choice test

Proficiency, Diagnostic, and Placement Tests

Proficiency tests measure a test taker's overall ability in English, usually defined independently of any particular instructional program. Proficiency tests are sometimes divided into subskills or modes of language (speaking, listening, writing, reading, vocabulary, and grammar).

The proliferation of standardized tests has often resulted in an emphasis on the testing of decontextualized skills such as sentence-level punctuation, grammar, and spelling. This undermines the mode in which cognition is most effective: the ability of the brain to seek out and assemble personal meaning. Proficiency tests are poor tests of achievement because, by design, their content has little or no relationship to the content of an instructional program. They may also poorly diagnose what specific knowledge a student has or is lacking.

Diagnostic and placement tests are administered to determine specific aspects of a student's proficiency in a second language. Placement tests determine the academic level or the grade level into which students need to be placed. In addition, placement tests can be used to monitor progress of English learners in acquiring English and to assist in redesignating English learners to mainstream classrooms (Slater, 2000).

Example of Concept   *Placement without Assessment*

I grew up in California, but I was put into an ESL class when I got to the community college because I applied late and that was the only writing class available. At the time I thought, what am I doing here? I'm a native speaker of English!

The students were from all over—from Japan, Iran, Iraq . . . The teacher had to constantly remind them that chitchat in their L1 would defeat the purpose of the class. That's what she thought, anyway.

Well, I passed that course and moved on to regular English classes . . . But that experience paid off in one way—that's when I decided I wanted to be an ESL teacher!

—*Viet Nyugen (2013)*

Example of Concept   *Aligning CELDT Levels and Instruction*

Sara, an eight-year-old third-grader, is from Honduras, and her family returns to Tegucigalpa periodically to visit the extended family. She has been in the United States for a year. She began Spanish-language schooling at the age of four in Honduras and has attained a basic level of reading in Spanish. Her mother was a teacher in Tegucigalpa and helps her to maintain her Spanish reading skills. Her CELDT scores were Listening and Speaking 165, Reading 190, and Writing 100.

Sara's total score, 455, places her at the Early Intermediate level for students in the third grade. Her teacher recognizes that at the level of Early Intermediate, Sara can already "read familiar vocabulary, phrases, and sentences chorally and independently," and therefore will design reading instruction to provide evidence that Sara can, among other objectives drawn from the Intermediate level of the ELD standards, "use complex sentences and appropriate vocabulary to express ideas and needs in social and academic settings."

Achievement Tests

An achievement test measures a student's success in learning specific instructional content, whether language (knowledge about English) or another subject (e.g., mathematics, science). A curriculum-based achievement test is given after instruction has taken place and contains only material that was actually taught. The staff of the instructional program usually prepares such a test.

However, the contemporary trend toward implementing national standards for achievement has caused a proliferation of achievement tests that are not aligned with specific curricular content. The pressure for students to perform well on these tests, which are often used by administrators as an index of academic success, may detract from time spent on language-development activities. Teachers who understand the needs of English learners can adjust their instruction to balance lesson planning with the need to prepare students to perform well on standardized achievement tests.

Example of Concept   *Preparing Students for Standardized Tests*

Third-grade teacher Jim Hughes does two particular things to prepare his students for standardized tests:

One is to expand their vocabulary—the vocabulary specifically found in the tests they must take. For example, the vocabulary of math includes words such as *about, approximately, estimate, round off, total, twice, double*—words they may know, but not their mathematical meanings. But, of course,

the students have to know the words in context, so we practice, practice, practice.

Second, I spend a lot of time encouraging the kids that they can do well on the standardized tests. I ask them to "try their best." I try to lower anxiety as much as possible by being nearby. Motivation, then, as well as reassurance are a big part of the "special" thing I try to give the children
—Jim Hughes (2004)

Competency Tests

More than half the states use minimum-competency testing programs to identify students who may be promoted or graduated (NCES, 2011). In some states, such as Florida, English learners in certain grades who have been in an ELD program for two or fewer years may be exempt from the state minimum-competency testing program. Many school districts mandate remedial instruction between terms for students who fail to meet minimum-competency standards. It is important that such supplementary instruction take into consideration the needs of English learners.

Example of Concept   *Competency Requirements*

The state of North Carolina requires that students pass "rigorous" competency tests in reading and mathematics in order to receive a North Carolina high school diploma. English learners must pass the competency tests as well as meet all state and local graduation requirements to graduate and receive a high school diploma. These students are eligible for certain types of accommodations while taking the tests—testing in a separate room; scheduled extended time; multiple test sessions; test administrator reads test aloud in English; students mark in test book; use of English or native-language dictionary or electronic translator. The student's committee for limited English proficiency determines the need and the type of accommodation. The use of accommodations must be documented and should be used routinely with the student by the classroom teacher (Public Schools of North Carolina, 2004, p. 3).

Methods of Assessment

Test scores, classroom grades, and teacher observation and evaluation are common bases for determining student progress. The judgments resulting from this testing may affect students' present adjustment to school and their future academic and social success. The social and economic pressures from testing often overshadow the curriculum and the affective goals of schooling.

Performance-based testing is a growing alternative to standardized testing, although standardized testing persists because of the economic and political investment in this type of assessment. For classroom purposes, teacher observation and evaluation— supplemented by other sources of data—remain potent allies for students' academic progress. Students can play a role in the assessment process by evaluating their own language development, content knowledge, and strategies for learning. This helps students become self-regulated learners who can plan their own learning activities and use of time and resources (O'Malley & Pierce, 1996).

Linking Assessment to the Integrated Curriculum

The use of an integrated curriculum promotes language and academic development for English learners. Units of study in literature, math, science, and social studies may be combined into an interdisciplinary program in which students can use a variety of communication systems (e.g., language, art, music, drama) to pursue open-ended assignments. Assessment is a natural part of this curriculum. Student outcomes are documented in a variety of ways—time capsules, surveys, creative works, posters, and so forth. Good records allow teachers to track individual progress and also reflect and store many observations about students' skills and interests.

Authentic Assessment

O'Malley and Pierce (1996) defined authentic assessment as "the multiple forms of assessment that reflect student learning, achievement, motivation, and attitudes on instructionally relevant classroom activities" (p. 4). Examples of authentic assessment include the use of portfolios, projects, experiments, current event debates, and community-based inquiries. Assessments are considered "authentic" if they stem directly from classroom activities, allow students to share in the process of evaluating their progress, and are valid and reliable in that they truly assess a student's classroom performance in a stable manner. The advantage of authentic assessment is that it is directly related to classroom performance and permits teachers to design and offer the extra mediation students may need as determined by the assessment.

Example of Concept   *Authentic Assessment*

At International High School in Queens, New York, authentic assessment is deeply embedded into all activities. In the Global Studies and Art interdisciplinary cluster, students researched a world religion that was unfamiliar to them. Their assignment was to create or re-create a religious artifact typical of the religion.

To begin the project, students brainstormed possible research questions. Project activities included visiting a museum that exhibits religious artifacts, researching in dyads, and communicating their research in progress to peers.

On the day of the final performance, students sat at tables of six, shared their findings, asked questions, and clarified what they had learned. The culminating activity was an informal conversation in yet another grouping so that students could expand their perspectives. Although students had their written reports at hand, they could not rely on them for their initial presentations or during the discussion (Walqui, 1999, p. 74).

Performance-Based Assessment

Performance-based testing corresponds directly to what is taught in the classroom and can easily be incorporated into classroom routines and learning activities. Methods for assessing a performance can be divided into two main types: *standardized* (e.g., tests, checklists, observations, rating scales, questionnaires, and structured interviews, in which each student responds to the same instructions under the same conditions) and *less standardized* (e.g., student work samples, journals, games, debates, story retelling, anecdotal reports, and behavioral notes, in which the scoring is tailored to the product in a less standard fashion). Using a combination of standardized and less standardized assessments provides a cross-check of student capabilities (Peregoy & Boyle, 2013).

Adapted Instruction

Administering a Classroom Test

Teacher-made tests can be used both formatively and summatively. Here are some guidelines:

- Tests should be measures of what has been taught. The same content standards that guide instruction should align with the assessment of instruction.
- Provide "word walls" or bilingual dictionaries to assist English learners with vocabulary.
- To avoid undue student anxiety, feature activities requiring a high degree of creativity or divergent thinking as homework or groupwork, and not as summative test items.

Questionnaires and surveys can help teachers learn about many students' skills and interests at once. An observation checklist allows teachers to circulate among students while they are working and monitor specific skills, such as emergent literacy skills, word-identification skills, and oral reading (Miller, 1995). The advantage of standardized assessment is its speed of scoring, using predetermined questions and answer keys.

Less standardized, or open-ended, assessments may feature longer problem-solving exercises, assignments that involve performances or exhibitions, and portfolios that contain student work gathered over a longer period of time. Despite the potential drawbacks of open-ended assessment, it can furnish valuable information about students' abilities.

Not all open-ended assessments are difficult to grade; teacher-made *scoring rubrics* can be determined in advance of an assignment and assist both teacher and student by communicating in advance the basis for scoring. Like objectives, scoring rubrics help to specify the outcome that is expected from a learning activity. Rubrics are not only used to score assignments after completion. They are also helpful when used formatively in the following ways:

- Students can gain a clear picture of the content addressed by the assignment.
- The level of achievement expected for each score level can be stated.
- The format of the assignment can be specified so students have a firm idea of the way to structure their work.
- Students can use the rubric to peer-assess each other's work, checking each aspect of the rubric as a pre-evaluation.

Teachers play an important role in assessing the developing skills of English learners. To assess bilingual students fairly, teachers must consider three sources of information: the results of assessment, their own understanding of the thinking processes that students use, and an understanding of the background knowledge from which students draw (Brisk, 1998). Overall, the responsibility for documenting the success of English learners is shared between teachers and school administrators.

Classroom Tests. Tests may be highly convergent (one right answer required) or may be open-ended, with many possible answers. Authentic tests of ability require students to have a repertoire of responses that call for judgment and skill in using language, skills, and knowledge.

Portfolio Assessment. The purposes of portfolio assessment are to maintain a long-term record of students' progress, to provide a clear and understandable measure of student productivity instead of a single number, to offer opportunities for improved student self-image as a result of showing progress and accomplishment, to recognize different learning styles, and to provide an active role for students in self-assessment (Gottlieb, 1995).

Portfolios can include writing samples (compositions, letters, reports, drawings, dictation), student self-assessments, audio recordings (retellings, oral think-alouds), photographs and video recordings, semantic webs and concept maps, and teacher notes about students. Portfolio records about students should be descriptive (what the child does when learning). Once every few weeks, the teacher reviews these records, making notes on the file about a student's strengths and weaknesses and making tentative conclusions that plan ways to help the student succeed (Barr, Blachowicz, Bates, Katz, & Kaufman, 2007).

Example of Concept *What's in a Student Portfolio?*

Mr. Zepeda gets baseline data from his students in order to assess their levels and to group them for instruction. He takes a running record as he listens to students read individually. Students write a friendly letter so Mr. Zepeda can determine their spelling development and their ability to express themselves in writing. In addition, he schedules individual conferences to learn about students' interests.

By the time of parent conferences, the students' portfolios contain writing samples; anecdotal records; photos; periodic running records; records of books the student has read; a complete writing project including prewriting, drafts, and final, published copy; a summary of the student's progress; and a list of goals set and accomplished. In preparation for the conference, Mr. Zepeda tells the students, "I want you to select the one piece of work that you feel best about. Write a one-page note to your parents explaining why you are proud of that piece of work and what you learned from doing it" (Herrell, 2000, p. 160).

Example of Concept *What's in a Teacher's Portfolio?*

What do teachers file in an assessment portfolio? Faltis and Coulter (2008) describe Mrs. MacPherson's language arts assessment for a sample student in her tenth-grade English class. In a three-ring binder she maintains a section for each student. In the section "Alex as a reader," she files a copy of the miscue analysis she did at the beginning of the year, along with other, shorter such assessments, some with annotations of her observations. She also has a set of sticky notes from informal observations she has made while walking around the class with a clipboard. A similar page of notes is entitled "Alex as a writer."

She keeps a page of skills and strategies that Alex has agreed to work on throughout year—Alex also has a set in his student portfolio that he refers to periodically. Again, she and he keep a similar page for writing. In this binder she also files results from district and state assessments and samples of Alex's work. In the front of the binder is a large spreadsheet with each student's name across the top and a set of English-language arts standards down the side—she checks off students' names when they have met the standards.

Portfolio Conference. When it is time for parent conferences, portfolios can provide the basis for dialogue. Juliana Ferry, a teacher at the Sequoyah School in Pasadena, California, asks students to make a presentation of their work to their parents. "The relationship shouldn't be adversarial," she says, "It's more of a collaboration" (Rivera, 2008, p. B6).

Standardized Tests

The term *standardized test* has come to mean large-scale, widely used tests standardized and published by large testing corporations. The benefits of standardized tests include speed in administration and convenience in scoring.

Between 2005 and 2007, twenty-three states across the United States added more than 11.3 million reading and math tests to their school curricula in order to keep up with NCLB requirements. New York alone has added more than 1.7 million tests. The school testing and testing services industry (which includes tutoring, test prep courses, and the tests themselves) is now estimated to be a $2.3 billion a year enterprise, with just five big companies controlling 90 percent of the statewide testing revenue (*Parade*, p. 10).

Norm- and Criterion-Referenced Tests. Large-scale standardized tests can be norm-referenced or criterion-referenced, or a combination of both. Norm-referenced tests compare student scores against a population of students with which the test has been standardized or "normed." Examples of norm-referenced tests are the Language Assessment Scales (LAS), a test designed to measure oral language skills in English and Spanish, and the Woodcock-Muñoz Language Assessment. Criterion-referenced tests are used principally to find out how much of a clearly defined domain of language skills or materials students have learned. In an ELD program with many levels, students may be required to pass criterion-referenced tests to progress from one level to the next.

Preparing Students for Standardized Tests. Many sources offer hints for successful test taking. Beck (2004) directed these to the student: Focus on one question at a time. Read the question carefully, making sure you understand the task involved. Read all the answer choices given, especially when the test asks for the *best* answer. If the question depends on reading comprehension, reread the selection as you consider each question. Make sure that each answer you mark corresponds to the question you are answering. If you do not understand a question, go on to the next one, answering the questions you know first—but make sure you mark an answer for each question. Go on to the next page if the test says "Continue" or "Go on." In a useful practice book for high-school students, Beck (2004) offered a series of sample examination questions covering multiple standards on the California English-Language Arts Content Standards.

Adapted Instruction

Thinking Skills for Common Core Standardized Tests

Under the Common Core standards, thinking skills are expected to play an ever-greater role in preparing students for college and career readiness. In science, students will formulate hypotheses and test evidence, providing explanations for phenomena observed and making use of cause-and-effect sentence structures. In mathematics, students will use specific vocabulary to pose and well as solve problems, and be able to support answers with the thinking processes that led them to their conclusions. In social sciences, students will draw information from original texts, weighing and comparing different points of view; as well as evaluating media sources for bias and validity. Students will be tasked with learning sophisticated language to match the demands of the content domains.

Williams (2007) questions the long-term effects of standardized testing on culturally and linguistically diverse students:

> What effect does the unrelenting emphasis on standardized literacy testing have on students' perception of the purposes and possibilities of literacy? By extension, what effect does testing have on their perception of the possibilities for themselves as readers and writers? . . . [T]eachers and researchers have argued that standardized testing works not from a set of objective standards somehow as constant as the North Star but from a set of cultural conceptions about literacy that are neither objective nor static. Students whose race or social class is not a part of the dominant culture often face more complex challenges in meeting the standards of that dominant culture. (pp. 70–71)

Nieto and Bode (2008) urge teachers to be proactive about testing:

> With a group of interested colleagues and parents, you can approach the local school committee and ask that standardized tests be kept to a minimum, that the results be used in more appropriate ways, and that students not be placed at risk because of the results of such tests. . . . [Y]ou can start an after-school tutoring program for students at your school. Try to get funding from your school system or the PTA, or even from a local business. (p. 128)

Teacher Observation and Evaluation

Teachers can document student progress and diagnose student needs by observing and evaluating students on an ongoing basis. They then communicate students' progress to students, to parents, and to administrators.

Observation-Based Assessment. As students interact and communicate using language, an observant teacher can note individual differences. Observations may be formal (e.g., miscue analysis, running record, Student Oral Language Observation Matrix [SOLOM]) or informal, such as anecdotal reports to record a cooperative or collaborative group working together; students telling a story, giving a report, or explaining information; or children using oral language in other ways. Multiple observations show student variety and progress (Crawford, 1993).

| **Example of Concept** | *Anecdotal Observations* |

Mrs. Feingold keeps a pad of 3" × 3" Post-it™ notes in the pocket of her jacket. When she observes a student's particular use of language, use of a particular learning style, or other noteworthy behavior, she jots the information on a note, including the student's name, date, and time of day. She then transfers this note to a small notebook for safekeeping.

Periodically, she files the notes by transferring them to a sheet of paper in each student's file. Just before parent conferences she duplicates this page—which contains as many as twelve notes side by side—as a permanent observational record of the student's language behaviors.

Adapted Instruction

Offering Feedback

There are various methods by which teachers can offer feedback: verbal praise, explaining a point of confusion, and informing if an answer is right or wrong; nonverbal feedback such as smiles, frowns, or nods; written feedback; individual, pair, group, or whole-class observations; promoting peer feedback; and immediate or delayed responses (Ong & Murugesan, 2007).

Student Self-Assessment. Student self-assessment can take several forms. Students can discuss their progress with one another; write reflection logs; use checklists and inventories; and participate in reading and writing conferences to determine their progress and needs for growth. They can ask themselves the following questions: What did I learn? What did I do well? What am I still confused about? What do I need help with? What do I want to learn more about? What am I going to work on next? (Gottlieb, 2007, p. 67).

Grading. A variety of approaches has been used to assign grades to English learners. Some schools that assign a *traditional A–F grade scale* in accordance with grade-level expectations do not lower performance standards for English learners in sheltered classes, although assignments are adjusted to meet the students' language levels. A *modified A–F grade scale* uses A–F grades based on achievement, effort, and behavior, with report card grades modified by a qualifier signifying work performed above, at, or below grade level. A third type of grade system is the *pass/fail grade scale* used by schools whose English learners are integrated into the regular classroom. This scale avoids comparing the English learners with English-proficient classmates (From the Classroom, 1991).

Some schools have begun to assign a numerical grade (1–4, with 4 being the highest score) according to a student's knowledge of state standards. For example, in second grade, if a child is required to "read fluently and accurately and with appropriate intonation and expression," the number grade reflects the mastery of this standard. Such ancillary factors as attendance and class participation do not influence this grade (Hernández, 2005).

Grading and assessment issues concern teachers of all students, but teachers of English learners face additional challenges. English learners' limited English affects their ability to communicate their content knowledge. Teachers and English learners may have different expectations and interpretations of the grade (Grognet, Jameson, Franco, & Derrick-Mescua, 2000). Answers to these issues are not easy. By working collaboratively with other teachers in the school, an overall schoolwide plan can be developed.

POINT ✦ COUNTERPOINT

Student Self-Assessment

Should students assess themselves? Farrell (2006) presents two sides of the argument:

POINT: Self-Assessment Works. "Self-assessment is easy to administer and it is quick. Also, students take more ownership in the assessment process, and may be more motivated to improve their language proficiency as a result" (p. 131).

COUNTERPOINT: Self-Assessment Is Not Helpful. "Both teachers and students may wonder if the students themselves are capable of assessing their own proficiency levels. Also, some peer assessment may be perceived of as a waste of time and unfair by the students if the teacher is not involved in the assessment process" (p. 131).

Implications for Teaching
Peer assessment works best when balanced with the teacher's formative and summative assessment.

Reflective teachers realize that students need to be motivated to "engage, aspire, take risks during learning endeavors" (Herrera, Murry, & Cabral, 2007, p. 260). Under standards-based assessment, grades should reflect mastery of the given curricular standards. Report-card grades best support instruction when students have taken part in authentic learning experiences and activities, have had opportunities for supervised practice, and have received timely feedback.

The following questions can guide decisions about a student's final grade:

- What information (scores) is the basis of the grade?
- Is this reflective of linguistic, academic, cognitive, and sociocultural aspects of performance?
- Are some aspects of learning weighted more than others?
- What role do cooperation, attitude, and motivation play in the final grade?

Adapted Instruction

A Grading and Assessment Plan: Equity for English Learners

- Grades belong to students. To increase a sense of responsibility and ownership, explain clearly the connection between class effort and grade criteria.
- Provide rubrics when work is assigned. If possible, show examples of desired work.
- Make "debriefing" a part of each assignment. Listen to students describe what was difficult and rewarding about the task. Take these factors into consideration during the next assignment.
- Distribute assessment across variable criteria to develop thinking skills and responsibility as well as emphasizing skill in reading and writing along.
- Develop a school-wide set of criteria for English learners that document progress across grade levels.
- Teach and test the acquisition of learning strategies as well as knowledge and facts.

Cautions about Testing

Tests are a significant part of the U.S. schooling system and are used in every classroom. When choosing standardized tests, teachers can consider the following guidelines (Worthen & Spandel, 1991) to help them determine the benefits and limitations of the test:

- Does the test correspond to the task that it measures?
- Does the score approximate the students' ability?
- How can the score be supplemented with other information?
- Does the test drive the curriculum?
- Is the test a fair sample of the students' skills and behaviors?
- Is the test being used unfairly to compare students and schools with one another?
- Are tests that involve minimum standards being used to make critical decisions regarding classification of students?

Cole (2007) explains what happens when testing dominates the conversation—and instruction—in the classroom:

> Teachers begin to explain the relevance or purpose of materials and activities not in terms of learning but in terms of state or national testing. When students ask "why" they have to do something, they are told it's for the test. . . . [W]e are not encouraging our students to learn for learning's sake. We are not showing them that the identities that they have available to them in this situation are valued because of their literacy, their numeracy, or their position in civic engagement. We are sending them the message that they are blips on a chart." (p. 7)

Reporting Assessment Results to Parents

Teachers are expected to communicate the results of assessment to parents, whether through grades on a report card or informal conferences (see Chapter 9) or by interpreting the results of standardized tests. Airasian (2005) gave the following advice to teachers: When explaining standardized test scores, start with general information about the test and its purpose. Describe the student's overall performance, with strengths and weaknesses; pick one or two areas (e.g., math and reading), and describe the percentile rank. To help the parent more fully understand the student's level of achievement, give the context of the student's general classroom performance. There is no need to explain everything, but rather give enough of an overview so that parents can get a clear idea of the child's assessment results.

Best Practices in Testing

The most effective assessment of what has been learned is that which most closely matches what is taught. Test content should reflect the curriculum, build on the experiences of students and be relevant to their lives, and be matched to their developmental level. If possible the conditions for instruction and assessment should be identical; the same type of material should be tested as was presented during instruction, with the same language and student interaction (Gottlieb, n.d.). The use of similar conditions helps students to access and remember what they have learned.

Identification, Assessment, and Placement of English Learners in the Schools

More than half the states have specific laws and provide procedural guidelines regarding identification procedures for English learners. Many states also have procedures for redesignating students and for placing them in mainstream classes. Generally speaking, students are first evaluated; then, if identified as needing ELD services, they are placed in suitable programs, if available. Ideally, the placement test results correspond directly to an instructional plan that can be implemented immediately by a classroom teacher. Once in a program, students are then periodically reevaluated for purposes of reclassification.

Identification Procedures for English Learners

A variety of methods are used to identify English learners needing services. The *home language survey,* a short form administered by school districts to determine the language spoken at home, is among the most frequently used methods of identifying students whose primary language is not English. *Registration* and *enrollment* information collected from incoming students can be used to identify students with a home language other than English. *Interviews* may provide opportunities to identify students. School districts are required by state and federal mandates to administer a placement test before assigning a new student to an instructional program if a home language survey indicates that the student's primary language is not English.

Assessment for Placement

Once students are identified, their level of English proficiency needs to be determined. Ideally, the assessment is done by staff with the language skills to communicate in the family's native language. Parents and students should be provided with orientation about the assessment and placement process and the expectation and services of the school system.

Various states in the United States use a mixture of measures to evaluate students for ELD services. These include the following: oral proficiency tests, teacher judgment, parent request, literacy tests in English, prior instructional services, writing samples in English, achievement tests in English, teacher ratings of English proficiency, oral proficiency tests in the native language, and achievement tests in the native language (Zehler, Fleischman, Hopstock, Stephenson, Pendzick, & Sapru, 2003).

Specific tests have been designed to help districts place English learners. For example, the Language Assessment Scales (LAS), a standardized test with mean scores and standard deviations based on various age groups, is designed to measure oral-language skills in English and Spanish. Another frequently used proficiency test is the Bilingual Syntax Measure (BSM), which measures oral proficiency in English and/or Spanish grammatical structures and language dominance.

Educators who draw from a variety of information sources can view students' needs in a broader context and thus design a language program to meet these needs. Teacher-devised checklists and observational data gathered as students participate in integrated learning activities can be used to confirm or adjust student placement (Lucas & Wagner, 1999).

As a caution, teachers and school personnel need to be aware that even after administering these placement tests and gathering placement information, appropriate academic placement may be difficult. First, placement tests measure only language proficiency. They say nothing about a student's academic background. Students may be highly prepared in certain subject areas and very weak in others. They may be very strong academically but have poor English skills, or, conversely, have excellent English skills and few academic skills. Placement by age can be a problem. Students may need much more time in the system to learn English, but placement in a lower grade may lead to social adjustment problems.

While acknowledging that NCLB has not provided enough help for urban school districts that are impacted by large numbers of English learners, some educational leaders recognize that the data provided by frequent testing can assist teachers in identifying students who need additional help (Domenech, 2008). Using ongoing assessment, teachers can help struggling students catch up before the end-of-year summative assessment documents school failure.

One example of assessment tracking is the English Language Proficiency Collaboration and Research Consortium (ELPCRC), a group of six states that use CTB/McGraw-Hill's LAS Links, a student tracking system that ties together assessment and instruction. Students are tested online, and the computer software evaluates performance and provides needed remediation. This system provides assessment–instruction integration that changes the role of teachers into managers rather than direct providers of instruction.

In summary, the procedures to identify and place English learners are as follows: When a student enrolls in a school district, administer the Home Language Survey. If the student has a primary language other than English, administer an English-language proficiency test. If the student is an English learner, administer achievement and placement tests in English and in the primary language. If the student is eligible for support services, notify parents of options and proceed with placement (Gottlieb, 2006).

Redesignation/Exit Procedures

School districts need to establish reclassification criteria to determine when English learners have attained the English-language skills necessary to succeed in an English-only classroom. The reclassification process may utilize multiple criteria including, but not limited to, the following:

- Be based on objective standards.
- Measure speaking, comprehension, reading, and writing.
- Ensure that all academic deficits are remediated.
- Include district evidence that students can participate meaningfully in the general program.

Some districts organize bilingual education advisory committees to ensure ethnic parent representation and participation in implementing redesignation criteria that are reliable, valid, and useful. National test norms or district, regional, or state norms can be employed for purposes of reclassification. States set various cutoff scores on language and achievement tests that are used as criteria for proficiency in the process of redesignation.

Example of Concept · *Criteria for Redesignating English Learners*

Verdugo Hills High School has various criteria for redesignating students. The school first asserts that "[r]edesignated students speak at least two languages. They learned English as a Second Language and proved their command of English by passing a redesignation test." The students must pass the following:

- CELDT (California English Language Development Test)
- ELA (English Language Arts) section of the CST (California Standards Test) with a score of Basic or higher
- Math and English or ESL 3/4 classes with a C or higher (Verdugo Hills High School, 2004)

Limitations of Assessment

Tests play a significant role in placing and reclassifying English learners. Often, pressure is applied for programs to redesignate students as fluent English-speaking in a short period of time and tests may be used to place English learners into mainstream programs before they are ready. Continuing support—such as tutoring, follow-up assessment, and primary-language help—is often not available after reclassification.

Standardized tests, though designed to be fair, are not necessarily well suited as measures of language ability or achievement for English learners. Both the testing situation and the test content may be rife with difficulties for English learners.

Anxiety. All students experience test anxiety, but this anxiety can be compounded if the test is alien to the students' cultural background and experiences. Allowing students to take practice exams may familiarize them with the test formats and reduce test anxiety.

Time Limitations. Students may need more time to answer individual questions due to the time needed for mental translation and response formulation. Some students may need a time extension or should be given untimed tests.

Rapport. When testers and students do not share the same language or dialect, the success of the testing may be reduced. Students may not freely verbalize if they are shy or wary of the testing situation. Rapport may also suffer if students resent the testing situation itself.

Cultural Differences. Students from some cultural groups may not feel comfortable making eye contact with a test administrator. Students from cultures that discourage individuals from displaying knowledge may not be quick to answer questions and may be reluctant to guess unless they are certain they are accurate. They may be embarrassed to volunteer a response or receive positive feedback about their performance (Cloud et al., 2000).

Problematic Test Content

For the most part, language placement tests are well suited for assessing language. Other tests, however, particularly achievement tests, may contain translation problems or bias that affect the performance of English learners.

Equivalent First- and Second-Language Versions. Translating an English-language achievement test into another language or vice versa to create equivalent vocabulary items may cause some lack of correspondence in the frequency of the items. For example, *belfry* in English is a much less frequently understood term than its Spanish counterpart, *campanario*.

Linguistic Bias. There are several forms of linguistic bias. *Geographic bias* happens when test items feature terms used in particular geographic regions but that are not universally shared. *Dialectical bias* occurs when a student is tested using expressions relevant to certain dialect speakers that are not known to others. *Language-specific bias* is created when a test developed for use with one language is used with another language.

Cultural Bias. Tests may be inappropriate not only because the language provides a dubious cue for students but also because the content may represent overt or subtle bias. The values of the dominant culture appearing in test items may be understood differently or not at all by English learners.

Cultural content appearing in tests may provide difficulty for students without that cultural background. Many students never experience common European American food items such as bacon; common sports in the United States may be unfamiliar; musical instruments may be mysterious to students; even nursery rhymes and children's stories may refer only to one culture.

Example of Concept *Cultural Bias in Standardized Tests*

Tae Sung, from Korea, looked at question number one.

1. **Her tooth came out so she put it**
    A. On top of the refrigerator
    B. Under the tree
    C. Under her pillow
    D. None of the above

In Korea, a child throws the lost tooth up on the roof so that the next one will grow in straight, but none of the answers said that. Tae Sung knew that "on top" meant up so he marked the first answer. Borden, from the Marshall Islands, also looked a long time at the question. In his country, you throw your tooth in the ocean for good luck. So Borden marked "none of the above" (Laturnau, n.d.).

Class Bias. Test content may represent a class bias; for example, the term *shallots* appeared on a nationally administered standardized achievement test, but only students whose families consume gourmet foods may be familiar with the term. Other such terms are *scallion* (another troublemaker from the onion family) and *vacuum cleaner.*

Content Bias. Even mathematics, a domain that many believe to be language-free, has been shown to cause difficulties, because language proficiency plays a relatively more important role than previously suspected.

Example of Concept   *Language in Mathematics Testing*

Using open-ended questions that ask the students to explain or describe can increase the difficulty of a math test. English learners can be overwhelmed by the words; not simply in decoding, but also in comprehending the problem as a whole. Complex problems must be stated in straightforward language.

In the Common Core State Standards that are being adopted by most states, the language load in mathematics classes will continue to be a challenge for English learners, with the additional requirement that students are going to be expected to engage in a wider range of complex problem solving. All students, including our English learners, will have to apply more linguistic skills in their math classes. Clearly teachers must reconsider the idea that "math is a universal language"—we definitely need language adaptation for our English learners. (Spencer, 2013)

Interpretation of Test Results

One last caution in the assessment of English learners is to understand the emphasis of the test: Is it on language proficiency or on content knowledge? When testing content, educators should select or devise tasks on which English learners can achieve, regardless of their language proficiency. When scoring the test, teachers must evaluate students' responses to distinguish those that are conceptually correct but may contain language problems from those that are conceptually incorrect.

The accompanying box offers attributes for the appropriate assessment of English learners.

Attributes of an Appropriate Assessment Plan for English Learners

- Both content knowledge and language proficiency are tested.
- Students' content knowledge and abilities in the native language as well as in English are assessed.
- Various techniques are used to measure content knowledge and skills (e.g., portfolios, observations, anecdotal records, interviews, checklists, exhibits, students' self-appraisals, writing samples, dramatic renditions, and criterion-referenced tests).
- The teacher is aware of the purpose of the assessment (e.g., whether the test is intended to measure verbal or writing skills, language proficiency, or content knowledge).

- Students' backgrounds, including their educational experiences and parents' literacy, are taken into account.
- Context is added to assessment tasks in the following ways:
  1. Incorporates familiar classroom material as a stimulus, such as brief quotations, charts, graphics, cartoons, and works of art
  2. Includes questions for small-group discussion and individual writing
  3. Mirrors learning processes with which students are familiar, such as the writing process and reading conferencing activities

- Administration procedures match classroom instructional practices (e.g., cooperative small groups, individual conferences, and assessment in the language of instruction).
- Extra time is given to complete or respond to assessment tasks.
- Other accommodations are made, such as simplifying directions in English and/or paraphrasing in the student's native language, as well as permitting students to use dictionaries or word lists.

Source: Based on August and Pease-Alvarez (1996) and Navarrete and Gustke (1996).

Technical Concepts

A good test has three qualities: validity, reliability, and practicality. A test must test what it purports to test (valid), be dependable and consistent (reliable), and be applicable to the situation (practical).

Validity

A test is *valid* if it measures what it claims to be measuring. A test has *content validity* if it samples the content that it claims to test in some representative way. For example, if a reading curriculum includes training in reading for inference, then a test of that curriculum would include a test of inference. *Empirical validity* is a measure of how effectively a test relates to some other known measure. One kind of empirical validity is *predictive:* how well the test correlates with subsequent success or performance. A second type of empirical validity is *concurrent:* how well the test correlates with another measure used at the same time. Teachers often apply this concept of concurrent validity when they grade examinations. Intuitively, they expect the better students to receive better scores. This is a check for concurrent validity between the examination and the students' daily performance.

Reliability

A test is *reliable* if it yields predictably similar scores when it is taken again. Although many variables can affect a student's test score—such as error introduced by fatigue, hunger, or poor lighting—these variables usually do not introduce large deviations in students' scores. A student who scores 90 percent on a teacher-made test probably has scored 45 on one-half of the test and 45 on the other half, regardless of whether the halves are divided by odd/even items or first/last sequence.

Practicality

A test may be valid and reliable but cost too much to administer either in time or in money. A highly usable test should be relatively easy to administer and score.

Many of the assessment practices and issues touched on in this chapter are further discussed in the online report "An Examination of Assessment of Limited English Proficient Students" (Zehler, Hopstock, Fleischman, & Greniuk, 1994).

One last criterion: Tests must be fair. This is not only true for individual tests, but for a testing system: "A legally defensible assessment system must stand on three pillars: validity, reliability, and fairness" (McDaniel & Wilde, 2008, p. 107).

Brewer, García, and Aguilar (2007), all key figures in Los Angeles Unified School District, call for an alternative accountability strategy for English learners:

> Congress should require and fund states to develop content-based standardized tests for EL students in their native languages. . . . [T]est scores shouldn't be factored into decisions about a school's proficiency until solid native-language tests are developed or EL students have time to learn the English they need to perform well. (p. A29)

Critics of NCLB are firm in contrasting its shortcomings with alternative visions. Alfie Kohn, author of *The Schools Our Children Deserve: Moving Beyond Traditional Classrooms and "Tougher Standards,"* has been a persistent critic of the standardized testing movement in general and of the emphasis on testing that underlies NCLB in particular. He points out that one does not need a federal law that tests children in order to identify schools that are underperforming; such schools are found in poor neighborhoods. A long-term plan to provide increased resources and better teachers is the necessary solution. He writes, "This law . . . must be replaced with a policy that honors local autonomy, employs better assessments, addresses the root cause of inequity and supports a rich curriculum" (Kohn, 2007, p. 7A).

Regardless of how valid, reliable, and practical a test may be, if it serves only the teachers' and the institution's goals, the students' language progress may not be promoted. Testing must instead be an integral part of a learning environment that encourages students to acquire a second language as a means to fulfill personal and academic goals.

LEARNING MORE

Further Reading

Scenarios for ESL Standards-Based Assessment (TESOL, 2001) is a useful resource offering principles for effective assessment of English learners, along with ideas for collecting and recording information, analyzing and interpreting assessment information, and using this information for reporting and decision making. An extensive set of examples drawn from K–12 instruction is included to assist the practitioner in using a wide range of assessment strategies including the use of journals and feedback forms, student conferences, performance tasks, commercially developed, norm-referenced tests, student observational and anecdotal records, rubrics, and assessment data-management systems.

Web Search

What are the procedures used to test and redesignate English learners in your state? What are the advantages of using multiple criteria to assess students' L1 and L2 proficiencies?

Exploration

Visit the language evaluation center in a local school district. Describe how English learners are identified. Ask for a copy of the home language survey (or equivalent), if available. Is there a coherent written plan available to parents about the process of identification, classification, and placement? Describe the testing procedure that follows the home language survey in which students are classified according to English-language level. Describe how this results in classroom placement. Once placed in classrooms, what kind of curriculum and instruction does each student receive?

Experiment

Go to the web practice site for the Test of English as a Foreign Language (TOEFL; online at http://toeflpractice.ets.org) and take a practice test. Compare your score with acceptable score ranges for international students. Would you be admitted to study in the United States if you were not already a native-English speaker?

MyEducationLab™

Authentic Assessment for ELLs

Authentic assessment may take many forms. In this video, classroom examples demonstrate that how students communicate their understanding is as important as how they solve the problem.

> To access the video, go to MyEducationLab (www.myeducationlab.com), choose the Díaz-Rico text, and log in to MyEducationLab for English Language Learners. Select the topic Assessment, and watch the video entitled "Authentic Assessment for ELLs."

Answer the following questions:

1. Why does this student task qualify as an example of performance-based assessment? What benefits are there to this type of assessment for ELLs?

2. What scaffolds does the teacher provide for the assessment task? Can you suggest others that would be appropriate for ELLs at lower levels of language proficiency?

Culture

*Cultural Diversity in the United States,
Culturally Responsive Schooling, and the Role
of the Family in Schools*

Part Four contains a broad look at culture, offering a historical background on cultural diversity and its treatment in the United States (Chapter 8), and exploring how culture influences every aspect of life, including schooling; how the intercultural educator employs culturally responsive schooling (Chapter 9);

and how schools can involve families (Chapter 10). The accompanying figure highlights Part Four of the theoretical model presented in the introduction. It is evident in the model that culture is a pervasive influence on schooling, permeating every other aspect.

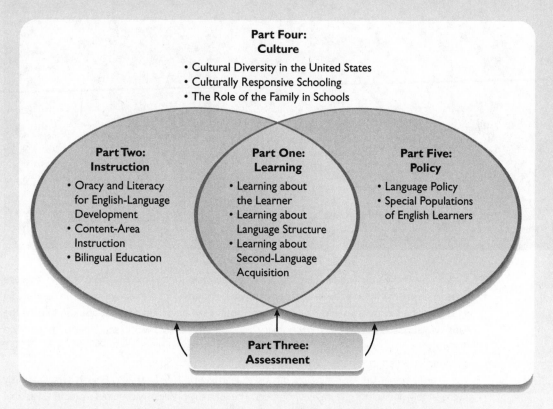

Theoretical Model for CLAD Culture: Cultural Diversity in the United States, Culturally Responsive Schooling, and the Role of the Family in Schools

8

Cultural Diversity

Immigration has brought the world into U.S. schools.

I grew up in New York City. My parents spoke to me in English, yet I picked up the Spanish language when I heard them speak to each other and when my grandmother spoke to me in Spanish. So I learned Spanish through informal exposure. I sound like a Spanish speaker, because I heard the language at home. But English is my primary language. My parents would send me to Puerto Rico for summer vacations, and that forced me to build on what I already knew. Plus, my aunt scolded me when I lacked the needed vocabulary to communicate in Spanish!

I believe that the facilitating conditions to learning both Spanish and English simultaneously were largely due to my cultural environment. The learning process was quite favorable. I was able to speak to my neighborhood friends and function in school with English. And at the same time I was able to speak to my extended family members in Spanish and attend church with my family in a Spanish service. My family and religious instruction were very instrumental in my upbringing. The communication that was facilitated through both languages was a motivation to keep both languages alive.

Darlene Purcell (2013)

They still come—a medical student from India who remains in Knoxville to set up a practice; a Danish au pair worker who meets a U.S. college student and extends her work visa; a Vietnamese grandmother who follows her daughter, who followed her teenage sons; a Mexican lawyer who sets up an import–export practice in Tijuana and San Diego; Romanian orphans brought to the United States through an adoption service; a Hong Kong capitalist who settles his family in San José while he commutes by jet to maintain his businesses. The immigration that has enriched the United States shows little sign of abating.

Each successive wave of immigration has had unique characteristics and a distinct impact on U.S. education. Whether attracted to the United States or forced here from their native country, immigrants have brought with them cultural, political, religious, and economic values, along with multiple tongues and various skills. Immigrants contribute material aspects of their culture (crafts, foods, technology) as well as nonmaterial aspects (family values, spiritual beliefs, medical practices). During the process of settlement, these immigrants require social and educational services to help them adapt to their new environment.

More than two-thirds of English learners in the United States are in the preschool through elementary age range. This population is diverse, with ethnic backgrounds originating in the peoples of Asia, the Middle East, Mexico, Central and South America, Africa, and the Caribbean, among others. Although Spanish speakers make up the majority of the English-learner population, even those in this group vary greatly on such factors as country of birth and family origin, rural/urban background and socioeconomic status, history of family education, and reasons for immigration to the United States. This diversity comprises a complex educational environment.

The extent of immigration and the policies that shape it have been controversial issues since the founding of this country. This great experiment—the United States of America—has required the innovation, fabrication, and synthesis of whole new patterns of existence. Those who have participated in this great cultural amalgamation have been themselves transformed. This transformation has not ended and will not end in the foreseeable future. We have the unique opportunity to enjoy and value it.

Historical Perspectives

The North American continent has received people from all over the world. Diverse immigrants have caused continuous intermingling and confrontation with indigenous populations and among themselves. In what was to become the United States, these contacts began when the Europeans arrived in the original thirteen colonies and met the many cultures of the Native Americans. Later, the colonists imported African slaves, who brought with them the various cultures of West Africa. Then, as settlers moved toward the interior, they encountered different native groups in the plains and pueblos. In the mid-nineteenth century, English-speaking Americans expanded into the Southwest, home to Native Americans as well as the Spanish-speaking heirs of land grants dating back to the sixteenth century. Finally, in the nineteenth and twentieth centuries, immigrant groups from all over the world poured into the United States, coming into contact with the descendants of all earlier groups.

From this contact came the expectation that these many cultures would merge into a homogeneous, shared national culture. The idea that the United States was a "melting pot" generated pressure on newcomers to conform in thought and behavior—to assimilate. For some, assimilation was easier than for others, and language, clothing, and other forms of distinction were easy to erase. For others, however, discarding traditions was not so easy. The Hassidic Jews, the Amish, the Hopi, the Navajo—those clinging to religious rites, lifestyles, or property without choosing to compromise—resisted assimilation pressures. These groups and others have created a more modern metaphor, that of the salad bowl: a mix in which the individual ingredients are not melted but, rather, retain their flavor and texture.

Another powerful metaphor is that of the kaleidoscope, in which the shifting patterns of culture, language, and race combine and recombine ceaselessly, yet are bound together by common ideals. The contributions of different ethnic cultures to the United States cannot be underestimated, yet the picture is not uniformly sunny. Dark and sordid episodes of conflict between, and discrimination against, various groups cloud the history of this nation. Minorities have systematically been denied opportunities and rights enjoyed the more privileged. Despite the hardships many have endured, ethnic groups in this country have become inseparable threads in the cultural tapestry of the United States.

Contributions

The North American continent had a myriad of indigenous cultures characterized by high levels of civilization before the European invasion began. These civilizations were either obliterated or they accommodated the arrival of new cultures through the creation of a hybrid New World. For the most part, European invaders attempted to replicate the life they had lived in the Old World, and those who were not a part of this mainstream of culture had the choice of assimilating or leading a separate existence. Those who could not assimilate were often treated as outsiders.

> **Did You Know?** According to author Kay Porterfield (2002), "Ancient American Indians were building pyramids before the Egyptians. They domesticated corn from a wild grass. They performed complicated surgeries. They also knew how to work with platinum and how to vulcanize rubber, two things Europeans could not do until the 1800s" (p. 1).

FIND OUT MORE ABOUT ...

Native American Contributions

Porterfield, K., & Keoke, E. (2003). *American Indian Contributions to the World: 15,000 Years of Invention and Innovation.* New York: Checkmark Books.

    This reference contains approximately 450 entries that detail and document the intentiveness of North, Meso-, and South American Indians.

Porterfield, K., & Keoke, E. (2005). *American Indian Contributions to the World: 15,000 Years of Invention and Innovation, Grades 4–9.*

A five-volume collection that introduces young readers to the advances that American Indians have made throughout history. Volumes include Food, Farming, and Hunting; Buildings, Clothing, and Art; Trade, Transportation, and Warfare; Medicine and Health; Science and Technology. (To order, visit www.infobasepublishing.com/search.aspx?q=porterfield.)

Many contributions of nonmainstream peoples remained just beneath the surface of the American dream—in some cases, *too* far beneath to influence the main paths of culture. For example, the spiritual heritage of the Native Americans—the deep and abiding respect for nature—has not had the impact on the dominant culture that may be necessary for the survival of the flora and fauna of the continent.

Native Americans. In many ways, the indigenous civilizations of precolonial North America were more highly developed than European cultures. The cities and roads of the Aztec culture astounded the European conquerors. The agricultural systems featured advanced forms of irrigation, with the cultivation of foods that were unknown to the Old World. Some of these foods (potato, corn, peanuts, and other grains) were later to provide 60 percent of Europe's diet and were responsible for the greatest explosion of population since the Neolithic Age (Feagin & Feagin, 1993). Substances from the New World (cocoa, tobacco, coca) were to provide Europeans with exhilarating addictions in the centuries to come.

Medicinal products from the Americas revolutionized the treatment of disease in Europe and still fascinate pharmacologists with as yet untapped treasures. The political systems of native peoples ranged from the religious theocracies in Mexico, sources of advanced astronomical and mathematical achievement unparalleled in the world of that day, to the democratic councils of the Algonquin, Iroquois, and other nations that were much admired by Benjamin Franklin and Thomas Jefferson (Hardt, 1992).

African Americans. The culture of African Americans has evolved from an African base that survived despite harshly limiting circumstances: Slaves could bring little or none of the material aspects of African culture with them. The aspects that survived did so in the hearts and minds of those who were forcibly moved to the New World. The present-day legacies of the African past are evident not only in the dance, music, literature, and religion of contemporary African Americans, but also in the sheer

> **Did You Know?**   Although African Americans comprise 14 percent of the U.S. population, they account for more than 42 percent of all students enrolled in public schools (Russell, 2008). The fact that only 2.4 percent of teachers are African American men and 5.6 percent are African American women leaves a racial and cultural gap in the preparation of African American teachers. In the top twenty urban school districts in America (with a total enrollment of 5 million students), more than 80 percent of the students are African American, yet more than 70 percent of teachers in urban schools are European American.

power of the patterns of everyday life and language that were strong enough to survive despite centuries of oppression. Ironically, the genre of music most associated with the United States—jazz—is permeated with African American influence. One could argue that the music of the United States would not exist in its current form without this influence. Even today the endlessly mutating forms of African American culture constitute an ongoing avant-garde, aspects of which are alternately embraced and denigrated by the wider society (some say, appropriated and abused by European American performers and producers—see Dyson, 1996).

Despite substantial discrimination, a long line of African American writers, such as James Weldon Johnson, Claude McKay, Richard Wright, Ralph Ellison, James

FIND OUT MORE ABOUT ...

African American Contributions in the Arts

African American Contributions to Theatrical Dance
www.theatredance.com

This website lists the characteristics of African dance that have contributed to various dance movements. Different types of dances are described.

Afrocentric Voices (www.afrovoices.com) profiles African American musicians, performers, and composers who pioneered forms of vocal music such as opera, art songs, and Negro spirituals composed for concert performance. These master musicians sponsored talented youth to pursue careers in classical music by advising, encouraging, mentoring, and establishing scholarships and competitions for young musicians.

> **Did You Know?**   Over his lifetime, Elijah McCoy, a Black Canadian American inventor, was granted fifty-two patents, most of which were for improvements in steam engines, although he did patent a folding ironing board and self-propelled lawn sprinkler. In 1916 he patented what he described as his greatest invention, the "graphite lubricator," which used powdered graphite suspended in oil to lubricate cylinders of "superheater" train engines. Others tried to copy his oil-dripping cup but none was as successful, prompting McCoy's customers to ask for "the real McCoy"—hence the expression (http://inventors.about.com/od/mstartinventors/a/Elijah_McCoy.htm).

FIND OUT MORE ABOUT ...

African American Contributors to Science

The Top Ten African American Inventors

http://teacher. scholastic.com/activities/bhistory
/inventors/ index.htm

> This teacher- and student-friendly website provides short introductions to ten African American inventors and links to other sites with further information.

African American Scientists Bibliography

(California Academy of Sciences Library)

> This archive contains weblinks to Benjamin Banneker, inventor; David Blackwell, mathematician

and games theorist; George R. Carruthers, research physicist and astroscientist; George W. Carver, inventor; Jewel P. Cobb, biologist and physiologist; Patricia Cowings, NASA scientist; Christine Darden, aerospace engineer; Mathew Henson, Arctic explorer; Fern Y. Hunt, mathematician; and a host of other notables in science (http://researcharchive.calacademy.org/research/ library/biodiv/biblio/Africansci-update.htm).

Baldwin, Imamu Baraka (LeRoi Jones), Maya Angelou, Toni Morrison, and Langston Hughes, have enriched U.S. literature and inspired new generations of poets, writers, and rappers. The religion of Black America has been a source of sustenance to African Americans since the arrival of the first slaves and has played a major role in fomenting protest for social justice. The nonviolent civil disobedience movement from the mid-1950s to the 1970s had religious underpinnings, with prominent minister-leaders such as the Reverend Martin Luther King, Jr.

African Americans have made substantial contributions to science. In the years preceding 1900, more than 1,000 patents were awarded to African American inventors, despite the fact that slaves were barred from applying for patents. For example, Jo Anderson, a slave in the Cyrus McCormick household, was the coinventor of the McCormick reaper. A slave of Jefferson Davis, president of the Confederate States of America, invented a boat propeller but was unable to patent the device. In the twentieth century, major scientists were active in such fields as aviation; electrical, mechanical, and construction engineering; rocketry; and many others. African Americans who have contributed in social science and philosophy include W. E. B. DuBois, Marcus Garvey, Elijah Muhammad, Frederick Douglass, E. Franklin Frazier, Oliver C. Cox, and Malcolm X (Appiah & Gates, 2003).

The story of Ernest E. Just illustrates the difficulties faced by African American scientists in their ascent to prominence. Just, a marine biologist, rose to become vice president of the American Society of Zoologists but was once refused admittance to Rockefeller Institute. Although Just authored over sixty scholarly papers and was a leading authority on egg fertilization, artificial parthenogenesis, and cell division, he was never appointed to a European American university. By contrast, George Washington Carver never aspired to take his place alongside European American scientists in their well-equipped, well-financed research facilities but revolutionized the agronomy of the peanut working in his small laboratory in Tuskegee.

Example of Concept

An African American History Curriculum

A partnership between the Baltimore City School System, the Reginald F. Lewis Museum, and local businesses has resulted in a new curriculum of forty-three lessons for elementary- and middle-school students grades 4–8 that features African American history. Field trips, primary-source reading materials, audio and video clips, and activities that provide for a variety of learning styles make history come alive for Baltimore's students. As of 2008, more than 1,400 students have visited local sites of importance to African American history (Weber, 2008).

Hispanics/Latinos. Hispanic contributions, which predate the landing of the Pilgrims at Plymouth Rock, have also been significant. Hispanic settlers in the Southwest helped lay the foundations for the agricultural, mining, and cattle industries on which early city and state economies were built (Hispanic Concerns Study Committee, 1987). This influence continues today. With the influx of Cubans during the 1960s, Miami was transformed, becoming a vibrant international and bicultural metropolis. New York and its environs contain more Puerto Ricans than the island of Puerto Rico. Los Angeles is now the second-largest Latin American city in the world.

Although Hispanics living in the United States can trace their roots to several different countries, a common denominator of Hispanic culture in the United States includes language, religious beliefs and practices, holidays, and life patterns. Values shared among Hispanics include the importance of interdependence and cooperation of the immediate and extended family and the importance of emotional relationships. As the mainstream culture comes into more contact with the Hispanic culture, it is beginning to recognize the importance of these family values.

In politics, Hispanic Americans have influenced urban life and education. The political impetus behind bilingual education stems from the culmination of Cuban immigrant pressure in Florida and the "Chicano Power" movement of the 1960s. A lasting contribution of this bilingual legislation may be current attempts to preserve the "small incidence" languages of Native Americans and Micronesia, linguistic resources that are endangered. Thus, Hispanic leadership has helped to preserve cultural resources in unforeseen ways.

Did You Know?

The Spanish governor of the Louisiana Territory, Bernardo de Galvez, provided the armies of General George Washington and General George Rogers Clarke with gunpowder, rifles, bullets, blankets, medicine, and supplies. Once Spain entered the Revolutionary War on the side of the Americans, Galvez raised an army of Spanish and Cuban soldiers, Choctaw Indians, and black former slaves that beat off the British attack in 1780 and gained control of the Mississippi River, thus frustrating a British plan to encircle the American colonies. After the war, because of the generous assistance that Galvez gave some European Americans who wanted to settle Texas, they named their city after him, Galveston (Padilla, 1998).

FIND OUT MORE ABOUT ...

Hispanic American Contributions

Impacto, Influencia, Cambio
www.smithsonianeducation.org/scitech
/impacto/graphic/index.html

This site highlights the lives and accomplishments of inventors, aviators, astronauts, and the everyday people of Latin America and the southwestern United States who have affected science and technology.

In literature and the other arts, Hispanic Americans have made significant contributions. An impressive folk tradition of Spanish songs and ballads has maintained a musical current containing the history, joys, and sorrows of the Mexican American, Puerto Rican, and Cuban experiences. Spanish radio and television stations and newspapers have played a major role in sustaining the language and reinforcing the values of Spanish America.

Spanish words have enriched the minds and tongues of North Americans. Fiction and poetry, in both languages, affirm Hispanic heritage and identity. Puerto Rican and Mexican American theater has dramatized the struggles for a voice. The public art of Mexico is a centuries-old tradition, with the colorful *steles* of the Aztecs and Mayans resonating through time and reappearing in the murals of the barrios and the public art of cities throughout the Southwest. Art, to the Hispanic, is a breath of culture, and artists, like intellectuals, are esteemed as cultural leaders. The culinary contributions of Hispanics are legion and include enchiladas from Mexico, black beans from Cuba, *mangú* from the Dominican Republic, and *pasteles* from Puerto Rico.

Asian Americans. Contributions of the Pacific Rim peoples to the United States will be of increasing importance in the twenty-first century. The economic power of Asian capital stems not only from Japanese post–World War II efforts but also from the Chinese diaspora that has provided capital for economic investment in much of Southeast Asia, Indonesia, Australia, and California. Although Chinese and Japanese immigration to western America was severely curtailed throughout the history of the United States, through sheer force of numbers and the volume of international trade, Asian economic and cultural influences on the United States have been consistent.

Did You Know? A Chinese American horticulturist helped to develop Florida's frost-resistant citrus fruit and paved the way for the state to compete in the citrus industry against California. Another Chinese American patented the process to make evaporated milk. There are Chinese American astronauts who go into space, and a Chinese American scientist helped to develop the fabric to make the space suits.

Source: Lin (2002, pp. 2–3).

Table 8.1 Websites with Resources for Teaching Asian Americans

www.asianamericanbooks.com	K–12 books and materials for Asian American cultural awareness
www.teachingforchange.org	Books, DVDs, CDs, and videos on the Asian American experience
www.chabotcollege.edu/Library/subjectindex /AsianAmericanStudies.htm	Asian Americans/Pacific Islanders Studies website index and list of reference books
www.csun.edu/asianamericanstudies	Resources for community activism; speakers' bureau
www.cetel.org/res.html	Gateway to online exploration of Asian American history, culture, media, and curricular resources
www.lib.uci.edu/online/subject/asiaamer.html	A comprehensive guide to information about Asian Americans and Pacific Islanders

The Asian population in the United States has grown forty-six percent between 1900 and 2010, to a total of 17 million, according to the U.S. Census Bureau (Trounson, 2012). This is four times the rate of growth of the U.S. population as a whole. Most Americans who identify as Asians live in cities, with New York City leading at 1.3 million; six of the top twelve cities are in California, led by Los Angeles at 483,585.

The cultures of Asia, characterized by unparalleled continuity from ancient times to the present, have contributed to Western culture in innumerable ways. The U.S. fascination with Asian cultures has included the martial arts, Eastern spiritual philosophies, fireworks, acupuncture, and Asian food, décor, and gardening.

The chief stumbling block to greater acceptance of Asian influences in the United States is the perceived linguistic barrier. The fact that more Asians speak English than the reverse closes the doors to a deeper knowledge of Asian cultures for many Americans. Perhaps the current generation of high-school students will begin to bridge this gap; Japanese is now taught in 563 U.S. schools, approximately 125 of which are in Hawaii, and Mandarin in eighty-five, of which almost half are in Washington state (Center for Advanced Research on Language Acquisition, 2001). Table 8.1 offers a variety of web-based resources for promoting the educational success of Asian Americans.

Arab Americans. Other groups as well have been ignored or remain invisible in the mainstream literature and education. However, events can propel a particular group to the forefront. Such is the case of Arab Americans, who are suddenly the object of

Did You Know?   In the summer of 1895, Kahlil Gibran arrived in New York from a small village in Lebanon. He became a well-known painter and writer. His most famous book, *The Prophet,* remains a bestseller sixty-two years after his death.

FIND OUT MORE ABOUT ...

Arab American Contributions

www.aaiusa.org
Divided into areas such as military, politics, sports, activism, business, law, entertainment, education, art

and literature, fashion, and science and medicine, this website lists and briefly describes leading Arab Americans in these fields.

much media attention. Because words such as *terrorism* and *anti-Americanism* arise, the ELD teacher may need to help students fight stereotypes and misinformation about this group.

Several waves of immigrants from Arabic-speaking countries have been settling in the United States since the 1880s. Unlike the previously mentioned groups, most Arab Americans have been able to assimilate into American life, and eighty percent of them are American citizens. They work in all sectors of society; are leaders in many professions and organizations; have a strong commitment to family, economic, and educational achievements; and are making contributions to all aspects of American life (Arab American Institute Foundation, n.d.).

Among other impressive contributions include those of surgeon Michael DeBakey, who invented the heart pump; comedian and actor Danny Thomas, the founder of St. Jude's Children's Research Hospital; and lawyer Edward Masry, who, along with Erin Brockovich, filed a class action lawsuit against Pacific Gas and Electric for polluting the drinking water of Hinkley, California. Through their efforts, PG&E paid out the largest toxic tort injury settlement in U.S. history, $333 million in damages (Suleiman, 1999).

Exploitation

The contributions of minorities to the cultural mainstream have not consistently been valued. On the contrary, many peoples in the cultural mix have been exploited. Their labor, their art, and their votes have been used and abused without adequate compensation.

From the beginning, European settlers exploited others. Many indentured servants worked at low wages for years to repay their passage to the New World. Native Americans brought food to the starving colonists and, in return, saw their fertile coastal lands taken away. Westward expansion features many a sordid tale of killing and robbery on the part of European settlers (Eckert, 1992). On the West Coast, Spanish missionaries also colonized native peoples, with somewhat more pious motives but a similar result. The Hispanic settlers in the West were in turn exploited by European Americans. Although superior firearms still carried the day, legal manipulations carried out in the English language systematically disenfranchised Hispanic settlers and caused a vast number of them to lose their property and water rights. Chinese settlers who were permitted into the West during the nineteenth century found that their labor was valued only in the meanest way, and the jobs available constituted "woman's work" such as laundry and cooking. And the story of exploitation of Africans brought to the New World is a tale of tears mixed with genocide and forced miscegenation.

In many cases, this exploitation continues to this day as the underclass of the United States, whether white, brown, or black, is inadequately paid and undereducated, forced to live without health benefits or adequate housing (see Table 8.2). Temporary jobs without benefits are the hallmark of the crueler, harsher world of the twenty-first century as economic and political forces polarize society.

The most difficult piece of the puzzle is the challenge of population growth. Creating jobs for a burgeoning population that will provide the financial means for the purchase of health care, education, housing, and an adequate diet is the issue. The population in 2050 is projected to consist largely of developing nations' peoples. The challenge is evident. Wrongs from the past cannot be righted, but present and future citizens can avoid those wrongs by understanding exploitative measures and working for change.

Table 8.2 Poverty Rates, Educational Attainment, Average Earnings, and Health Insurance by Race and Origin

Race and Origin	Poverty Rates (3-year average 2001–2003)	Educational Attainment (high-school graduate or more)	Average Earnings in 2002 for All Workers, 18 Years and Older			Health Insurance: People without Coverage (3-year average 2001–2003)
			Total	Not High-School Graduate	High-School Graduate	
White	10.2%	85.1%	$37,376	$19,264	$28,145	14.2%
Non-Hispanic White	8.2	89.45	39,220	19,423	28,756	10.6
Black	23.7	80.0	28,179	16,516	22,823	19.6
American Indian/Alaska Native	23.2	—	—	—	—	27.5
Asian	10.7	87.6	40,793	16,746	24,900	18.5
Asian and/or Native Hawaiian and other Pacific Islanders	10.8	—	—	—	—	18.6
Hispanic origin (of any race)	21.9	57.0	25,827	18,981	24,163	32.8

Source: Adapted from U.S. Census Bureau (2004a, 2004b, 2004c).

The Impact of a Changing Population

By the year 2010, one of every three Americans will be either African American, Hispanic American, or Asian American. (See Chapter 1 for demographic trends.) This represents a dramatic change from the image of the United States throughout its history. In the past, when Americans have looked in the mirror, they have seen a largely European American reflection. Immigration, together with differing birthrates among various populations, is responsible for this demographic shift. Along with the change in racial and ethnic composition has come a dramatic change in the languages spoken in the United States and the languages spoken in U.S. schools.

In the midst of the changing demographics in the United States, two minority groups—immigrants and economically disadvantaged minorities within the country—face similar challenges. Both immigrants and indigenous minorities must adjust to the demands of modern technological societies and must redefine their cultural self-identity. Economic and educational achievement is not equally accessible to these minorities.

Poverty among Minority Groups

A key difficulty for many minorities is that of poverty. Almost one-quarter (twenty-four percent) of African Americans and more than one-fifth (twenty-two percent) of Hispanic Americans live in poverty (U.S. Census Bureau, 2004c). Worse, Blacks and Hispanics are even more likely not to be simply poor, but to be *extremely* poor—with incomes under half the poverty level of Whites. Although the vast majority of the poor are non-Latino Whites (4.3 million), since 2000, more than 600,000 Latino children have fallen into poverty; and in 2005, one in every three Black children living in America was poor.

Since 2002, for every five children who fell into poverty, four fell into extreme poverty (living with an annual income below $7,412 for a family of three, $18,660 for a family of four). Unfortunately the number of children in extreme poverty grew 11.5 percent, almost twice as fast as the 6.0 percent rate of increase for child poverty overall (Children's Defense Fund, 2004c).

Contrary to popular perceptions about poor families, seventy percent of children in poverty lived in a family in which someone worked full- or part-time for at least part of the year. Almost one in three poor children (31.4 percent) lived with a full-time year-round worker. One of the results of poverty, according to the Department of Agriculture, is that poor households are "food insecure" (without enough food to fully meet basic needs at all times due to lack of financial resources). This was the case for one out of every six households with children in 2002 (Children's Defense Fund, 2004a).

Between 2000 and 2010, the number of children living in poverty in the United States increased by forty-one percent, to almost one-fourth of all children (Emanuel, 2012). Impoverishment leads to devastating educational challenges: lower preschool attendance, poorer health leading to increased school absences, and lower graduation rates (one-third of poor children will not graduate from high school).

The percentage of poor children, represented by the share qualifying for free and/or reduced-price school lunches, is significantly higher (seventy-two percent) in schools with high numbers of English learners compared with schools with few English learners (about forty percent). In fact, poverty was cited as a "serious problem" by more than forty percent of principals and teachers at schools affected by English learners versus twenty percent or less of staff at other schools. Student health problems, likely also related to poverty, were identified as "serious" and "moderate" more frequently in high- than in low-English-learners-affected schools (Cosentino de Cohen, & Clewell, 2007, p. 3).

Poverty does not mean merely inadequate income; rather, it engenders a host of issues, including insufficient income and jobs with limited opportunity, lack of health insurance, inadequate education, and poor nutrition. Poor children are more likely to die in infancy, have a low birth weight, and lack health care, housing, and adequate food (Children's Defense Fund, 2004b). Poor children are at least twice as likely as nonpoor children to suffer stunted growth or lead poisoning or to be kept back in school. They score significantly lower on reading, math, and vocabulary tests when compared with similar nonpoor children (Children's Defense Fund, 2004c).

Among people living below the poverty line, fifty-six percent speak a language other than English, compared with forty-one percent for those above the poverty line (Gorman & Pierson, 2007). English learners often face severe educational shortfalls, as one researcher noted: "Compared with affluent schools, ELs attend schools which are likely to experience higher teacher turnover, allocate fewer resources to classrooms, and face more challenging conditions overall" (Merino, 2007, p. 1).

Poverty plays a large role in the education of America's youth. It affects the ability of the family to devote resources to educational effort. This situation, coupled with social and political factors that affect minority children in schools, stacks the deck against minority-student success. Demographic trends ensure that this will be a continuing problem in the United States.

Poverty affects not only individuals, but also entire school districts. Many U.S. school districts are facing multiple stresses because of economic factors linked to the recession in 2007–2008. In California, which educates 1.4 million English learners, some districts have declining enrollments, which result in declining revenues; the instructional year has been reduced to less than 180 days; teachers as well as counselors have been laid off; families are experiencing higher levels of unemployment; and more families are in poverty, with more students qualifying for free or reduced-price meals (EdSource, 2012). These desperate financial straits negatively affect the quality of education provided for English learners.

The Education of Minorities

The economy of the United States in the future will rest more on Asian American and Hispanic American workers than at present. As a consequence, the education of these populations will become increasingly important. Consider that in 2010, forty-three percent of students enrolled in public elementary and secondary schools were minorities—an increase of twenty-two percent from 1987, largely due to the growth in the Hispanic population (Aud et al., 2012). Of these, 9.7 percent were English learners. Of these minorities, 88.9 percent of Asian Americans had a high-school diploma and 52.4 percent had bachelor degrees. In contrast, only 62.9 percent of Hispanics had high-school diplomas and 13.9 percent had college degrees. Eighty-eight percent of non-Hispanic Whites, on the other hand, had high-school diplomas and more than a thirty percent had bachelor degrees (U.S. Census Bureau, 2012a). The extent of the problem becomes clearer.

Minority students typically live in racially isolated neighborhoods and are more likely to attend segregated schools. More than one-third (thirty-eight percent) of Hispanic students and Black students (thirty-seven percent) attended schools with minority enrollments of ninety to 100 percent. Seventy-seven percent of Hispanics and seventy-one percent of Blacks were enrolled in schools where minorities constitute fifty percent or more of the population.

In addition, minority children are overrepresented in compensatory programs in schools. In the 1999–2000 school year, fifteen percent of Black and fourteen percent of Native American students were enrolled in special education, a significantly higher proportion than White and Hispanic (eleven percent) and Asian/Pacific Islander students (six percent) (NCES, 2003a, 2003b). Subsequent researchers have found that African American students, in particular, are overrepresented in specific categories: emotional disturbance, intellectual disability, and learning disabilities (LD), (de Valenzuela, Copeland, Qi, & Park, 2006). The same researchers found that "African American, Hispanic, Native American, and ELL students were more likely to be identified with a potentially stigmatizing disability (i.e., LD) and less likely to be identified with a socially valued special education identifier (i.e., GL [gifted])" (p. 436).

Thus, nearly a half-century after *Brown v. Board of Education,* a student who is Black, Latino, or Native American remains much less likely to succeed in school. A major factor is a disparity of resources—inner-city schools with large minority populations have been found to have higher percentages of first-year teachers, higher enrollments, fewer library resources, and less in-school parental involvement, characteristics that have been shown to relate to school success (U.S. Government Accounting Office, 2002).

One scholar characterizes the gap between the educational achievement of Latinos and Whites as "the struggle for cognitive justice" (García, 2012, p. 195). He states,

> Although the professed goal of American society is that all children and youth are offered opportunities to study and learn in healthy, dynamic, and safe environments in which a broad rage of social and cultural funds are readily displayed and shared . . . income inequality is surely linked to lessened prospects for attaining a good education and a responsible life for the self, the family, and the greater society. What is at stake here is the argument for a cultural citizenship that is a full and first-class citizenship. This is especially true for immigrant families. Vital to this situation is a poignant and absolute opposition to any brand of second-class citizenship. (p. 196)

With its emphasis on a narrow technological paradigm that fails to recognize any type of intelligence that does not score highly on instruments defining "intelligence quotient," García adds that the educational system in America excludes those who cannot understand this viewpoint enough to participate in it, let alone succeed. For Latino and Latina youth (as do many contemporary scholars, he spells this *Latin@* to indicate the terms "Latino" and "Latina" are combined), too often this results in what García calls "a knowledge connection to nowhere" (p. 196).

On an encouraging note, Hispanic students represent the largest and fastest-growing minority group taking the SAT and now account for 13.5 percent (206,584) of all SAT takers compared to 7.8 percent (94,677) ten years ago, showing that the number of Hispanics taking the test has more than doubled between 1999 and 2009 (College Board, 2009).

The conclusion is inescapable: The educational system of the United States has been fundamentally weak in serving the fastest growing school-age populations. Today's minority students are entering school with significantly different social and economic backgrounds from those of previous student populations and therefore require educators to modify their teaching approaches to ensure that these students have access to the American dream.

Immigration and Migration

The United States has historically been a nation of immigrants, but the nature and causes of immigration have changed over time. The earliest settlers to the east coast of North America came from England and Holland, whereas those to the South and West came mainly from Spain. In the early eighteenth century, these settlers were joined by involuntary immigrants from Africa. Subsequent waves of immigrants came from Scotland, Ireland, and Germany, and later from central and eastern Europe. Immigration from the Pacific Rim countries was constrained by severe immigration restrictions until the last decades of the twentieth century.

However, imperialistic policies of the United States, primarily the conquest of the Philippines, Puerto Rico, Hawaii, and the Pacific Islands, caused large influxes of these populations throughout the twentieth century. The wars in southeast Asia and Central America throughout the 1970s and 1980s led to increased emigration from these areas. In the 1990s, immigrants arrived from all over the world. In 2008, forty-five percent of all legal immigrants came from just five countries—Mexico, China, the Philippines, India, and Vietnam (McCabe & Meissner, 2010). In 2010, nearly 40 million of the approximately 209 million residents of the United States were foreign born (Jones-Correa, 2012). Data from the 2010 U.S. Census show that as of 2009, 22.5 percent of all public school students were either foreign-born or have at least one foreign-born parent (Shah, 2012).

In 2010, Mexico was the largest region of origin of immigrants to the United States, with twenty-nine percent of the total; Asia the second largest source, at twenty-four percent; and "Other Latin America and the Caribbean" third, with twenty-eight percent. This compares to 1970, when sixty percent of all immigrants were Europeans and Mexicans only eight percent. Currently, there are 11,478,413 immigrants living in the United States from Mexico (Jones-Correa, 2012). Central American immigration to the United States is a recent phenomenon, with sixty-three percent of Central Americans having arrived in the United States since 1990, including fifty-eight percent Salvadorans, nearly seventy percent Guatemalan, and seventy-four percent Honduran. Together, these three nationalities make up six percent of U.S. immigrants, with 1.1 million Salvadorans, 798,682 Guatemalans, and 467,943 Hondurans (Rosenblum & Brick, 2011).

Seven southern states experienced the most rapid change in demographics between 1990 and 2009: North Carolina, Georgia, Arkansas, Nevada, Tennessee, South Carolina, and Nebraska. None of these had attracted significant numbers of immigrants before 1990, but in each of them, the immigrant population increased by at least 200 percent between 1990 and 2000. Immigration to these new receiving areas is overwhelmingly Latin American in origin, and in many southern and midwestern states, a significant portion of this migrant flow is undocumented (Jones-Correa, 2012). Attracted to agriculture, construction, meat processing, furniture manufacturing, and other jobs in smaller towns and cities, Latino migrants have dramatically altered local populations, bringing demands for new kinds of food and other cultural features and bringing a third racial demographic to the traditional Black/White dynamic in these areas.

Causes of Immigration

Migration is an international phenomenon. Throughout the world, populations are dislocated by wars, famine, civil strife, economic changes, persecution, and other factors. The United States has been a magnet for immigrants seeking greater opportunity and economic stability. The social upheavals and overpopulation that characterized nineteenth-century Europe and Asia brought more than 14 million immigrants to the United States in the forty-year period between 1860 and 1900. A century later this phenomenon can be witnessed along the border between the United States and Mexico. Politics and religion as well as economics provide reasons for emigration. U.S. domestic and foreign policies affect the way in which groups of foreigners are accepted. Changes in immigration policy, such as amnesty, affect the number of immigrants who enter the country each year.

FIND OUT MORE ABOUT ...

Economic Factors

U.S. Immigration Facts
www.rapidimmigration.com/usa
/1_eng_immigration_facts.html

This site provides general facts about recent U.S. immigration and then discusses immigrant entrepreneurs and economic characteristics of immigrants.

Economic Factors in Immigration. The great disparity in the standard of living attainable in the United States compared to that of many developing countries makes immigration attractive. Self-advancement is uppermost in the minds of many immigrants and acts as a strong incentive despite the economic exploitation often extended to immigrants (e.g., lower wages, exclusion from desirable jobs).

Immigration policy has corresponded with the cycles of boom and bust in the U.S. economy; the Chinese Exclusion Act of 1882 stopped immigration from China to the United States because of the concern that Chinese labor would flood the market. The labor shortage in the western United States resulting from excluding the Chinese had the effect of welcoming Japanese immigrants who were good farm laborers. Later, during the Great Depression of the 1930s, with a vast labor surplus in the United States, the U.S. Congress severely restricted Philippine immigration, and policies were initiated to "repatriate" Mexicans back across the border.

When World War II transformed the labor surplus of the 1930s into a severe worker shortage, the United States and Mexico established the Bracero Program, a bilateral agreement allowing Mexicans to cross the border to work on U.S. farms and railroads. The border was virtually left open during the war years. However, despite the economic attractiveness of the United States, now, as then, most newcomers to this society experience a period of economic hardship.

Political Factors in Immigration. Repression, civil war, and change in government create a "push" for emigration from foreign countries, whereas political factors within the United States create a climate of acceptance for some political refugees and not for others. After the Vietnam War, many refugees were displaced in southeast Asia. Some sense of responsibility for their plight caused the U.S. government to accept many of these people into the United States. For example, Cambodians who cooperated with the U.S. military immigrated to the United States in waves: first, a group including 6,300 Khmer in 1975; second, 10,000 Cambodians in 1979; third, 60,000 Cambodians between 1980 and 1982 (Gillett, 1989a).

The decade of the 1980s was likewise one of political instability and civil war in many Central American countries, resulting in massive civilian casualties. In El Salvador, for example, such instabilities caused the displacement of 600,000 Salvadorans who lived as refugees outside their country (Gillett, 1989b). Through the Deferred Enforced Departure program of the U.S. government, nearly 200,000 Salvadoran immigrants were given the right to live and work legally in the United States.

Other populations, such as Haitians claiming political persecution, have been turned away from U.S. borders. U.S. policy did not consider them to be victims of political repression, but rather of economic hardship—a fine distinction, in many cases, and here one might suspect that racial issues in the United States make it more difficult for them to immigrate. It would seem, then, that the grounds for political asylum—race, religion, nationality, membership in a particular social group, political opinion—can be clouded by confounding factors.

In sum, people are pushed to the United States because of political instability or political policies unfavorable to them in their home countries. Political conditions within the United States affect whether immigrants are accepted or denied.

Religious Factors in Immigration. Many of the early English settlers in North America came to the New World to found colonies in which they would be free to establish or practice their form of religious belief. Later, Irish Catholics left Ireland in droves because their lands were taken by Protestants. Many eastern European Jews, forced to emigrate because of anti-Semitic pogroms in the nineteenth century, came to the United States in great numbers. Current immigration policies permit refugees to be accepted on the basis of religion if the applicant can prove that persecution comes from the government or is motivated by the government (Siskind Susser, n.d.).

Family Unification. The risks associated with travel to the New World have made immigration a male-dominated activity since the early settlement of North America. In some cases, such as that of the Chinese in the nineteenth century, immigration laws permitted only young men to enter. Initial Japanese immigration, which was not restricted as severely as Chinese, involved predominantly young men between the ages of twenty and forty. Similarly, today's Mexican immigrant population consists largely of young men who have come to the United States to work and send money home. Once settled, these immigrants seek to bring family members to the United States. Family unification is a primary motivation for many applications to the Bureau of Citizenship and Immigration Services (BCIS) in the Department of Homeland Security.

Unfortunately, too often the mainstream media in the United States focus on anti-immigration stories, particularly against Mexicans. Rarely featured in the media, however, are analyses of the reasons behind persistent Mexican emigration attempts: Today, the majority of Mexicans are poorer and more economically insecure that they were just a few years ago (Bigelow, 2007). Under the North American Free Trade Agreement (NAFTA), manufacturing wages in Mexico declined nine percent between 1994 and 2004, poverty in rural areas increased from fifty-four percent to eighty-one percent, and almost 1.5 million Mexican farmers lost their land because of cheap corn imports from the United States. These facts argue for a more compassionate stance toward Mexican English learners who are recent immigrants.

Educational Attainment. Immigrants' overall education attainment rates lag behind those of the U.S.-born population. Among adults aged twenty-five and older in 2007, similar percentages of the foreign- and U.S.-born populations had bachelor's degrees (twenty-seven percent versus twenty-eight percent, respectively), but a lower proportion of the foreign-born (forty-four percent) than the U.S.-born (fifty-six percent) population had completed some college but had not earned a bachelor's degree (Crissey, 2009).

Civic Engagement. Foreign- and U.S.-born children of immigrants are the fastest-growing component of the U.S. population. It is vitally important to the future political and economic success of U.S. society that these young people engage fully in educational practices that prepare them as citizens and productive workers. Stevik, Stevik, and Labissiere (2008) compared the patterns of civic engagement of immigrant and nonimmigrant youth in Miami, Florida—the city within the United States that has the highest proportion of immigrants. The researchers found that immigrants devote considerable activity to using their bilingual skills to help other immigrants.

It is possible to infer that they also help other immigrants to succeed in school, suggesting that educators might draw upon these individuals to assist others.

Immigrants also become heavily engaged in politically related activities in response to discrimination. This is also true of native minorities: In the face of exclusion and unequal treatment, marginalized groups often become reactive, responding to the "us-against-them" rhetoric of prejudice with a tendency to solidify ethnic identity (Pérez, 2012). This promotes ethnic group solidarity and political mobilization, with consequences such as increased student participation in campaigns to increase access to higher education.

Migration

Americans have always been restless. Historically, crowding and the promise of greater economic freedom were reasons for moving west. The gold rush attracted, for the most part, English-speaking European Americans from the eastern United States, but other minority groups and immigrants were also drawn to the search for instant wealth. Miners from Mexico, Peru, and Chile increased California's Latino population; Greeks, Portuguese, Russians, Poles, Armenians, and Italians flocked to the San Francisco Bay area. During the Depression, many of these populations migrated once again to California's central valley to find work as farm laborers. With the rise of cities, rural populations sought economic advancement in urban environments. Many African Americans migrated to northern cities after World War I to escape prejudice and discrimination.

Today, many immigrants are sponsored by special-interest groups such as churches and civic organizations that invite them to reside in the local community. Once here, however, some groups find conditions too foreign to their former lives and eventually migrate to another part of the United States. For example, a group of Hmong families sponsored by Lutheran charities spent two years in the severe winter climate of the Minneapolis area before resettling in California. Hispanics, on the other hand, are migrating from cities in the Southwest, New York, and Miami toward destinations in the Midwest and middle South.

Based on the 2000 census, Americans continue to move. The most mobile population between 1995 and 2000 was Hispanics (fifty-six percent), followed by Asians (fifty-four percent), Native Americans and Alaska Natives (fifty percent), and Blacks (forty-nine percent). The least mobile population was non-Hispanic Whites (forty-three percent). Of the regions in the United States, the South had the highest level of net domestic immigration of non-Hispanic Whites, Blacks, Asians, and Hispanics (Schachter, 2003).

Immigration Laws and Policies

Economic cycles in the United States have affected immigration policies, liberalizing them when workers were needed and restricting immigration when jobs were scarce. These restrictive immigration policies were often justified with overtly racist arguments. Asian immigration was targeted for specific quotas. The first Asian population that was specifically excluded was the Chinese, but the growth of Japanese immigration as a result of this quota prompted Congress to extend the concept of Chinese exclusion to Japan (1908) and the rest of Asia. The immigration laws of the 1920s (the National Origins Acts of 1924 and 1929) banned most Asian immigration and established quotas that favored northwestern European immigrants. The quota system, however, did not apply to Mexico and the rest of the Western Hemisphere. In 1943, Congress symbolically ended the Asian exclusion policy by granting ethnic Chinese a token quota of 100 immigrants a year. The Philippines and Japan received similar tiny quotas after the war.

Did You Know? Although Hispanics are the most urbanized ethnic/ racial group in the United States (ninety percent living in metropolitan areas in 2000), the nonmetro Hispanic population is now the most rapidly growing demographic group in rural and small-town America. By 2000, half of all nonmetro Hispanics lived outside traditional southwest cities. Many of these Hispanics are newly arrived undocumented young men from rural, depressed areas of Mexico. In spite of their relatively low education levels and weak English skills, employment rates exceeded those of all other nonmetro Hispanics and non-Hispanic Whites.

Source: Kandel and Cromartie (2004).

U.S. Foreign Policy. As the United States grew as a capitalist nation, economic forces had a great influence on U.S. foreign policy. In the early growth of commercial capitalism from 1600 to 1865, new settlers were a source of labor; Africans were enslaved to provide plantation labor, and poor Europeans such as Irish Catholics were recruited abroad for low-wage jobs in transportation and construction. In the phase of industrial capitalism (1865–1920), U.S. treaties with Europe and intervention in European affairs (World War I) maintained the labor supply until the 1924 Immigration Act, which provided overall limits on immigration (favoring immigrants from Europe over other regions of the world). U.S. imperialist policies in Asia (conquest of the Philippines and Hawaii) ensured a supply of raw materials and a home for U.S. military bases in the Pacific, but immigration policy denied access to the United States for the majority of Asians.

The Immigration and Nationality Act Amendments of 1965 brought about vast changes in immigration policy by abolishing the national origins quota system and replacing it with a seven-category preference system for allocating immigrant visas—a system that emphasizes family ties and occupation. Although there is a per-country limit for these preference immigrants, certain countries—People's Republic of China, India, Mexico, and the Philippines—are "oversubscribed," and hopeful immigrants are on long waiting lists, some extending for as many as twelve years (U.S. Department of State, 2004).

An additional provision in the 1965 act is the diversity immigrant category, in which 55,000 immigrant visas can be awarded each fiscal year to permit immigration opportunities for persons from countries other than the principal sources of current immigration to the United States. No one country can receive more than seven percent of the available diversity visas in any one year (U.S. Department of State, 2004).

The Refugee Act of 1980 expanded the number of persons considered refugees, again allowing more immigrants to enter the United States under this category. As a result of these policy changes, immigrants from Latin America and Asia began to enter the United States in unprecedented numbers, eclipsing the previous dominance of Europeans.

Legal Status. Many immigrants are *documented*—legal residents who have entered the United States officially and live under the protection of legal immigration status. Some of these are officially designated *refugees,* with transitional support services and assistance provided by the U.S. government. Most immigrants from Cambodia, Laos, Vietnam, and Thailand have been granted refugee status. *Undocumented* immigrants are residents without any documentation who live in fear of being identified and deported.

Being in the United States illegally brings increased instability, fear, and insecurity to school-age children because they and their families are living without the protection, social services, and assistance available to most immigrants. With the passage of the Immigration Reform and Control Act in 1986, however, undocumented children are legally entitled to public education.

Immigration from Mexico and Central America tends to depend not so much on a steady stream as on ebbs and flows that correspond to such factors as availability of jobs and fear of deportation. Esquivel and Becerra (2012) report that the number of illegal immigrants from Mexico residing in the United Stages fell from 7,000,000 in 2007 to about 6,000,000 in 2011, whereas the number of legal immigrants increased from 5.5 million to 5.8 million. The change from 2007 to 2011 reflects the weak U.S. economy, increased border enforcement, the rise in deportations, growing danger along the Mexican border, and a long-term decline in the Mexican birthrate.

FIND OUT MORE ABOUT ...

U.S. Immigration Policy

U.S. Department of State, Bureau of Consular Affairs, Visa Bulletin

http://travel.state.gov/visa/frvi/bulletin/bulletin_1360 .html

The Visa Bulletin, updated monthly, provides information about immigrant numbers and eligibility criteria for various categories.

United States Immigration Policy

www.cbo.gov/doc.crfm?index-7051

This paper, written in 2007, provides an overview of U.S. immigration policy, a summary of current U.S. immigration law, statistics, enforcement efforts, and requirements for naturalization.

Resources Available to Immigrants. The Emergency Immigrant Education Program (EIEP; No Child Left Behind, Title III, subpart 4) provides assistance to school districts whose enrollment is affected by immigrants. The purpose of the program is to provide high-quality instruction to immigrant children and youth, to help them with their transition into U.S. society, and to help them meet the same challenging academic content and student academic achievement standards as all children are expected to meet (NCLB, Sec. 3241). School districts and county offices of education qualify for EIEP funding if they have an enrollment of at least 500 eligible immigrant pupils and/or if the enrollment of eligible immigrant pupils represents at least three percent of the total enrollment (online at www.policyarchive.org/handle/10207 /bitstream5/3254.pdf).

The Dream Act. The Development, Relief, and Education of Alien Minors (DREAM) Act was introduced in the U.S. Congress in 2001; its purpose was to provide federal legislation that would open a path for undocumented students to obtain legal resident status. The bill would have enabled undocumented high-school graduates to apply for up to six year's conditional residency status if they entered the United States before age sixteen and had been continuously present for five years prior to the law's enactment; had received a high-school diploma or its equivalent; and had demonstrated good moral character. The six-year residency requirement was to be used to attend college, or the individual was to spend two years in the U.S. Armed Forces.

The DREAM Act of 2010 came close to passing, but it was defeated in the U.S. Senate. In the meantime, many states have acted to allow undocumented college students to pay in-state tuition rates, easing the burden on families. The states cannot overturn the Illegal Immigration Reform and Immigrant Responsibility Act (IIRIRA) of 1996 (8 U.S.C. 1623), which denies immigrants such benefits, however, and out-of-state students paying higher tuition have sued to hold states to the IIRIRA tenets. In 2012, the Obama administration pledged not to enforce deportation for some undocumented college students, providing relief for hundreds of thousands of such would-be DREAM Act beneficiaries.

How far have we come? The Puritans brought to New England a religion based on a monochromatic worldview. They outlawed Christmas and disapproved of celebration. The United States of America has struggled with this severe cultural reductionism since its founding. As the splendor and the celebratory spirit of the Native American and immigrant cultures have been recognized, the people of the United States have opened up to accept the beauty and brilliant hues that Native Americans and immigrants have contributed. As more and more diverse groups settle and resettle throughout the continent, customs and traditions mingle to create an ever-new mix. The salad bowl, the kaleidoscope—these are metaphors for diversity in taste, in pattern, and in lifestyle. The American portrait is still being painted, in ever-brighter hues.

LEARNING MORE

Further Reading

Lies My Teacher Told Me by J. Loewen (1995) is a fascinating book that questions many of the "facts" presented in U.S. history textbooks. According to the author, "African American, Native American, and Latino students view history with a special dislike" (p. 12). Perhaps the Eurocentric every-problem-is-solved approach in the texts deadens students to the true nature of the controversies and to the richness of the stories of history.

Web Search

Using a search engine (e.g., Google), enter "contributions of _____" (the group of students who are most represented in your school). Based on what you find, share your findings with the school staff and then prepare a lesson (with the help of the students and their parents) that highlights the contributions of the group.

Exploration

Visit a local school district office (or use the Internet) to find out which ethnic groups are represented in your state and school district. Prepare a presentation for the staff at your school and brainstorm how you can be more proactive in including these groups in the curriculum.

Collaboration

Determine what school-site activities involve minority groups. Are the activities confined to flags, food, and fiestas? Are the activities confined to specific months (e.g., African Americans discussed only during Black History Month)? Work with other teachers to develop an overall year plan that incorporates contributions of various groups to the richness of the United States.

MyEducationLab™

Multicultural Education

Administrators from Hans Christian Andersen School discuss their conceptions of multicultural education. They also deal with issues of evaluating students' and their own performances. They share their thoughts about political correctness.

To access the video, go to MyEducationLab (www.myeducationlab.com), choose the Díaz-Rico text, and log in to MyEducationLab for English Language Learners. Select the topic Cultural-Based Instruction, and watch the video entitled "Multicultural Education."

Answer the following questions:

1. What advantages of a multicultural curriculum are discussed? What do these administrators mean when they say that schools are desegregated but not integrated?

2. What is meant in this video by "politically correct"?

3. Several administrators describe students' pride in their cultural heritage. How does this relate to students' pride in being a successful student? Discuss the differences in the definition of a "successful student." How does one define success?

9

Culturally Responsive Schooling

Students show more interest in reading when the curriculum includes content that is relevant to their culture.

Unlike my grandmother, the teacher did not have pretty brown skin and a colorful dress. She wasn't plump and friendly. Her clothes were of one color and drab. Her pale and skinny form made me worry that she was very ill. . . . The teacher's odor took some getting used to also. Later I learned from the girls this smell was something she wore called perfume. The classroom . . . was terribly huge and smelled of medicine like the village clinic I feared so much. Those fluorescent light tubes made an eerie drone. Our confinement to rows of desks was another unnatural demand made on our active little bodies. . . . We all went home for lunch since we lived a short walk from the school. It took coaxing, and sometimes bribing, to get me to return and complete the remainder of the school day.

Joe Suina (1985, writing his impressions on entering school at age 6)

The narrative of this Pueblo youth illustrates two cultural systems in contact. Suina was experiencing a natural human reaction that occurs when a person moves into a new cultural situation—culture shock. He had grown up in an environment that had subtly, through every part of his life, taught him appropriate ways of behavior—for example, how people looked (their color, their size, their dress, their ways of interacting) and how space was structured (the sizes of rooms, the types of lighting, the arrangement of furniture). His culture had taught him what was important and valuable. The culture Suina grew up in totally enveloped him and gave him a way to understand life. It provided him with a frame of reference through which he made sense of the world.

Culture is so pervasive that often people perceive other cultures as strange and foreign without realizing that their own culture may be equally mystifying to others. Culture, though largely invisible, influences instruction, policy, and learning in schools (see the figure on page 217). Members of the educational community accept the organization, teaching and learning styles, and curricula of the schools as natural and right, without realizing that these patterns are cultural. And the schools are natural and right for members of the culture that created them. As children of nondominant cultures enter the schools, however, they may find the organization, teaching and learning styles, and curricula to be alien, incomprehensible, and exclusionary.

Unfortunately, teachers—who, with parents, are the prime acculturators of society—often have little training regarding the key role of culture in teaching and learning. Too often, culture is incorporated into classroom activities in superficial ways—as a group of artifacts (baskets, masks, distinctive clothing), as celebrations of holidays (Cinco de Mayo, Martin Luther King, Jr. Day), or as a laundry list of stereotypes and facts (Asians are quiet; Hispanics are family-oriented; Arabs are Muslims). Teachers who have a more insightful view of culture and cultural processes are able to use their understanding to

Table 9.1   The Skills and Responsibilities of the Intercultural Educator

Understand Culture and Cultural Diversity
Explore key concepts about culture.
Investigate ourselves as cultural beings.
Learn about students' cultures.
Recognize how cultural adaptation affects learning.

Strive for Equity in Schooling
Detect unfair privilege.
Combat prejudice in ourselves and others.
Fight for fairness and equal opportunity.

Promote Achievement with Culturally Responsive Schooling
Respect students' diversity.
Work with culturally supported facilitating or limiting attitudes and abilities.
Sustain high expectations for all students.
Marshal parental and community support for schooling.

Source: Díaz-Rico (2000).

move beyond the superficial and to recognize that people live in characteristic ways. They understand that the observable manifestations of culture are but one aspect of the cultural web—the intricate pattern that weaves and binds a people together. Knowing that culture provides the lens through which people view the world, teachers can look at the "what" of a culture—the artifacts, celebrations, traits, and facts—and ask "why."

Teachers in the twenty-first century face a diverse student population that demands a complicated set of skills to promote achievement for all students. As intercultural educators, teachers understand culturally responsive schooling and can adapt instruction accordingly. Table 9.1 outlines the skills and responsibilities of the intercultural educator. This chapter addresses culturally responsive schooling and the struggle to achieve equity in schooling. This chapter also includes using culturally responsive pedagogy to promote student achievement.

Understanding Culture and Cultural Diversity

As an initial step in learning about the complexity of culture and how the culture embodied within the school affects diverse students, the following sections examine the nature of culture. Knowledge of the deeper elements of culture—beyond superficial aspects such as food, clothing, holidays, and celebrations—can give teachers a crosscultural perspective that allows them to educate students to the greatest extent possible. These deeper elements include values, belief systems, family structures and child-rearing practices, language and nonverbal communication, expectations, gender roles, and biases—all the fundamentals of life that affect learning.

The Nature of Culture

Does a fish understand water? Do people understand their own culture? Teachers are responsible for helping to pass on cultural knowledge through the schooling process. Can teachers step outside their own culture long enough to see how it operates and to understand its effects on culturally diverse students? A way to begin is to define culture.

The term *culture* is used in many ways. It can refer to activities such as art, drama, and ballet or to items such as pop music, mass media entertainment, and comic books. The term *culture* can be used for distinctive groups in society, such as adolescents and their culture. It can be used as a general term for a society, such as the "French culture." Such uses do not, however, define what a culture is. As a field of study, culture is conceptualized in various ways (see Table 9.2).

The definitions in Table 9.2 have common factors but vary in emphasis. The following definition of culture combines the ideas in Table 9.2:

> Culture is the explicit and implicit patterns for living, the dynamic system of commonly agreed-upon symbols and meanings, knowledge, belief, art, morals, law, customs, behaviors, traditions, and/or habits that are shared and make up the total way of life of a people, as negotiated by individuals in the process of constructing a personal identity.

Table 9.2 Definitions of Culture

Definition	Source
The sum total of a way of life of a people; patterns experienced by individuals as normal ways of acting, feeling, and being	Hall (1959)
That complex whole that includes knowledge, belief, art, morals, law, and custom, and any other capabilities acquired by humans as members of society	Tylor (in Pearson, 1974)
Mental constructs in three basic categories: *shared knowledge* (information known in common by members of the group), *shared views* (beliefs and values shared by members of a group), and *shared patterns* (habits and norms in the ways members of a group organize their behavior, interaction, and communication)	Snow (1996)
Partial solutions to previous problems that humans create in joint mediated activity; the social inheritance embodied in artifacts and material constituents of culture as well as in practices and ideal symbolic forms; semi-organized hodgepodge of human inheritance. Culture is exteriorized mind and mind is interiorized culture	Cole (1998)
Frames (nationality, gender, ethnicity, religion) carried by each individual that are internalized, individuated, and emerge in interactions	Smith, Paige, and Steglitz (1998)

Postmodern writers have added much to the study of the interplay between culture and the individual by emphasizing the importance of performativity: People act out the roles in culture that display the identities they wish to have known, and they often do this at odds to, or in defiance of, the surrounding ambiance. Moreover, people in the postmodern world take on temporary identities and then shrug off identities that no longer fit. Therefore one must add another paragraph to the preceding definition of culture:

> To understand culture, one must look beyond the obvious to understand how values, codes, beliefs and social relations are continually being reshaped by shifting parameters of place, identity, history, and power. Rather than individuals being excluded for differing from cultural norms, people with dissonant, flexible, complex, and hybrid racial and ethnic identities struggle to generate new meanings within accommodating contexts as they use experimentation and creativity to rework existing configurations of knowledge and power and thus extend the possibilities of being human, even in the face of an uncertain outcome.

The important idea is that culture involves both observable behaviors and intangibles such as beliefs and values, rhythms, rules, and roles. The concept of culture has evolved over the last fifty years away from the idea of culture as an invisible, patterning force to that of culture as an active tension between the social "shortcuts" that make consensual society possible and the contributions and construction that each individual creates while living in society. Culture is not only the filter through which people see the world but also the raw dough from which each person fashions a life that is individual and satisfying.

Because culture is all-inclusive (see the figure on page 217), it includes all aspects of life. Snow (1996) listed a host of components (see Table 9.3).

Cultures are more than the mere sum of their traits. There is a wholeness about cultures, an integration of the various responses to human needs. Cultures cannot be taught merely by examining external features such as art and artifacts. For example, a

Table 9.3 Components of Culture

Daily Life			
Animals	Hobbies	Medical care	Sports
Clothing	Housing	Plants	Time
Daily schedule	Hygiene	Recreation	Traffic and transport
Food	Identification	Shopping	Travel
Games	Jobs	Space	Weather

The Cycle of Life		
Birth	Divorce	Rites of passage
Children	Friends	Men and women
Dating/mating	Old age	
Marriage	Funerals	

Interacting		
Chatting	Functions in communication	Parties
Eating	Gifts	Politeness
Drinking	Language learning	Problem solving

Society			
Business	Education	Government and politics	Science
Cities	Farming	Languages and dialects	Social problems
Economy	Industry	Law and order	

The Nation		
Holidays	Cultural borrowing	National issues
Geography	Famous people	Stereotypes
History		

Creative Arts		
Arts	Genres	Music
Entertainment	Literature	Television

Philosophy, Religion, and Values

Source: Based on Snow (1996).

teacher who travels to Japan may return laden with kimonos and chopsticks, hoping these objects will document Japanese culture. But to understand the culture, that teacher must examine the living patterns and values of the culture that those artifacts represent.

Key Concepts about Culture

Despite the evolving definitions of culture, theorists agree on a few central ideas. These concepts are first summarized here and then treated with more depth.

Culture Is Universal. Everyone in the world belongs to one or more cultures. Each culture provides templates for the rituals of daily interaction: the way food is served, the way children are spoken to, the way needs are met. These templates are an internalized way to organize and interpret experience. All cultures share some universal characteristics. The manner in which these needs are met differs.

Culture Simplifies Living. Social behaviors and customs offer structure to daily life that minimizes interpersonal stress. Cultural patterns are routines that free humans from endless negotiation about each detail of living. Cultural influences help unify a society by providing a common base of communication and common social customs.

Culture Is Learned in a Process of Deep Conditioning. Cultural patterns are absorbed unconsciously from birth, as well as explicitly taught by other members. Culture dictates how and what people see, hear, smell, taste, and feel, and how people and events are evaluated. Cultural patterns are so familiar that members of a culture find it difficult to accept that other ways can be right. As cultural patterns are learned or acquired through observation and language, seldom are alternatives given. The fact that cultural patterns are deep makes it difficult for the members of a given culture to see their own culture as learned behavior.

Culture Is Demonstrated in Values. Every culture deems some beliefs and behaviors more desirable than others, whether these be about nature, human character, material possessions, or other aspects of the human condition. Members of the culture reward individuals who exemplify these values with prestige or approval.

Culture Is Expressed Both Verbally and Nonverbally. Although language and culture are closely identified, the nonverbal components of culture are equally powerful means of communication about cultural beliefs, behaviors, and values. Witness the strong communicative potential of the obscene gesture! In the classroom, teachers may misunderstand a student's intent if nonverbal communication is misinterpreted.

Example of Concept *Nonverbal Miscommunication*

Ming was taught at home to sit quietly when she was finished with a task and wait for her mother to praise her. As a newcomer in the third grade, she waited quietly when finished with her reading assignment.	Mrs. Wakefield impatiently reminded Ming to take out a book and read or start another assignment when she completed her work. She made a mental note: "Ming lacks initiative."

Societies Represent a Mix of Cultures. The patterns that dominate a society form the *macroculture* of that society. In the United States, European American traditions and cultural patterns have largely determined the social behaviors and norms of formal institutions. Within the macroculture, a variety of *microcultures* coexist, distinguished by characteristics such as gender, socioeconomic status, ethnicity, geographical location, social identification, and language use.

Generational experiences can cause the formation of microcultures. For example, the children of Vietnamese who immigrated to the United States after the Vietnam War often became native speakers of English, separating the two generations by language. Similarly, Mexicans who migrate to the United States may find that their children born in the United States consider themselves "Chicanos."

Individuals who grow up within a macroculture and never leave it may act on the assumption that their values are the norm. When encountering microcultures, they may be unable or unwilling to recognize that alternative beliefs and behaviors are legitimate within the larger society.

Culture Is Both Dynamic and Persistent. Human cultures are a paradox—some features are flexible and responsive to change, and other features last thousands of years without changing. Values and customs relating to birth, marriage, medicine, education, and death seem to be the most persistent, for humans seem to be deeply reluctant to alter those cultural elements that influence labor and delivery, marital happiness, health, life success, and eternal rest.

Culture Is a Mix of Rational and Nonrational Elements. Much as individuals living in western European post-Enlightenment societies may believe that reason should govern human behavior, many cultural patterns are passed on through habit rather than reason. People who bring a real tree into their houses in December—despite the mess it creates—do so because of centuries-old Yule customs. Similarly, carving a face on a hollow pumpkin is not a rational idea. Those who create elaborate altars

---

Did You Know? **The Persistence of Cultural Values** The Sarmatians, like their neighbors the Scythians, were nomadic people who lived just north of the Black Sea in ancient times. They had one outstanding trait in particular—a unique love of their horses, such that graves were almost always found with horse bones, bridles, and other accoutrements buried next to the human remains. Thousands of years later, in the twentieth century, their descendants, the Ossetians, waged a fierce cultural skirmish with government officials of the Union of Soviet Socialist Republics (USSR). The issue? The Ossetians insisted on killing a man's horse when he died and burying it with the corpse. The Soviets mandated that it was a crime to waste the People's resources. For many years, subterfuge persisted—a deceased man's horse mysteriously would become sick or disabled and had to be shot, and graves would be reopened in the dead of night to accommodate one more body. (More information at www.ossetians.com/eng.)

Did You Know? Extreme dedication to the concept of standardized testing is deeply ingrained in Chinese parents. Government officials in the Sui dynasty (circa 605 CE) began a competitive examination system that later in the Tang dynasty attracted candidates from all over the country. Test-takers hoped that by attaining a high score on the examination they might qualify for positions of power and influence in the civil service of imperial government. Do students today complain about the rigors of "test week"? Scholars taking the imperial exams were often locked in bare, isolated cells, or in cubicles with other candidates, taking twenty-four to seventy-two hours to complete a test that covered military strategy, civil law, revenue and taxation, agriculture, and geography, as well as works by Confucius and some of his disciples. (Read more about China's Imperial examinations: www.sacu.org/examinations.html.)

in their homes or take food to the grave of a loved one for the Mexican celebration of Day of the Dead do so because of spiritual beliefs.

Cultures Represent Different Values. The fact that each culture possesses its own particular traditions, values, and ideals means that actions can be judged only in relation to the cultural setting in which they occur. This point of view has been called *cultural relativism*. In general, the primary values of human nature are universal—for example, few societies condone murder. However, sanctions relating to actions may differ.

Attempting to impose "international" standards on diverse peoples with different cultural traditions causes problems. This means that some cardinal values held by teachers in the United States are not cultural universals but instead are values that may not be shared by students and their families. For example, not all families value children's spending time reading fiction; some may see this as a waste of time. Some families may not see value in algebra or higher mathematics; others might consider art in the classroom to be unimportant.

Even Diverse Societies Have a Mainstream Culture. The term *mainstream culture* refers to those individuals or groups who share values of the dominant macroculture. In the United States, this dominant or core culture is primarily shared by members of the middle class. Mainstream American culture is characterized by the following values (Gollnick & Chinn, 2006):

- Individualism and privacy
- Independence and self-reliance
- Equality
- Ambition and industriousness
- Competitiveness
- Appreciation of the good life
- Perception that humans are separate from and superior to nature

Culture Affects People's Attitudes toward Schooling. For many individuals, educational aspiration affects the attitude they have toward schooling: what future job or profession they desire, the importance parents ascribe to education, and the investment in education that is valued in their culture. Cultural values also affect the extent to which families are involved in their children's schooling and the forms this involvement takes. Family involvement is discussed in Chapter 10.

Adapted Instruction

Working with Attitudes toward Schooling

In working with diverse students, teachers will want to know:

- What educational level the student, family, and community desire for the student
- What degree of assimilation to the dominant culture (and to English) is expected and desired

Culture Governs the Way People Learn. Any learning that takes place is built on previous learning. Students have learned the basic patterns of living in the context of their families. They have learned the verbal and nonverbal behaviors appropriate for their gender and age and have observed their family members in various occupations and activities. The family has taught them about love and about relations between friends, kin, and community members. They have observed community members cooperating to learn in a variety of methods and modes. Their families have given them a feeling for music and art and have shown them what is beautiful and what is not. Finally, they have learned to use language in the context of their homes and communities. They have learned when questions can be asked and when silence is required. They have used language to learn to share feelings and knowledge and beliefs. Culture appears to influence learning styles, the way individuals select strategies, and the way they approach learning (Shade & New, 1993).

The culture that students bring from the home is the foundation for their learning. Although certain communities exist in relative poverty—that is, they are not equipped with middle-class resources—poverty should not be equated with cultural deprivation. Every community's culture incorporates vast knowledge about successful living. Teachers can utilize this cultural knowledge to organize students' learning in schools.

Example of Concept *Culturally Specific Learning Styles*

Students can acquire knowledge by means of various learning modalities, which are often expressed in culturally specific ways. The Navajo child is often taught by first observing and listening, and then taking over parts of the task in cooperation with and under the supervision of an adult. In this way, the child gradually learns all the requisite skills. Finally, the child tests himself or herself privately—failure is not seen by others, whereas success is brought back and shared. The use of speech in this learning process is minimal (Phillips, 1978).

In contrast, acting and performing are the focus of learning for many African-American children. Children observe other individuals to determine appropriate behavior and to appreciate the performance of others. In this case, observing and listening culminates in an individual's performance before others (Heath, 1983b). Reading and writing may be primary learning modes for other cultures such as traditionally educated Asian students.

Investigating Ourselves as Cultural Beings

The Personal Dimension

For intercultural educators, self-reflection is vital. By examining their own attitudes, beliefs, and culturally derived beliefs and behaviors, teachers begin to discover what has influenced their value systems. Villegas and Lucas (2002) summarized this self-reflection in eight components (see Table 9.4). Some of these components are further addressed in Chapter 10.

Table 9.4 Components of the Personal Dimension of Intercultural Education

Component	Description
Engage in reflective thinking and writing.	Awareness of one's actions, interactions, beliefs, and motivations—or racism—can catalyze behavioral change.
Explore personal and family histories by interviewing family members.	Exploring early cultural experiences can help teachers better relate to individuals with different backgrounds.
Acknowledge group membership.	Teachers who acknowledge their affiliation with various groups in society can assess how this influences views of, and relationships with, other groups.
Learn about the experiences of diverse groups by reading or personal interaction.	Learning about the histories of diverse groups—from their perspectives—highlights value differences.
Visit students' families and communities.	Students' home environments offer views of students' connections to complex cultural networks.
Visit or read about successful teachers.	Successful teachers of children from diverse backgrounds provide exemplary role models.
Appreciate diversity.	Seeing difference as the norm in society reduces ethnocentrism.
Participate in reforming schools.	Teachers can help reform monocultural institutions.

Source: Based on Villegas and Lucas (2002).

CULTURAL SELF-STUDY:

Self-Exploration Questions

- Describe yourself as a preschool child. Were you compliant, curious, adventuresome, goody-goody, physically active, nature loving? Have you observed your parents with other children? Do they encourage open-ended exploration, or would they prefer children to play quietly with approved toys? Do they encourage initiative?

- What was the knowledge environment like in your home? What type of reading did your father and mother do? Was there a time when the members of the family had discussions about current events or ideas and issues? How much dissent was tolerated from parental viewpoints? Were children encouraged to question the status quo? What was it like to learn to talk and think in your family?

- What kind of a grade-school pupil were you? What is your best memory from elementary school? What was your favorite teacher like? Were you an avid reader? How would you characterize your cognitive style and learning style preferences? Was the school you attended ethnically diverse? What about your secondary school experience? Did you have a diverse group of friends in high school?

- What is your ethnic group? What symbols or traditions did you participate in that derived from this group? What do you like about your ethnic identity? Is there a time now when your group celebrates its traditions together? What was the neighborhood or community like in which you grew up?

- What was your experience with ethnic diversity? What were your first images of race or color? Was there a time in your life when you sought out diverse contacts to expand your experience?

- What contact do you have now with people of dissimilar racial or ethnic backgrounds? How would you characterize your desire to learn more? Given your learning style preferences, how would you go about this?

Cultural Self-Study

Self-study is a powerful tool for understanding culture. A way to begin a culture inquiry is by investigating one's personal name. For example, ask, "Where did I get my name? Who am I named for? In which culture did the name originate? What does the name mean?" Continue the self-examination by reviewing favorite cultural customs—such as holiday traditions, home décor, and favorite recipes. More difficult self-examination questions address the mainstream U.S. values of individual freedom, self-reliance, competition, individualism, and the value of hard work. Ask, "If someone in authority tells me to do something, do I move quickly or slowly? If someone says, 'Do you need any help?' do I usually say, 'No, thanks. I can do it myself'? Am I comfortable promoting myself (e.g., talking about my achievements in a performance review)? Do I prefer to work by myself or on a team? Do I prefer to associate with high achievers and avoid spending much time with people who do not work hard?" These and other introspective questions help to pinpoint cultural attitudes. Without a firm knowledge of one's own beliefs and behaviors, it is difficult to contrast the cultural behaviors of others. However, the self-examination process is challenging and ongoing. It is difficult to observe one's own culture.

Learning about Students' Cultures

Teachers can use printed, electronic, and video materials, books, and magazines to help students learn about other cultures. However, the richest source of information is local—the life of the community. Students, parents, and community members can provide insights about values, attitudes, and habits. One method of learning about students and their families, ethnographic study, has proved useful in learning about the ways that students' experiences in the home and community compare with the culture of the schools.

Ethnographic Techniques

Ethnography is an inquiry process that seeks to provide cultural explanations for behavior and attitudes. Culture is described from the insider's point of view, as the classroom teacher becomes not only an observer of the students' cultures but also an active participant (Erickson, 1977). Parents and community members, as well as students, become sources for the gradual growth of understanding on the part of the teacher.

For the classroom teacher, ethnography involves gathering data in order to understand two distinct cultures: the culture of the students' communities and the culture of the classroom. To understand the home and community environment, teachers may observe and participate in community life, interview community members, and visit students' homes. To understand the school culture, teachers may observe in a variety of classrooms, have visitors observe in their own classrooms, audio- and videotape classroom interaction, and interview other teachers and administrators.

Observations. The classroom teacher can begin to observe and participate in the students' cultures, writing up field notes after participating and perhaps summing up the insights gained in an ongoing diary that can be shared with colleagues.

Such observation can document children's use of language within the community; etiquettes of speaking, listening, writing, greeting, and getting or giving information; values and aspirations; and norms of communication.

When analyzing the culture of the classroom, teachers might look at classroom management and routines; affective factors (students' attitudes toward activities, teachers' attitudes toward students); classroom talk in general; and nonverbal behaviors and communication. The thoughts and intentions of the participants can also be documented.

Interviews. Structured interviews use a set of predetermined questions to gain specific kinds of information. Unstructured interviews are more like conversations in that they can range over a wide variety of topics, many of which the interviewer would not necessarily have anticipated. As an outsider learning about a new culture, the classroom teacher would be better served initially using an unstructured interview, beginning with general questions and being guided in follow-up questions by the interviewee's responses. The result of the initial interview may in turn provide a structure for learning more about the culture during a second interview or conversation. A very readable book about ethnography and interviewing is *The Professional Stranger: An Informal Introduction to Ethnography* (Agar, 1980).

Home Visits. Home visits are one of the best ways in which teachers can learn what is familiar and important to their students. The home visit can be a social call or a brief report on the student's progress that enhances rapport with students and parents. Scheduling an appointment ahead of time is a courtesy that some cultures may require and provides a means for the teacher to ascertain if home visits are welcome. Dress should be professional. The visit should be short (twenty to thirty minutes) and the conversation positive, especially about the student's schoolwork. Viewing the child in the context of the home provides a look at the parent–child interaction, the resources of the home, and the child's role in the family. One teacher announces to the class at the beginning of the year that she is available on Friday nights to be invited to dinner. Knowing in advance that their invitation is welcomed, parents and children are proud to act as hosts.

Example of Concept | *A Home Visit*

Home visits can be an effective way for a teacher not only to demonstrate accessibility and interest to students and their families, but also to learn about the family and the context in which the student lives.

One teacher announced to her class that she would be available on Friday evenings to be invited to eat in students' homes. That set of a bit of competition! Students passed the "request for invitation" to their families, and she was booked solidly from fall through the winter holidays. When she would begin class on Monday mornings with thanks to the host student, and describe the tastiest part of the menu, eyes would sparkle with the memory of having had a special guest at home.

Students as Sources of Information. Students generally provide teachers with their initial contact with other cultures. Teachers who are good listeners offer students time for shared conversations by lingering after school or opening the classroom during lunchtime. Teachers may find it useful to ask students to map their own neighborhood. This is a source of knowledge from the students' perspectives about the boundaries of the neighborhood and surrounding areas.

Parents as Sources of Information. Parents can be sources of information in much the same way as their children. The school may encourage parent participation by opening the library once a week after school. This offers a predictable time during which parents and teachers can casually meet and chat. Parents can also be the source for information that can form the basis for classroom writing. Using the Language Experience Approach, teachers can ask students to interview their parents about common topics such as work, interests, and family history. In this way, students and parents together can supply knowledge about community life.

Community Members as Sources of Information. Community members are a rich source of cultural knowledge. Much can be learned about a community by walking or driving through it, or stopping to make a purchase in local stores and markets. One teacher arranged to walk through the neighborhood with a doctor whose office was located there. Other teachers may ask older students to act as tour guides. During these visits, the people of the neighborhood can be sources of knowledge about housing, places where children and teenagers play, places where adults gather, and sources of food, furniture, and services.

Through community representatives, teachers can begin to know about important living patterns of a community. A respected elder can provide information about the family and which members constitute a family. A community leader may be able to contrast the community political system with the city or state system. A religious leader can explain the importance of religion in community life. Teachers can also attend local ceremonies and activities to learn more about community dynamics.

The Internet. Websites proliferate that introduce the curious to other cultures. Webcrawler programs assist the user to explore cultural content using keyword prompts.

Participating in Growth Relationships. Self-study is only one means of attaining self-knowledge. Teachers who form relationships with individuals whose backgrounds differ from their own, whether teacher colleagues or community members, can benefit from honest feedback and discussions that help to expand self-awareness. Intercultural educators are not free from making mistakes when dealing with students, family and community members, and colleagues whose culture differs from their own. The only lasting error is not learning from these missteps or misunderstandings.

Sociocultural Consciousness. Villegas and Lucas (2007) invite teachers who were raised in middle-class, monolingual communities to develop a "sociocultural consciousness" (p. 31) that impels them to examine the role of schools in both perpetuating and challenging social inequities. Understanding the role that differential distribution of wealth and power plays in school success helps teachers to commit to the ethical obligation of helping all students learn.

How Cultural Adaptation Affects Learning

As immigrants enter American life, they make conscious or unconscious choices about which aspects of their culture to preserve and which to modify. When cultures meet, they affect each other. Cultures can be swallowed up (*assimilation*), one culture may adapt to a second (acculturation), both may adapt to each other (*accommodation*), or they may coexist (*pluralism or biculturalism*). Contact between cultures is often not a benign process. It may be fraught with issues of prejudice, discrimination, and misunderstanding. Means of mediation or resolution must be found to alleviate cultural conflict, particularly in classrooms.

Fears about Cultural Adaptation. Pryor (2002) captured the nature of immigrant parents' concerns about their children's adjustment to life in the United States:

> In the United States, some immigrant parents live in fear that their children will be corrupted by what they believe to be the materialistic and individualistic dominant culture, become alienated from their families, and fall prey to drugs and promiscuity. Their fears are not unfounded, as research shows that the longer that immigrants live in the United States, the worse their physical and mental health becomes. . . . One Jordanian mother stated, "I tell my son (who is 8 years old) not to use the restroom in school. I tell him he might catch germs there that he could bring home, and make the whole family ill. I really am afraid he may get drugs from other kids in the restroom." (p. 187)

Many immigrant parents are overwhelmed with personal, financial, and work-related problems; they may have few resources to which to turn for help. In the process of coming to terms with life in a foreign country, they may be at odds with the assimilation or acculturation processes their children are experiencing, causing family conflict.

| **Example of Concept** | *Holding on to Sikh Heritage in the United States* |

Sikhs began coming to the United States in large numbers in the 1980s because of religious persecution in India, gradually numbering about 500,000 across America. Sikh communities across North America began to realize that their children needed to acquire Punjabi in order to maintain their religious practice (Sikhism is the world's fifth largest religion). Now there are about 150 *gurdwaras,* or Sunday schools, to teach how to speak and write Punjabi and maintain the culture and values of the Sikh religion.

According to Jasdeep Singh, who has two young sons who attend weekly classes, his parents' generation has their ties to India to support their ethnic identity. But young people need more. "I think my generation is the one that's actually seen the value of Punjabi schools." (Abdulrahim, 2011, p. AA3)

Assimilation. When members of an ethnic group are absorbed into the dominant culture and their culture gradually disappears in the process, they are said to assimilate. *Cultural assimilation* is the process by which individuals adopt the behaviors, values, beliefs, and lifestyle of the dominant culture. *Structural assimilation* is participation in the social, political, and economic institutions and organizations of mainstream society. It is structural assimilation that has been problematic for many immigrants. Teachers may strive to have students assimilate culturally but be blind to the fact that some of their students will not succeed because of attitudes and structures of the dominant society.

Acculturation. When individuals adapt effectively to the mainstream culture, they are said to *acculturate*. To acculturate is to adapt to a second culture without necessarily giving up one's first culture. Some researchers have emphasized the importance of acculturation for success in school.

Schools are the primary places in which children of various cultures learn about the mainstream culture. Sometimes culture is taught explicitly as a part of the ELD curriculum (Seelye, 1984). According to Cortés (2013):

> Acculturation of students should be a primary goal of education because it contributes to individual empowerment and expands life choices. However, this acculturation should be additive, not subtractive. Subtractive acculturation can disempower by eroding students' multicultural abilities to function effectively within both the mainstream and their own ethnic milieus, as well as in their relations with those of other cultural backgrounds. But today even traditional additive acculturation is not enough. For our multicultural twenty-first century, education should strive to develop student multicultural capacities by embracing what I call "multiculturation," the blending of *multiple* and *acculturation*.

Accommodation. A two-way process, accommodation happens when members of the mainstream culture change in adapting to a minority culture, the members of which in turn accept some cultural change as they adapt to the mainstream. Thus, accommodation is a mutual process. To make accommodation a viable alternative in schools, teachers need to demonstrate that they are receptive to learning from the diverse cultures in their midst, and they also need to teach majority students the value of "interethnic reciprocal learning" (Gibson, 1991).

Example of Concept   *Accommodating Students' Culture*

[I]n non-Indian[*] classes students are given opportunities to ask the teacher questions in front of the class, and do so. Indian students are given fewer opportunities for this because when they do have the opportunity, they don't use it. Rather, the teacher of Indians allows more periods in which she is available for individual students to approach her alone and ask their questions where no one else can hear them. (Philips, 1972, p. 383)

[*]Native American

Pluralism. Assimilation, not acculturation, was the aim of many immigrants who sought to become part of the melting pot. More recently, minority groups and their advocates have begun to assert that minority and ethnic groups have a right, if not a responsibility, to maintain valued elements of their ethnic cultures. This *pluralist* position is that coexistence of multicultural traditions within a single society provides a variety of alternatives that enrich life in the United States. Pluralism is the condition in which members of diverse cultural groups have equal opportunities for success, in which cultural similarities and differences are valued, and in which students are provided cultural alternatives. Integration creates the conditions for cultural pluralism. Merely mixing formerly isolated ethnic groups does not go far enough, because groups rapidly unmix and resegregate.

Biculturalism. Being able to function successfully in two cultures constitutes biculturalism. Darder (1991) defined *biculturalism* as

> a process wherein individuals learn to function in two distinct sociocultural environments: their primary culture, and that of the dominant mainstream culture of the society in which they live. It represents the process by which bicultural human beings mediate between the dominant discourse of educational institutions and the realities they must face as members of subordinate cultures. (pp. 48–49)

What is it like to be bicultural in the United States? Bicultural people are sometimes viewed with distrust. An example is the suspicion toward Japanese Americans during World War II and the resulting internment. Parents may also feel threatened by their bicultural children. Appalachian families who moved to large cities to obtain work often pressured their children to maintain an agrarian, preindustrial lifestyle, a culture that is in many ways inconsistent with urban environments (Pasternak, 1994). Similarly, families from rural Mexico may seek to maintain traditional values after immigrating to the United States even as their children adopt behaviors from the U.S. macroculture. The process of becoming bicultural is not without stress, especially for students who are expected to internalize dissimilar, perhaps conflicting, values.

Cultural Congruence. In U.S. schools, the contact of cultures occurs daily. In this contact, the congruence or lack thereof between mainstream and minority cultures has lasting effects on students. Students from families whose cultural values are similar to those of the European-American mainstream culture may be relatively advantaged in schools, such as children from those Asian cultures who are taught that students sit quietly and attentively. In contrast, African American students who learn at home to project their personalities and call attention to their individual attributes (Gay, 1975) may be punished for efforts to call attention to themselves during class.

Teachers, who have the responsibility to educate students from diverse cultures, find it relatively easy to help students whose values, beliefs, and behaviors are congruent with U.S. schooling but often find it difficult to work with others. The teacher who can find a common ground with diverse students will promote their further education.

Stages of Individual Cultural Contact. Experiencing a second culture causes emotional ups and downs. Reactions to a new culture vary, but there are distinct stages in the process of experiencing a different culture (Brown, 2007). These same emotional stages can occur for students. The intensity will vary depending on the degree of similarity between home and school culture, the individual child, and the teacher.

The first state, *euphoria*, may result from the excitement of experiencing new customs, foods, and sights. This may be a "honeymoon" period in which the newcomer is fascinated and stimulated by experiencing a new culture.

The next stage, *culture shock*, may follow euphoria as cultural differences begin to intrude. The newcomer is increasingly aware of being different and may be disoriented by cultural cues that result in frustration. Deprivation of the familiar may cause a loss of self-esteem. Depression, anger, or withdrawal may result.

The final stage, *adaptation to the new culture*, may take several months to several years. Long-term adjustment can take several forms. Ideally, the newcomer feels capable of negotiating most new and different situations. On the other hand, individuals who do not adjust as well may feel lonely and frustrated. A loss of self-confidence may result. Eventually, successful adaptation results in newcomers being able to actively express themselves and to create a full range of meaning in the situation.

Example of Concept   *Diagnose Your Vulnerability to Culture Shock*

The *Intercultural Effectiveness Scale (IES)* is a self-assessment available from the Kozai Group (http://www.intercultural.org/kozai.php) that "evaluates competencies critical for effective interaction with people from different cultures." Those who take this self-assessment receive a diagnostic booklet that explains which self-reported personality strengths and challenges might lead to more or less success when interacting with other cultures. According to the website of the Intercultural Communication Institute, "[The *IES*] is useful in crosscultural and diversity courses to increase awareness and self-analysis for improvement."

Source: Printed with permission of The Intercultural Communication Institute. (2013). The Intercultural Effectiveness Scale (IES). Online at www.intercultural.org/kozai.pho.

Striving for Equity in Schooling

Teachers who were themselves primarily socialized in mainstream American culture may not be aware of the challenges faced by individuals from nondominant cultures as they strive to succeed in U.S. schools. Bonilla-Silva (2003) contended that European Americans have developed powerful rationalizations and justifications for contemporary racial inequality that exculpate them from responsibility for the status of people of color. This constitutes a new racial ideology he called "color-blind racism" (p. 2), which is a way of committing or participating in racist practices while not believing that oneself is racist (also called "racism without racists" [p. 1] and "new racism" [p. 3]).

To create school environments that are fair for all students, teachers need to achieve clarity of vision (Balderrama & Díaz-Rico, 2005) about the social forces that advantage some members of society and disadvantage others. This work entails recognizing that society is becoming increasingly polarized, moving toward a vast separation between the rich and the poor. Class and racial privilege, prejudice, and unequal opportunity are barriers to success. Awareness of unfair practices is the first step toward remedy.

Detecting Unfair Privilege

For European American middle-class teachers to accept the work of achieving equity in education, they must at some point examine their own complicity in the privileges of being white and middle class in a society predicated on inequity. *Privilege* is defined as the state of benefiting from special advantages, favors, or rights accorded to some, to the exclusion of others. McIntosh's (1996) article "White Privilege and Male Privilege" is a useful tool for exploring the advantage experienced by those who are white, male, or middle-class in order to become aware of the many social advantages they have reaped at the expense of those who are nonwhite, non-middle-class, or female. Figure 9.1 presents some of the privileges that the dominant race/class/gender enjoys.

Fighting for Fairness and Equal Opportunity

Schools in the United States have not been level playing fields for those of nonmainstream cultures. Teachers can remedy this in both academic and extracurricular areas. According to Manning (2002), teachers should

> consider that all learners deserve, ethically and legally, equal access to curricular activities (i.e., higher-level mathematics and science subjects) and opportunities to participate in all athletic activities (i.e., rather than assuming all students of one race will play on the basketball team and all students of another race will play on the tennis or golfing teams). (p. 207)

Cultural fairness can extend to the social and interpersonal lives of students, those daily details and microinteractions that also fall within the domain of culture. Teachers who invest time to get to know their students, as individuals as well as cultural beings, address issues of fairness through a personal commitment to equality of treatment and opportunity.

Figure 9.1 The Privileges of the Dominant Race/Class/Gender

I can rent or purchase housing in an affordable, desirable area, with neighbors who will be neutral or pleasant to me.

My children will see their race represented in curricular materials.

When I purchase, my skin color does not suggest financial instability.

I can criticize our government without being seen as a cultural outsider.

"The person in charge" is usually a person of my race.

Traffic cops do not single me out because of my race.

My behavior is not taken as a reflection on my race.

If my day is going badly, I need not suspect racial overtones in each negative situation.

I can imagine many options—social, political, or professional—without wondering if a person of my race would be allowed to do what I want to do.

Source: Adapted from McIntosh (1996).

Establishing a Climate of Safety

Many students live in terror of school because they are bullied. Bullying is an issue of power, and those who lack power and social capital—such as immigrants—are often targets. English learners may suffer from racial and ethnic stereotyping; cultural and language barriers and concerns over legal status may lead to many incidents not being reported to authorities. Classroom discussion about current or historical events involving immigrant communities can also help prevent bullying by humanizing those groups to other students.

Gay, lesbian, bisexual, and transgender (GLBT) students also report a high level of being bullied. According to a 2009 survey of more than 7,200 middle- and high-school students, nearly eighty-five percent of LGBT students say they are verbally harassed, and forty percent report physical harassment because of their sexual orientation (Kosciw, Greytak, Díaz, & Bartkiewicz, 2010). GLBT teens commit suicide at three to four times the rate of other students. Almost eighty percent of teens say their teachers do little or nothing to stop anti-LGBT bullying when they see it. Reece-Miller (2010) calls the gay, lesbian, bisexual, transgender, and queer/questioning (LGBTQ) students "the silent minority," whose needs are largely ignored in K–12 schools.

Educators have a legal responsibility to respond to students' bullying one another. If a student is teased because of perceived sexual orientation, "Some teachers and principals don't get involved. This might seem like an issue best left out of the classroom, but there's a population of gay, lesbian, bisexual and transgender (GLBT) students who feel unsafe at school" (Martin, 2011, p. 9).

Educators can create safe schools for GLBTIQ (now including "intersex") students:

- Establish a student club ("gay-straight alliance") where students can talk about issues related to sexual orientation.
- Provide anti-bullying training, emphasizing GLBT issues.
- Develop the presence of supportive staff (who are not necessarily GLBTIQ themselves).
- Include GLBTIQ figures in the curriculum. (Martin, 2011)

| **Example of Concept** | *Reducing Verbal Emotional Violence* |

Tired of battling students' verbal put-downs of one another in his eighth-grade social studies classroom, John Ash led a discussion on what it felt like to both send and receive put-downs. Using definitions, examples, and student input, Ash showed students how to identify and react to this kind of verbal violence.

In less than a month, Ash had drastically reduced the incidents of verbal violence in his classroom. "Some people think 'safe' refers only to physical safety," he said. "But it also means emotional safety. If I don't provide an environment where students are safe emotionally, how much learning do you think will occur?" (Moorman & Haller, 2011)

Combating Prejudice in Ourselves and Others

If diversity is recognized as a strength, educators will "avoid basing decisions about learners on inaccurate or stereotypical generalizations" (Manning, 2002, p. 207). Misperceptions about diversity often stem from prejudice.

The Dynamics of Prejudice. One factor that inhibits cultural adaptation is prejudice. Prejudice takes various forms: excessive pride in one's own ethnic heritage, country, or culture so that others are viewed negatively; *ethnocentrism*, in which the world revolves around oneself and one's own culture; a prejudice against members of a certain racial group; and stereotypes that label all or most members of a group. All humans are prejudiced to some degree, but it is when people act on those prejudices that discriminatory practices and inequalities result.

A closer look at various forms of prejudice, such as racism and stereotyping, as well as resulting discriminatory practices can lead to an understanding of these issues. Teachers can then be in a position to adopt educational methods that are most likely to reduce prejudice.

Example of Concept *Xenophobia in U.S. History*

Sutherland (1989) described the Centennial of 1876, which was held in Philadelphia:

> [T]he Centennial impressed everyone. Its 167 buildings and 30,000 exhibits covered 236 acres in Fairmount Park. The Main Exhibition Building, housing the principal exhibits of manufactured products and scientific achievements, measured 1,800 feet long and 464 feet wide, the largest building in the world. . . . [A] total of thirty-five foreign nations provided exhibits or entertainment in one form or another. . . . [W]herever they went on the fairgrounds, visitors saw and heard xenophobic expressions of prejudice. Foreign-looking people of all races and nationalities, were they Orientals, Turks, Slavs, Egyptians, or Spaniards, were "followed by large crowds of idle boys, and men, who hooted and shouted at them as if they had been animals of a strange species." (pp. 263, 264, 268)

Racism. Racism is the view that a person's race determines psychological and cultural traits—and, moreover, that one race is superior to another. Racism can also be cultural when one believes that the traditions, beliefs, languages, artifacts, music, and art of other cultures are inferior. On the basis of such beliefs, racists justify discriminating against or scapegoating other groups. As important as is the facet of symbolic violence that racism represents, of equal importance is the fact that goods and services are distributed in accordance with such judgments of unequal worth.

Racism is often expressed in hate crimes, which are public expressions of hostility directed at specific groups or individuals. These may take the form of harassment (scrawling graffiti on people's homes; pelting houses with eggs; burning crosses on lawns; children playing in yards being subjected to verbal taunts; hate-filled e-mails sent to individuals or groups; swastikas carved into public textbooks, school desks, or other property; etc.) or, at the extreme, assaults and murder directed toward minorities. Schools are often prime sites in which hate crimes are committed. This fact underscores the urgency of educators' efforts to understand and combat racism.

Example of Concept
Racial Tension—Differing Points of View

When racial tensions erupted between Black and Asian students at South Philadelphia High School, Asian students shared their concerns about the events at a news conference with community advocates. They charged that school security guards did not protect them. In turn, the security spokesman said, "What gets lost in all of this is the fact that the school, the community, and the students have worked hard over the past two years to foster a positive learning environment."

Through a translator, ninth-grader Chaofei Zheng said that he wants to get an education, make friends, and improve his English; that there are nice students at the school and he doesn't understand the reason for the attacks that sent several Asian students to a hospital.

Amina Velazquez, a senior who is Black and Puerto Rican, said that Asian students tend to stay within their own groups, making it hard to get to know them. Valazquez, a member of student government, suggested that if Asian students participated in more activities, they would be further integrated into the school community. She noted that for some, language barriers make interaction difficult.

Superintendent Michael Silverman had a fourth viewpoint. The racial tension "started in the community and came to school—I don't know how you separate the school from the community." (Matheson, 2009, Associated Press, (www.accessmylibrary.com/article-1G1-213640674/us-school-racial-tensions.html)

Teaching against Racism. Students and teachers alike must raise awareness of racism in the attempt to achieve racial equality and justice. Actively listening to students in open discussion about racism, prejudice, and stereotyping can increase teachers' understanding of how students perceive and are affected by these concepts. School curricula can be used to help students be aware of the existence and impact of racism. Science and health teachers can debunk myths surrounding the concept of race. Content-area teachers can help students develop skills in detecting bias.

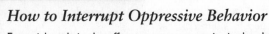

Adapted Instruction
How to Interrupt Oppressive Behavior

Essential tools in the effort to promote equity in the classroom and school environment are the skills that work toward social justice. All too frequently students join in mockery or discriminatory behaviors because they cannot stand up to peer pressure—instead, they turn away, or they "go with the crowd." In such situation, students can "act toward" social justice in the following ways:

- Interrupting the behavior by voicing disapproval: "I don't think that's funny."

- Interrupting and educating others by explaining why the behavior is wrong.

- Supporting others who are proactive by siding with them physically or verbally.

- Replacing hurtful behaviors by initiating and organizing opposite, proactive responses. (McClintock, 2000)

Stereotypes. Often resulting from racist beliefs, stereotypes are preconceived and oversimplified generalizations about a particular ethnic or religious group, race, or gender. The danger of stereotyping is that people are not considered as individuals but are categorized with all other members of a group. A stereotype can be favorable or unfavorable, but, whether it is positive or negative, the results are negative: The perspective on an entire group of people is distorted.

Example of Concept *Comparisons within a Cultural Group*

Mrs. Abboushi, a third-grade teacher, discovers that her students hold many misconceptions about the Arab people. Her goal becomes to present them with an accurate and more rounded view of the Arab world. She builds background information by using a world map on which the students identify the countries featured in the three books they will read: *Ibrahim* (Sales, 1989), *The Day of Ahmed's Secret* (Heide & Gilliland, 1990), and *Nadia, the Willful* (Alexander, 1983).

After reading and interactively discussing the books, students are divided into groups of four, each receiving a copy of one of the books. Students prepare a Cultural Feature Analysis chart that includes the cultural features, setting, character and traits, family relationships, and message. Groups share their information and Mrs. Abboushi records the information on a large chart. During the follow-up discussion, students discover that not all Arabs live the same way, dress the same way, or look the same way. They recognize the merging of traditional and modern worlds, the variability in living conditions, customs and values, architecture, clothing, and modes of transportation (Diamond & Moore, 1995, pp. 229–230).

Adapted Instruction

Antiracist Activities and Discussion Topics

- Recognize racist history and its impact on oppressors and victims.
- Understand the origins of racism and why people hold racial prejudices and stereotypes.
- Be able to identify racist images in the language and illustrations of books, films, television, news media, and advertising.
- Identify specific ways of developing positive interracial contact experiences.
- Extend the fight against racism into a broader fight for universal human rights and respect for human dignity.

Source: Bennett (2003, pp. 370–373).

Programs to Combat Prejudice and Racism. The Southern Poverty Law Center distributes Teaching Tolerance magazine, a free resource sent to over 600,000 educators twice a year that provides antibias strategies for K–12 teachers. Carnuccio (2004) describes the Tolerance.org website, a web project of the Southern Poverty Law Center (available at www.splcenter.org), as an "extremely informative resource":

The project has done an excellent job of collecting and disseminating information on the advantages of diversity. . . . The site features pages designed specifically for children, teens, teachers, and parents. *Planet Tolerance* has stories for children to read and listen to and games for them to play. Teens can find ideas on how to bring diverse groups together in their schools. Teachers' pages feature articles, films and books to order, lesson ideas, and a forum in which to share ideas with other teachers. The pamphlet *101 Tools for Tolerance* suggests a variety of ideas for community, workplace, school, and home settings. *Parenting for Tolerance* offers ways for parents to guide their children to develop into tolerant adults. (p. 59)

Example of Concept   *Combating Anti-Muslim Bias*

In the wake of the 2001 World Trade Center bombings, the 2.5 million Muslims in the United States have reported widespread negative bias. Educators have taken the lead in combatting this bias.

Southeastern Michigan is a richly diverse area that includes a large Arab American community. But in this divided region, kids from different backgrounds rarely meet. For the past twenty years, the group Generation of Promise has chosen sixty high-school juniors for a ten-month program that gives them the opportunity to showcase their culture and learn about others.

"We attempt to take students who are leaders in those communities, who can influence their peer groups, and expose them to that diversity in a real, intimate way," says Christine Geoghegan, director of Generation of Promise. That can happen through trips to a mosque in Dearborn or by attending a Shabbat dinner at the home of a Jewish student.

In 2010, Maya Edery, an Israeli American, was paired with Mohamad Idriss, a native of Lebanon who is Muslim. They have become close friends.

"You can coordinate the most sophisticated program," says Geoghegan. "But what changes people is people—access to relationships they're otherwise not having." (www.tolerance .org/magazine/number-39-spring-2011/feature/ combating-anti-muslim-bias)

Institutional Racism. "[T]hose laws, customs, and practices that systematically reflect and produce racial inequalities in American society" (Jones, 1981) constitute institutional racism. Classroom teaching that aims at detecting and reducing racism may be a futile exercise when the institution itself—the school—promotes racism through its policies and practices, such as underreferral of minority students to programs for gifted students or failing to hire minority teachers in classrooms where children are predominantly of minority background.

Classism. In the United States, racism is compounded with classism, the distaste of the middle and upper classes for the lifestyles and perceived values of the lower classes. Although this classism is often directed against linguistic and cultural minorities—a typical poor person in the American imagination is urban, black, and young, either a single teen mother or her offspring—portraying poverty that way makes it easier to stigmatize the poor (Henwood, 1997).

Classism has engendered its own stereotype against poor European Americans— for example, the stereotyped European American indigent who is called, among other things, "White trash" (Wray & Newitz, 1997). Poor whites, who outnumber poor minorities, may bear the brunt of a "castelike" status in the United States as much as linguistic and cultural minorities do.

Discrimination. Discriminatory practices tend to legitimize the unequal distribution of power and resources between groups defined by such factors as race, language, culture, gender, and/or social class. Blatant discrimination, in which differential education for minorities is legally sanctioned, may be a thing of the past, but discrimination persists. De facto segregation continues; most students of color are still found in substandard schools. Schools with a high percentage of minority enrollment tend to employ faculty who have less experience and academic preparation. Teachers may communicate low expectations to minority students. The "hidden curriculum" of tracking and differential treatment results in schools that perpetuate the structural inequities of society. Thus, school becomes a continuation of the discrimination experienced by minorities in other institutions in society (Grant & Sleeter, 1986).

In the past, those in power often used physical force to discriminate. With the spread of literacy, the trend moved away from the use of physical force toward the use of shame and guilt. The school plays a part in this process. The values, norms, and ideology of those in power are taught in the school. Skutnabb-Kangas (1981, 1993) called this *symbolic-structural violence*. Direct punishment is replaced by self-punishment, and the group discriminated against internalizes shame associated with cultural differences. The emotional and intellectual bonds of internalized injustice make the situation of minorities more difficult.

Example of Concept   *Avoiding "Microaggressions"*

Teachers may be unaware of the effect of their interactions with students from underrepresented groups. Derald Wing Sue's *Microaggressions in Everyday Life: Race, Gender, and Sexual Orientation* (2010) offers an analysis of how careless, unintended slights and inadvertent social cues can take massive tolls on the psychological well-being and academic achievement of minority groups. (*Hint:* Never sigh, "Oh, boy..." in frustration when teaching a group of African American youth.)

Reducing Interethnic Conflict

If interethnic conflict occurs, taking immediate, proactive steps to resolve the conflict is necessary. Table 9.5 presents a scenario in which conflict resolution is needed and describes a twelve-skill approach to mediation.

Johnson and Johnson (1979, 1994, 1995) emphasized the usefulness of cooperative, heterogeneous grouping in the classroom in the resolution of classroom conflict. Explicit training for elementary students in negotiation and mediation procedures has proved effective in managing conflict, especially when such programs focus on safely expressing feelings, taking the perspective of the other, and providing the rationale for diverse points of view (Johnson, Johnson, Dudley, & Acikgoz, 1994).

Table 9.5 Applying a Twelve-Skill Approach to Interethnic Conflict

Scenario: A group of four European American girls in tenth grade had been making fun of Irena and three of her friends, all of whom were U.S.-born Mexican Americans. One afternoon Irena missed her bus home from high school, and the four girls surrounded her when she was putting books in her locker. One girl shoved a book out of the stack in her hands. Irena shoved her back. Just then, a teacher came around the corner and took Irena to the office for discipline. The assistant principal, Ms. Nava, interviewed Irena to gain some background about the situation. Rather than dealing with Irena in isolation, Ms. Nava waited until the next day, called all eight of the girls into her office, and applied the twelve-skill approach to conflict resolution.

Skill	Application of Skills to Scenario
1. The win–win approach: Identify attitude shifts to respect all parties' needs.	Ms. Nava asked each girl to write down what the ideal outcome of the situation would be. Comparing notes, three of the girls had written "respect." Ms. Nava decided to use this as a win–win theme.
2. Creative response: Transform problems into creative opportunities.	Each girl was asked to write the name of an adult who respected her and how she knew it was genuine respect.
3. Empathy: Develop communication tools to build rapport. Use listening to clarify understanding.	In turn, each girl described what she had written above. The other girls had to listen, using eye contact to show attentiveness.
4. Appropriate assertiveness: Apply strategies to attack the problem not the person.	Ms. Nava offered an opportunity for members of the group to join the schools' Conflict Resolution Task Force. She also warned the group that another incident between them would result in suspension.
5. Cooperative power: Eliminate "power over" to build "power with" others.	Each girl was paired with a girl from the "other side" (cross-group pair) to brainstorm ways in which teens show respect for one another.
6. Managing emotions: Express fear, anger, hurt, and frustration wisely to effect change.	Ms. Nava then asked Irena and the girl who pushed her book to tell their side of the incident without name-calling.
7. Willingness to resolve: Name personal issues that cloud the picture.	Each girl was asked to name one underlying issue between the groups that this incident represented.
8. Mapping the conflict: Define the issues needed to chart common needs and concerns.	Ms. Nava mapped the issues by writing them on a wall chart as they were brought forth.
9. Development of options: Design creative solutions together.	Still in the cross-group pairs from step 5 above, each pair was asked to design a solution for one of the issues mapped.
10. Introduction to negotiation: Plan and apply effective strategies to reach agreement.	Ms. Nava called the girls into her office for a second day. They reviewed the solutions that were designed and made a group plan for improved behavior.
11. Introduction to mediation: Help conflicting parties to move toward solutions.	Each cross-group pair generated two ideas for repair if the above plan failed.
12. Broadening perspectives: Evaluate the problem in its broader context.	The eight girls were asked if racial conflict occurred outside their group. Ms. Nava asked for discussion: Were the same issues they generated responsible for this conflict?

Source: Based on www.crnhq.org.

Especially critical is the role of a mediator in establishing and maintaining a balance of power between two parties in a dispute, protecting the weaker party from intimidation, and ensuring that both parties have a stake in the process and the outcome of mediation. In contrast, those programs that teach about "group differences,"

Example of Concept   *Conflict Resolution in New Jersey*

Real estate development in the West Windsor–Plainsboro School District in the 1980s and 1990s brought into one rural area a population that was diverse in income, culture, race, and ethnicity. Increasing incidents of racial unrest in the schools and in the community at large caused school administrators to set into motion a program of conflict resolution in K–12 classrooms. Among its components were the following:

- A peacemaking program at the elementary level to teach children how to solve problems without resorting to aggression
- Training for middle school students in facilitating positive human relations
- A ninth-grade elective course in conflict resolution
- An elective course for grade 11 and 12 students to prepare student mediators for a peer-mediation center
- An annual "human relations" retreat for student leaders and teachers that encouraged frank and open conversations about interpersonal and race relations

- A planned welcome program for newcomers at the school to overcome feelings of isolation
- A minority recruitment program for teachers
- Elimination of watered-down, nonrigorous academic courses in lieu of challenging courses, accompanied by a tutoring program for academically underprepared high-school students

Within three years, the number of incidences of vandalism, violence, and substance abuse in the school district was reduced considerably. The people of West Windsor and Plainsboro "accomplished much in their quest to rise out of the degradation of bigotry" (Bandlow, 2002, pp. 91–92; Prothrow-Smith, 1994).

involve exhortation or mere verbal learning, or are designed directly for "prejudice reduction" are usually not effective.

Educators should not assume that cultural contact entails cultural conflict. Perhaps the best way to prevent conflict is to include a variety of cultural content and make sure the school recognizes and values cultural diversity. If conflict does occur, however, there are means to prevent its escalation. Teachers should be aware of conflict resolution techniques before they are actually needed.

Adapted Instruction

Resolving Conflicts in the Classroom

- Resolve to be calm in the face of verbalized anger and hostility.
- To defuse a problem, talk to students privately, encouraging the sharing of perceptions on volatile issues. Communicate expectations that students will be able to resolve their differences.
- If confrontation occurs, set aside a brief period for verbal expression. Allow students to vent feelings as a group.
- Do not tolerate violence or personal attacks.

Promote Achievement with Culturally Responsive Schooling

Intercultural educators who understand students' cultures can design instruction to meet children's learning needs. They invite students to learn by welcoming them, making them feel that they belong, and presenting learning as a task at which students can succeed. Teaching styles, interaction patterns, classroom organization, curricula, and involvement with parents and the community are factors within the teacher's power to adapt.

The intercultural educator uses culturally responsive schooling practices to promote the school success of culturally and linguistically diverse (CLD) students. As Richards, Brown, and Forde (2004) stated, "In a culturally responsive classroom, effective teaching and learning occur in a culturally supported, learner-centered context, whereby the strengths students bring to school are identified, nurtured, and utilized to promote student achievement" (n.p.).

The four major components of culturally responsive schooling that promote achievement (see Table 9.1 on page 242) are as follows.

- Respect students' diversity.
- Work with culturally supported facilitating or limiting attitudes and abilities.
- Sustain high expectations for all students.
- Marshal parental and community support for schooling.

This section examines each of these components in turn.

Respecting Students' Diversity

Traditionally, educators have used the word *diversity* to denote racial differences. However, today's school population is diverse in a number of ways: academic ability, multiple intelligences, learning styles, thinking styles, gender, attitudes, culture and ethnicity, socioeconomic status, home language, and developmental readiness (Kagan, 2007). Differentiated instruction has come to mean the responsibility that teachers must assume in diversifying classroom practices to ensure that individual students will succeed.

Differentiated instruction involves first assessing students to get to know them in a variety of ways. Then, instructional components must be diversified. Differentiated instruction is an approach in which teachers assess students to determine how they differ on an array of characteristics and then modify instruction to honor that diversity. Ongoing assessment helps teachers maintain a flexible understanding of students' needs.

Acknowledging Students' Differences. Imagine a classroom of thirty students, each with just one unique fact, value, or belief on the more than fifty categories presented in Table 9.3 ("Components of Culture," p. 245). Culture includes diversity in values, social customs, rituals, work and leisure activities, health and educational practices, and many other aspects of life. Each of these can affect schooling and are discussed in the following sections, including ways that teachers can respond to these differences in adapting instruction.

Values are "beliefs about how one ought or ought not to behave or about some end state of existence worth or not worth attaining" (Bennett, 2003, p. 64). Values are particularly important to people when they educate their young, because education is a primary means of transmitting cultural knowledge.

Example of Concept

Teacher Whose Values Nurture Latino/as

Teachers play an indispensable part within the learning environment of the school. They engage and nurture student learning via a variety of social and personal situations. . . . Inherent in this process is the teacher's ideology as reflected in the pedagogical practices that the teacher exemplifies. The desired pedagogical practices will most likely include her or his curricular understandings embedded within constructs of diversity; pluralism; integrated pedagogy; knowledge acquisition and learning; first and second language acquisition and learning; academic content; democratic understandings; social justice; and . . . the new millennium of technology, multicomplex information systems, multicultural communications, and global collaboration and competition.

. . . Latinos/as need to be respected for whom they are and for what they bring to school. Unquestionably, Latino/a students need to be connected socially, emotionally, and academically to their schools. Latina/o students must experience teachers and a school curriculum that accepts them for whom they are and encourages them to grow to whom they can become. . . . Teachers and the schools that support them are prepared to do right by their students by daring to love and care genuinely for their students, their historicities, and their ethnicities.

—*Rudolfo Chávez Chávez (1997, n.p.)*

Social customs cause people to lead very different daily lives. These customs are paced and structured by deep habits of using time and space. For example, *time* is organized in culturally specific ways.

Example of Concept

Cultural Conceptions about Time

Adela, a Mexican American first-grade girl, arrived at school about twenty minutes late every day. Her teacher was at first irritated and gradually exasperated. In a parent conference, Adela's mother explained that braiding her daughter's hair each morning was an important time for the two of them to be together, even if it meant being slightly late to school. This family time presented a value conflict with the school's time norm.

Other conflicts may arise when teachers demand abrupt endings to activities in which children are deeply engaged or when events are scheduled in a strict sequence. In fact, schools in the United States are often paced very strictly by clock time, whereas family life in various cultures is not regulated in the same manner. Moreover, teachers often equate speed of performance with intelligence, and standardized tests are often a test of rapidity. Many teachers find themselves in the role of "time mediator"—helping the class to adhere to the school's time schedule while working with individual students to help them meet their learning needs within the time allotted.

Adapted Instruction

Accommodating Different Concepts of Time and Work Rhythms

- Provide students with choices about their work time and observe how time spent on various subjects accords with students' aptitudes and interests.

- If a student is a slow worker, analyze the work rhythms. Slow yet methodically accurate work deserves respect; slow and disorganized work may require a peer helper.

- If students are chronically late to school, ask the school counselor to meet with the responsible family member to discuss a change in morning routines.

Space is another aspect about which social customs differ according to cultural experience. Personal space varies: In some cultures, individuals touch one another frequently and maintain high degrees of physical contact; in other cultures, touch and proximity cause feelings of tension and embarrassment. The organization of the space in the classroom sends messages to students: how free they are to move about the classroom, how much of the classroom they "own," how the desks are arranged. Both the expectations of the students and the needs of the teacher can be negotiated to provide a classroom setting in which space is shared.

Adapted Instruction

Accommodating Different Concepts of Personal Space

- If students from the same culture and gender (one with a close personal space) have a high degree of physical contact and neither seems bothered by this, the teacher does not have to intervene.

- The wise teacher accords the same personal space to students no matter what their culture (e.g., does not touch minority students more or less than mainstream students).

Some *symbolic systems* are external, such as dress and personal appearance. For example, a third-grade girl wearing makeup is communicating a message that some teachers may consider an inappropriate indicator of premature sexuality, although makeup on a young girl may be acceptable in some cultures. Other symbolic systems are internal, such as beliefs about natural phenomena, luck and fate, vocational expectations, and so forth.

Each culture incorporates expectations about the proper ways to carry out *rites, rituals, and ceremonies*. School ceremonies—for example, assemblies that begin with formal markers such as the Pledge of Allegiance and a flag salute—should have nonstigmatizing alternatives for those whose culture does not permit participation.

Adapted Instruction

Culturally Influenced School Dress Codes

- Boys and men in some cultures (e.g., rural Mexico) wear hats; classrooms need to have a place for these hats during class time and provision for wearing the hats during recess.
- Schools that forbid "gang attire" yet permit privileged students to wear student council insignia (i.e., sweaters with embroidered names) should forbid clique-related attire for all.
- A family–school council with representatives from various cultures should be responsible for reviewing the school dress code on a yearly basis to see if it meets the needs of various cultures.
- Permission for religious garb (e.g., Islamic head scarves, Sikh ritual knives, Hassidic dress) should be a part of the school dress code.

Rituals in some elementary classrooms in the United States are relatively informal. For example, students can enter freely before school and take their seats or go to a reading corner or activity center. Students from other cultures may find this confusing if they are accustomed to lining up in the courtyard, being formally greeted by the principal or head teacher, and then accompanied in their lines as they enter their respective classrooms.

Rituals are also involved in parent conferences. Greeting and welcome behaviors, for example, vary across cultures. The sensitive teacher understands how parents expect to be greeted and incorporates some of these behaviors in the exchange.

Crosscultural variation in *work and leisure activities* is a frequently discussed value difference. Young people, particularly those in the U.S. mainstream-culture middle class, are trained to use specific tools of play, and their time is structured to attain skills (e.g., organized sports, music lessons). In other cultures, such as that of the Hopi Nation in Arizona, children's playtime is relatively unstructured, and parents do not interfere with play. Cultures also vary in the typical work and play activities expected of girls and of boys. All these values have obvious influence on the ways children work and play at school.

Adapted Instruction

Accommodating Diverse Ideas about Work and Play

- Many high-school students arrange class schedules in order to work part time. If a student appears chronically tired, a family–teacher conference may be needed to review priorities.
- Many students are overcommitted to extracurricular activities. If grades suffer, students may be well advised to reduce activities to regain an academic focus.
- Plagiarism in student work may be due to unclear conceptions about the permissability of shared work.
- Out-of-school play activities such as birthday parties should not be organized at the school site, such as passing out invitations that exclude some students.

Health and medicine practices involve deep-seated beliefs, because the stakes are high: life and death. When students come to school with health issues, teachers need to react in culturally compatible ways. Miscommunication and noncooperation can result when teachers and the family view health and disease differently. For example, community health practices, such as the Cambodian tradition of coining (in which a coin is dipped in oil and then rubbed on a sick person's back, chest, and neck), can be misinterpreted by school officials who, seeing marks on the child, call Child Protective Services.

Adapted Instruction

Health and Hygiene Practices

- Families who send sick children to school or, conversely, keep children home at the slightest ache may benefit from a conference with the school nurse.
- All students can profit from explicit instruction in home and school hygiene.

The *economic, legal, political,* and *religious institutions* that support and govern family and community life have an influence on behavior and beliefs. Interwoven into U.S. institutions are religious beliefs and practices. In the United States, religious practices are heavily embedded but formally bounded: witness the controversy over Christmas trees in schools but the almost universal cultural and economic necessity for increased consumer spending at the close of the calendar year.

Schools in the U.S. have been responsive to the need for sensitivity about events they sponsor that seem to be too closely tied to religious holidays. In fact, the role of religion in the schools is often fiercely debated. The Anti-Defamation League discusses issues of religion in the public schools at the website http://archive.adl.org/religion_ps_2004/teaching.asp. A few guidelines include the following: Religious symbols may be used as teaching aids in the classroom, but may not be used as classroom decoration; music, art, literature, and drama with religious themes may be included in the curriculum, provided that their overall effect does not endorse religion; and school assemblies or concerts may include religious music or drama as long as that inclusion does not appear to endorse religion over non-religion, or one religion over another.

Religious beliefs underlie other cultures even more fundamentally. Immigrants with Confucian religious and philosophical beliefs, for example, subscribe to values that mandate a highly ordered society and family through the maintenance of proper social relationships. In Islamic traditions, the Koran prescribes proper social relationships and roles for members of society. When immigrants with these religious beliefs encounter the largely secular U.S. institutions, the result may be that customs and cultural patterns are challenged, fade away, or cause conflict within the family.

Adapted Instruction

Muslim Students in the ELD Classroom

Muslim students from all over the world are appearing in U.S. classrooms, ranging from Bosnian, Somalian, and Afghani refugees in K–12 schools to Malaysians, Bangladeshis, Fijians, and Saudis in university classrooms. These students visit or immigrate from societies that could not be more diverse—cosmopolitan versus rural, progressive versus traditional, multilingual versus monolingual cultures. What they share as Muslims is a frame of reference in which religion plays a significant, public role in society, with spiritual matters playing a larger role in daily discourse than is encouraged in the secular West. Moreover, gender separation is deep and abiding.

Teachers are urged to approach controversial issues with tact and consideration. As far as coeducational activities, it is best to begin by including students in large mixed-gender groups rather than in mixed-gender pairs to allow students time to adjust to working in close proximity with strangers of the opposite sex. (Schmitt, 2009)

Students come to school already steeped in the learning practices of their own family and community. They come with *educational expectations,* but many of the organizational and teaching practices of the school may not support the type of learning to which students are accustomed. Teachers who can accommodate students' proclivities can gradually introduce student-centered practices while supporting an initial dependence on the teacher's direction.

Did You Know?

Polynesian students coming from the South Pacific may have experienced classroom learning as a relatively passive activity. They expect teachers to give explicit instruction about what to learn and how to learn it and to carefully scrutinize homework daily. When these students arrive in the United States and encounter teachers who value creativity and student-centered learning, they may appear passive as they wait to be told what to do (Funaki & Burnett, 1993).

Teachers who seek to understand the value of education within the community can interview parents or community members (see Chapter 10).

Adapted Instruction

Accommodating Culturally Based Educational Expectations

- Classroom guests from the community can share methods for teaching and learning that are used in the home (e.g., modeling and imitation, didactic stories and proverbs, direct verbal instruction).

- Children from cultures that expect passive interaction with teachers (observing only) can be paired with more participatory peers to learn to ask questions and volunteer.

Cultures differ in the *roles* people play in society and the *status* accorded to these roles. For example, in the Vietnamese culture, profoundly influenced by Confucianism, the father ranks below the teacher, who ranks only below the king. Such a high status is not accorded to teachers in U.S. society, where, instead, medical doctors enjoy this type of prestige. Such factors as gender, social class, age, occupation, and education level influence the manner in which status is accorded to various roles. Students' perceptions about the roles possible for them in their culture affect their school performance.

Immigrants to the United States often come from cultures in which men and women have rigid and highly differentiated *gender roles*. The gender equality that is an ostensible goal in classrooms in the United States may be difficult for students of these cultures. For example, parents may spend much time correcting their sons' homework while ascribing little importance to their daughters' schoolwork.

To enlighten students about the achievements of women, Martínez's *500 Years of Chicana Women's History* (*500 Años de la Mujer Chicana*) is an invaluable reference for English-learner classrooms, especially those with Spanish-English bilingual skills. Text and pictures featuring social and political issues over the long history of Mexican American women's struggles will fascinate and enlighten English learners, provoking rich discussions and writing.

Sexual identification is also a part of gender issues. Gay, lesbian, or bisexual adolescents who face a hostile school climate or undergo harassment, and/or verbal or physical abuse may become truant, drop out, or resort to suicide or substance abuse (Nichols, 1999).

Adapted Instruction

Gender-Role Expectations

- Monitor tasks performed by boys and girls to ensure they are the same.
- Make sure that boys and girls perform equal leadership roles in cooperative groups.
- If families in a given community provide little support for the scholastic achievement of girls, a systematic effort on the part of school counselors and administrators may be needed to help families accommodate their beliefs to a more proactive support for women.

The belief that education can enhance *social economic class status* is widespread in the dominant culture of the United States, but individuals in other cultures may not have similar beliefs. In general, individuals and families at the upper-socioeconomic-status levels are able to exert power by sitting on college, university, and local school boards and thus determining who receives benefits and rewards through schooling. However, middle-class values are those that are generally incorporated in the culture of schooling. The social class values that children learn in their homes largely influence not only their belief in schooling but also their routines and habits in the classroom.

Adapted Instruction

The Influence of Social Class on Schooling

- Students who are extremely poor or homeless may need help from the teacher to store possessions at school.
- A teacher who receives an expensive gift should consult the school district's ethics policies.
- A high grade on a school assignment or project should not depend on extensive family financial resources.

In various cultures, expectations about *age-appropriate activities* for children and the purpose of those activities differ. Middle-class European Americans expect children to spend much of their time playing and attending school rather than performing tasks similar to those of adults. Cree Indian children, on the other hand, are expected from an early age to learn adult roles, including contributing food to the family. Parents may criticize schools for involving children in tasks that are not related to their future participation in Cree society (Sindell, 1988).

Cultures also differ in their criteria for moving through the various (culturally defined) life cycle changes. An important stage in any culture is the move into adulthood, but the age at which this occurs and the criteria necessary for attaining adulthood vary according to what *adulthood* means in a particular culture.

Adapted Instruction

Accommodating Beliefs about Age-Appropriate Activities

- Child labor laws in the United States forbid students from working for pay before a given age. However, few laws govern children working in family businesses. If a child appears chronically tired, the school counselor may need to discuss the child's involvement in the family business with a responsible family member.
- Cultural groups in which girls are expected to marry and have children at the age of fifteen or sixteen (e.g., Hmong) may need access to alternative schools.

In the United States, *occupation* very often determines income, which in turn is a chief determinant of prestige in the culture. Students thus may not see all occupations as desirable for them or even available to them and may have mixed views about the role education plays in their future occupation.

Some cultural groups in the United States are engaged in a voluntary way of life that does not require prolonged schooling (e.g., the Amish). Other groups may be involuntarily incorporated into U.S. society and relegated to menial occupations and ways of life that do not reward and require school success (e.g., Hispanics in the Southwest). As a result, they may not apply academic effort (Ogbu & Matute-Bianchi, 1986).

Example of Concept   *Collaborative Relationships*

Conchas (2006) studied the Medical Academy at Baldwin High School (California), a school-within-a-school that prepares students for careers in health-related occupations. A positive learning environment connected students and teachers across race, gender, and class differences. Both immigrant and U.S.-born Latinos formed a strong sense of belonging and identification with other students in the program; strong collaborative relationships led to academic success.

Adapted Instruction

Occupational Aspirations

- At all grade levels, school subjects should be connected with future vocations.
- Teachers should make available at every grade an extensive set of books on occupations and their requirements, and discuss these with students.
- Role models from minority communities can visit the classroom to recount stories of their success. Successful professionals and businesspeople can visit and explain how cultural diversity is supported in their place of work.

Child-rearing practices have wide implications for schools. Factors such as who takes care of children, how much supervision they receive, how much freedom they have, who speaks to them and how often, and what they are expected to do affect their behavior on entering schools. Many of the misunderstandings that occur between teachers and students arise because of different expectations about behavior, and these different expectations stem from early, ingrained child-rearing practices.

Because the largest group of English learners in California is of Mexican ancestry, teachers who take the time to learn about child-rearing practices among Mexican immigrants can help students adjust to schooling practices in the United States. An excellent source for this cultural study is *Crossing Cultural Borders* (Delgado-Gaitan & Trueba, 1991).

As the numbers of school-provided breakfasts and lunches increase, *food preferences* are an important consideration. Furthermore, teachers who are knowledgeable about students' dietary practices can incorporate their students' background knowledge into health and nutrition instruction.

Besides customs of what and when to eat, eating habits vary widely across cultures, and "good" manners at the table in some cultures are inappropriate or rude in others. For example, Indochinese consider burping, lip smacking, and soup slurping to be common behaviors during meals, even complimentary to hosts. Cultural relativity is not, however, an excuse for poor or unhygienic eating, and teachers do need to teach students the behaviors that are considered good food manners in the U.S. mainstream context.

Dealing with Food Preferences

- In addition to knowing in general what foods are eaten at home, teachers will want to find out about students' favorite foods, taboo foods, and typical foods.

- Eating lunch with students—even on a by-invitation basis—can provide the opportunity to learn about students' habits.

- If a student's eating habits alienate peers, the teacher may need to discuss appropriate behaviors.

In many cultures, *arts and crafts* performed at home—such as food preparation; sewing and weaving; carpentry; home building and decoration; religious and ritual artistry for holy days, holidays, and entertaining—are an important part of the culture that is transmitted within the home. Parents also provide an important means of access to the humanities and the visual and performing arts of their cultures. The classroom teacher draws on the resources of the community and then shares these with all the members of the classroom.

Example of Concept   *Preserving Traditional Vietnamese Music*

Lac Hong is the largest group in the United States that promotes traditional Vietnamese performing arts. Children as young as four begin singing traditional folk songs, eventually learning to play the moon-shaped lute (*dan nguyet*), the one-stringed monochord (*dan bau*), or the sixteen-string zither (*dan tranh*). Classes are led by Mai Nguyen, a former music professor from the Saigon National Conservatory, who immigrated to Orange County, California, at the end of the Vietnam War.

"The students are not just learning music," Nguyen says, "they are learning culture—and the culture is still alive." (Tran, 2008, p. B3)

Educating Students about Diversity. Both mainstream students and CLD students benefit from education about diversity, not only cultural diversity but also diversity in ability, gender preference, and human nature in general. This engenders pride in cultural identity, expands the students' perspectives, and adds cultural insight, information, and experiences to the curriculum.

Did You Know?   James Banks (1994) explained the difference between studying the cultures of other countries and the cultures within the United States. According to Banks, teachers may implement a unit on the country of Japan but avoid teaching about Japanese internment in the United States during World War II (Brandt, 1994).

Global and Multicultural Education. ELD teachers—and mainstream teachers who teach English learners—can bring a global and multicultural perspective to their classes.

> Language teachers, like teachers in all other areas of the curriculum, have a responsibility to plan lessons with sensitivity to the racial and ethnic diversity present in their classrooms and in the world in which their students live. . . . [Students] can learn to value the points of view of many others whose life experiences are different from their own. (Curtain & Dahlberg, 2004, p. 244)

Table 9.6 lists some cultural activities that Curtain and Dahlberg recommended for adding cultural content to the curriculum.

The goal of multicultural education is to help students "develop cross-cultural competence within the American national culture, with their own subculture and within and across different subsocieties and cultures" (Banks, 1994, p. 9). Banks introduced a model of multicultural education that has proved to be a useful way of assessing the approach taken in pedagogy and curricula. The model has four levels, represented in Table 9.7 with a critique of strengths and shortcomings taken from Jenks, Lee, and Kanpol (2002).

There is a clear distinction between multiculturalism and globalism, although both are important features of the school curriculum: "Globalism emphasizes the cultures and peoples of other lands, and multiculturalism deals with ethnic diversity within the United States" (Ukpokodu, 2002, pp. 7–8).

Table 9.6 Sample Cultural Activities for Multicultural Education

Activity	Suggested Implementation
Visitors and guest speakers	Guests can share their experiences on a variety of topics, using visuals, slides, and hands-on materials.
Folk dances, singing games, and other kinds of games	Many cultures can be represented; cultural informants can help.
Field trips	Students can visit neighborhoods, restaurants, museums, or stores that feature cultural materials.
Show-and-tell	Students can bring items from home to share with the class.
Read books about other cultures	Age-appropriate fiction or nonfiction books can be obtained with the help of the school or public librarian.
Crosscultural e-mail contacts	Students can exchange cultural information and get to know peers from other lands.

Source: Curtain and Dahlberg (2004).

Nieto and Bode (2008) make the point that multicultural education does more than merely celebrate diversity:

> [M]ulticultural education does not simply involve the affirmation of language and culture. Multicultural education confronts not only issues of difference but also issues of power and privilege in society. This means challenging racism and other biases as well as the inequitable structures, policies, and practices of schools and, ultimately, of society itself. Affirming language and culture can help students become successful and

Table 9.7   Banks's Levels of Multicultural Education, with Critique

Level	Description	Strengths	Shortcomings
Contributions	Emphasizes what minority groups have contributed to society (e.g., International Food Day, bulletin board display for Black History Month).	Attempts to sensitize the majority white culture to some understanding of minority groups' history.	May amount to "cosmetic" multiculturalism in which no discussion takes place about issues of power and disenfranchisement.
Additive	Adding material to the curriculum to address what has been omitted (reading *The Color Purple* in English class).	Adds to a fuller coverage of the American experience, when sufficient curricular time is allotted.	May be an insincere effort if dealt with superficially.
Transformative	An expanded perspective is taken that deals with issues of historic, ethnic, cultural, and linguistic injustice and equality as a part of the American experience.	Students learn to be reflective and develop a critical perspective.	Incorporates the liberal fallacy that discussion alone changes society.
Social action	Extension of the transformative approach to add students' research/action projects to initiate change in society.	Students learn to question the status quo and the commitment of the dominant culture to equality and social justice.	Middle-class communities may not accept the teacher's role, considering it as provoking students to "radical" positions.

Source: Model based on Banks (1994); strengths and shortcomings based on Jenks, Lee, and Kanpol (2002).

well-adjusted learners, but unless language and cultural issues are viewed critically through the lens of equity and social justices, they are unlikely to have a lasting impact in promoting real change. (pp. 4–5)

Similar to Banks's superficial-to-transformative continuum is that of Morey and Kilano (1997). Their three-level framework for incorporating diversity identifies as "exclusive" the stereotypical focus on external aspects of diversity (what they called the four *f*'s: food, folklore, fun, and fashion); "inclusive," the addition of diversity into a curriculum that, although enriched, is fundamentally the same structure; and "transformed," the curriculum that is built on diverse perspectives, equity in participation, and critical problem solving. Howard (2007) has suggested that a transformative approach to diversity has five basic phases: building trust, engaging personal culture, confronting issues of social dominance and social justice, transforming educational practices, and engaging the entire school community. Thus, it is clear that pouring new wine—diversity—into old bottles—teacher-centered, one-size-fits-all instruction—is not transformative.

In general, research suggests that substantive changes in attitudes, behaviors, and achievement occur only when the entire school environment changes to demonstrate a multicultural atmosphere. Parents are welcomed in the school, and programs are instituted that permit interactions between students of different backgrounds. In such schools, all students learn to understand cultures different from their own. Minority students do not internalize negativity about their culture and customs. Cooperative learning groups and programs that allow interaction between students of diverse backgrounds usually result in fewer incidents of name-calling and ethnic slurs as well as in improved academic achievement (Nieto & Bode, 2008).

It is not easy for culturally and linguistically diverse (CLD) students to maintain pride in their cultures if these cultures suffer low status in the majority culture. Students feel conflict in this pride if their culture is devalued. When the languages and cultures of students are highly evident in their schools and teachers refer to them explicitly, they gain status. Schools that convey the message that all cultures are of value—by displaying explicit welcome signs in many languages, by attempts to involve parents, by a deliberate curriculum of inclusion, and by using affirmative action to promote hiring of a diverse faculty—help to maintain an atmosphere that reduces interethnic conflict.

Example of Concept   *Action Research for Curricular Change*

Diane Red and Amy Warner are two fourth-grade teachers who are dissatisfied with the four-week unit on "Explorers" in the social studies curriculum. They were concerned that the unit was too focused on the European viewpoint and did not adequately represent the perspectives of the indigenous people of the Americas. They modified the readings to include books that presented a range of perspectives on Columbus. In an action research project, they asked students to tally the number of times in each book that Europeans were pictured versus the native Tainos or Caribs from the islands where Columbus landed, and used the tallies as data in their research. In the modified lessons, they used K-W-L charts, and included many opportunities for discussion. Their "action research" focused on gathering evidence to evaluate the success of their "renovated" approach.

Source: Nolan and Hoover (2008).

How the Identity of a Young Child Is Affected by Learning a New Language. Researchers who study English learners within a critical and sociocultural perspective view the individual as socially situated within a network of social relations, using language as a social practice. Within this matrix, language helps to forge a complex identity that changes over time and space. Litowitz (1997) queried the teacher's role in creating these identities: It is important to reexamine not only "what we are asking the learner to *do* but whom we are asking the learner to *be*" (p. 479).

Identity is affected by the child's linguistic and social capital. Children of the socioeconomic elite are granted an advantage toward school success by the ability to establish a school-success-supported identity, including the attraction of peers that share the advantage of similar capital. Day (2002) studied the social relationships of a Punjabi-speaking English learner in a Canadian elementary school, showing the critical role his relationships played in the identities he could negotiate and the access, participation, and opportunities for language learning he could therefore gain. Similarly, Gutierrez (1994) studied three different classrooms in which the contexts for learning were constructed differently, leading to differential access to learning on the part of Latino elementary children.

English learners are particularly challenged when asked to negotiate a dual-language environment. In a two-year study of four Mandarin/English bilingual students in a California school, McKay & Wong (1996) traced how students actively used flexible identities to position and reposition themselves, to resist positioning, and to set up "counter-discourses" that shaped their investment toward learning English. In a similar study, Hunter (1997) analyzed the multiple and often contradictory positioning of Roberto, a Portuguese/English bilingual child, whose identity in relation to school expectations often conflicted with his identity among peers, and the effect this had on his second-language acquisition.

Validating Students' Cultural Identity. "An affirming attitude toward students from culturally diverse backgrounds significantly impacts their learning, belief in self, and overall academic performance" (Villegas & Lucas, 2002, p. 23). Cultural identity—that is, having a positive self-concept or evaluation of oneself and one's culture—promotes self-esteem. Students who feel proud of their successes and abilities, self-knowledge, and self-expression, and who have enhanced images of self, family, and culture, are better learners.

Oakes and Lipton (2007) believe that students should view their cultural identities as integral to their school success, not as something they must "overcome":

> Perhaps schools' greatest challenge is to create a school culture that supports college attendance for students whose lives do not conform to [the profile of a person with high scores on standardized tests, whose parents went to college, whose main language is mainstream, unaccented English, and who have middle-class perspectives and financial support]. The school culture must position college success as expected and inevitable not just for students who change [identities] or for students who are exceptions to stereotypes, but for students who have no need or no intention to slight their family's background and culture as they acquire skills and knowledge that are genuinely useful for college success. (p. 354)

Of course, the most powerful sense of self-esteem is the result not solely of one's beliefs about oneself but also of successful learning experiences. Practices of schooling that damage self-esteem, such as tracking and competitive grading, undermine authentic cooperation and sense of accomplishment on the part of English learners.

Classroom Practices That Validate Identity. Díaz-Rico (2008) suggested that through observations, shared conversations during lunchtime or before or after school, and group participation, teachers can gain understanding about various individuals and their cultures. Teachers can also ask students to interview their parents about common topics such as work, interests, and family history and then add a reflective element about their relationship and identification with these aspects of their parents' lives.

Adolescents acquire identities through sociocultural groups, such as language and cultural groups, as well as through activities in which they engage (athletics, band, computers, gangsta, goth). They are also labeled by schools (students in honors or special education, English learners, "at-risk," "leaders"). These identities may influence school behavior, as some groups pressure members not to invest in school success, but rather to adopt resistance or apathetic attitudes.

Example of Concept

Students' Co-creation of Pro-School-Success Identities

Willet (1995) described three female first-grade English learners, Nahla (an immigrant from Palestine), Etham (a native of the Maldive Islands), and Yael (a native Israeli), who were allowed to sit together during their daily thirty-minute pull-out ELD class. In contrast, a fourth student, Xavier, a Mexican American, was placed between two English-speaking girls who did not help him because he was a boy. Over the year of Willett's study, the three girls solidified identities as good students by cooperating and supporting one another, whereas Xavier became more reliant on the teacher and gained the reputation of a needy, dependent child. In this way, the social environment was a factor in the creation of identity.

Example of Concept

A School-Compatible Identity

Julie, a five-year-old child of Polish-speaking immigrant parents (in Canada), was able to form relationships with other kindergarten children by making a set of allies among children who would stick up for her when another child attempted to subordinate her or to exclude her from co-play activities. Moreover, she was able to create alliances with adults in her classroom by obeying key conventions of the schoolroom: She was silent upon adult command, moved smoothly through transitions between activities, showed adept use of tools such as scissors and paste, and often greeted adults who entered the classroom with excited smiles and hugs. Together, these behaviors resulted in adults attributing to her the personality of a pleasant and easygoing child—a "nice little girl"—and she was deemed "ready" for grade 1. She was then recommended for promotion—whereas some other English learners in the same class were not (Toohey & Norton, 2003).

Instructional Materials That Validate Identity. Classroom texts are available that offer literature and anecdotal readings aimed at the enhancement of identity and self-esteem. *Identities: Readings from Contemporary Culture* (Raimes, 1996) includes readings grouped into chapters titled "Name," "Appearance, Age, and Abilities," "Ethnic Affiliation and Class," "Family Ties," and so forth. The readings contain authentic text and may be best used in middle- or high-school classes.

A book that is useful for a comparison of Asian cultural values with those of mainstream American culture is Kim's (2001) *The Yin and Yang of American Culture.* This book presents a view of American culture—its virtues and vices—from an Eastern perspective and may stimulate discussion on the part of students. *Exploring Culturally Diverse Literature for Children and Adolescents* (Henderson & May, 2005) helps readers understand how stories are tied to specific cultural and socio-political histories, opening readers' minds to literature written from the "insider's" versus the "outsider's" point of view.

Promoting Mutual Respect among Students. The ways in which we organize classroom life should make children feel significant and cared about—by the teacher and by one another. Classroom life should, to the greatest extent possible, prefigure the kind of democratic and just society we envision and thus contribute to building that society. Together, students and teachers can create a "community of conscience," as educators Asa Hillard and George Pine call it (Christensen, 2000, p. 18).

Mutual respect is promoted when the curriculum includes multiple points of view and when students are given the chance to genuinely talk to one another about topics that concern them. The instructional conversation is a discourse format that encourages in-depth conversation (see Chapter 5).

Example of Concept   *A Cultural Heritage Project*

Promoting research projects is a way for students to participate in school in ways related to their personal identities. One teacher based a unit plan on this standard from the Michigan Curriculum Standard from Social Studies: *Students will gain knowledge about the past to construct meaningful understandings of our diverse cultural heritage.* In this unit, students were to compare two aspects of cultural heritage from information obtained from the Internet, culminating in an individual report on a favorite artist or inventor as

well as a group PowerPoint presentation and simulated interview with the historical figure.

The Puerto Rican group compared Ladislao Martinez and Alvin Medina, one traditional and one contemporary *cuatro* (folk guitar) player. They contrasted the two players, drawing on sound clips that included current musical favorites. A rich context of time and place gave each participant a personal connection to the topic (Conley, 2008).

Adapting to Students' Culturally Supported Facilitating or Limiting Attitudes and Abilities

A skilled intercultural educator recognizes that each culture supports distinct attitudes, values, and abilities. These may facilitate or limit the learning situation in U.S. public schools. For example, the cultures of Japan, China, and Korea, which promote high academic achievement, may foster facilitating behaviors, such as the ability to listen and follow directions; attitudes favoring education and respect for teachers and authorities; attitudes toward discipline as guidance; and high-achievement motivation. However, other culturally supported traits may hinder adjustment to the U.S. school, such as lack of experience participating in discussions; little experience with independent thinking; strong preference for conformity, which inhibits divergent thinking; and distinct sex-role differentiation, with males more dominant.

Example of Concept   *Overcoming Reluctance to Participate Orally*

Asian students are more likely to speak up in class when the participation is structured, such as in a debate that has definite rules for whose turn it is to talk. Unstructured class discussions in which one must aggressively promote one's turn may make many Asian students feel anxious and uncomfortable,

because this does not mirror the home environment, where often students speak only when requested to do so by a parental authority (Tateishi, 2007–2008). Small-group discussion with leaders whose task is to involve all members can be a means of conducting classroom talk.

Similarly, African American family and cultural values that encourage independent action, self-sufficiency, and imagination and humor may facilitate adjustment to the classroom, but dialect speakers with limited experiences with various types of Standard English patterns may be hindered. The Mexican American cultural values that encourage cooperation, the affectionate and demonstrative parental relationships, children assuming mature social responsibilities such as child care and translating family matters from English to Spanish, and an eagerness to try out new ideas may all facilitate classroom success. On the other hand, such attitudes as depreciating education after high school, especially for women; explicit sex-role stereotyping favoring limited vocational roles for women; and dislike of competition may go against classroom practices and hinder classroom success (Clark, 1983).

Cooperation versus Competition. Triandis (1995) stated that the most important difference between cultures that can be identified in schools is the contrast between individualist and collectivist value systems. Traditional U.S. classrooms mirror middle-class European American values of competition: Students are expected to do their own work; are rewarded publicly through star charts, posted grades, and academic honors; and are admonished to do their individual best. In the Cree Indian culture, however, children are raised in a cooperative atmosphere, with siblings, parents, and other kin sharing food as well as labor (Sindell, 1988). In the Mexican American culture, interdependence is a strength; individuals have a commitment to others, and all decisions are made together. Those who are successful have a responsibility to others to help them succeed.

Because about seventy percent of the world's population lives in a collectivist culture (including Native Americans, Native Hawaiians, Latin American, African Americans, Asians, and Arab groups), according to Tileston and Darling (2008), it is probably wiser for teachers to emphasize interdependence among students rather than aggressive and competitive competition. Some balance must be achieved in the classroom between the individual competitive culture of the dominant U.S. culture and the collaborative preferences of students from group-oriented, cooperative cultures.

The Use of Language. In learning a second language, students (and teachers) often focus on the form. Frequently ignored are the ways in which that second language is used (see the section on pragmatics in Chapter 2). The culture that underlies each language prescribes distinct patterns and conventions about when, where, and how to use the language (see Labov, 1972). Heath's (1983b) *Ways with Words* noted that children in "Trackton," an isolated African American community in the South, were encouraged to use spontaneous verbal play, rich with metaphor, simile, and allusion. In contrast, the children of "Roadville," a lower-middle-class European American community in the South, used language in more restricted ways, perhaps because of habits encouraged by a fundamentalist religious culture. Heath contrasted language usage in these two cultures: verbal and nonverbal communication (the "said" and the "unsaid"), the use of silence, discourse styles, the nature of questions, and the use of oral versus written genres.

Both *verbal and nonverbal means* are used to communicate. More than sixty-five percent of the social meaning of a typical two-person exchange is carried by nonverbal cues (Birdwhistell, 1974). *Kinesic* behavior, including facial expressions, body movements, postures, and gestures, can enhance a message or constitute a message in itself. *Paralanguage*—the nonverbal elements of the voice—is an important aspect of speech that can affirm or belie a verbal message. *Proxemics*, the communication of interpersonal distance, varies widely across cultures. Last but not least, *olfactics*—the study of interpersonal communication by means of smell—constitutes a factor that is powerful yet often overlooked.

People throughout the world employ *silence* in communicating. As with other language uses, however, silence differs dramatically across cultures. In the United States, silence is interpreted as expressing embarrassment, regret, obligation, criticism, or sorrow (Wayne in Ishii & Bruneau, 1991). In Asian cultures, silence is a token of respect. Particularly in the presence of the elderly, being quiet honors their wisdom and expertise. Silence can also be a marker of personal power. In many Native American cultures, silence is used to create and communicate rapport in ways that language cannot.

Intercultural differences exist in *asking and answering questions*. In middle-class European American culture, children are exposed early on to their parents' questioning. While taking a walk, for example, a mother will ask, "See the squirrel?" and, later, "Is that a squirrel? Where did that squirrel go?" The questions are asked to stimulate conversation and to train children to focus attention and display knowledge. In the Inuit culture, on the other hand, adults do not question children or call their attention to objects and events in order to name them (Crago, 1993).

Responses to questioning differ across cultures. Students from non-Western cultures may be reluctant to attempt an answer to a question if they do not feel they can answer absolutely correctly. Students do not share the European-American value of answering questions to the best of their ability regardless of whether that "best" answer is absolutely correct or not.

Cultures may differ in *discourse styles* that influence conversations: the way conversations open and close, the way people take turns, the way messages are repaired to make them understandable, and the way in which parts of the text are set aside. These differences in discourse are stressful for second-language learners. Multiply this stress by the long hours children spend in school, and it is no wonder that English learners may feel subjected to prolonged pressure.

Example of Concept   *Classroom Discourse Patterns*

Discourse in the classroom can be organized in ways that involve children positively, in ways that are culturally compatible. A group of Hawaiian children, with the help of an encouraging and participating adult, produced group discourse that was co-narrated, complex, lively, imaginative, and well connected. Group work featured twenty-minute discussions of text in which the teacher and students mutually participated in overlapping, volunteered speech and in joint narration (Au & Jordan, 1981).

In contrast, Navajo children in a discussion group patterned their discourse after the adults of their culture. Each Navajo student spoke for an extended period with a fully expressed statement, and other students waited courteously until a clear end was communicated. Then another took a similar turn. In both communities, children tended to connect discourse with peers rather than with the teacher functioning as a central "switchboard." If the teacher acted as a central director, students often responded with silence (Tharp, 1989a).

Adapted Instruction

How Students Tell You They Don't Understand

Arabic (men): *Mish fahem*

Arabic (women): *Mish fahmeh*

Armenian: *Yes chem huskenur*

Chinese (Cantonese): *Ngoh m-ming*

Chinese (Mandarin): *Wo bu dung*

Persian: *Man ne'me fah'mam*

Japanese: *Wakarimasen*

Korean: *Juh-neun eehae-haji mot haget-ssum-nida*

Russian: *Ya nye ponimayu*

Spanish: *No comprendo*

Vietnamese: *Toi khong hieu*

Yiddish: *Ikh veys nikht*

In addition to ways to say "I don't understand" in 230 languages, J. Runner's webpage has translations in many languages for the following phrases: "Hello, how are you?" "Welcome," "Good-bye," "Please," "Thank you," "What is your name?" "My name is . . . ," "Do you speak English?" "Yes," and "No." There is also a link to Internet Language Resources; see www.elite.net/~runner/jennifers/understa.htm.

Source: Runner (2000).

Oral versus written language creates learning differences. Orality is the foundation of languages. Written expression is a later development. In fact, of the thousands of reported languages in use, only seventy-eight have a written literature (Edmonson, 1971). Research has suggested that acquiring literacy involves more than learning to read and write. Thinking patterns, perception, cultural values, communication style, and social organization can be affected by literacy (Ong, 1982; Scribner & Cole, 1978).

In studying oral societies, researchers have noted that the structure and content of messages tend to be narrative, situational, and oriented toward activity or deeds, although abstract ideas such as moral values are often implicit. In contrast, the style of literacy is conceptual rather than situational. Words are separate from the social context of deeds and events, and abstract ideas can be extracted from written texts. In an oral society, learning takes place in groups because narration must have an audience. This contrasts with a literate society, in which reading and writing can be solitary experiences. In an oral society, much reliance is placed on memory, as this is the principal means of preserving practices and traditions (Ong, 1982).

Example of Concept   *Characteristics of One Oral Culture*

Hmong immigrants in the United States demonstrate the comparative disadvantage faced by individuals from an oral culture when expected to perform in a literate environment. Hmong individuals may become frustrated in the abstract world of school. The very concept of independent study is alien to this culture because learning always occurs in community groups. Learning among strangers and doing homework, a solitary endeavor, run counter to traditional group practices and may distance children from their families. As Hmong children become literate and engage in independent study, parents may become disturbed over the loss of centrality and power in their children's lives, which may produce family tension (Shuter, 1991).

Participation Styles. The way teachers are taught to teach is a reflection of the expectations of U.S. culture. Teachers raised in a mainstream culture have elements of that culture embedded in their personal teaching approach. The selection of a particular teaching method reflects cultural values more than it argues for the superiority of the method. Some of these elements may need to be modified to meet the needs of students from other cultures. The accompanying Example of Concept illustrates the way the culturally preferred participation style of one group of students differed from their teachers'.

Example of Concept   *Culturally Preferred Participation Styles*

In classrooms on the Warm Springs (Oregon) Reservation, teacher-controlled activity dominated. All the social and spatial arrangements were created by the teacher: where and when movement took place; where desks were placed and even what furniture was present in the room; and who talked, when, and with whom. For the Warm Springs students, this socialization was difficult. They preferred to wander to various parts of the room, away from the lesson; to talk to other students while the teacher was talking; and to "bid" for one another's attention rather than that of the teacher.

For the Native American children, the small-reading-group structure in which participation is mandatory, individual, and oral was particularly ill fitting. They frequently refused to read aloud, did not utter a word when called on, or spoke too softly to be audible. On the other hand, when students controlled and directed interaction in small-group projects, they were much more fully involved. They concentrated completely on their work until it was completed and talked a great deal to one another in the group. Very little time was spent disagreeing or arguing about how to go about a task. There was, however, explicit competition with other groups.

A look at the daily life of the Warm Springs children revealed several factors that would account for their willingness to work together and their resistance to teacher-directed activity. First, they spend much time in the company of peers with little disciplinary control from older relatives. They also spend time in silence, observing their elders and listening without verbal participation. Speech seems to be an optional response rather than a typical or mandatory feature of interaction. One last characteristic of community life is the accessibility and openness of community-wide celebrations. No single individual directs and controls all activity, and there is no sharp distinction between audience and performer. Individuals are permitted to choose for themselves the degree of participation in an activity. Schooling became more successful for these students when they were able to take a more active part.

Source: Adapted from Philips (1972, pp. 370–394).

Teacher–Student Interactions. The teacher–student relationship is culturally mandated in general ways, although individual relationships vary. Students who have immigrated may bring with them varying notions of teacher–student interactions. For example, in some cultures, learning takes place in an absolutely quiet classroom where the teacher is in complete control and authority is never questioned. In other cultures, students talk among themselves and are able to engage with teachers in cooperative planning. Attitudes toward authority, teacher–student relationships, and teacher expectations of student achievement vary widely. Yet the heart of the educational process is in the interaction between teacher and student. This determines the quality of education the student receives.

Adapted Instruction

Encouraging Positive Relationships

Although it may appear daunting to be able to accommodate the various teacher–student relations represented by different cultural groups in a classroom, there are several ways teachers can learn about their students to provide a learning environment.

- Express care and respect equally to all students.
- Openly communicate acceptance of students and be accessible to them.
- In classroom discussions and in private, encourage students to talk about their expectations for learning.

Source: Adapted from Lemberger (1999).

Example of Concept

"Retooling" to Improve Teacher–Student Relationships

Even teachers of color find they need to "retool" their practice when assigned to a classroom of culturally and linguistically diverse students. An African American teacher who taught for many years in a predominantly white suburban school said, "When I first found myself teaching classes of mostly black kids, I went home frustrated every night because I knew I wasn't getting through to them, and they were giving me a hard time. It only started getting better when I finally figured out that I had to re-examine everything I was doing" (Howard, 2007, p. 17).

To learn more about a student's actions for reactions in the context of their cultural backgrounds, teachers might pause for a reflection:

- If a student's background is very different from my own, what cultural assumptions do I bring to the situation that may be impeding my understanding of the student?
- What is it that I need to understand about this student's background that might be affecting the situation?
- How might speaking with the student's family help to further my cultural understanding?

Classroom Organization. The typical organization of U.S. classrooms is that of a teacher-leader who gives assignments or demonstrates to the students, who act as audience. Teacher presentations are usually followed by some form of individual study. Learning is then assessed through recitation, quizzes, or some other performance. Small-group work, individual projects, or paired learning require distinct participation structures, ways of behaving and speaking. Learning how to behave in these settings may require explicit cultural adaptation. Many students new to U.S. classrooms have never before taken part in group problem solving, story retelling, or class discussion. Such activities entail social as well as linguistic challenges. Teachers can help students by providing clear instructions and ample models, by calling on more self-confident students first, and by assigning self-conscious students minor roles at first in order not to embarrass them. Teachers who are sensitive to varying cultural styles organize other means for students to demonstrate language and content knowledge, and they act as observers and guides rather than directors or controllers of student activity.

Example of Concept *Class Discussions*

A Vietnamese student who moved to the United States describes his reaction to a class discussion:

> As a student in Vietnam, I learned not to ask questions, not to raise my hand, or to have much contact with the teacher. I listened, took notes, and memorized the material. The teacher was always right. Imagine my surprise when I entered a U.S. classroom and listened as my classmates talked, argued, and discussed! The teacher encouraged discussion and even listened to what the students had to say. This felt very different to me.

Source: Dresser (1993, p. 120).

Curriculum. Many aspects of the school curriculum are highly abstract and contain themes and activities for which many CLD students have little referent. Some teachers, rather than finding ways in which students can become familiar with academically challenging content, are quick to devise alternative activities of lower academic worth. Research on Alaska Native education suggests a number of abuses perpetrated in the name of "being sensitive to children's cultural backgrounds." Teachers often exempt Alaska Native students from standards applicable to other students. For example, they assign an essay on "Coming to the City from the Village" as a substitute for a research paper. Too many lessons are created featuring stereotypic content (kayaks and caribou) that demonstrates a shallow cultural relevance (Kleinfeld, 1988).

Avoiding bias means more than using "politically correct" terminology that does not incorporate prejudice. It also means protecting the authenticity of sources. Reese (2007) comments on the distortions often displayed when children are presented with literature about Native Americans: Indians are portrayed either as savages, or on the other extreme, as poetic, romantic figures with a message about living in harmony with the earth. Reese, a Pueblo Indian, calls for literature that reflects the heterogeneity of the Native American experience in ways that counter culturally and historically inaccurate mythmaking. She offers valuable guidelines for evaluating and selecting Native American literature for classroom use, especially featuring markers of cultural authenticity.

Example of Concept   *The Eurocentric Curriculum*

What is a Eurocentric perspective, and why is that limiting for today's students? Because the United States began as a set of British colonies, many perspectives published even in contemporary textbooks reflect a European point of view. For example, in geography, Europe and the United States are centered side-by-side, with the rest of the world at the margins. Parts of the world are named according to their position relative to Europe, for example, the "Middle East" (Hernandez, 2001). Students may become depressed when their native countries and regions play so small a role in the curricula and texts, and the world of information does not include their issues and perspectives.

In her article "Educating Teachers for Cultural and Linguistic Diversity: A Model for All Teachers," Parla (1994) discussed issues related to the multicultural classroom and includes information on cultural sensitivity, linguistic diversity, and teaching strategies that can help teachers grow in their understanding of cultural issues and translate that understanding into classroom practice. The article can be found at www.ncela.gwu.edu/files/rcd/BE022361/Educating_Teachers_For_Cultural.pdf.

Adapted Instruction

Assessing Ethnic, Linguistic, and Gender Biases in the Curriculum

The following checklist can help teachers assess the extent to which ethnic, linguistic, and gender biases exist in the curriculum:

- What groups are represented in texts, discussion, and bulletin board displays? Are certain groups invisible?

- Are the roles of minorities and women presented in a separate manner from other content, isolated or treated as a distinct topic?

- Are minorities (and women) treated in a positive, diversified manner, or stereotyped into traditional or rigid roles?

- Are the problems faced by minorities presented in a realistic fashion, with a problem-solving orientation?

- Is the language used in the materials inclusive, or are biased terms used, such as masculine forms (*mankind, mailman*)?

- Does the curriculum foster appreciation of cultural diversity?

- Are experiences and activities other than those common to middle-class European American culture included?

Sustaining High Expectations for All Students

Jussim (1986) offered a general framework for the relationship between teacher expectations and student achievement. Teachers develop initial expectations based on a student's reputation, on previous classroom performance, or on stereotypes about racial, cultural, and linguistic groups. These expectations form the basis for differential treatment of students and for the rationalization for such treatment. Students, in turn, react to this differential treatment in ways that confirm the teacher's expectations. Thus, teachers have a high degree of effect on student achievement: Student effort and persistence are shaped, in part, by students' perception of the teacher's expectations.

Expecting high achievement from English learners and communicating these expectations require specific educational programs that draw attention to the hidden curriculum of the school, quality of interaction between teachers and students, diverse learning styles, the use of the community as a resource, and a commitment to democratic ideals in the classroom (Gollnick & Chinn, 2006).

Assessing Students' Ability and Achievement Validly. A major responsibility of the intercultural educator is to ensure that students' abilities are truly developed by instructional experiences. Many students' abilities are underestimated because their second-language skills do not adequately convey their talents. Sometimes unfamiliarity with the students' culture compounds the language barrier. Validity and bias in testing are addressed in Chapter 7.

Challenging Students to Strive for Excellence as Defined by Their Potential. Teachers tread a fine line between expecting too much of their students, causing frustration on students' part through stress and overwork, and expecting too little by watering down the curriculum, leading to boredom and low academic achievement. Ongoing formative assessment, combined with a sensitive awareness of students' needs and a willingness to be flexible, helps the teacher to monitor and adjust the instructional level to students' abilities.

Teachers' behavior varies with the level of expectation held about the students. Students of whom much is expected are given more frequent cues and prompts to respond to, are asked more and harder questions, are given a longer time to respond, are encouraged to provide more elaborate answers, and are interrupted less often (Good & Brophy, 1984). Teachers tend to be encouraging toward students for whom they have high expectations. They smile at these students more often and show greater warmth through nonverbal responses such as leaning toward the students and nodding their heads as students speak (Woolfolk & Brooks, 1985). The online report *Expectations and Student Outcomes* (Cotton, 1989) is a useful resource in learning about how expectations are communicated to students.

Students' responses to teacher expectations seem to be highly influenced by cultural background and home discourse patterns. Some cultures encourage students to set internal standards of worth, and peer pressure devalues dependence on teachers for approval.

Motivating Students to Become Active Participants in Their Learning. Learner autonomy is a key element of constructivist learning—teachers help students to construct new knowledge, providing scaffolds between what students already know and what they need to learn. Learner autonomy occurs when learners feel that studying is taking place due to their own volition. This autonomy is the basis for self-managed, self-motivated instruction. Such autonomy must be supported in a systematic way by the teacher and curriculum in order for the learner to benefit.

Educators acknowledge that it is impossible to teach learners everything they need to know while they are in class. Therefore, a major aim of classroom instruction should be to equip learners with learning skills they can employ on their own. These include the following:

- Efficient learning strategies
- Identification of their preferred ways of learning
- Skills needed to negotiate the curriculum
- Encouragement to set their own learning objectives
- Support for learners to set realistic goals and time frames
- Skills in self-evaluation (Nunan, 1989, p. 3)

Student autonomy is at risk in the climate of coercive adherence to standardized test scores as the sole criterion of effective instruction. Certainly there is a place for choice in topics and freedom to voice divergent views as the core of democratic schooling (see Giroux & McLaren, 1996).

Encouraging Students to Think Critically. An important aspect of schooling in a democracy is the ability to think for oneself, analyze ideas, separate fact from opinion, support opinions from reading, make inferences, and solve problems. The ability to think critically can enhance self-understanding and help students approach significant issues in life with analytical skills. This includes critical thinking, preparing students to be problem solvers who can analyze, evaluate, synthesize, and design when offered real-life situations—students who can make connections between divergent ideas and face the world with compassion and empathy (Mintz & Yun, 1999). An organized introduction to this complex field, presenting lesson plans that have been remodeled to include critical thinking strategies, is available from www.critical thinking.org/pages/index-of-articles/1021/.

Critical thinking includes the ability to look for underlying assumptions in statements, to detect bias, to identify illogical connections between ideas, and to recognize attempts to influence opinion by means of propaganda. These skills are fundamental to the clear thinking required of autonomous citizens in a democracy.

Helping Students Become Socially and Politically Conscious. "Sociocultural consciousness means understanding that one's way of thinking, behaving, and being is influenced by race, ethnicity, social class, and language" (Kea, Campbell-Whatley, & Richards, 2004, p. 4). Students as well as teachers need to have clarity of vision about their sociocultural identities and their role in the institutions that maintain social and economic distinctions based on social class and skin color.

Political and social consciousness is hard-won. It requires teachers to offer students a forum in which to discuss social and political events without partisan rancor; to investigate issues in the national and local press that have possible multiple perspectives; and to find a way to support students' voices about their lives and feelings.

Bulletin boards on which student writing can be posted, weekly current event discussions, and class newsletters are projects that can encourage autonomous student thinking, writing, and discussion.

An excellent resource for student projects in the community, including those that deal with social justice issues, is Lewis's *The Kid's Guide to Social Action: How to Solve the Social Problems You Choose—And Turn Creative Thinking into Positive Action.* This book explains how to organize students to carry out projects such as having a proclamation issued, circulating a petition, and calling public officials—important ways that students can become involved in social issues and influence public policy in a democracy.

This chapter has emphasized the profound influence of culture on people's perceptions, feelings, and actions, and the variety of ways in which individuals experience contact with other cultures. Let us revisit briefly Joe Suina, the Pueblo youth whose contact with school created cultural conflict for him. How could the school have been more accommodating? Ideally, Suina's teacher would be a Pueblo Indian and would share his culture. Classrooms in a Pueblo school would resemble the home, with intimate spaces and furniture designed for student comfort. If these conditions are not feasible, a non-Pueblo teacher would accommodate to the ways of the students in the same way that students are expected to accommodate to the school.

Teachers can play an important role in learning about their students' communities and cultures and in reducing the culture shock between home and school by working actively toward the creation of culturally responsive instruction. The best way for a teacher to understand culture is first to understand himself or herself and the extent to which mainstream U.S. cultural values are explicitly or implicitly enforced during instruction. A teacher who understands his or her own teaching and learning styles can then ask to what extent each student is similar or dissimilar. This goes a long way toward understanding individual differences. The key for the intercultural educator is to be sensitive, flexible, and open.

LEARNING MORE

Further Reading

Victor Villaseñor's *Rain of Gold* (1992) is a fascinating history of his family's experience as Mexican immigrants to southern California. Read the book and identify passages that illustrate the following Mexican values: the importance of religion, the woman as center of home and family, respect for the mother, protection of women's virtue, the ideal woman as pure, how to be a man, the role of the man as protector of the family, the importance of tradition, respect for life, death as a part of life, respect for work, respect for learning, importance of honor, and acceptance of passion as a part of life.

Web Search

Explore the Southern Poverty Law Center's website at www.splcenter.org. The most current issue of *Teaching Tolerance,* the organization's magazine for teachers, is available to read online, and by clicking other buttons you can discover ideas and resources for teachers, parents, teens, and children. Also investigate www.tolerance.org. This site also provides invaluable information for teachers, parents, teens, and children. Share your findings with your colleagues and plan how to incorporate some of the lessons and ideas from this site into your overall school plan.

Exploration

Ask several educators how they celebrate the birthday of Dr. Martin Luther King, Jr. on the legal holiday of his birth. Find a commemoration in your area and attend. How does this stimulate you to follow the ideals of Dr. King?

Collaboration

View the movie *Stand and Deliver*, which is about the success of Jaime Escalante, the outstanding mathematics teacher at Garfield High School in Los Angeles. Watch the scene two or three times in which a grandmother comes to Escalante's house. Role-play with a friend the elaborate greeting ritual with which Mr. Escalante warmly welcomes the elderly woman. Discuss with a friend or classmate a form of greeting that might be appropriate for an elderly family member who visits a classroom.

MyEducationLab™

The Importance of Culture

In this video, teachers and other English-learner education experts discuss the role of culture in the process of second language acquisition, especially as it plays out in classroom interactions among students and teachers. Various aspects of culture are highlighted, including what people do, think, and believe about what constitutes appropriate ways to interact in the classroom; cultural norms concerning the meaning of eye contact, gestures, and facial expressions; and how much distance to maintain from others during conversations. The importance of learning about and validating students' home cultures is emphasized.

To access the video, go to MyEducationLab (www.myeducationlab.com), choose the Díaz-Rico text, and log in to MyEducationLab for English Language Learners. Select the topic Diversity, and watch the video entitled "The Importance of Culture."

Answer the following questions:

1. How would you define "culture"? Provide three examples of how it applies to classroom interactions and student learning.

2. The video emphasizes learning about and validating students' home cultures. Describe several ways you can modify instruction to better involve students' families and their resources.

3. In the video, mention is made of the friction and emotional stress that may occur when cultural norms are violated. Identify one specific cultural aspect that might be a source of friction or stress due to differences between home and school norms. How might you resolve the issue while at the same time respecting the home culture?

4. How can teachers promote tolerance by integrating home and school learning experiences? How can teachers solicit the help of parents as cultural mediators.

10

The Role of the Family in Schools

Families are responsive partners with schools when their children find joy and meaning in education.

© Michael Newman/PhotoEdit, Inc.

"Let's sing 'Eency Weency Spider' in English, Spanish, and Hawaiian," says teacher Rosa Hernandez to her Head Start classroom filled with excited preschoolers and parents. Inside the colorful and welcoming environment, both generations settle down for a lesson. They start by making the hand gestures for spiders. Miss Rosa then reads a book aloud, asking students and parents to repeat key phrases.

"My goal is to prepare students for kindergarten, but it's also to empower these families," says Hernandez. "Sometimes when children first arrive here, their self-esteem is low. But once they start working with their parents inside the classroom, their self-esteem becomes higher and they participate more."

Sherry Posnick-Goodwin (2010/2011, p. 10)

High school graduation—and beyond that, higher education or further career preparation—is a long road for many students. Those who are the first in their families to graduate from high school or college often look back and credit their parents, caregivers, or family members for the encouragement, support, and motivation that it took to achieve success. In reality, it is often the close partnership of families and educators that creates school success. What can educators do to strengthen home–school collaboration? What role do families play in schooling?

The terms that educators use to talk about the home–school relationship is important. Some educators prefer to speak of parent *participation,* because for many, the word *involvement* connotes that the school is acting *upon* the families rather than acting *together* in an equal relationship. Most family members are more comfortable in a two-way partnership in which educators respect and learn from families and where partners share the responsibility for the child's success.

Family as a broad term includes birth, step-, and adoptive parents; other custodial relations such as foster parents and other caregivers; and intergenerational families that raise children. When a teacher communicates to any of these responsible parties the great honor and joy it is to be that child's teacher, counselor, or principal, the door is open for a creative and productive partnership.

Marshaling Family and Community Support for Schooling

Family and community involvement supports and encourages students and provides opportunities for families and educators to work together in educating students. Families need to become involved in different settings and at different levels of the educational process. Family members can help teachers to establish a genuine respect for their children and the strengths they bring to the classroom. They can work with their own children at home or serve on school committees. Collaborative involvement in school restructuring includes family and community members who help to set goals and allocate resources.

Parental involvement in the school is influenced by cultural beliefs. The U.S. system was developed from small, relatively homogeneous local schools with considerable community and parental control. The pattern of community and parental involvement continues today with school boards, PTAs, and parent volunteers in the schools. This pattern is not universal outside the United States. In cultures in which teachers are accorded high status, parents may consider it improper to discuss educational matters or bring up issues that concern their children. Many Asian-American parents, for example, have high expectations for their children's academic success, but are reluctant to become involved in the classroom, believing education is the responsibility of the school (Fuller & Olson, 1998).

Other factors that make family involvement difficult are school procedures such as restrictive scheduling for family–teacher conferences and notification to parents that students' siblings are not welcome at school for conferences and other events. These procedures tend to divide families and exclude parents. School staffs can involve the community by talking with parents and community liaisons to work out procedures that are compatible with cultural practices.

It is important that parents not be used in a compensatory manner or given the message that they need to work to bring their children "up" to the level of an idealized norm. This approach often makes parents feel that they are the cause of their children's failure in school. Attributing students' lack of success to parental failure does not recognize that the school itself may be the culprit by failing to meet students' needs.

Whether parents are willing to come to school is largely dependent on their attitude toward school, a result in part of the parents' own school experiences. This attitude is also a result of the extent to which they are made welcome by the schools. Invitational barriers can exclude parents as well as students. On the other hand, teachers who are willing to reach out to parents and actively solicit information from them about their children and their hopes for their children's schooling are rewarded with a richer understanding of students' potential.

Bilingual, Bicultural Home–School Partnerships

In some ways, the easiest home–school partnerships to sustain are those in which the teacher and the parents share the same language and culture. Although the majority of the U.S. teachers are not bilingual speakers of English, a small but increasing number of teachers are bilingual and bicultural. Teachers who share the language and culture of the student have an edge in rapport. This argues for more hiring of such specialists.

Home–School Communication: Telephone Calls. When the teacher, counselor, or principal shares the home language and culture of the community, communication with a student's family is facilitated in many ways. A teacher may find that phone calls to the home in the home language often promote rapport: Teachers can introduce themselves, listen to concerns, and answer questions that might arise. If there is no home phone, it is important to find what time of day the given family member can answer a mobile phone. Calls to the home in which only the school employee speaks English are not likely to be effective.

Example of Concept   *Tips on Telephoning Families*

When making a call to a student's home, these tips can help:

Pre-call:
- Be prepared. Have information readily available that the family member might need (a referral, a date/time).
- Have a pen and paper handy.

Begin:
- Identify yourself and the name of the child you are calling about.

- State the reason you are calling (information about . . . make an appointment . . . returning a call . . .).

During the call:
- Take brief notes of the conversation.
- If you don't understand what is said, ask to have it repeated.
- If you need to call back, ask for a suitable time.

Language-Specific Listening. Listening skills are as language-specific as vocabulary and grammar. A teacher who shares the home language of the family is familiar with the norms of turn taking that communicate respect and is probably more able to achieve a deeply effective conversation that shares and compares perspectives about the child. Even more than what it said, often the unconscious rhythms of intonation and the nuances of vocabulary choice between same-language speakers can sustain rapport, despite the need to address not only a student's successes, but also mistakes and challenges. Engaging the parents in support of a student sometimes requires a level of directness that is easier for family members to accept when couched in the home language.

Home–School Newsletters. If students are biliterate, the teacher can help them to produce a class newsletter with featured articles in the language(s) of the home. If a student wrote it, students are more likely to read it at home and share it with family members. Such a newsletter may feature homework tips that come from students, with study hints that match the developmental levels of the students and offer creative ideas that appeal to peers. Students can add puzzles and short stories to such a newsletter for younger children in order to entertain and involve siblings.

Example of Concept — *Using Social Media to Communicate with Families*

Parent conferences online, virtual school events lifestreamed, and educational events broadcast on YouTube are ways to bring parents into Net 2.0 communication with teachers (www.classroom20.com/group/virtualconferencesforeducatorsandparents).

Acquiring a Third, Fourth, or Fifth Language. Educators with dual-language skills might find it easier to learn words or phrases in yet a third language if there is a third heritage language in the community. It might be easier for biliterate educators to understand the need to post signs in alternative languages. Exposing students to role models of multicompetent language use is vital.

Same-Language, Dissimilar-Culture Home–School Partnerships

Many teachers have learned Spanish or some other language in order to function as bilingual teachers. Others share a heritage language with students. Even speaking the same language, they may still find cultural differences that need to be bridged to facilitate family involvement.

Intralanguage Differences and Dialects. Predominant world languages such as Spanish and Arabic are spoken differently around the world. Part of the students' linguistic heritage is knowledge of these differences. Taking the time to compare and enjoy differences in dialect helps students to acknowledge such diversity and accommodate the contrasting vocabulary and idioms of various dialects. Thus the same-language, different-culture teacher can model from an insider's point of view support for the classroom heritage as a global language.

Students with interrupted schooling may lack literacy in the home language and thus rely exclusively on oral speech. Thus, an important feature of dialect difference may be differing access to orally transmitted folklore. This is a fragile family asset, yet one worth exploring.

Cultural Differences in Same-Language Groups. The United States has been settled by waves of immigrant groups, some of whom—such as Panamanians and Mexicans, for example—share a language but have very distinct cultures. These are cultural differences that go far beyond values; they represent alternative lifestyles, distinct dialects, and sometimes different racial histories. A teacher who speaks the same heritage language of a family may have to guard against assuming rapport based on cultural similarities, especially if the family is from a different part of the world.

Some community members who speak the same language but are from different cultures may be openly antagonistic toward others, because of divisions such as "gang" rivalries, "turf" conflicts, or religious differences. Even postcolonialism may play a role, as in Puerto Ricans (citizens of the United States because of the legacy of colonialism) who may resent more recently immigrated Mexicans or Cubans who live in the same community. The wise teacher takes cultural differences into consideration when reaching out to the community.

If the community is divided because of culture—such as neighborhoods in Chicago that are "either Puerto Rican or Mexican"—no amount of interpersonal skill or intercultural communication may be enough to surmount the culture clash. But intercultural communication is still key.

Some student populations have very different cultures despite a shared ethnic background. When interacting with these students and their families, a teacher may have to interact on a case-by-case basis to know which families participate in which culture.

| **Example of Concept** | *Same Language, Contrasting Cultures* |

Students at Montebello High School (in the Los Angeles area) may look to outsiders as a mostly homogenous population—93 percent Latino, 70 percent low income—but the 2,974 Latino students are split between those who are connected to their recent immigrant roots and those who are more Americanized. In the "TJ" (for Tijuana) side of the campus, students speak Spanish; take ESL classes; and participate in soccer, *folklorico* dancing, and the Spanish club. On the other side of campus, students speak mostly English, play football and basketball, and participate in student government. The two groups are not mutually hostile, but as senior Lucia Rios says, "It's like two countries." The differences in values between the two groups stems from their families' values—the recent immigrants are focused on economic survival and do not have the cash to pay for extracurricular activities. Another difference is musical taste (soccer players listen to Spanish music in the locker room, whereas football players listen to heavy metal and rap). (Hayasaki, 2004, pp. A1, A36–A37)

Intracultural Values Differences. Just because one shares the same language and culture as one's students, it is not necessarily true that one shares the same values. It is also possible that the teacher's personal values may be at odds with those of parents.

A teacher who needs to discuss with family members ways in which family values must change to increase support for their children's schooling may do so more effectively when using a heritage language. For example, this scene illustrates a classic situation in which a teacher must confront a family member (presumably the original conversation upon which this episode is based took place in Spanish!):

> In a scene from the motion picture *Stand and Deliver,* Jaime Escalante, the high-school math teacher, and his wife have dinner in the Mexican restaurant owned by the father of Anna, a young women whose parents have pulled her out of school to serve as a waitress. Escalante calls the owner's attention to the math mistake Anna has made on the bill and asks the man to allow his daughter to return to school. The man is enraged: How can the teacher "eat my food and then insult my values?" But Anna returns to math class . . .

Rapport is not automatic between those speaking the same heritage language. Sociopolitical differences may also create tensions between a teacher and family members, as between Vietnamese immigrants in California who fought for and against South Vietnam in the Vietnam War. Similar conditions may affect other immigrant groups whose homeland conflicts find them bitter enemies even in the New World. In these cases, deep values differences create community divisions, and the same-language professional may be viewed warily by the community or implicitly expected to choose sides.

Same-Culture Generational Differences. Generational differences may also create value differences. One example is the difference in values and lifestyles shown by the generations of Japanese who immigrated to the United States. *Isseis* were the first generation of Japanese who immigrated at the end of the nineteenth and the beginning of the twentieth century. They were fully Japanese in their cultural values and material culture. *Niseis* (second generation) were American born and culturally marginal between being American and Japanese (but really more American). *Sanseis* (third generation), *yonseis* (fourth generation), *goseis* (fifth generation), and so on, are descendants of the original Isseis, so many generations removed from Isseis that most have little contact with Japanese culture and language, having assimilated into American society. *Shin Isseis* (new first generation) are Japanese who immigrated to America after World War II. Because immigration from Japan was prohibited from 1924 until 1952, this was the first generation of Japanese who came after the war; they are ethnically Japanese. There are also descendants in the school population of significant numbers of Japanese married to Americans (see www.library.ca.gov /services/docs/japanese.pdf). An American-born public-school teacher who speaks Japanese may, therefore, have widely differing values and lifestyles from a recent Japanese immigrant.

Despite deep similarities in cultural values, historical circumstances may have created cultural differences, such as those that exist between Taiwan Chinese and those from the People's Republic of China. Two teachers who speak Mandarin may represent different sociopolitical histories. Teachers of Mandarin in a dual-language immersion setting may have differing values from the parent community. Thus, when values are concerned, the same language does not guarantee rapport.

Different-Language Home–School Partnerships Requiring Intercultural Communication

Because learning a second language requires a long-term commitment, teachers would do well to begin at any point in their professional lives to learn the dominant language of the community in which they work. This is not always feasible in schools in which children enroll from families of many diverse language backgrounds. Even speaking the dominant second language of a community does not guarantee rapport with all families; bilingual teachers may have many students who speak other languages in the same classroom. For the most part, teachers who do not speak the home language of the family must rely on intercultural communication skills to create a working relationship with the family. There are many aspects of the parents' culture to be learned; this reciprocity is important when expecting the families to work with the school.

Patterns That Support Learning at Home. A prime understanding that the educator must achieve is how the basic lifestyles and living patterns of the family affect the student. It is important to understand the family's habits to the extent that educators can help the child to find the time and place to accomplish homework. What resources can each family access? Is there time to go to the local public library? Who in the family uses a computer or smartphone? It takes deep cultural knowledge on the part of the teacher to assign the type, frequency, and extent of homework that the family can support.

Tapping Family Funds of Knowledge. Each family contributes expertise to the neighborhood. Having grown up within such a network helps the same-culture educator to honor "neighborhood knowledge" and to find a way to match schoolwork with nonacademic, yet invaluable, knowledge from the community (González, Moll, & Amanti, 2005).

> Jaime's father, uncle, and sometimes his older brother work together to install marble countertops in kitchens and bathrooms. Mrs. Montañez, Jaime's third-grade teacher, sent home a request for Jaime to bring small samples to class of the marble used in the installations, along with the name used for of each type of marble. The class took time to search where in the world marble quarries can be found and how the marble travels to their town. Then everyone in the class measured their kitchen tables or counters and calculated how much it would cost to convert that area to marble. Jaime was proud to be the inspiration for lessons in geography, geology, and math. His father, uncle, and brother all came to the class's culminating open-house presentations on The World of Marble.

Curriculum that draws in and builds upon community knowledge can be tied to grade-level curriculum standards. The important aspect is that it also draws in community members—particularly fathers, uncles, and older brothers—whose interest in schooling supports the success of their sons, brothers, nephews, nieces, sisters, and daughters.

Reaching Out to Workers in the Community. Various workers visit every community on a daily or weekly basis, representing utility companies, delivery services, social service workers, and other such personnel. Although funds for class field trips may be difficult to obtain, students can use their mobile phones to record brief interviews with these workers, using a small laminated card as an introduction that explains the educational purpose of such an encounter. Students can ask such workers simple questions and bring the results back to class. This helps to create prevocational awareness.

Finding a Volunteer Coordinator. The teacher who is more connected to the daily routines of families may know when a parent or caregiver might be free to spend an hour helping in the classroom. It is vital to identify the person who serves as the informal community organizer. Educators who are "tuned in" can find out who talks to whom, and when, and who that special "someone" is who functions as the social hub of a neighborhood. This can assist the teacher to get help from parents in the classroom. These insights can help to convert those unanswered requests for help into the opposite—a full schedule of eager volunteers!

Finding Community Advocates. Some parents are vocal about school-related issues and can work to organize others. This type of leadership is invaluable when working to create high-quality educational experience for English learners.

Example of Concept   *A Voice for Parents*

Elsa Nuñez is running for a seat on the Pajaro Valley Unified School District (PVUSD), California, school board. She is the mother of four PVUSD students and has been vocal in advocating for ways to speed up her children's acquisition of English. After five years in PVUSD schools, her ninth-grade twin girls are still classified as English learners.

She says, "Since I've been involved in my children's education, parents started approaching me, and they had the same concerns I had. They looked up to me to be their voice."

Nuñez adds that some people say that Spanish-speaking parents are not concerned about their children's education. She disputes this: "It's not because they don't care. It's because they don't know how."

A San José native, Nuñez went to Mexico to live when she was twenty-four, and then returned with her family. She wants her children to retain Spanish and their Mexican culture, but is transferring her children to an all-English high school in Aptos rather than attending Watsonville High. "It's too easy in this community to go back and forth with the language," she says.

Crosscultural Differences. Reaching out to families whose culture differs in multiple dimensions from that of the teacher requires an extraordinary investment to gain an in-depth understanding of cultural differences (see Chapter 9). Families from different cultures approach the interaction with the school in very different ways.

Example of Concept   *Cultural Differences in Parent Involvement*

A major difference between Russian parents and those from other cultural groups is the assertive way in which Russian parents often approach classroom teachers to inquire about their children's academic progress. Russian parents also approach teachers even though they do not speak English very fluently. The children translate for them as they inquire about homework or progress in class (Gaitan, 2006, p. 60).

Avoiding Cultural Deficit Assumptions. Because most teachers are themselves the product of U.S. schools, they often have internalized what Fránquiz, Salazar, and DeNicolo (2011) called "majoritarian tales" (p. 282), defined as "a mindset of positions, perceived wisdoms, and shared cultural understandings" (p. 282), about non-White racial and ethnic groups. One such belief is the notion that parents of English learners do not value their children's education. Such a belief places the blame for school failure on parents and masks the socioeconomic inequities that force families in poverty to make hard choices about family resources and parental attention. Over time, these beliefs that position members of certain groups as deficient become the norm about how teachers view families and students.

Fránquiz et al. (2011) propose that teachers who have personal knowledge and experience with families who are involved might produce a competing story, a "counterstory," that exposes and challenges deficit views of families. In fact, Solórzano and Yosso (2002) invite teacher action research with "counter-storytelling" at its core—research that creates new narratives in which families and teachers together find new ways to shape collaboration within the vision of a dual-language community.

Parents can help to combat deficit attitudes by volunteering to share aspects of the home culture and language. In this way they become cultural mediators.

Example of Concept   *A Parent Fosters Cultural Pride*

One Chinese American parent successfully intervened in a school situation to the benefit of her daughter and her classmates:

After my daughter was teased by her peers because of her Chinese name, I gave a presentation to her class on the origin of Chinese names, the naming of children in China, and Chinese calligraphy. My daughter has had no more problems about her name. What is more, she no longer complains about her unusual name, and she is proud of her cultural heritage. (Yao, 1988, p. 224)

Involving Parents as Cultural Mediators

Teachers can allow parents to act as cultural mediators in several ways:

- Establish an explicit open-door policy so parents will know they are welcome.

- Send written information home about classroom assignments and goals, and encourage parents to reply.

- Call parents periodically when things are going well and let them know when they can call you.

- Suggest specific ways parents can help in assignments.

- Get to know the community by visiting the community, and letting parents know when you are available to visit homes or talk at some other location.

- Arrange several parent conferences a year and let parents talk about their child's achievement.

- Solicit parents' views on education through a simple questionnaire, telephone interviews, or student or parent interviews.

Source: Adapted from Banks (2004).

Structuring Parent and Community Partnerships

In one little-known requirement under No Child Left Behind, school districts receiving more than $500,000 per year in Title I funds (which support the education of children from low-income families) are expected to spend one percent of those funds on programs to engage parents. But the usual strategies—sending home notes in backpacks and holding parents' nights—are not as effective with families where English is not spoken.

"Strong parent involvement is one factor that research has shown time and time again to have positive effects on academic achievement and school attitudes" (Ovando & Collier, 1998, p. 270). Fortunately, over the past decade successful programs have developed and various guidelines are available to help school personnel, parents, and communities work together to ensure parental rights, parental involvement, successful programs, and school-community partnerships that benefit students.

Recognizing Parental Rights

Parents have numerous rights that educators must respect and honor in spite of the challenges they may present to the school. These include (1) the right of their children to a free, appropriate public education; (2) the right to receive information concerning education decisions and actions in the language parents comprehend; (3) the right to make informed decisions and to authorize consent before changes in educational placement occur; (4) the right to be included in discussions and plans concerning disciplinary action toward their children; (5) the right to appeal actions when they do not agree; and (6) the right to participate in meetings organized for public and parent information (Young & Helvie, 1996).

Issues in Parental Involvement

Schools attempting to increase parental involvement have encountered issues in five areas of concern: language, survival and family structure, educational background and values, knowledge about education and beliefs about learning, and power and status. Ovando and Collier (1998) offered questions within each area that can provide a valuable guide as school personnel begin to address and overcome misconceptions regarding parents and that will open dialogue for fruitful collaborations and programs (see Table 10.1).

Table 10.1 Questions Regarding Parent–School Relationships

Area of Concern	Questions
Language	How does educators' language (jargon?) affect home–school communication?
	Do community members support using the home language in school?
Family structure	How do the struggles of day-to-day survival affect the home–school partnership?
	How will differences in family structure affect the relationship?
Educational background, attitudes toward schooling	Do school expectations match the parents' educational backgrounds?
	What do educators assume about the attitudes of parents toward schooling?
Knowledge and beliefs about education	How do parents learn about school culture, their role in U.S. schools, and the specific methods being used in their child's classroom? Would they be comfortable reinforcing these methods at home?
	How do parents and teachers differ in the perception of the home–school relationship?
Power and status	How does the inherent inequality of the educator–layperson relationship affect the partnership?
	Do programs for parents convey a message of cultural deficiency?
	To what degree are language-minority community members a part of the school in instructional and administrative positions?

Source: Adapted from Ovando and Collier (1998, pp. 301–309).

Programs in Action

As schools and parents have looked for ways in which they can partner in order to help children achieve success in school, several have developed family literacy projects. One of the first was the Párajo Valley Family Literacy project in Watsonville, California. Project founder and author Dr. Alma Flor Ada designed a parental involvement program that would help parents recover a lost sense of dignity and identity. She began with a "meet the author" program by telling her own stories and explaining her feelings about writing in Spanish. Each subsequent session included reading and discussing children's books and sharing experiences. Videotapes showing parents discussing and enjoying the books were circulated in the community. The major components of this project were the collaboration of the school and parents in a shared enterprise and the reciprocal interaction between parents and children that encourages both to enjoy literature (Ada, 1989).

A second such project was the Hmong Literacy Project initiated by Hmong parents in Fresno, California. As their children became more assimilated in the United States and less appreciative of their cultural roots, the parents felt the need to preserve their oral history and maintain their culture through written records. Therefore, they asked for literacy lessons in Hmong (a language that has been written for about only thirty years) and in English. Throughout the program, these parents developed not only the asked-for literacy skills but also skills in math and computers that allowed them to help their children academically. Through the *Hmong Parents Newsletter,* communication was increased between the school and the community, leading to greater parent participation in school activities (Kang, Kuehn, & Herrell, 1996).

Parents and older siblings can be encouraged to work with preschool and school-age children in a variety of activities. Rather than recommending that parents speak English more at home, teachers can encourage parents to verbalize in their home language with children in ways that build underlying cognitive skills. Parents can sit with the child to look at a book, pointing to pictures and asking questions; they can read a few lines and let the child fill in the rest or let the child retell a familiar story. Children can listen to adults discuss something or observe reading and writing in the primary language. Schools can assist communities with implementing literacy or cultural classes or producing a community primary-language newspaper. The school can also educate students and parents on the benefits of learning the home language of the parents and can find ways to make dual-language proficiency a means of gaining prestige at school.

Example of Concept   *Home and School Connection*

Here one teacher describes the success of a nonfiction publishing party hosted by the students:

> Parents and many extended family members came, as did neighbors and youth organization leaders with whom the students were involved. At various places around the room, reports were visible with yellow comment sheets. Visitors could sit at a desk or table, read, and comment on what they had read.
>
> Language was not a barrier: Many parents encouraged their children to read to them in English and translate the stories into the native language. They were proud of the English that their child had learned and proud that the child remembered the native language well enough to translate. Many students encouraged their parents to try saying the name of the objects in the pictures that accompanied many of the reports in English. Everywhere I looked, I saw proud children beaming as they showed their work off to the people they cared about and who cared about them. (Cho Bassoff, 2004, para. 9 and 10)

PreK–3 education environments for young Hispanic children should feature rich language stimuli, with many opportunities for students and teachers to talk with one another in both Spanish and English. This also includes families as part of the dialogue. As Garcia and Jensen (2007) note, "Spanish-speaking parents are more likely to involve themselves in schools and classrooms in which Spanish is regularly spoken" (p. 37).

The New York City Model. The New York City Department of Education Office of Family Engagement has involved large numbers of family members by holding workshops early in the morning and on weekends, when parents who hold multiple jobs are likely to be free. They provide translators in more than a dozen languages and rehearse in class how parents can speak up as advocates for their children and how to help children of every age with schoolwork in every subject. In this way, the barriers to academic success for English learners are coming down (Russakoff, 2009).

Example of Concept   *Parent Training Sessions*

Parents of kindergarten English learners at Lillian Elementary School in Los Angeles were invited to two Saturday workshops in October and two more in December, where they were taught by teachers how to help their children learn to recognize alphabet letters and learn sight words such as *here* and *the*.

In a math lesson, teacher Gloria Sigala urged parents to teach their children the concept of a pair, or circles, triangles, and rectangles. Even though many parents are immigrants who work long hours to support their families, educators are seeing that time parents spend helping their children pays off. Teachers say that the kindergarteners are more confident and attentive in class (Quiñoñes, 2008).

Example of Concept   *Home–School Partnerships to Combat Truancy*

When students began skipping classes in high school, several teachers and staff became concerned. The district's ELD and bilingual staff and several school principals met individually with students and parents to search for the reasons the school system wasn't working. Community meetings were held with parents, teachers, school principals, central office administrators, and the school superintendent to strengthen the home–school partnership, and included informal potluck suppers and teacher- and parent-facilitated roundtable discussions. Numerous suggestions and positive actions came from these meetings—including the powerful links that were made between the district and the families (Zacarian, 2004, pp. 11–13).

The Importance of Leadership Positions. One researcher has documented the effect of Latinos in positions of power within schools as an important message to Latino parents. When parents saw their own ethnicity reflected in leadership positions—at the administrative and governance level—in schools, they were more willing to participate in home–school connective activities, which ultimately manifest as increased school involvement (Shah, 2009).

Overcoming Families' Reluctance to Become Involved. One factor that makes Latino parents reluctant to volunteer in schools is that they have less experience in schools: More than forty percent of Latina mothers of public-school children have less than a high-school education, compared with less than six percent for white mothers and a just over eighteen percent for African American mothers (Gándara, 2010). Because they have, on average, the lowest education level of any major ethnic group in the United States, Latino family members are often reluctant to be involved in their children's schools—even more so if they do not speak English. In fact, Gándara, Rumberger, Maxwell-Jolly, and Callahan (2003) found that schools with high percentages of Latino English learners had significantly fewer adult volunteers.

Fear of Reprisal. Some children in U.S. schools, or family members, are illegal immigrants, which introduces emotional, if not legal, complexity into the family's relation to the schools. Because immigration has been used as a wedge issue by national, state, and local political parties, many families whose members are undocumented live in fear of exposure, arrest, or denial of services by school authorities.

Although schools are prohibited against using residence status as grounds for denying educational services by *Plyler v. Doe* [457 U.S. 202 (1982)], a case in which the Supreme Court of the United States prohibited states to limit the rights afforded to people (specifically children) based on their status as immigrants, the "push-back" against this statute by some state and local authorities often intimidates immigrants and causes families to limit their contacts with schools. Thus, politics complicates the schooling of English learners.

School–Community Partnerships

In addition to developing partnerships with parents, schools are also reaching toward communities to help them in educating all children. Community-based organizations (CBOs)—groups committed to helping people obtain health, education, and other basic human services—are assisting students in ways that go beyond traditional schooling (Dryfoos, 1998). Adger (2000) found that school–CBO partnerships support students' academic achievement by working with parents and families, tutoring students in their first language, developing students' leadership skills and higher education goals, and providing information and support on issues such as health care, pregnancy, gang involvement, and so on (see Chapter 11).

Schools have evolved a variety of successful strategies to work with families to further the academic progress of English learners. The ideas and programs featured in this chapter provide basic concepts and examples. Educators who meet families halfway—that is, who share, or have learned, the heritage language, or who make efforts to understand the families' values and behaviors—will communicate clearly that the partnership is important. In this light, the whole community understands that the school is a source of support, the heart of the neighborhood. This level of trust takes a wholehearted effort to develop and sustain.

LEARNING MORE

Further Reading

Can teachers use Twitter to help parents stay involved with the classroom? Dana Wilber's book *iWrite* (Heinemann, 2010) features a section on microblogging and Twitter in her chapter, "Upcoming Technologies That May Make a Difference in the English Classroom."

Web Search

The National Coalition for Parent Involvement in Education (www.ncpie.org) is one of many sites that offer tips on involving families. It features such links as Young-chan Han's article "Working with Immigrant, Refugee Students and Families To Help Them Understand School Transportation Services" that contains tips for helping families learn about school bus service and other issues related to transportation (see http://content .yudu.com/A1rhdl/STNApril2011/resources/38.htm).

Exploration

Using the resource given below, answer these four questions:

1. How do Latino parents define "parental involvement"?
2. What do Latino parents see as challenges to parental involvement?
3. How do educators view parental involvement? Is this different from your answer to question #1?
4. How do Latino students view their parents' role in schooling?

Zarate, M. E. (2007). Understanding Latino parental involvement in education (#2069). Los Angeles: The Tomás Rivera Policy Institute. (www.trpi.org/archiv/)

Collaboration

Find out the family–school collaboration plan in a local school district. With a partner, attend a school-sponsored family event.

MyEducationLab™

Embracing Home Experiences of Culturally Diverse Students

This video discusses the importance of embracing the experiences of Culturally Diverse Students. Parents of English Learners provide experiences and learning opportunities for their children that can be beneficial to all students in the classroom. Encouraging students and families to share their experiences is an important part of culturally-sensitive instruction.

To access the video, go to MyEducationLab (www.myeducationlab.com), choose the Díaz-Rico text, and log in to MyEducationLab for English Language Learners. Select the topic Diversity, and watch the video entitled "Embracing Home Experiences of Culturally Diverse Students."

Answer the following questions:

1. In what ways can a teacher make "being unique" a strength in the classroom?
2. How could you establish a classroom culture that encourages students share their funds of knowledge?
3. What specific things can you do to encourage parents of English Learners to share their experiences and learning in your classroom?

Policy

Language Policy and Special Populations of English Learners

Language policies and specific program models constitute Part Five. Rather than summarizing the policy "big picture"—at the national or state levels—Chapter 11 begins with the role of the classroom teacher in daily policymaking and proceeds from that level to a more comprehensive overview. Chapter 12 contains a description of the issues surrounding identification and referral of culturally and linguistically diverse (CLD) learners to special school services. (See accompanying figure.)

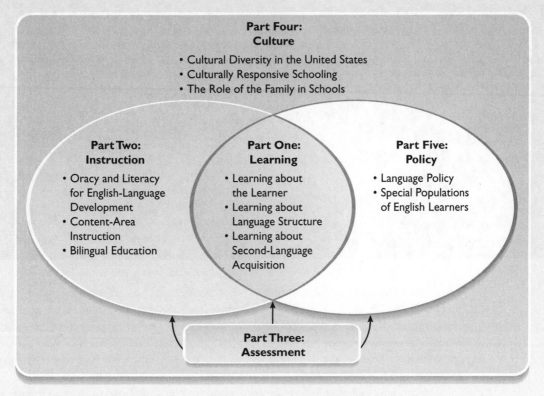

Model for CLAD Policy: Language Policy and Special Populations of English Learners

11

The Role of Educators in Language Policy

Interacting with the community brings recognition to the student as well as the school.

© PhotosIndia.com LLC/Alamy

The dropout crisis in the twenty-first century is not a losing battle. Not only do we know what the problem is and why it is so pervasive, particularly in low-income communities, and communities of color specifically, but we also know what works. Decades of strong research and examples of model practices demonstrate that policy matters, institutional culture matters, and individual actions and behaviors matter. Separately, these factors say something important. But together, these factors can be powerful sources of understanding and action.

We are now in a place where we need to merge complex understandings with political will to truly transform the crisis facing our communities. This transformation can only occur if researchers, educators, policymakers, parents, students and community stakeholders work together. If we transform the way our institutions function, we will transform the educational opportunities for our students and communities particularly those who have been historically left behind.

We must be bold and forward looking, particularly in the context where challenges loom and injustice often prevails, especially for the most vulnerable children and communities.

Louie Rodríguez (2013)

Teachers have a significant influence over the daily lives of students in their classroom. They can actively create a climate of warmth and acceptance for culturally and linguistically diverse (CLD) learners, supporting the home language while fostering the growth of a second language. Conversely, they can allow policies of the school to benefit only the students whose language and culture are in the majority by, for example, condoning the exclusive use of the dominant language. This permits majority-language students to gain advantage at the expense of those students who speak minority languages. Teachers make policy day by day, by the actions they take in the classroom, by the professional commitments they honor, and by the stance they take on the importance of their students' primary languages.

Policies about language—and, to a lesser extent, about culture (lesser only because the cultural patterns of schooling are less obvious)—determine the organization and management of schooling (see the figure on page 311). Such factors as class size, allocation of classrooms, availability of primary-language instruction, availability of support services for CLD learners, and funds for curricular materials are determined by policies that are made by decisions at the federal, state, local, or school level. The questions of *who makes policy* and *who influences policy* are important. Can teachers influence policy on a scale larger than their single classroom—on a schoolwide level, on a districtwide level, on the level of a community as a whole, on a statewide or national basis? Or are policy decisions too remote from the daily life of classrooms for teachers to be influential?

Policies can be formal and official, or they can be informal, such as efforts to create and manipulate attitudes toward languages and language variations (Corson, 1990). Both formal and informal policies have an impact on second-language teaching. Like it or not, teachers work under conditions that are highly affected by social and political conditions. Ideally, teachers' decisions further the academic success of English learners. If this is not the case, the academic future of these students is undermined or undone.

This chapter focuses on policy in language matters rather than on the more pervasive topic of cultural matters for two reasons. First, language policy is a current zone of contention for educators, and thus awareness in this area is urgent. Second, cultural patterns of schooling are more difficult to examine and, although equally important to the day-to-day lives of students and teachers alike, are not the subject of current controversy to the extent of such topics as bilingual education. However, the role of teachers in creating and executing policy in this area is also crucial.

A Critical Approach to Language Policy

Several sociologists and social philosophers who study language and society have urged a wider perspective on the social tensions that underlie arguments about the language(s) used in schooling. A critical perspective, one that looks at broad social issues of dual-language proficiency and language policy, has developed from the work of five theorists in particular: James Tollefson, Michel Foucault, Norman Fairclough, Pierre Bourdieu, and Jim Cummins.

Tollefson: Power and Inequality in Language Education

Tollefson (1995) has examined issues of language equity—the social policies and practices that lead to inequity for non-native language speakers—in various international contexts and laid the foundation for a worldwide vision of language equity issues. He contrasted two ways to study language behavior: *descriptive* and *evaluative* (Tollefson, 1991). A descriptive approach seeks to understand the relationship of language behavior and social participation. It examines such linguistic phenomena as *diglossia* (why low-status versus high-status language is used in various contexts); *code shifting* (why bilingual speakers choose one language over another in social contexts); *relations of dominance* (how language is used to establish and maintain social position); and *register shifts* (how the formality/informality of language shapes rules and norms of interaction).

An evaluative approach, on the other hand, looks at such language policy issues as efforts to *standardize* or *purify language*, attempts to *preserve* or *revive endangered languages*, and movements to *establish national languages* or *legislate language usage*. In these separate domains of inquiry, those who study language descriptively focus on language as it is actually used, and those who take an evaluative perspective describe shaping or changing language behavior.

Language diversity can be seen as a problem, as a right, or as a resource (Galindo, 1997; Ruíz, 1984). The view that dual-language proficiency is a *problem* that must be remedied is, at best, socially and economically shortsighted—and, at worst, the foundation for linguistic genocide (defined by Skutnabb-Kangas, 1993, as "systematic extermination of a minority language"; see also Skutnabb-Knagas, 2000). The position that language diversity is a *right* has been the basis for the court cases and congressional mandates that have created bilingual education; however, these movements have probably been successful because of the emphasis on transitional efforts, with bilingual education seen as a right that expires when a student makes the shift into English.

The idea that language diversity is a *resource*, that dual-language proficiency is a valuable asset, is gaining some adherents in the United States, particularly among those who do business with second-language populations in the United States and abroad. The work of Tollefson and his colleagues (see Pennycook, 1994; Skutnabb-Kangas,

Example of Concept   *Multilingualism as a Resource*

Salvador Sarmiento, a teacher in a third-grade bilingual classroom, responded to the pressures of increased assessment demands from NCLB,	the focus on skills-based instruction, and negative climate toward bilingual education in a unique way—by starting a Spanish-language unit on

dance. He brought in CDs on the merengue to use during physical education class. Students read from books about Latin dance and wrote poems in response. Mr. Sarmiento choreographed a dance routine for the students to perform for parent night.

When students from other classes begged their teachers for a chance to dance, the third-grade students wrote letters to the other teachers explaining how they could teach their students to dance. Having a real reason to write a letter in English made them pay careful attention to grammar and spelling.

At the end of the grading period, most of these third-grade students met or surpassed the benchmark expectation in both English and Spanish. Salvador's passion for dance "paid off" in enriched linguistic, cultural, and education learning opportunities (Sarmiento, 2008).

2000) has documented that fights for language equity have profound ramifications for social as well as economic policy on a worldwide basis.

Tollefson's work in providing a larger context for viewing the struggles of minority-language speakers is useful in policy settings in which an economic argument is made for English-only schooling (that English-only schooling furthers economic success for English learners). Ironically, English-only schooling will not be as valuable as dual-language proficiency—attaining advanced skills in more than one language—as the source of employment advancement for most job seekers in the coming global economy.

Foucault: The Power of Discursive Practices

Foucault, a twentieth-century social historian, traced the spread of power relations in the modern world, relations that are sustained by means of networks shaped largely by language practices. In several important treatises, Foucault outlined the links between power and language. He documented ways in which authorities have used language to repress, dominate, and disempower social groups in favor of social norms that are favorable to those in power; yet conversely, certain social groups have appropriated or acquired language practices that mimic those in power and thus have shaped power to their own ends. Foucault (1979, 1980) emphasized that the struggle for power is "a struggle for the control of discourses" (Corson, 1999, p. 15). In this same vein, Gramsci (1971) conceptualized social power as hegemonic; that is, people are influenced to follow invisible norms and forms of cultural power, even when it is not to their advantage to do so. Thus, the forms of power that benefit the dominant class influence and shape the behavior of subordinated classes, sometimes to their detriment.

Foucault's contribution to the study of language policy, although indirect, is profound. He has shown that language is not neutral; discursive practices are inseparable from the workings of power, and in fact are the direct vehicle for the circulation of power. Power, however, is neutral; it can be a creative force for those who use discourse masterfully, as well as a destructive force that excludes those without effective language practices.

Fairclough: Critical Language Analysis

Although Foucault laid the foundation for the study of the role of language in the workings of power, Fairclough (1989, 1997) has offered a structured means to analyze linguistic features of discourse in order to discover the power messages that are conveyed. Fairclough conceives of discourse as a nested set of boxes: first, the text itself that constitutes the message; second, the institutional influence on the message; and third, the social/cultural influence on the message. Any text, whether spoken or written, has features at these three levels. These levels constitute the power that the message carries. Fairclough's critical language analysis (CLA) offers tools to tease out the hidden messages of power in a discourse (Table 11.1).

Table 11.1 Fairclough's Critical Language Analysis

Box Level	Description	Questions to Ask
First (innermost)	Describes features of the text	In order to read the message "between the lines," ask the following: What is the style of writing, level of vocabulary, complexity of syntax, and tone of the message? What is assumed that the reader knows? What features of gendered language are noticeable? Who is responsible for the actions, opinions, or stance taken in the text? Where did the text originate? What interaction generated it? What is said? What is unsaid but implied? What is the tone of the message?
Second (middle layer)	Probes the institutional influence on the text	To interpret this influence, ask: What social group or agency (a school, television, schooling, friendship, etc.) supplied the context for the message? What was the institutional origin of the message? Who supplied the platform, the paper, the computer, or the microphone? Who stands to benefit from the message? How was the text influenced by an institution?
Third (outermost layer)	Examines the sociocultural context	What sociocultural factors came into play? How did society's attitudes/treatment of age, gender, culture influence the text? How might the text have been different had its origin been a person of different culture, gender, or age? What hidden messages can be understood about this message knowing its social origin?

Source: Based on Fairclough (1989).

CLA can be used to scrutinize a parent newsletter sent home from an elementary school to Spanish-speaking parents. The intent of the newsletter is to explain to parents how to help their child with homework:

- At the level of text, the newsletter appears to be a word-for-word translation of the reverse side, a letter to English-speaking parents. The text has been written on a word processor, in dual columns like a newspaper. There are no illustrations—merely a page full of text. The content has ten paragraphs, each explaining a different feature of "homework tips."
- At the institutional level, the sheet is part of a "School Open House" packet distributed with about six other papers, some of which are in Spanish and some of which are not. The text was written by an assistant principal and translated by an aide.
- At the sociocultural level, the text assumes that the parents welcome the advice of the school authorities and that the parents' role is to help the students complete the assignments sent home by the teachers. There is no mention of a role for parents as collaborating with the teacher to determine the worth or value of the assignments.

In contrast, another teacher works with students to write a "Homework Help" manual, a six-page "little book" composed by students themselves in cooperative groups. Each group decides on a title for their book and brainstorms the book's content. Will it include recommendations of a special place to study at home? Will it mention adequate lighting? Will it discuss how to deal with the distractions of television or of siblings? Will it advise students how to solicit help from parents? Will it advise parents how to communicate to teachers the comparative worth of different types of assignments? Will the book be in more than one language? Each group adds the ideas that the members choose. When the books are ready, the teacher asks each student to take the book home, discuss it with the family, and then come back to class with feedback about whether the suggestions are apt.

Examined with the analytical tools of CLA, these little books are a very different product from the parent newsletter previously described.

- At the level of text, this effort is an individual product, with personalized artwork, student-generated ideas, and student-generated language that is understandable to family members.
- At the institutional level, both the existing habits of the family and the needs of the school are respected, and communication between home and school is built into the project.
- At the sociocultural level, the student is positioned as a consultant on the family's habits and values, and family is positioned as a valued partner in teaching and learning.

Thus, CLA, a structured means of creating awareness of hidden levels of language, can be used to examine assumptions that lie beneath schooling practices. This awareness operates unconsciously but smoothly in skilled power players but is useful as a conscious tool for those who could benefit from an increased understanding of power, particularly as it operates at the institutional and sociocultural levels. As an analytic tool, it is simple yet easy enough to teach to children as they become aware of what is said—and not said—in discourse.

Bourdieu: Language as Social Capital

The French anthropologist Bourdieu considered language to be *cultural capital*— that is, a part of the social "goods" that people accumulate and use to assert power and social class advantage. In a capitalist society, those who are native speakers of a high-status language have cultural capital, whereas those who speak a lower-status language must work hard to overcome the lack of such capital. *Social capital* is a major form of cultural capital. Social capital for children in most middle-class families includes being provided transportation to public libraries, buying additional school-related materials, visiting museums, being given music or art lessons, traveling, having homework supervised, benefitting from tutors, attending school functions, and even moving into the best school districts (Chang, 2005).

Bourdieu (1977) emphasized that schools act as agents of an economic system to reproduce the existing distribution of capital. Schools permit the "haves" (those already possessing cultural capital) to succeed at the expense of the "have-nots," those who are comparatively lacking in the linguistic skills, prior knowledge, or other social resources to succeed. Education plays a key role in the determination of social success, and permits further understanding of the challenges faced by those whose language skills are not deemed of social importance.

The unique contribution of Bourdieu was his recognition that language, along with other intangible social factors, is an asset, as are physical resources. In a class-room, a teacher's predilection is to be attracted toward social capital—to those children who already appear to be successful—and to shun those who appear to lack this attraction. One might also deduce that a teacher's attention, admiration, and reinforcement are therefore aspects of a teacher's social capital that he or she can deploy at will. Bourdieu placed schooling, with its behaviors and practices, squarely in the center of the surrounding economic reality, with policies that act as currency— currency that functions every bit as powerfully as does hard cash.

Cummins: Language Policies as Emancipatory

Cummins (2001) clearly delineated educational practices that function as collabora-tive relations of power and set these against counterpractices that are coercive in nature. Cummins cautioned that children who enter schools in which diversity is *not* affirmed soon grasp that their "difference" is not honored but, rather, is suspect. If students are not encouraged to think critically, to reflect, and to solve problems, they are being submitted to a "transmission model" of pedagogy. The resulting sense of reduced worth undermines achievement. Pressuring students to conform, or to participate in schooling practices that are unfair or discriminatory, causes them to lose their identity as human beings: They are subjected to what Cummins (1989) called "identity eradication." To counteract this devaluation of students, teachers' and students' roles must be redefined.

Cummins thus took a critical pedagogy stance, in line with Paulo Freire's (1985) call for a liberating education of "transforming action," in which teachers are dedicated to social change. Unfortunately, many teachers are unaware of the power practices that either help students to develop or hinder them from developing a sense of control over their own lives. They are equally unaware of the ways in which spoken and unspoken language can circulate messages of dominance or subordination— features of institutional racism and disempowerment. Cummins's work, together with the work of other critical pedagogists, highlights the need for structural changes within schools that support positive attitudes, strong personal and social identities on the part of English learners, and academic success.

To summarize the contributions of the critical language theorists, power relations hidden within language issues are a characteristic of societies around the world. The tools of the social language critic work to clarify and reveal the covert power relations that language enables. Language is a chief vehicle for deploying power, whether constructively or destructively. The power potential of any message, verbal or nonverbal, can be systematically analyzed. Language is a kind of social asset, and schools are agencies through which language is used to benefit or to detract from the accrual of social wealth. Schooling practices can empower or disempower, depending on the language and cultural policies within the school.

Language Policy: The Classroom

Teachers *can* influence language policy, and those who are experts on the education of English learners *should* be influential. If teachers do not influence policy, decisions will be made by others: by the force of popular opinion, by politicians, by bureaucrats, by demagogues. The influence of teachers will not be felt, however, by wishing or hoping. Teachers need to examine closely the possibilities that exist for influence on policy and then work hard to make this influence a reality. This influence can be wielded by teachers in different ways in various social and political arenas: by monitoring procedures and curricula within the classroom itself, at the school level, and at the level of the local school district; by encouraging support within the community; by working within state commissions and professional organizations; and by lobbying for federal policies that benefit English learners. As Villegas and Lucas (2007) note: "Teaching is an ethical activity, and teachers have an ethical obligation to help all students learn. To meet this obligation, teachers need to serve as advocates for their students, especially those who have been traditionally marginalized in schools" (p. 32).

Educational Equity in Everyday Practices

Equitable educational practices require discipline and vigilant self-observation on the part of classroom teachers (Tollefson, 1991). Practicing gender, socioeconomic, racial, and cultural equity means that males and females from minority and majority races and cultures, whether rich or poor, receive equal opportunity to participate, such as being given equally difficult questions to answer during class discussion, along with adequate verbal and nonverbal support.

Cultural equity calls for teachers to accept students' personalization of instruction; to use multicultural examples to illustrate points of instruction; to listen carefully to the stories and voices of the students from various cultures; and to tie together home and school for the benefit of the students. Issues of socioeconomic equity arise, for example, when assignments for at-home projects are evaluated more highly when they incorporate a wealth of resources that some families can provide and others cannot.

In a democratic classroom, even the teacher must not play an autocratic role, usurping the rights of others to be treated fairly and with respect. As Faltis and Coulter (2008) explain, students must be taught the interpersonal skills they need to solve problems that interfere with learning. In this way, the classroom functions smoothly and the focus is on learning.

Teachers must endeavor to extend the rich, close relationship of mentor and protégé to all students. Referrals to special education on the one hand, and to gifted or enriched instruction on the other, should not unfairly favor or target students of one gender, race, or culture. (If school site or district criteria result in de facto lack of equity in these areas, teachers may need to ask for a review of the criteria.) Practicing "everyday equity" ensures the possibility of equal opportunity for all. The following classroom policies promote inclusion for students:

- Teachers value the experiences of culturally different children.
- The primary language is seen as a worthy subject for instruction and as a means by which students can acquire knowledge.
- Classroom strategies guarantee boys and girls equal access to the teacher's attention.

Marshall and Oliva (2006) sum up the role of socially conscious educators:

School leaders sometimes do equity work when they implement equity-related policies. . . . Some go further, demanding better than the letter of the law, for example, by joining in political coalitions or in legal actions for school finance equity, for the preservation of bilingual programs, and the like. However, the activist, interventionist stance of social justice leadership goes even further, inspired not just by an intellectual ideal, but also by moral outrage at the unmet needs of students and a desire for a caring community where relationships matter. . . . Social justice leadership reconnects with emotional and idealistic stances. It supports leaders' . . . efforts to conceptualize and articulate models of leadership that incorporate democratic community engagement, spirituality and emotion, and caring and compassion. (pp. 7–8)

The Social Environment of the Classroom

Students come to school for social as well as academic reasons. School practices in noncurricular areas, such as discipline, and in extracurricular activities, such as school clubs, should be nondiscriminatory. These activities provide ways in which the school climate can foster or retard students' multicultural competence (Bennett, 2003). If the school climate is accepting of the linguistic and cultural identities of students, these identities will develop in ways that are consonant with an academic environment. If not, a resistance culture may develop that rejects schooling, with outcomes such as high dropout rates and high incidences of school vandalism. The formal and the hidden curriculum of a school need to be consistent with each other so that they support diversity and achievement. The social climate of the school can be one of acceptance for all students in the following ways:

- Culturally and linguistically diverse students are grouped heterogeneously.
- Children and staff learn about the cultural practices of the families represented in the school.
- Students can win prestige positions in extracurricular activities regardless of their ethnic or cultural background.
- Dress codes do not discriminate against some subcultures while allowing others to dress as they wish.
- School staff members (e.g., office personnel) are equally courteous to all students and visitors.

The Policies Embodied in Teachers' Plans

Teachers can be explicit about issues of equity and multicultural inclusion in planning yearly units and daily lessons. Teachers are responsible for obtaining materials that are nonbiased and promote positive role models from a variety of ethnic groups and for designing and planning instruction that makes success possible for all students (see Díaz-Rico, 1993). This responsibility cannot be transferred to other decision-making bodies. Materials are readily available that describe multicultural education (see Bennett, 2003; Harris, 1997; Nieto & Bode, 2008). Teachers can plan for culturally and linguistically fair instruction in the following ways:

- Students' interests and backgrounds are taken into consideration when planning instruction.
- Materials depict individuals of both genders and of various races and cultures in ways that suggest success.
- Materials for bilingual and multicultural instruction receive equitable share of budgeted resources.
- Daily plans include adequate time for development of primary-language skills.

Example of Concept   *A Social Justice Issue in a Math Lesson*

Mr. Rodriguez challenged his high-school math class to test the numbers of English learners in honor classes in their high school against the proportion expected through mathematical chance. Concluding that the disproportionately small number was unlikely to occur randomly, the teacher encouraged his students to present their results to the school administration. This moved the content of the math class from dry, disconnected content to a connection with socially and personally relevant issues (Zacarian, 2011).

Policy at the School Level

An exemplary teacher's greatest contribution at the school site may be the positive outcomes evident throughout the school as that teacher's students provide leadership, goodwill, and academic models for other students. However, a school site can be the setting for scores of such students when school personnel take explicit roles in school-site decision making.

Collaboration with Colleagues

Schools can benefit greatly when teachers work together. Sharing resources, working together to plan instruction, and teaching with one another add insight and vitality to a job that is often isolating. It is vital that personal relations be established and maintained with all colleagues at a school site to ensure that the staff are not polarized along lines of cultural, linguistic, or philosophical differences. Decisions that are often made collaboratively are the following:

- Extra-duty assignments are adjusted for teachers who must translate letters sent home to parents or develop primary-language materials.
- Primary-language materials and other materials are freely shared among professional staff.
- Primary-language instructors are socially integrated with the mainstream staff.

School-Site Leadership

School authorities, particularly principals, can support ELD and bilingual instruction in many ways. Often, principals are the leading advocates for funding increases at the district level. Principals can work with teachers to configure classes and class sizes to the benefit of English learners. Appointing a lead or mentor teacher can help new teachers adjust to and meet the needs of English learners. Lead teachers may be able to develop professional presentations that showcase student abilities or program features. Districtwide principals' meetings or school board meetings may be venues where these presentations can be seen and heard. By communicating to others about students' abilities as well as innovative program structures for English learners, principals begin to develop a climate of acceptance for linguistic and cultural diversity. This can be accomplished in the following ways:

- Marking policies are monitored to ensure that all students have equal opportunity to receive high grades.
- Staff members who have expertise in English-language development or expertise in primary-language instruction are given time to be of assistance to other teachers.
- Teachers with English-language development or primary-language assignments are given an equal share of mentoring and supervisory assistance.
- Leaders in the school set an example of respect and encouragement for diverse language abilities and cultures within the school.

FIND OUT MORE ABOUT ...

School-Site Leadership

Professional Development for Teachers in Culturally Diverse Schools

www.cal.org/resources/digest/profdvpt.html

A digest that describes a set of necessary conditions concerning school and district policies in order for teachers to effectively teach second-language learners. In addition, it documents several schools that have successfully restructured their academic programs to include all students.

Leading for Diversity: How School Leaders Can Improve Interethnic Relations

http://escholarship.org/uc/item/9g91h7ff

A report based on case studies of twenty-one schools across the United States in which the leadership had taken proactive steps to improve relations between the varying student groups. It provides two sample dilemmas and discusses how to assess the school context, set priorities, and develop a plan.

The Academic Ambiance of the School

Schools that are noted for academic excellence attract community attention because of the success of their students and alumni. Academic competitions outside of schools are one way in which certain schools garner academic laurels and gain the reputation for an academic ambiance. The better examples of this type of competition tend to promote problem solving rather than simple recall skills. Competitions that require inventive thinking are also available, and the fact that these are less language dependent may be more attractive to English learners. Schools can foster an academic ambiance in a variety of ways:

- Teachers who sponsor academically oriented extracurricular activities are given extra pay, just as athletic coaches are.
- Funds are available for students to travel to intellectual competitions.

- Individuals from diverse cultural and linguistic backgrounds are actively solicited for teams that compete for academic awards.
- Some intellectual activities such as contests are held in the primary language.

Involving Parents/Families

Encouraging parents and families to participate in school activities is vital. The extra step of sending families letters, reports, and notices in their home language helps to build rapport and extend a welcome to the school. These language policies constitute the daily message that home languages are important and valued. Families can receive the message that they are valued in many ways:

- Representative family committees can advise and consent on practices that involve CLD students.
- Parents/guardians can use the school library to check out books with their children.
- School facilities can be made available for meetings of community groups.

Example of Concept   *Involving Families and Communities*

A simple invitation invited families, school district employees, local businesses, and community members to Community Literacy Day at the new elementary school in town. Each individual was asked to bring a favorite book to share. A table of book choices was available with volunteers to help match volunteer, book, and grade level. The program was a huge success. Each classroom had several readers, and some visitors went to more than one class (Guth, 2002).

FIND OUT MORE ABOUT ...

Parental Involvement

Parental Involvement: Title I, Part A
www.ed.gov/programs/titleiparta/parentinvguid.doc
   This guidance document from the U.S. Department of Education explains the parental involvement

responsibilities of the state and local education agencies and the school under the No Child Left Behind legislation.

Policy in Local School Districts

The policies of local school districts are shaped by the values of the community. This may create frustration for teachers who feel that educational decisions are not in the hands of educators. On the other hand, teachers who take responsibility for helping to shape the community's beliefs and values may find that their leadership as teachers is very welcome.

Professional Growth and Service

Serving on district curriculum adoption committees is one way in which teachers can share and contribute their expertise. Teacher-led presentations to other teachers, staff, or community members are also important contributions. These activities deliver the message that teachers are knowledgeable and interested in the community at large. Consider the following ideas for teacher involvement:

- Teachers' opinions are consulted for materials purchased by school district and community libraries.
- Teachers participate in leadership training for English-language-development programs.

FIND OUT MORE ABOUT ...

Professional Development

Professional Development for Language Teachers
www.cal.org/resources/digest/0303diaz.html

This digest discusses professional development and lists six strategies for teachers to help them with their development.

The School Board

Teachers are very much aware that school policies are determined by the beliefs of school board members as well as by legal precedents set by state and federal laws and court decisions. Part of the advocacy position suggested by Cazden (1986) is the need for teachers to espouse and support appropriate program for English learners before local boards. In cooperation with parent groups, teachers can be effective in marshaling support for programs designed for language-minority groups. School board policies can be influenced in positive ways:

- Policy committees can place recommendations before the school board in a timely manner, with clear, concise, well-researched presentations.
- Frequent attendance at school board meetings sends the message that the meetings are monitored by those who support language-minority students' achievement.

Community Support for English Learners

A supportive community offers a home for linguistic and cultural diversity. This support takes many forms: affirming variety in neighbors' lifestyles, patronizing minority businesses, fund-raising for college scholarships for English learners, and providing community services that are user-friendly for all.

The Public Forum

Communities accept other languages being spoken in the community if there is little fear of economic or political encroachment by immigrants. By supporting English learners and their rights, teachers can see that situations such as that which occurred in Monterey Park, California, do not recur. A Monterey Park city council member led a fight to halt the use of public funds for the purchase of Chinese-language books for the city's library. The criticism was that these books solely benefit the Chinese community. Those who supported the initiative did not recognize that the Chinese population has as much right to be supported by the government as any other group and that English-speaking Americans studying Chinese might benefit from these books (Dicker, 1992). In this case, local policy was being affected by the linguistic chauvinism of one community leader.

Policies of community agencies such as the library can be influenced by the following teacher-led activities:

- Librarians can file teachers' lesson plans in the library and make specific materials accessible to students.
- Teachers can justify to librarians the need for primary-language materials.
- Teachers can conduct classes open to parents in community arenas, including the library.
- Schools can work together with parents to encourage the use of community resources such as libraries.

Community Organizations

Service organizations are often run by community leaders who set the tone for the community and who are a source of employment for workers. Business leaders sometimes have strong ideas about education. They usually enjoy dialogue with professional educators and seek to be updated on current beliefs and practices. It is in this dialogue that professional educators need to present the foundation for current pedagogy. The leaders of community organizations want to help schools improve so that their children and their workers will be productive. Obtaining this help is easier when requests are concrete and the justification is strong. Ways in which community organizations can interact with schools include the following:

- Sending representatives to school career days to talk about the importance of more than one language in the workplace.

- Establishing partnerships with schools to support activities such as student internships, tutoring, and mentoring.
- Establishing partnerships with school districts to help finance language programs.

State Commissions and Professional Organizations

Outside the immediate community, a larger community awaits. Statewide commissions or state boards of education are opportunities for teachers to be involved in writing statewide curricula, adopting textbooks, and serving on advisory boards. National professional organizations often have state counterparts. Joining Teachers of English to Speakers of Other Languages (TESOL) or the National Association for Bilingual Education (NABE) puts educators in contact with language development specialists nationally and internationally. These organizations' publications carry news from state affiliates, and newsletters from the state organizations carry news of local associations. If there is no local organization, why not start one?

The Voice of the Expert

Attending district or regional professional conferences is a beginning step toward developing one's own expertise on linguistic and cultural issues and teaching practices. Successful teachers may be able to join with colleagues to develop school-level or district-level presentations about a particular area of instruction. Reading articles in professional magazines and journals helps to develop particular expertise, as does advanced university course work. Some journals, such as TESOL's *Essential Teacher* (see www.tesol.org for submission guidelines), and publishers solicit publications from teachers. This is one way to share successful classroom practices.

Professional Leadership Roles

A career is developed over a lifetime. Expertise in particular areas continues to grow along with teaching experience. One can envision a more just and equitable society thirty years from now as today's new teachers reap the harvest of the support for linguistic and cultural diversity that they have promoted. Those who are willing to take responsibility within professional organizations by serving on committees, drafting proposals, attending meetings, calling members, stuffing envelopes, and other activities are those who can be called on to serve in leadership positions. Leadership roles can come in various forms:

- Mentors and other experienced teachers can invite beginning teachers to professional meetings so the organizations can benefit from fresh energy.
- Teachers can start a local affiliation of a national organization.

Legislation and Public Opinion

State and national legislators are responsive to popular opinion as expressed by letters of support and phone calls on controversial issues. Bilingual education and language issues often arouse strong emotions, perhaps because language itself is so closely connected to the soul of a person or because language policies affect the criteria for employment vital to economic survival and success in the United States (Heath, 1983a). Legislators need to hear from professionals in the field to balance the effect of those who perceive language and cultural diversity as a threat. The debate that takes place within a legislature brings to public attention the issues involved in any complex area of public life and allows a public forum for criticizing government policies (Jewell, 1976). The strong backing of professional organizations supports legislators who have the courage to promote dual-language education. Public policy can be supported in the following ways:

- Organizations can send subscriptions to professional magazines to legislative libraries.
- Teachers and parents can organize letter-writing campaigns and visit legislators personally to convey interest in language-minority issues.

Opposing Linguicism

Linguicism refers to discrimination based on the language one speaks. Proponents of English as the official language of the United States see its dominance threatened and consider it the "glue" that holds the United States together. Of the twenty-eight states with Official English laws, twenty-three have passed these since 1981, indicating a rise in language restriction in the late twentieth century. Opponents of this Official English movement do not see the dominance of English in this country being threatened; in fact, they cite research indicating that it is other, non-English languages that are threatened both in the United States and worldwide by English.

The First Amendment to the Constitution of the United States requires that Congress shall pass no law "abridging the freedom of speech." If citizens in this country cannot retain the language and culture of their choice, then their liberty and citizenship rights are severely limited.

The alternative put forward by the National Association for Bilingual Education (NABE), the National Education Association (NEA), and others advocates of bilingual and bicultural education is a bilingual English Plus philosophy: good for both families and for America's ability to compete in a global, multilingual world (Reyhner, 2007).

Influencing Federal Policies

In countries where more than one language is spoken, rarely do these languages share an equal social status. Speakers of the dominant language are those who make social policy, including language policy. These policies can range from support for the subordinate language, to benign neglect, to overt language suppression. Decisions are primarily made on political and economic grounds and reflect the values of those in political power (Bratt Paulston, 1992). Citizens have a duty to affect these policies.

Federal Funds for Innovation

The U.S. Department of Education provides billions of dollars in grants to states and school districts to improve elementary and secondary schools. With the help of these monies, numerous schools have restructured using dual-language and other enrichment models that actively engage CLD and mainstream students.

Notices about competitions for funds and special programs are usually available from state and county offices of education. By working with district grant specialists, teachers can write successful grant proposals. Individuals who have competed successfully for funding may be willing to offer workshops for others to increase the general expertise in such areas.

Federal Legislation

Programs such as Title III of the No Child Left Behind Act originate in Congress. Part of the Elementary and Secondary Education Act, this legislation must be reauthorized periodically. At such intervals, public opinion plays a large role in determining the continuation of programs that benefit English learners. When bills are introduced that commit federal funds on a large scale to minorities, conservative forces within Congress often target these programs for extinction. At these times, lobbying efforts are needed to communicate the need for these programs.

- Teachers can request that professional organizations send cards and letters to congressional representatives.
- E-mail campaigns can bring critical aspects of pending legislation to the attention of congressional leaders.

The National Spirit

A national spirit is created in part by individuals who voice their opinions freely. A national magazine, for example, offers a platform to writers whose opinions can be influential. Teachers need to exercise their writing skills frequently and at length in order to participate in national arguments that are rehearsed in the media.

Controversial actions and media figures also shape the national spirit. When demagogues arise who voice reactionary or incendiary viewpoints, the population at large must take steps to defuse their voices. Letters to national networks voicing opposition to and distaste for antiminority or racist viewpoints, for example, are necessary in order that these media do not glorify controversial figures and give them undue voice. The United States operates on a system of checks and balances. Those who oppose racism or bigotry must speak up and must speak as loudly as the voices of separation and intolerance. Often, teachers of English learners must become

FIND OUT MORE ABOUT ...

Grant Proposals and Exemplary Programs

U.S. Department of Education

www.ed.gov/fund/landing.jhtml

Provides links to sites that answer questions about the grant process, enables a search of the Department of Education's programs by topic (for example, English Language Acquisition), and makes available application packages along with information about deadlines and contacts.

School Reform and Student Diversity: Case Studies of Exemplary Practices for LEP Students

www.ncela.gwu.edu/pubs/schoolreform

This article describes programs in eight schools that "have created exemplary learning environments for language-minority students who have limited English proficiency" (Introduction, para. 4). All of them combine LEP program features with more general restructuring.

advocates for their concerns until the voices of the minority community become skilled enough to speak for themselves and powerful enough to be heard. Teachers who share the culture and language of the minority community have a natural function as community leaders.

- Teachers can make policymakers aware of the need for workers proficient in more than one language.
- With school administrators, teachers can generate community support to advocate for programs for CLD students.

In a nation consisting of more than 300 million people, the majority of whom share English as the language of daily interchange, the language skills and rights of minorities are a fragile resource. Social and political forces on a national scale may seem overwhelming. Indeed, as much as individualism is a part of the national mythology of the United States, by working together with colleagues and district personnel, by joining and becoming leaders in professional organizations, teachers can exert national influence for constructive change in the education of CLD learners. This constructive change is possible at every level from the national to the local by the use of appropriate professional activities.

At the classroom level where teachers are most comfortable, language policy means creating an educational and social climate that makes school a place where all students are comfortable, where all students meet success in learning. The days are past when the failure of large numbers of CLD learners can be blamed on students' personal shortcomings or supposed deficiencies in family background. When students fail to learn, schools and teachers have failed.

If teachers are willing to step outside the confines of the classroom to help students be successful, then it is time to learn how to influence policy on a larger scale. The belief that teachers have no role in language planning and language politics is a denial of professional responsibility, an abdication of authority. A teacher who believes in the potential for success of CLD learners is in a strong position to fight for the recognition of their rights and the allocation of resources that make educational success possible.

LEARNING MORE

Further Reading

Rebecca Freeman's (2004) *Building on Community Bilingualism* demonstrates how schools that serve bilingual communities can promote English-language development, academic achievement, *and* expertise in other languages. Through an ethnographic account of bilingualism and education in the Puerto Rican community in Philadelphia, she shows how individual teachers and teams of educators have organized their policies, programs, and practices to promote bilingualism through schooling on the local school and school district levels. The book concludes by outlining how educators working in other contexts can develop language policies, programs, and practices that address the needs of the students and communities they serve.

Web Search

The Center for Applied Linguistics' Website (www.cal.org) provides several links to other organizations that deal with public policy and language issues (go to www.cal.org/links /index.html). In addition, several language policy and planning digests provide insights into what teachers can do (www.cal.org/resources/digest/subject.html).

Exploration

The case studies of the eight exemplary schools in the School Reform and Student Diversity document (http://www2.ed.gov/pubs/SER/Diversity/index.html) are divided into the following sections: school and community context; learning environment; curriculum and instructional strategies; program for LEP students; school structure; and district support. Choose one of these areas and examine your school and district according to the model from the article.

Collaboration

Based on your exploration, work with colleagues and your administration to implement some of your findings. Conversely, collaborate with your district grant specialist to work on funding for a program at your site.

MyEducationLab™

Community Support for Culturally Diverse Students and Families

In this video, Christine Slater expresses the need for pre-service teachers to bridge the gap between the school and the community. She discusses the importance of understanding the implications of a network of adults who are associated with each child.

To access the video, go to MyEducationLab (www.myeducationlab.com), choose the Díaz-Rico text, and log in to MyEducationLab for English Language Learners. Select the topic Diversity, and watch the video entitled "Community Support for Culturally Diverse Students and Families."

Answer the following questions:

1. It is often a preconceived notion for teachers that mothers and fathers are the only adults in contact with their students. Explain how a community can provide a network of adults that provide support for children.

2. In what ways does the support community impact academic achievement for children learning English as a second language?

3. How can a teacher help to align community and schooling in a more coherent way?

12
Culturally and Linguistically Diverse Learners and Special Education

English learners who are blind can achieve communicative competence by interacting with mainstream peers.

© Amy Etra/PhotoEdit, Inc.

Each generation of English learners in the United States undergoes distinct life experiences, and classroom interactions that reflect these experiences will help them to learn to stimulate their growth in oracy and literacy. In the 1990s, teachers reached out to new arrivals through thematic units on such topics as immigration, reading *How Many Days to America?* (Bunting, 1991) and *If You Sailed on the Mayflower in 1620* (McGovern, 1969). However, today's English learners are more likely to have been born in the United States, and to be living in rural or inner-city environments. Today's learners have diverse ways of thinking, learning, and reacting to instruction. New kinds of multicultural books and multimedia materials are needed that reflect the lived experiences of these learners. The materials need to depict students of varied abilities, delivered in a way that is universally accessible. Perhaps they can create these books themselves in class, so their voices can be heard by other learners.

How can schools make more effective use of special education to provide services to those who need them, while maintaining most CLD students in mainstream classroom placement?

Culturally and linguistically diverse (CLD) learners, as any other cross-section of today's learners, may need special education services. Often, mainstream classroom teachers find themselves responsible for teaching students with special education needs who also need to acquire English. A consultation model introduces constructive ways for teachers of CLD learners and other certified personnel to collaborate in order to meet the needs of such special learners.

> Given the rapid demographic changes that have occurred in schools, communities, and workplaces, a major concern in the field of special education and rehabilitation today is the provision of effective services to multilingual/multicultural diverse populations. . . . [C]hildren and youth of these diverse groups will form a major part of the future workforce in this country. Therefore, the services provided in schools as well as in rehabilitation play an important role in strengthening this workforce for our society. (Chang, 2005)

This chapter includes such topics as identifying CLD learners with special instructional needs, teaming with resource or special education teachers, and teaching strategies for inclusion. The emphasis will be on students who need additional instructional mediation, because those students' needs tend to surface in an obvious way. However, similar principles—if not strategies—can be applied to CLD learners who are gifted and talented.

Researchers who have looked at the special education services available to English learners (e.g., Baca & Cervantes, 1984; Figueroa, 1993; González, 1994) have found a host of issues, including cultural differences as well as language issues.

Both special education and special education–CLD learner interface have come under attack from those who criticize the current models of service delivery. Sleeter (1986) believed that the process that labels certain students as "handicapped" without a critical look at the social and cultural conditions of regular schooling needed to be examined. Stainback and Stainback (1984) advocated that special education and regular education be merged and that all students receive individualized education. Others (Artiles & Trent, 1994; Bernstein, 1989; Figueroa, Fradd, & Correa, 1989) have addressed the over- or underrepresentation of CLD students in special education. Few believe, however, that the current special education system, including the treatment of CLD learners within that system, will undergo vast systemic reform in the near future.

Jesness (2004) outlines the complexity of the situation when special education and ELD are mixed: "Placing learning disabled children in classes designed for English learners is as unethical and harmful as placing English learners in classes meant to serve the learning disabled and mentally challenged" (p. 82). Certainly those who have been educated in English for only a short time deserve an adequate period of adjustment. However, the Individuals with Disabilities Education Act (IDEA) specifically allows referral and placement for English learners and young children with developmental delays, which may include language acquisition.

In their call for a restructuring of bilingual special education, Baca and de Valenzuela (1994) offered three primary goals: (1) Classrooms should conform to the needs of students rather than students conforming to the classroom; (2) efforts should be made to increase the academic performance of CLD special education students; and (3) teachers should be actively involved throughout the assessment process, with assessment-based curricular adaptations becoming a major part of the intervention process before a student is referred for special education services, and a diagnostic teaching model put in place instead of a remedial approach. These goals provide a direction for the efforts to augment and improve the overall delivery of education to CLD learners. But first, who are these learners? What educational and policy issues does their education raise?

Scenarios and Issues

The issues surrounding culture, learning, and second-language acquisition are complex. The needs of many students can be addressed only with the aid of careful diagnostic work and documentation of student progress. However, many cases involve similar situations and evoke consistent fundamental questions.

Who Are CLD Learners with Special Needs?

Because of the complexity of the issues that underlie special educational services for CLD learners, both personal and academic, it is helpful to personalize these issues with cases drawn from the field. Each scenario does not represent any student in particular but rather a composite of several students created from similar circumstances.

Elisa's Memory. Elisa's third-grade teacher, Stephanie Robinson, is wondering if Elisa has a memory problem. She did not attend kindergarten, and in first grade the instruction was primarily in Spanish. In second grade, the only class taught in English was social studies. Now that she is being asked to learn to read in English, Elisa doesn't seem to remember words that she has read before. When she reads aloud, she can decode most new words adequately but acts as though each word is new each time—there is little sense of recognition or increase in comprehension when she reencounters a word. Mrs. Robinson is just about to make a referral to special education. Does she have adequate grounds for referral?

Losing ELD Services after Referral. Alsumana comes from a family that recently emigrated from Papua New Guinea. His mainstream classroom teacher has successfully made a case for referral to testing, but Ron Patton, his pull-out ELD teacher, is not supportive of this referral because in the past, when a student was placed into a special education environment, that student lost access to ELD services. Because, in Ron's opinion, success in school ultimately depends on the child's acquisition of English, he would like to ensure that CLD learners are not deprived of any other services that would help them. How can he remain involved if Alsumana is placed in special education?

Conflict over Referral. Mrs. Espinoza, the fourth-grade classroom teacher, is struggling with Luke. Luke's parents emigrated from Romania and settled in a rural area in the school district. Luke attends school only reluctantly and says that he would rather be working with his father outdoors. Mrs. Espinoza insists his poor performance in school is due to his attitude toward schooling and not to a learning disability. The school social worker, however, has advocated all year for Luke to be referred for a special education evaluation. During this time, he has made little academic progress. Should he be referred to special education?

Social and Emotional Adjustment. New arrivals are "fresh meat" for the gangs in the area around Bud Kaylor's elementary school. Bud has taught ELD and fifth grade for six years, and although he finds rewards in the challenges of an urban school, he sees the fear and threats that students experience outside the school environment as detrimental to their learning. One student, José Luis, seems overcome by fear in the school setting and never speaks a word. Bud feels that psychological counseling could be a way to deal with the social and emotional problems José Luis seems to be experiencing. Should he refer José Luis for help?

Sonia Doesn't Read. Fifth-grader Sonia is a native-Spanish speaker from the Dominican Republic. She did not attend school until the second grade. She was taught to read in Spanish, but now that she does not have access to Spanish reading instruction, she is falling behind. She attends a resource program, but the resource teacher sees that the problems that show up in English (poor oral language, limited vocabulary development, difficulties with writing, and poor comprehension) limit Sonia's progress. Should Sonia be referred to special education?

Tran the Troubled. Tran is a new student in the fourth grade. His family lives a fairly isolated life in a community of immigrants from Vietnam, but his parents want Tran to grow up speaking English, so they speak to his sister and him in English. However, because the parents both work, they leave Tran for long periods with his grandmother, who speaks only Vietnamese. Tran acts like a dual personality. In class, his performance is uneven; he does not volunteer and does not complete work, yet he seeks constant attention and approval from his teacher. On the playground, his teacher sees in Tran a quick intelligence that comes out when he interacts with the other boys. The teacher is unsure how to handle Tran; he may have a learning disability, but his school problems may be due to extreme cultural differences between home and school. Does she have adequate grounds for referral for psychological testing?

Issues Underlying the Scenarios

Each of these scenarios reflects a particular aspect of the relationship between three distinct domains—learning, second-language acquisition, and special education services in the schools—and these domains are set in a background of cultural issues. Table 12.1 outlines the relationships between the scenarios and underlying issues.

Table 12.1   Scenarios and Issues in Special Educational Services for English Learners

Scenario	Issues
Elisa's Memory. Does Elisa, a third-grade student who demonstrates low English reading skills, have a memory problem connected with a learning disability?	At what point is a learning problem considered a language-acquisition delay and not a learning disability?
Losing ELD Services after Referral. Will Alsumana, a recent immigrant, be deprived of ELD services if he is placed in special education?	Should ELD services be available to special education students?
Conflict over Referral. Does Luke's poor performance in school indicate a learning disability, or is it due to his low academic motivation?	What role do family attitudes and values play in the issue of special education referral?
Social and Emotional Adjustment. Should his teacher refer José Luis to psychological counseling to deal with his social and emotional problems in an urban school?	What is the role of psychological counseling in second-language acquisition?
Sonia Doesn't Read. Should Sonia, a fifth-grader with limited prior schooling experience and low English skills, be referred to special education?	What is the role of special education for immigrant students with little prior literacy experience?
Tran the Troubled. Tran's quick intelligence shines on the playground but not in the classroom. Is he learning disabled?	What role does cultural difference play in a case in which a student has classroom learning problems?

These scenarios and the issues surrounding the education of CLD learners are centered on two basic questions: How can these students' language acquisition, cultural adjustment, and emotional/motivational difficulties be distinguished from learning problems? And how can these issues best be addressed? Special education–CLD learner issues are complex, yet a central dilemma focuses the essential debate: How can a school district avoid inappropriate referrals and placements yet ensure access for CLD learners who are learning disabled? The ELD–special education interface brings with it a set of collaboration issues. What is the role of the ESL specialist (or the CLAD teacher) in referral, assessment, and subsequent services to students who may be placed in special education?

Principles for the Education of CLD–Special Education Students

Several basic principles characterize fair and effective processes for determining the educational services appropriate for the CLD learner who may be experiencing learning difficulties. These principles may be used to guide initial identification and early intervention, diagnostic evaluation and testing, and, if necessary, placement in a special education learning environment. The principles address five domains: the responsibility of students for learning, students' need for self-knowledge, goals for instruction, relationship of educational services to mainstream instruction, and the need for informed decision making. Table 12.2 presents each of these five domains and its accompanying principle.

Table 12.2 Principles for the Education of English-Learning Special Education Students

Domain	Principle
Responsibility of students for learning	English learners need to become self-responsible, active students who know how to learn. They need linguistic and nonlinguistic strategies, including metalinguistic and metacognitive, that may be generalizable across learning contexts.
Students' need for self-knowledge	Students need to understand their own learning styles and preferences, as well as discover their intrapersonal strengths and weaknesses in a variety of areas, including both linguistic and nonlinguistic (logical-mathematical, musical, and spatial) domains.
Goals for instruction	Students need meaningful and relevant language and academic goals that promote effective communication and learning, in social as well as academic domains.
Relationship of educational services to mainstream instruction	Any education setting must provide educational content and approaches that facilitate students' abilities to make smooth transitions to mainstream instruction.
Need for informed decision making	Educational decisions concerning CLD learners should involve ELD specialists, parents, and other professionals making collaborative, informed judgments that are based on a thorough, fair assessment of the child's language acquisition stage, culture, and individual needs and talents.

Source: Based on Wallach and Miller (1988).

The Disproportionate Representation of Culturally and Linguistically Diverse Children in Special Education

The Individual with Disabilities Education Act (IDEA) entitles all individuals with disabilities to a free, appropriate public education (FAPE) and mandates nondiscriminatory assessment, identification, and placement of children with disabilities. The law stipulates that children not be labeled "disabled" if their poor school achievement is due to ethnic, linguistic, or racial difference. Currently, the assessment and placement of CLD students have become major issues in special education (Burnette, 2000), including overidentification (i.e., students are classified into a disability category when they do not have genuine disabilities); underidentification (i.e., students' disabilities are overlooked and not addressed in their educational programs); and misidentification (i.e., students' disabilities are assigned to inappropriate disability categories) (Brusca-Vega, 2002).

Overrepresentation in Disability Programs

In the United States, some ethnic groups continue to be overrepresented in programs for those who are mildly mentally retarded (MMR) or seriously emotionally disturbed (SED). Overrepresentation of CLD learners in MMR programs was the basis for litigation in a number of court cases in the 1970s. The cases addressed the lack of due-process procedural safeguards, improper intelligence testing in the student's second language, and inadequate training of evaluators and special educators, resulting in mandated remedies in these areas (Coutinho & Oswald, 2004).

If the proportion of special education students of a given ethnic background exceeds the proportion of this group in the general population, then overrepresentation is a problem because the educational treatment that students receive is not equivalent to that received by the general student population (Macmillan & Reschly, 1998); because disproportionate placement in special education settings can segregate students by race; and because being labeled as a special education student has potentially negative effects on students' self-esteem and on teachers' perception of students (Valles, 1998).

Although the court cases of the 1970s helped to reduce the number of CLD students being sent into special education classes, recent expansion of disability categories to include mild learning disabilities and developmental delays has resulted in an increase in the number of bilingual students being served in remedial education classes (Connor & Boskin, 2001). Some researchers have cautioned that aptitude (or lack of it) is a cultural construction—cultural groups differ in what is considered a disability. For example, when students do not use expected classroom discourse rules, the teacher may judge them to be disabled.

Example of Concept   *Misunderstanding Is Construed as Disability*

Mrs. Patterson asked a "known-answer" question to the class to see who had read the science pages assigned as homework. "Who can tell me, in what system is 100 degrees the boiling point of water?" Mario looked down, but Mrs. Patterson was eager to have him participate. "Mario?" she asked. Mario looked up and squinted. "Metric" he answered softly. Mrs. Patterson shook her head and asked, "Who can help Mario? Is it Fahrenheit or centigrade?" (She thought sadly, *Mario never knows the answer. Maybe he has a learning disability.* But Mario thought, puzzled, *What was wrong with "metric"?*)

Underrepresentation in Gifted Programs

Conversely, CLD students are underrepresented in gifted education with the exception of Asian American students, who are overrepresented in proportion to the general population in the United States. According to Ryan (2008), African American, Latino, and Native American students have been historically underrepresented in gifted programs. These students may be underrepresented by as much as 30 to 70 percent (p. 53). Ford (1998) suggested that the issue of underrepresentation of Hispanic and African American students is compounded by several problems: the widely differing definitions of *gifted* across the school districts of the United States, the inadequacy of relying solely on standardized tests for admission to such programs, the lack of training on the part of teachers to recognize diverse talents as they nominate students, the confusing nature of the nomination process for minority parents, the lack of self-nomination on the part of minority students, lack of diversity on the part of selection panels, and inadequate training of assessment personnel who act as gatekeepers for gifted programs. The following list provides recommended remediation for underrepresentation (Ford, 1998):

- Use valid identification instruments (e.g., Raven's Matrices instead of the Wechsler Scale for Children–Revised).

- Collect multiple types of information from various sources (including both descriptive and quantitative data).
- Provide support services prior to identification (such as help with study skills and time management).
- Train teachers and school personnel on culturally derived learning styles.
- Increase family involvement in identification and support.
- Increase awareness of research on giftedness in minorities.

Example of Concept   *Gifted "School within a School"*

Paris Doby, an African American senior on the verge of graduation, attends the Crenshaw Gifted Magnet High School (CGMHS) in South Central Los Angeles—one of the roughest neighborhoods. Gifted students take separate core classes but share physical education and electives with other students on campus.

"High school has been a great experience," says Paris. "I have kind of a legendary feeling. I feel almost *obligated* to do great things. I am very excited about attending UCLA next year" (Posnick-Goodwin, 2011, p. 18).

Identification, Referral, and Early Intervention

Classroom teachers, along with parents and other school-site personnel, are responsible for identifying CLD learners with special instructional needs. When a classroom teacher initially identifies a student who may need additional mediation, a phase of intensive focus begins that may, or may not, result in a placement in special education.

Typically, the most common reasons for referral to special education for English learners are the "high-incidence" diagnoses: learning disability (LD), mild cognitive delays, speech and language delays and disorders, attention-deficit/hyperactivity disorder (ADHD), and/or emotional or behavior disorders. However, lack of understanding of cultural and language issues has led some educators to be overly cautious about referring English learners for special education services (Echevarria & Graves, 2007).

English-language-development educators may find it useful to learn some professional terms used in special education (see Table 12-3).

Table 12.3   Special Education Acronyms

IDEA	The Individuals with Disabilities Education Act (1975): Federal legislation that guarantees to individuals with disabilities a free and appropriate public education, alongside nondisabled peers.
IEP	Individualized Education Plan: Written plan negotiated by a school-based team and parents that contains goals and services proposed for a student receiving special education.
RSP	Resource Specialist Program: Program providing materials and support for students with identified disabilities who are assigned to a general education classroom more than fifty percent of the school day.

SDC	Special Day Class: Self-contained classroom that provides services to special education students with intensive needs who cannot be educated in a general education or RSP classroom.
SST	School Study Team (also called School Screening Team): Group comprised of the classroom teacher, administrator, and educational specialists who review a student's performance in the classroom if that student has been referred for special education evaluation. The team may also include parents.

The Referral Process: The Roles of the Classroom Teacher and the ELD Specialist

The School Screen Team or otherwise-named entity is a school-site committee that bears responsibility for receiving and acting on an initial referral by the classroom teacher for a student who is in need of additional mediation in learning. The team not only reviews the classroom teacher's specific concerns about the student but also makes suggestions for modifying the learning environment for the student within the regular classroom and provides guidance, training, and assistance in implementing *initial interventions* that may prove helpful in educating the student in question.

How can the classroom teacher decide if a student might have a disability requiring referral to special education? Friend and Bursuck (2006) offered these questions to assist in the decision-making process:

- What are specific examples of a student's needs that are as yet unmet in the regular classroom?
- Is there a chronic pattern that negatively affects learning? Or, conversely, does the difficulty follow no clear pattern?
- Is the student's unmet need becoming more serious as time passes?
- Is the student's functioning significantly different from that of classmates?
- Do you discover that you cannot find a pattern?

One last consideration is the discrepancy between the student's performance in the first and second languages. If the problem does not occur when the child receives instruction in the primary language, it is likely that the situation has resulted from second-language acquisition rather than from a learning disability.

After receiving a referral from the classroom teacher, the school ELD or bilingual specialist, as a member of the team, may be asked to fill out a data sheet containing test data, school history, language preferences, and other information about the student. Thus, this person plays an important role in investigating the following aspects of the CLD learner's case.

Background Experience and Previous School Settings. Does the student have a previous history of difficulty? In this case, contacting a previous teacher and checking records from previously attended schools can provide important background information. A file containing the history of special education services, if it exists, is not routinely transferred with a student unless specifically requested by the receiving school personnel.

Response to the Classroom Environment. Does the student seem uncomfortable or unaccustomed to a classroom environment? A history of previous schooling may uncover evidence of little or no prior schooling.

Cultural and Linguistic Background. The home language survey given on entering a school should properly identify the home language. If the home culture of the CLD learner is new to the classroom teacher, it may be useful to perform an ethnographic study of that culture (see Chapter 9).

Level of Acculturation. Contacting parents to determine the degree of acculturative stress that the family of the student is experiencing can provide important insights. Observing the student interacting with other students, staff, and parents in the home, school, and community can help the specialist identify possible acculturation problems.

Learning Styles. Observation of the student across a variety of academic tasks and content areas may show the need for curricular interventions that provide instructional variety.

Physical Health. The school nurse may provide or obtain a student's health record and developmental history, as well as a record of vision and hearing examinations and determination of overall physical health and diet.

Academic and Learning Problems That CLD Learners May Experience

CLD learners and students with learning disabilities may experience similar difficulties. This creates a challenge to determine whether a learning impairment is due to the students' second-language-acquisition process or to an underlying learning disability that warrants a special education placement. Gopaul-McNicol and Thomas-Presswood (1998) noted the following possible characteristics of CLD learners that may overlap with those of students with learning disabilities.

- *Discrepancies between verbal and nonverbal learning.* Exposure to enriching and meaningful linguistic experiences and activities may have been limited in a student's culture.
- *Perceptual disorders.* If a CLD student's home language is nonalphabetic, he or she may have difficulty with alphabetic letters. If a student was not literate in L1, he or she may have difficulty with sound–symbol relationships.
- *Language disorders.* A student may experience difficulty processing language, following directions, and understanding complex language.
- *Metacognitive deficits.* CLD learners, if from a nonliterate background, may lack preliteracy behaviors and strategies, such as regulatory mechanisms (planning, evaluating, monitoring, and remediating difficulties), or may not know when to ask for help.
- *Memory difficulties.* Lack of transfer between the first and second language or limited information retention in the second language may be present.

- *Social–emotional functioning.* CLD learners may experience academic frustration and low self-esteem. This may lead to self-defeating behaviors such as learned helplessness. Limited second-language skills may influence social skills, friendships, and teacher–student relationships.
- *Difficulty attending and focusing.* CLD learners may exhibit behavior such as distractibility, short attention span, impulsivity, or high motor level (e.g., finger tapping, excessive talking, fidgeting, inability to remain seated). These may stem from cognitive overload when immersed in a second language for a long period of time.
- *Culture/language shock.* Students experiencing culture or language shock may show uneven performance, not volunteer, not complete work, or seek constant attention and approval from the teacher.
- *Reading dysfunctions.* CLD learners may exhibit a variety of reading problems. These problems may include slow rate of oral or silent reading (using excessive lip movement or vocalization in silent reading); short perceptual span (reading word by word rather than in phrases); mispronunciation, omission, insertion, substitutions, reversals, or repetition of words or groups of words in oral reading; lack of comprehension; and inability to remember what has been read.
- *Written expression skill deficits.* Writing may present an additional area of difficulty for CLD learners, at the level of grammar and usage or at the level of content. Teachers often judge writing as "poor" if it lacks the following characteristics: variety in sentence patterns; variety in vocabulary (choosing correct words and using synonyms); coherent structure in paragraphs and themes; control over usage, such as punctuation, capitalization, and spelling; and evidence that the writer can detect and correct his or her own errors.

One cannot expect a newcomer to English to demonstrate proficiency in these skills immediately. Some writing skills may not be a part of the student's native culture, and thus acquiring these requires acculturation as well as second-language acquisition.

Similarities between Ethnic Language Variations and Learning Disability Symptoms

A systematic analysis of three sets of language users (native-English speakers, CLD learners, and students with learning disabilities) reveals similarities in abilities and dysfunctions between CLD learners and students who are learning disabled. This overlap in language characteristics highlights the difficulty in identifying an English learner as possibly learning disabled.

Early Intervention

The classroom teacher's primary concern is to determine if a student's academic or behavioral difficulties reflect factors other than disabilities, including inappropriate or inadequate instruction. If a student is not responsive to alternative instructional or behavioral interventions over a period of several weeks or months, there is more of a chance that a placement in special education will be necessary (García & Ortiz, 2004; Ortiz, 2002).

The School Screen Team works with the classroom teacher to design intervention strategies that address the CLD learner's second-language-acquisition, language development, and acculturation needs, and decides if formal referral to testing is warranted.

A key to the diagnosis of language-related disorders is the presence of similar patterns in both the primary and the secondary languages. The classroom teacher adopts an experimental attitude, implementing strategies over a period of time and documenting the effect these innovations have on the student in question.

Adapted Instruction

Instructional Modifications for CLD Students

Although many of the strategies recommended below are appropriate for all students, they are particularly critical for CLD students suspected of a learning disability:

- Design lessons in which students use a variety of modes of information input—visual, tactile, and auditory.
- Within each lesson, balance instructional time that involves direct, "hands-on" experience with time for explicit, direct instruction of strategies and skills.
- Make sure that students fully comprehend information; use frequent "checking for understanding."
- If a student shows signs of fatigue, allow time for stretching or take a brief relaxation break.
- Between asking a question and expecting an answer, pause to allow time for students to create a thoughtful response.
- Be a positive listener.
- Ask questions that require answers matched to students' English proficiency.

Roles of Classroom Teachers and ELD Teachers during the Process of Determining Eligibility for Additional Services

Both classroom teachers and the ELD teacher may play a variety of roles during the process of determining a student's eligibility for additional services:

- *Organizer.* The classroom teacher, with the help of the ELD teacher, organizes student records, records of interventions attempted and the relative success thereof, records of parent contact, and records of contact with other community agencies.
- *Instructor.* The ELD teacher may be able to advise the classroom teacher about adapting learning environments to greater diversity in students' learning styles, devising initial intervention strategies, and using curriculum-based assessment to document student achievement.
- *Investigator.* The ELD teacher or a bilingual paraprofessional may accomplish preliminary testing in the student's L1, study students' culture and language, and interview parents.

- *Mentor to students*. The classroom and ELD teacher may get to know the student and family, suggest a testing environment compatible with the student's culture, and prepare the student for the evaluation process.
- *Colleague*. The ELD teacher and the classroom teacher act as helpful colleagues, sharing expertise about L2 acquisition effects, potential crosscultural misunderstandings, and possible effects of racism or discrimination on CLD learners and families. They collaborate to resolve conflicts, work with translators, and draw on community members for information, additional resources, and parental support. This collaboration is discussed later in this chapter.

Testing for Special Education

The School Screen Team, after reviewing the evidence provided by the classroom teacher and analysis of the early intervention accommodations, approves or denies the request for special education testing. If approved, such testing will take place only after parental approval has been secured in writing. A school psychologist or licensed professional evaluator performs the testing. Figure 12.1 offers some fundamentals that must be in place to ensure the validity of such testing.

Bilingual students must be tested in both languages to qualify for special education services. The most difficult students to refer to testing are those who may have language delay or mild learning disabilities, aggravated by the need to acquire English (Jesness, 2004). Some students may have had their prior schooling interrupted, making assessment of their ability a confusing process. The most important figure in this quandary is the bilingual psychologist, who can administer dual-language evaluation and make a reasoned determination for the student as to what kind of educational program is most appropriate.

Figure 12.1   Assumptions in Psychological Testing

1. The person administering testing is licensed and certified, and has adequate training concerning the following:
   - Administration, scoring, and interpretation of the test
   - Pitfalls and limitations of a particular test
   - Capability to establish rapport and understand the nonverbal language and cultural beliefs/practices of the person being tested
   - Oral ability in the language of the person or provision made for a trained interpreter
2. Instruments chosen for assessment have norms that represent the population group of the individual being tested.
3. The person being tested understands the words used and can operate from a worldview that understands what is expected from the testing situation.
4. Behavior sampled is an adequate measure of the individual's abilities.

Some caveats about these assumptions:

1. Translated tests may not be equivalent to their English forms in areas such as content validity and the amount of verbalization that can be expected from different cultures. Even having discrete norms for different languages may not provide norms for different cultures.

(continued)

Figure 12.1   Continued

2. Many individuals do not have testing experience or experience with test materials, such as blocks or puzzles. Conversely, what they do have expertise in may not be measured in the test. The individual's learning style or problem-solving strategies can be culturally bound.

3. Individuals who have the following characteristics will do well on tests. These are consistent with the dominant U.S. American mainstream culture and may not be present, or may be present to a limited degree, in an individual from another culture:

    *   Monochronic orientation: focus on one task at a time
    *   Close proximity: can tolerate small interpersonal space
    *   Frequent and sustained eye contact
    *   Flexibility in response to male or female examiner
    *   Individual orientation: motivated to perform well in testing situation
    *   Understanding of verbal and nonverbal aspects of majority culture
    *   Internal locus of control: taking responsibility for one's own success
    *   Field-independent cognitive style: can perceive details apart from the whole
    *   Reflective, methodological, analytical cognitive style

Source: Gopaul-McNicol, Sharon-Ann; Thomas-Presswood, Tania. *Working with Linguistically and Culturally Different Children: Innovative Clinical and Educational Approaches*, 1st Ed., © 1999. Adapted and Electronically reproduced by permission of Pearson Education, Inc., Upper Saddle River, New Jersey.

The Descriptive Assessment Process

Evaluating CLD learners for possible placement in a special education classroom involves attention to linguistic and cultural factors that may impede the school success of the student. A *descriptive assessment* (Jitendra & Rohena-Díaz, 1996) process in three phases takes these factors into account.

The first phase is descriptive analysis, in which an oral monologue, an oral dialogue, and observation of the student in class are used together to ascertain if the student has a communicative proficiency problem. If this is the case, the assessment may end, and the student may be referred to a speech/language therapist for additional mediation in language development. Alternatively, the student may be referred for additional mediation in language development *and* the evaluation process may continue, indicating that the student has a communicative proficiency problem as well as other problems.

If there is evidence of some other learning problem, the second phase begins—explanatory analysis. The assessor examines extrinsic factors, such as cultural or ethnic background or level of acculturation, that determine if normal second-language-acquisition or crosscultural phenomena can account for the student's learning difficulties. If these factors do not account for the described difficulties, the examination continues to the third phase: assessment for the presence of intrinsic factors, such as a learning disability. This three-phase evaluation process helps to ensure that linguistic and cultural differences receive thoughtful consideration in the overall picture of the student's academic progress.

Family Support for Evaluation

During the evaluation process, the classroom teacher who keeps the family informed about the process reaps the benefit of knowing that family members understand the need for professional assessment and support the student's need for additional mediation of learning. Teacher–family conferences play an important part in sustaining support.

Example of Concept   *Helping the Family Understand Their Child's Level of Achievement*

Mrs. Said keeps three demonstration portfolio folders for use during family conferences. One folder displays average work for the grade level (all names have been removed from such work samples), one folder displays superior work, and a third folder contains work samples that are below grade level.

During conferences, family members compare their child's work with these samples to gain a context for achievement at that grade level. If their child's performance is not at grade level, they often are more willing to support the provision of additional help for their child.

Collaboration among ESL–ELD Resource Teachers and Special Educators

Organizing a collaborative program requires cooperation between professionals who are concerned for the welfare of the student. Teachers can play a variety of collaborative and consultative roles within school contexts, using a variety of problem-solving strategies to design successful ways to create student success.

Definition and Principles of Collaboration

Collaboration is "a style for direct interaction between at least two coequal parties voluntarily engaged in shared decision making as they work toward a common goal" (Friend & Cook, 1996, p. 6). This definition pinpoints several necessary principles: Professionals must treat one another as equals; collaboration is voluntary; a goal is shared (that of finding the most effective classroom setting for the student under consideration); and responsibility is shared for participation, decision making, and resources, as well as accountability for outcomes. These are predicated on a collegial working environment of mutual respect and trust.

Collaboration among Professionals

In a well-designed program for educating English learners, much collaborative planning takes place among staff members. If there is an ELD specialist in the school, that professional often engages in planning with content teachers to integrate content instruction with language-development objectives; with classroom/mainstream teachers in grade-level team meetings; with bilingual teachers to choose complementary materials in the first and second languages; with resource teachers to share diagnostic tools and other forms of assessment; with program, school, and district administrators to design and implement services, offer in-service workshops, and set policies for grading, record keeping, and redesignation; and with curriculum coordinators to create model units of instruction that incorporate content and English-language-development standards.

English-language-development services, whether delivered by the classroom teacher or by an ELD resource teacher, should continue during the period of referral and testing, and then continue if a student receives special education services.

Working with an Interpreter

Teachers who do not share a primary language with the student under consideration may benefit from collaborative relations with an interpreter. However, instructional aides who are hired as teaching assistants should not be automatically pressed into service as translators or interpreters. Interpretation is a professional service that should be provided by trained and certified personnel. Figure 12.2 gives guidelines for successful cooperative relations with interpreters.

Relationship of Continued ELD with Other Services

English-language-development services are a continuing resource for students throughout the initial intervention, testing, and recommendation phases of special education referral. An ELD teacher may work with the student directly, continuing to implement early intervention strategies, or help the student indirectly by working with other teachers, parents, and peers.

Direct Services. Working directly with the student, the ELD teacher may tutor or test the child in the curricular material used in the classroom, or chart daily measures of the child's performance to see if skills are being mastered. The ELD teacher may work specifically on those areas in which the student requires additional mediation or continue to teach the student as a part of an ELD group in the regular classroom.

Indirect Services. Supplementing the classroom teacher's role, the ELD teacher may consult with other teachers on instructional interventions; devise tests based on the classroom curricula and give instruction on how to develop and use them; show how to take

Figure 12.2 How to Work with an Interpreter

1. Meet regularly with the interpreter to facilitate communication, particularly before meeting with a student or parent.
2. Encourage the interpreter to chat with the client before the interview to help determine the appropriate depth and type of communication.
3. Speak simply, avoiding technical terms, abbreviations, professional jargon, idioms, and slang.
4. Encourage the interpreter to translate the client's own words as much as possible to give a sense of the client's concepts, emotional state, and other important information. Encourage the interpreter to refrain from inserting his or her own ideas or interpretations, or from omitting information.
5. During the interaction, look at and speak directly to the client. Listen to clients and watch their nonverbal, affective response by observing facial expressions, voice intonations, and body movements.
6. Be patient. An interpreted interview takes longer.

Source: Adapted from López (2002).

daily measures of a child's academic and social behavior; establish parent groups for discussion of and help with issues of concern; train older peers, parent volunteers, and teacher aides to work with younger children as tutors; and offer in-service workshops for teachers that focus on special interest areas such as curriculum-based assessments, cultural understanding, and second-language-acquisition issues (West & Idol, 1990).

If the evaluation process results in the recommendation of special education services, the ELD teacher helps write the student's Individual Educational Plan (IEP). Collaboration between ELD, special educators, the classroom teacher, parents, and the student is vital to the drafting and approval of an IEP that will result in academic success. The plan for continued ELD services are a part of the document.

Teaching Strategies for the CLD Special Learner

Modified instruction can accommodate different instructional needs within the classroom and foster learning across academic content areas. *Inclusion* is a term often used to describe the provision of instruction within the conventional/mainstream classroom for students with special needs or talents. Although primarily associated with the education of exceptional students, this term has also been used for the varying degrees of inclusion of CLD learners in the mainstream classroom (Florida Department of Education, 2003).

The mainstream classroom of an included student is a rich, nonrestrictive setting for content instruction and language development activities. The three components of an exemplary program for CLD learners—comprehensible instruction in the content areas using primary language and SDAIE, language arts instruction in English, and heritage (primary) language maintenance or development—are present.

The teacher makes every effort for the student to be "as dynamically a part of the class as any student that is perceived as routinely belonging to that class" (Florida Department of Education, 2003, n.p.). Overall, teaching for inclusion features teaching practices that showcase learners' strong points and support the areas in which they may struggle.

The task for the teacher becomes more complex as the increasingly varied needs of students—those who are mainstream (non-CLD/non-special-education), mainstream special education, CLD learner, CLD learner–special education—are mixed in the same classroom. Such complexity would argue that an inclusive classroom be equipped with additional educational resources, such as teaching assistants, lower student to teacher ratio, and augmented budget for instructional materials. The chief resource in any classroom, however, is the breadth and variety of instructional strategies on which the experienced teacher can draw. The following sections suggest multiple strategies in the areas of listening skills, reading, and writing.

Adapting Listening Tasks

Techniques to teach listening skills have been grouped in Table 12.4 into the three phases of the listening process (before listening, during listening, and after listening).

Adapting Reading Tasks

Reading assignments for inclusion students, listed in Table 12.5, follow the three-part division of the reading process (before reading, during reading, and after reading, alternatively named "into," "through," and "beyond").

Table 12.4 Strategies for Additional Mediation for Included Students According to the Listening Process

Phase	Strategies
Before listening	• Directly instruct listening strategies. • Arrange information in short, logical, well-organized segments. • Preview ways to pay attention. • Preview the content with questions that require critical thinking. • Establish a listening goal for the lesson. • Provide prompts indicating that the information about to be presented is important enough to remember or write down.
During listening	• Actively involve students in rehearsing, summarizing, and taking notes. • Use purposeful, curriculum-related listening activities. • Model listening behavior and use peer models. • Teach students to attend to teacher cues and nonverbal signs that denote important information. • Use verbal, pictorial, or written prelistening organizers to cue students to important information. • Teach students to self-monitor their listening behavior using self-questioning techniques and visual imagery while listening.
After listening	• Discuss content. Use teacher questions and prompts to cue student response (e.g., "Tell me more"). • Integrate other language arts and content activities with listening as a follow-up.

Source: Based on Mandlebaum and Wilson (1989).

Table 12.5 Strategies for Additional Mediation for Included Students According to the Reading Process

Phase	Strategies
Before/into reading	• Check readability levels to see if students can achieve comprehension. • Locate or adapt versions of the reading so reading level will match students who are below the level of the class. • Preview reading materials with students to set a purpose for reading. • Bridge to students' existing knowledge or create new schemata for content. • Pre-teach vocabulary words that are essential to the lesson. • Provide outlines or summaries if necessary. • Peers, volunteers, and/or paraprofessionals may read simpler versions one-on-one to students.

Phase	Strategies
During/through reading	• Use study guides to emphasize important features of the reading. • Help students to focus by providing a noise-free listening area. • Provide pictures or other multimodal input to supplement reading. • Pause occasionally to pinpoint vocabulary that is defined in surrounding context.
After/beyond reading	• Discuss what has been read to clarify content, using a list of questions to be peer-read. • Review key vocabulary to deepen comprehension. • Use formative assessment to ask comprehension questions one-on-one with students. • Allow students to follow-up a reading with a diverse set of creative activities to encourage multimodal response.

Adapting Writing Tasks

Writing is used in two main ways in classrooms: to capture and demonstrate content knowledge (taking notes, writing answers on assignments or tests) and to express creative purposes. If the acquisition of content knowledge is the goal, students can often use a variety of alternatives to writing that avoid large amounts of written work (both in class and homework). In general, teachers of students with special needs in inclusive settings change the response mode to oral when appropriate (Smith, Polloway, Patton, & Dowdy, 2003).

Adapted Instruction

Strategies for Content Writing

• Provide a written outline of key content from lecture notes to reduce the amount of board copying.
• Allow group written responses through projects or reports, with the understanding that each member takes an equal turn in writing.

A Focus on Self-Expression. When students write for self-expression, they should follow a well-defined writing process, with provision for generating ideas, drafting, and peer editing. Students can use a stamp that indicates "first draft" to distinguish drafts from polished, or *recopied*, versions; this helps to honor rough drafts as well as completed writing. (See Chapter 4 for a discussion of the writing process.)

Assistive Technology

The term *assistive technology* in schools covers a broad range of support, ranging from low-tech—such as monoculars and large-print books for the visually impaired—to high-tech—such as customized wheelchairs and special-purpose software. With the

Adapted Instruction

Strategies for Writing Conventions

- To help CLD learners with spelling, display a word bank on a classroom wall with commonly used words that native speakers would already know.
- Help students select the most comfortable method of writing (i.e., cursive or manuscript).
- For the purpose of improving handwriting, make available an optional calligraphy center where students can practice elegant forms of handwriting, with correct models available of cursive styles.

help of computers, teachers are able to adapt customized curricula for students based on their ability and capacity for learning; to monitor students' performance in real time; and to increase their participation, motivation, and self-confidence. Tablet computers, for example, can use preformatted templates after reading a book to fill in answers about genre, characters, and plot; this prepares students to write their own stories. Technology can help a special education student with mainstream peers.

One parent whose child has difficulty with auditory processing was enthusiastic about the use of a tablet computer: "... it was a game changer for my daughter in her general ed classroom. She has access to content she didn't have before. She can practice many times" (Fisher & Frey, 2012, p. 10).

Adapting Homework Tasks

Special education students, like English learners, may need homework to be adapted to fit their needs:

- Adapted format—shorter assignments, alternative response formats (e.g., oral rather than written)
- Adapted expectations for performance—longer time until due date, grade based on effort rather than performance, provision for extra credit opportunities
- Scaffolded performance—arrangements made for teacher, aide, peer tutor, or study group assistance; auxiliary learning aids sent home with student (calculator, study guides)
- Monitored performance—student checks in frequently with teacher or parent (Hibbard & Moutes, 2006, p. 95)

Assessing Student Performance in the Mainstream Classroom

A key feature of instruction for inclusion is continuous student assessment. Ongoing assessment accomplishes three purposes: It evaluates the curriculum using immediate, measurable results; pinpoints which instructional tasks and strategies are responsible for student success; and provides a basis for communicating this success to the student, parents, and collaborating team members. A variety of means are available to assess the success of the student in response to the curriculum, instructional strategies, and social aspects of the inclusion environment.

Methods of Assessing the Success of Included Students

Direct observation and *analysis of student products* are two ways to assess the success of included students. Direct observation, by the teacher or by a collaborating team member, can determine if the student has opportunities to speak in class, has enough academic engaged time and time to complete assigned tasks, and is receiving teacher feedback that communicates high expectations and immediate contingencies for completion or noncompletion of work, correct responding, or misbehavior.

Analysis of student products can help team members determine which instructional activities have been successful and which may need to be modified. Throughout this process, formative assessment gives students feedback about their performance and ways they can improve.

Assessing Students' Work

For students who need a significantly modified curriculum, the issue of assigning grades should be addressed before the Individualized Education Plan (IEP) is approved. Teachers working together in the classroom collaborate to establish guidelines for achievement and assign grades. Alternative grading systems are appropriate as long as the school district ensures that the grading practices and policies are not discriminatory. The grading process may include teachers' writing descriptive comments that offer examples of student performance or of certain instructional approaches or strategies that have proven successful, or observations about students' learning styles, skills, effort, and attitude.

The widespread emphasis on standards-based instruction means that grades should reflect student mastery of required material. Most teachers find pass–fail and checklist-type grades more helpful for students with disabilities than letter and number grades; yet many school districts mandate letter grades on report cards. This often results in a high percentage of low grades given to included students.

Testing Accommodations for Students with Disabilities

Testing materials or procedures should enable students to participate in assessments in a way that assesses their abilities rather than their disabilities. Under the 2004 reauthorization of the Individuals with Disabilities Education Act (IDEA), states must have guidelines in place for assessment accommodation and must report the number of students using accommodations during state and district assessments. The purpose of these assessment accommodations is to more accurately measure the student's knowledge and skills.

Table 12.6 gives examples of various types of test accommodations.

Table 12.6 Categories of Assessment Accommodations

Type of Accommodation	Examples
Information presentation	Use large print, use braille, repeat or read aloud directions
Equipment and material	Use a calculator, amplification equipment, manipulatives
Response	Point, mark answers in book, scribe or record responses
Setting	Use an individual carrel, student's home, or a separate room
Timing/scheduling	Provide extended time, frequent breaks

Source: National Center in Educational Outcomes (2011).

Thompson and Thurlow (2002) proposed applying principles of Universal Design when creating and administering tests, such as allowing all examinees to adjust font size or, using a computer, to access other-language translations of the test. In this way, those needing accommodations would have immediate access to these alterations.

Using the Results of Assessment

Ongoing assessment monitors the extent to which the student's IEP is being fulfilled. Assessment activities should be detailed to the greatest extent possible when the IEP is approved so that all members of the collaborating team are aware of their roles and responsibilities. In this way, the results of assessment are immediately compared to the performance stipulated in the IEP and progress is ensured.

Keeping parents informed as full participating members of the collaborating team ensures that they know what they can do at home to assist their child. Persistence and positive feedback in this effort help parents stay motivated and engaged.

Universal Design for Special Populations of English Learners

English learners with special needs include those with learning disabilities and vision, hearing, health, and mobility impairments. These conditions add complexity to the second-language-acquisition challenges these learners face. Educators have begun to view the education of these learners from a unified perspective: Universal Instructional Design (UID), which is based on Universal Design (UD).

Principles of Universal Design have been used to make products and environments "usable by all people, to the greatest extent possible, without the need for adaptation or specialized design" (Connell, Jones, Mace, Mueller, Mullick, Ostroff, Sanford, Steinfield, Story, & Vanderheiden, 1997, p. 1). The seven principles of Universal Design are as follows:

1. Equitable use (useful to people with diverse abilities)
2. Flexibility in use (accommodates individual preferences and abilities)
3. Simple and intuitive use (easy to understand, regardless of the user's experience, knowledge, language skills, or current concentration level)

4. Perceptible information (necessary information is communicated effectively to the user, regardless of ambient conditions or the user's sensory abilities)
5. Tolerance for error (adverse consequences of accidental or unintended actions are minimized)
6. Low physical effort (efficient, comfortable, and relatively effortless)
7. Size and space for approach and use (affords approach, reach, and manipulation regardless of user's body size, posture, or mobility)

Universal Instructional Design

With an augmented emphasis on learning styles and other learner differences, UD, now called *Universal Instructional Design*, has moved into education. Application of UID goes beyond merely physical access for all students (e.g., wheelchair ramps and sign language translators), ensuring access to information, resources, and tools for students with a wide range of abilities, disabilities, ethnic backgrounds, language skills, and learning styles. Burgstahler (2008) noted that

> Universal Instructional Design principles . . . give each student meaningful access to the curriculum by assuring access to the environment as well as multiple means of representation, expression, and engagement. (p. 1)

Table 12.7 offers an overview of the principles of UID and some suggested applications of these principles in the education of English learners with special needs. UID does not imply that one universal size fits all but rather that a diversity of opportunities will work for many different students. Educators may find more information

Table 12.7 Principles of Universal Instructional Design Applied to English Learners with Special Needs

Principle	Definition	Application
Inclusiveness	A classroom climate that communicates respect for varying abilities	Use bilingual signage and Braille bilingual materials; welcome and respect aides and assistants; supply multiple reading levels of texts.
Physical access	Equipment and activities that minimize sustained physical effort, provide options for participation, and accommodate those with limited physical abilities	Use assistive technologies such as screen readers and online dictionaries; make online chatrooms available for deaf and hearing-impaired students.
Delivery methods	Content is delivered in multiple modes so it is accessible to students with a wide range of abilities, disabilities, interests, and previous experiences	Employ a full range of audiovisual enhancement, including wireless headsets and captioned video; build in redundant modes (e.g., audiotaped read-along books, typed lecture notes, and study guides).
Information access	Use of captioned videos and accessible electronic formats; in printed work, use of simple, intuitive, and consistent formats	Ensure that information is both understandable and complete; reduce unnecessary complexity; highlight essential text; give clear criteria for tests and assignments.

(continued)

Table 12.7 Continued

Principle	Definition	Application
Interaction	Accessible to everyone, without accommodation; use of multiple ways for students to participate	Set up both heterogeneous groups (across second-language ability levels) and homogeneous groups (same language-ability level); instruct students on how to secure a conversational turn.
Feedback	Effective prompting during an activity and constructive comments after the assignment is complete	Employ formative assessment for ongoing feedback.
Demonstration of knowledge	Provision for multiple ways students demonstrate knowledge—group work, demonstrations, portfolios, and presentations	Offer different modes to all students so that special-needs students are not the only ones with alternatives.

Sources: Burgstahler (2002), Egbert (2004), and Strehorn (2001).

in the *Parent's Guide to Universal Design for Learning,* online at www.ncld.org /checklists-a-more/parent-advocacy-guides/a-parent-guide-to-udl.

Adapted Instruction

Assistive Technology for the Visually Impaired

Reese (2006) describes many ways that ELD programs can accommodate the visually impaired with assistive technology; audio books; and magnifiers, large print, print-enlarging devices, or Braille for written materials. For accessing materials at a distance such as a chalkboard, mildly impaired students can use monocular telescopes or bioptic lenses.

Teaching Blind English Learners

Because eighty percent of learning is visual (Seng, 2005), blind English learners are a special concern. Table 12.8 offers considerations to help teachers who are not trained to teach the blind so they can deliver effective instruction to these students.

Table 12.8 Addressing the Needs of Blind Students

Aspects of Concern	Questions and Suggestions
Understanding degrees of blindness	Is the student partially or totally blind? Residual vision should be used to the maximum extent possible.
Understanding the background	How and when did the student become blind—at the age of eight or nine (certain visual memory will be retained) or blind at birth (ideas and images will be conceived differently)?
Setting up a readers service	Textbooks are usually translated into Braille one chapter at a time, but a pool of volunteers can read to blind students or tape-record books.

Aspects of Concern	Questions and Suggestions
Technological help	Computer software can download material and transcribe it into Braille dots. Blind students can use the computer sound synthesis software such as text to speech and voice recognition—some software can be downloaded for free.
In the classroom	Because the blind student cannot see the classroom board, the teacher has to be more vocal and repeat every word put on the board. When plans or diagrams are used, they can be embossed by sticking string to cardboard.
Reactions of other students	Many sighted students come forward willingly to help their blind classmates both in the classroom and in the community.
Teaching tips	Use talking books and taped dialogues for reading comprehension lessons; use real objects in lessons; and use field trips to bring culture, exposure, and experiences to the blind students.

Teaching English Learners with Hearing Impairments

More than forty percent of school-age deaf and hard-of-hearing students are from ethnically and racially diverse families (Schildroth & Hotto, 1994). Deaf students in the public school setting face the challenge of three different cultures: their own ethnic background, the Deaf community, and that of mainstream hearing people (Qualls-Mitchell, 2008). Working with such cultural diversity, it is helpful to encourage students to appreciate and respect one another's differences, and to develop an awareness of the needs of others. Using signing, multimodal presentation of information, imagery, and highly motivating materials helps deaf students become active learners. Biographies that represent role models are motivating for all students. Qualls-Mitchell (2008) presents fifteen different resources for teachers of hearing-impaired students, including Moore and Panara's (1996) *Great Deaf Americans*, a source book for biographies representing diverse populations.

Hearing loss can be *conductive* (damage or obstruction in the outer or middle ear), *sensorineural* (damage to the inner ear), *mixed* (both of previous), or *central* (involving the central nervous system and/or brain). Each type of hearing loss requires distinct intervention, conductive damage being the easiest to remediate using a hearing aid. Table 12.9 features teaching strategies for those with hearing impairments.

Table 12.9 Instructional Strategies for Students with Hearing Impairments

Services Available	
• Speech/language training from a specialist	• Note-taking assistance
• Amplification systems	• Instruction for teachers and peers in sign language
• Interpreter using sign language	• Counseling
• Captioned videotapes and television	• Increased use of visual materials

(continued)

Table 12.9 Continued

Classroom Management
• Arrange desks in a semicircle to facilitate speech-reading.
• Reduce distracting ambient noise.
• Speak clearly, with good enunciation.
• Use gestures to facilitate understanding when speaking.

Student–Teacher Interaction
• Seat the student close to the teacher and face the student when talking.
• Speak face to face, using natural speech.

Academic Assistance
• List key points on the chalkboard.
• Use several forms of communication.
• Give short, concise instructions and have the student repeat key points privately to ensure comprehension.
• Appoint a peer buddy to help the student stay abreast of the class during oral reading.

Social Skills Development
• Create opportunities for group work.
• Model patience and respect during communication.
• Teach social cues and unspoken rules of conversation if the student seems to make inappropriate interactions.

Source: Based on Pierangelo and Giuliani (2001).

Teaching English Learners with Autism Spectrum Disorders

> In a "sensory break area" where students with autism can take a time out if needed and calm themselves, Will plays a board game and works at casual conversation with speech pathologist Amy Gold. "Turn-taking with a game is concrete, and from this he learns about conversational turn-taking," explains Gold. (Goodwin, 2010, p. 11)

This child is a part of a growing population of students with autism, the fastest growing special education population in the United States. According to Baio (2012, n.p.), autism spectrum disorders (ASDs) are "a group of developmental disabilities characterized by impairments in social interaction and communication and by restricted, repetitive, and stereotyped patterns of behavior. Symptoms typically are apparent before age 3 years." Autism is difficult to diagnose in children because the symptoms are complex and the exact biologic nature of the disorders has not been determined.

Researchers estimate that in 2012, one in eighty-eight children in the United States had some form of autism (Baio, 2012). The prevalence of autism in the U.S. population varies geographically and racially; researchers suspect that increased efforts to identify and label children who show signs of autism are a function of access to services, rather than representing difference in the populations, because the rate for White children is reported to be 1 in 83, compared to 1 in 127 for Latinos and 1 in 98 for African Americans. With improved access to special educations services for culturally and linguistically diverse young children, this picture may change.

Education is considered the primary treatment for autism. Classroom interventions include behavioral training, speech and language therapy, and one-on-one work with motor disorder skills. Many of these students also require ELD services.

Teaching CLD learners in U.S. classrooms is a challenge on a scale without precedent in modern education. As the social and economic stakes are raised, students who fail to reach their potential represent a loss to society as a whole. Each student—including those with special needs, whether for additional mediation or acceleration of instruction—is a treasure box, with his or her individual and specific talents, cultural background, and life experiences locked inside. Opening this treasure chest and releasing these talents to the world is an educational adventure of the highest order. The teacher with crosscultural, language, and academic development training holds the key.

LEARNING MORE

Further Reading

Ask your school or local public librarian for a list of biographies, autobiographies, or other genres that will raise your awareness of a specific disability: autism, attention-deficit/hyperactivity disorder, or a physical, emotional, or learning disability.

Web Search

Go online to see if the following organizations' websites offer specific suggestions for the education of CLD students:

- Alexander Graham Bell Association for the Deaf
- American Association for the Deaf-Blind
- American Association on Mental Retardation
- American Council of the Blind
- American Society for Deaf Children
- Autism Society of America, Inc.
- Beach Center on Families and Disability
- Challenge (Attention Deficit Disorder Association)
- Children with Attention Deficit Disorders (ChADD)

Exploration

Visit a special education classroom in which instruction takes place in one or more primary languages. Discuss with the teacher the availability of special education materials in the language(s). Ask if there are parent guides to the Individualized Education Plan (IEP) process in the languages represented in the class.

Experiment

Try "Second-Language Lead Me Blindfolded," a variation of the "Lead Me Blindfolded" game, in which a partner leads you around the block blindfolded and you must rely on that partner for cues. Choose a partner who will speak to you only in a foreign language with which you are not familiar as you are led around.

MyEducationLab™

The Inclusive Classroom

With inclusion, students of all abilities are educated together in the general education classroom. Children with special needs are not isolated, but are involved in all aspects of the classroom, curriculum, and learning activities. The classroom diversity that results requires that the teacher function as part of a cooperative team that includes specialists that offer special services.

To access the video, go to MyEducationLab (www.myeducationlab.com), choose the Díaz-Rico text, and log in to MyEducationLab for English Language Learners. Select the topic Special Needs and Inclusion, and watch the video entitled "The Inclusive Classroom."

Answer the following questions:

1. What are the elements of an effective inclusive classroom for English learners?
2. What can the teacher of culturally and linguistically diverse (CLD) students do to create an effective inclusive classroom?
3. The inclusion of children with special needs adds to the diversity of the classroom. Evaluate the rewards and challenges of an inclusive classroom for culturally and linguistically diverse (CLD) students. Explain your answer.

References

Abdulrahim, R. (2011). Holding on to Sikh heritage in the U.S. *Los Angeles Times,* May 7, AA3.

Abedi, J., Hofstetter, C. H., & Lord, C. (2004). Assessment accommodations for English language learners: Implications for policy-based empirical research. *Review of Educational Research, 74*(1), 1–28.

Ada, A. (1989). Los libros mágicos. *California Tomorrow,* 42–44.

Adams, T. L. (2003). Reading mathematics: More than words can say. *The Reading Teacher, 56*(8), 786–795.

Adger, C. (2000). School/community partnerships to support language minority student success. Online at http://escholarship.org/uc/item/8k29w24p.

Agar, M. (1980). *The professional stranger: An informal introduction to ethnography.* Orlando, FL: Academic Press.

Airasian, P. (2005). *Classroom assessment: Concepts and applications* (5th ed.). Boston: McGraw-Hill.

Alexander v. Sandoval. (2001). 532 US 275, Docket No. 99-1908.

Alexander, S. (1983). *Nadia, the willful.* New York: Dial.

Allan, K. K., & Miller, M. S. (2005). *Literacy and learning in the content areas* (2nd ed.). Boston: Houghton Mifflin.

Allen, E., & Seaman, J. (2011). Learning on demand: Online education in the United States, 2010. Babson Park, MA: Babson Research Group. Online at www.babson.edu/News-Events/babson-news/Pages/111109OnLineLearningStudy.aspx.

Alpan, O. (2013). Personal communication.

Alsonso-Zaldivar, R. & Tompson, T. (2010, July 30). 87% of Hispanics value higher education, 13% have college degree. *USA Today,* Online at www.usatoday.com/news/education/2010-07-30-poll-hispanic-college_N.htm.

Alvarez, J. (2007). My English. In R. Spack (Ed.), *Guidelines: A cross-cultural reading/writing text* (pp. 30–35). New York: Cambridge University Press.

Amselle, J. (1999). Dual immersion delays English. *American Language Review, 3*(5), 8.

Andrews, L. (2001). *Linguistics for L2 teachers.* Mahwah, NJ: Erlbaum.

Anstrom, K. (1996). *Federal policy, legislation, and education reform: The promise and the challenge for language minority students.* In A. Kindler (Ed.), National Clearinghouse of Bilingual Education. Washington, DC: George Washington University, Institute for the Study of Language and Education.

Anstrom, K., & DiCerbo, P. (1999). *Preparing secondary education teachers to work with English language learners: Mathematics.* Center for the Study of Language and Education, Graduate School of Education & Human Development, the George Washington University.

Anstrom, K., Steeves, K. A., & DiCerbo, P. (1999). *Preparing secondary education teachers to work with English language learners: Social Studies.* Center for the Study of Language and Education, Graduate School of Education & Human Development, the George Washington University.

Appiah, K. A., & Gates, H. L. (2003). *Africana.* New York: Perseus.

Arab American Institute Foundation. (n.d.). *Quick facts about Arab Americans.* Washington, DC: Author. Retrieved January 13, 2005, from www.aaiusa.org/educational_packet.htm.

Arias, I. (1996). *Proxemics in the ESL classroom.* Retrieved September 2, 2004, from http://exchanges .state.gov/forum/vols/vol34/no1/p32 .htm.

Artiles, A. J., & Trent, S. C. (1994). Overrepresentation of minority students in special education: A continuing debate. *Journal of Special Education, 27*(4), 410–437.

Asher, J. (1982). *Learning another language through actions: The complete teachers' guidebook.* Los Gatos, CA: Sky Oaks.

Au, K., & Jordan, C. (1981). Teaching reading to Hawaiian children: Finding a culturally appropriate solution. In H. Trueba, G. Guthrie, & K. Au (Eds.), *Culture and the bilingual classroom: Studies in classroom ethnography* (pp. 139–152). Rowley, MA: Newbury House.

Aud, S., Hussar, W., Johnson, F., Kena, G., Roth, E. (NCES), Manning, E., Wang X., & Zhang, J. (2012). *The condition of education.* Washington, DC: National Center for Educational Statistics.

Auerbach, E. (1993). Putting the P back in "participatory." *TESOL Quarterly, 27*(3), 543–545.

August, D., Hakuta, K., & Pompa, D. (1994). *For all students: Limited English proficient students and Goals 2000.* Washington, DC: National Clearinghouse for Bilingual Education.

August, D., & Pease-Alvarez, L. (1996). *Attributes of effective programs and classrooms serving English language learners.* Santa Cruz, CA: Center for Research on Cultural Diversity and Second Language Learning.

Avery, E. (2012). Cursive connects us to our past and future. *California Educator, 16*(9), 44.

Babbitt, N. (1976). *Tuck everlasting.* New York: Bantam Books.

Baca, L., & Cervantes, H. T. (1984). *The bilingual special education interface.* Columbus, OH: Merrill.

Baca, L., & de Valenzuela, J. S. (1994). *Reconstructing the bilingual special education interface.* Online at http://www.eric.ed.gov/ERICWebPortal/search/detailmini.jsp?_nfpb=true&_&ERICExtSearch_SearchValue_0=ED381023&ERICExtSearch_SearchType_0=no&accno=ED381023.

Baker, C. (2001). *Foundations of bilingual education and bilingualism* (3rd ed.). Clevedon, Eng.: Multilingual Matters.

Baio, J. (2012). *Prevalence of autism spectrum disorders—Autism and Developmental Disabilities Monitoring Network, 14 Sites, United States, 2008.* Atlanta, GA: Centers for Disease Control. Online at http://www.cdc.gov/mmwr/preview/mmwrhtml/ss6103a1.htm?s_cid=ss6103a1_w.

Balderrama, M. V., & Díaz-Rico, L. T. (2006). *Teacher performance expectations for educating English learners.* Boston: Allyn & Bacon.

Bandlow, R. (2002). Suburban bigotry: A descent into racism and struggle for redemption. In F. Schultz (Ed.), *Annual editions: Multicultural education 2002–2003* (pp. 90–93). Guilford, CT: McGraw-Hill/Dushkin.

Banks, C. (2004). Families and teachers working together for school improvement. In J. Banks & C. Banks (Eds.), *Multicultural education: Issues and perspectives* (5th ed., pp. 421–442). Hoboken, NJ: Wiley.

Banks, J. (1994). *An introduction to multicultural education.* Boston: Allyn & Bacon.

Barfield, S. C., & Uzarski, J. (2000). Integrating indigenous cultures into English language teaching. *English Teaching Forum, 47*(1), 2–9.

Barna, L. M. (2007). Intercultural communication stumbling blocks. In R. Spack (Ed.), *Guidelines: A cross-cultural reading/writing text* (pp. 66–74). New York: Cambridge University Press.

Barr, R., Blachowicz, C. L. Z., Bates, A., Katz, C. & Kaufman, B. (2007). *Reading diagnosis for teachers: An instructional approach.* Boston: Pearson.

Barrett, J. (1978). *Cloudy with a chance of meatballs.* New York: Scholastic Books.

Beck, M. (2004). *California standards assessment workbook.* White Plains, NY: Longman.

Beeghly, D. G., & Prudhoe, C. M. (2002). *Litlinks: Activities for connected learning in elementary classrooms.* Boston: McGraw-Hill.

Bennett, C. (2003). *Comprehensive multicultural education: Theory and practice* (5th ed.). Boston: Allyn & Bacon.

Bernard, B. (1995). *Fostering resiliency in kids: Protective factors in the family school and community.* San Francisco: West Ed Regional Educational Laboratory.

Bernstein, D. K. (1989). Assessing children with limited English proficiency: Current perspectives. *Topics in Language Disorders, 9,* 15–20.

Bialystok, E. (2009). Bilingualism: The good, the bad, and the indifferent. *Bilingualism: Language and Cognition, 12*(1), 3–11.

Bigelow, B. (2007). Rethinking the line between us. *Educational Leadership, 64*(6), 47–61.

Bilingual Education Act, Pub. L. No. (90-247), 81 Stat. 816 (1968).

Bilingual Education Act, Pub. L. No. (93-380), 88 Stat. 503 (1974).

Bilingual Education Act, Pub. L. No. (95-561), 92 Stat. 2268 (1978).

Bilingual Education Act, Pub. L. No. (98-511), 98 Stat. 2370 (1984).

Bilingual Education Act, Pub. L. No. (100-297), 102 Stat. 279 (1988).

Bilingual Education Act, Pub. L. No. (103-382) (1994).

Birdwhistell, R. (1974). The language of the body: The natural environment of words. In A. Silverstein (Ed.), *Human communication: Theoretical explorations* (pp. 203–220). Hillsdale, NJ: Erlbaum.

Bitter, G. G., & Legacy, M. E. (2007). *Using technology in the classroom* (7th ed.). Boston: Pearson.

Bitter, G. G., & Pierson, J. M. (2004). *Using technology in the classroom* (6th ed.). Boston: Pearson.

Block, C. C., & Israel, S. E. (2005). *Reading first and beyond.* Thousand Oaks, CA: Corwin Press.

Bonilla-Silva, E. (2003). *Racism without racists: Color-blind racism and the persistence of racial inequality in the United States.* Lanham, MD: Rowman & Littlefield.

Bourdieu, P. (with Passeron, J.). (1977). *Reproduction in society, education, and culture.* Los Angeles: Sage.

Brahier, D. J. (2009). *Teaching secondary and middle school mathematics* (3rd ed.). Boston: Pearson.

Brandt, R. (1994). On educating for diversity: A conversation with James A. Banks. *Educational Leadership, 51,* 28–31.

Brass, J. J. (2008). Local knowledge and digital movie composing in an after-school literacy program. *Journal of Adolescent & Adult Literacy, 51*(5), 464–473.

Bratt Paulston, C. (1992). *Sociolinguistic perspectives on bilingual education.* Clevedon, UK: Multilingual Matters.

Brewer, D., García, M., & Aguilar, Y. F. (2007, September 7). Some children left behind. *Los Angeles Times,* A29.

Brisk, M. E. (1998). *Bilingual education: From compensatory to quality schooling.* Mahwah, NJ: Erlbaum.

Brown, D. (2007). *Principles of language learning and teaching* (5th ed.). Englewood Cliffs, NJ: Prentice Hall.

Brown, S. (2006). *Teaching listening.* New York: Cambridge University Press.

Brown, S. C., & Kysilka, M. L. (2002). *Applying multicultural and global concepts in the classroom and beyond.* Boston: Allyn & Bacon.

Bruder, M. B., Anderson, R., Schultz, G., & Caldera, M. (1991). *Ninos especiales* program: A culturally sensitive early intervention model. *Journal of Early Intervention, 15*(3), 268–277.

Brusca-Vega, R. (2002). Disproportionate representation of English language learners in special education. In *Serving English language learners with disabilities: A resource manual for Illinois educators.* Retrieved February 9, 2005, from www.isbe.state.il.us/spec-ed/bilingualmanual2002.htm.

Buckmaster, R. (2000, June 22–28). First and second languages do battle for the classroom.

(Manchester) Guardian Weekly (Learning English supplement), 3.

Buell, M. Z. (2004). Code-switching and second-language writing: How multiple codes are combined in a text. In C. Bazerman & P. Prior (Eds.), *What writing does and how it does it* (pp. 97–122). Mahwah, NJ: Erlbaum.

Buettner, E. G. (2002). Sentence-by-sentence self-monitoring. *The Reading Teacher, 56*(1), 34–44.

Bunting, E. (1990). *How many days to America? A Thanksgiving story.* New York: Clarion.

Burgstahler, S. (2008). *Creating video products that are accessible to people with sensory impairments.* Retrieved October 27, 2008, from www.washington.edu/doit/Brochures/Technology/vid_sensory.html.

Burgstahler, S. (2002). *Universal design of instruction.* Retrieved January 25, 2005, from www.washington.edu/doit/Brochures/Academics/instruction.html.

Burnette, J. (2000). *Assessment of culturally and linguistically diverse students for special education eligibility.* ERIC Clearinghouse on Disabilities and Gifted Education (ED #E604).

Burns, M. S., Griffin, P., & Snow, C. E. (Eds.). (1999). *Starting out right: A guide to promoting children's reading success.* Washington, DC: National Academy Press.

Caine, R. N., Caine, G., McClintic, C., & Klimek, K. (2004). *Brain/mind learning principles in action: The fieldbook for making connections, teaching, and the human brain.* Thousand Oaks, CA: Sage.

Caine, R., & Caine, G. (1994). *Making connections: Teaching and the human brain.* Menlo Park, CA: Addison Wesley.

Calderón, M. (2007). Adolescent literacy and English language learners: An urgent issue. *ESL Magazine, 56,* 9–14.

Calderón, M., & Slavin, R. (2001). Success for all in a two-way immersion school. In D. Christian & F. Genesee (Eds.), *Bilingual education.* Alexandria, VA: Teachers of English to Speakers of Other Languages.

California Department of Education (CDE). (1992). *Handbook for teaching Korean-American students.* Sacramento: Author.

California Department of Education (CDE). (1994). *Physical education framework.* Retrieved October 18, 2004, from www.cde.ca.gov/ci/cr/cf/allfwks.asp.

California Department of Education (CDE). (1998a). *English-language arts content standards.* Retrieved March 17, 2005, from www.cde.ca.gov/be/st/ss/engmain.asp.

California Department of Education (CDE). (2004). *Visual and performing arts standards.* Retrieved October 18, 2004, from www.cde.ca.gov/be/st/ss/vamain.asp.

California Department of Education (CDE). (1999). *Reading/language arts framework for California public schools.* Sacramento: Author. Retrieved September 10, 2004, from www.cde.ca.gov/cdepress/lang_arts.pdf.

California Department of Education (CDE). (2012). *English language development standards.* Sacramento: Author. Retrieved September 10, 2004, from www.cde.ca.gov.

California Department of Education (2005). *A study of the relationship between physical fitness and academic achievement in California using 2004 test results.* Sacramento, CA: Author.

California State Code of Regulations. (1998). *Title 5, Division 1, Chapter 11: English language learner education. Subchapter 4. English language learner education.* Retrieved May 16, 2001, from www.cde.ca.gov/prop227.html.

Canale, M. (1983). From communicative competence to communicative language pedagogy. In J. Richards & R. Schmidt (Eds.), *Language and communication* (pp. 2–27). New York: Longman.

Carlson, L. M. (1994). *Cool salsa: Bilingual poems on growing up Latina in the United States.* New York: H. Holt. (Reprinted in 2013 from Square Fish Publishers [Macmillan]).

Carlson, L. M. (2005). *Red hot salsa: Bilingual poems on being young and Latina in the United States.* New York: H. Holt.

Carnuccio, L. M. (2004). Cybersites. *Essential Teacher, 1*(3), 59.

Carrasquillo, A., & Rodríguez, V. (2002). *Language minority students in the mainstream classroom.* Clevedon, UK: Multilingual Matters.

Cartagena, J. (1991). English only in the 1980s: A product of myths, phobias, and bias. In S. Benesch (Ed.), *ESL in America: Myths and possibilities*(pp. 11–26). Portsmouth, NH: Boynton/Cook.

Casey, J. (2004). A place for first language in the ESOL classroom. *Essential Teacher, 1*(4), 50–52.

Casteñada v. Pickard, 648 F.2d 989 (5th Cir. 1981).

CATESOL. (1998). *CATESOL position statement on literacy instruction for English language learners, grades K–12.* Online at www.catesol.org/ppapers.html.

Cavanaugh, C. (2006). *Clips from the classroom: Learning with technology.* Boston: Allyn & Bacon.

Cazden, C. (1986). ESL teachers as language advocates for children. In P. Rigg & D. S. Enright (Eds.), *Children and ESL: Integrating perspectives* (pp. 9–21). Alexandria, VA: Teachers of English to Speakers of Other Languages.

Center for Advanced Research on Language Acquisition. (2001). *K–12 less commonly taught languages.* Retrieved January 12, 2005, from http:// carla.acad.umn.edu:591/k12.html.

Center for Research on Education, Diversity, and Excellence (CREDE). (2004). *Observing the five standards of practice.* Retrieved April 8, 2005, from www.cal.org/crede/pubs/rb11.pdf.

Chamot, A. U., Barnhardt, S., El-Dinary, P. B., & Robbins, J. (1999). *The learning strategies handbook.* White Plains, NY: Longman.

Chandler, D. (2007). *Semiotics: The basics.* London: Taylor & Francis.

Chang, B., & Au, W. (2007–2008). Unmasking the myth of the model minority. *Rethinking Schools, 22*(2), 14–19.

Chang, J-M. (2005). *Asian American children in special education: Need for multidimensional collaboration.* Retrieved February 2, 2005, from www.dinf.ne.jp/doc/english/Us_Eu/ada_e/pres_com/pres-dd/chang.htm.

Chávez Chávez, R. (1997). *A curriculum discourse for achieving equity: Implications for teachers when engaged with Latina and Latino students.* Online at http://education.nmsu.edu/faculty/ci/ruchavez/publications/hispanic_dropout_project.htm.

Children's Defense Fund. (2004a). *Defining poverty and why it matters for children.* Retrieved January 15, 2005, from www.childrensdefense.org/familyincome/childpoverty/default.asp.

Children's Defense Fund. (2004b). *Each day in America.* Retrieved January 15, 2005, from www.childrensdefense.org/data/eachday.asp.

Children's Defense Fund. (2004c). *2003 facts on child poverty in America.* Retrieved January 13, 2005, from www.childrensdefense.org/familyincome/childpoverty/basicfacts.asp.

Cho Bassoff, T. (2004). Compleat Links: Three steps toward a strong home–school connection. Online at www.tesol.org/read-and-publish/journals/other-serial-publications/compleat-links/compleat-links-volume-1-issue-4-%28autumn-2004%29/three-steps-toward-a-strong-home-school-connection.

Chomsky, N. (1959). Review of B. F. Skinner "Verbal Behavior." *Language, 35,* 26–58.

Christensen, L. (2000). *Reading, writing, rising up: Teaching about social justice and the power of the written word.* Milwaukee, WI: Rethinking Schools.

Civil Rights Act, Pub. L. No. (88-352), 78 Stat. (1964).

Clark, B. (1983). *Growing up gifted: Developing the potential of children at home and at school* (2nd ed.). Columbus, OH: Merrill.

Cloud, N., Genesee, F., & Hamayan, E. (2000). *Dual language instruction.* Boston: Heinle and Heinle.

Cohen, A. (1996). *Second language learning and use strategies: Clarifying the issues. Working Paper Series #3.* Minneapolis: University of Minnesota Center for Advanced Research on Language Acquisition.

Cohen, E., Lotan, R., & Catanzarite, L. (1990). Treating status problems in the cooperative classroom. In S. Sharon (Ed.), *Cooperative learning: Theory and research* (pp. 203–229). New York: Praeger.

Coiro, J. (2003). Exploring literacy on the Internet. *The Reading Teacher, 56*(5), 458–460.

Cole, K. (2007). Pressures and promise in the mainstream classroom. In K. Cole, C. Collier, & S. Herrera (Eds.), *Making the right investments: Strengthening the education of English language and bilingual learners: Research conference proceedings* (pp. 3–11). Harrisburg, PA: Center for Schools and Communities.

Cole, M. (1998, April 16). *Cultural psychology: Can it help us think about diversity?* Presentation at the annual meeting of the American Educational Research Association, San Diego.

College Board (2009). 2009 college-bound seniors are most diverse group ever to take SAT® as more minority students prepare for higher education. Online at http://www.collegeboard.com/press/releases/206201.html.

College Board (2011). *2011 SAT trends.* Online at http://professionals.collegeboard.com/data-reports-research/sat/cb-seniors-2011/tables.

College Board (2012). *The 8th annual report to the nation.* Accessed May 21, 2012, from www.collegeboard.org/freepubs.

Collier, V. (1987). Age and rate of acquisition of second language for academic purposes. *TESOL Quarterly, 21*(4), 617–641.

Collier, V. P. (1995). Acquiring a second language for school. Washington, DC: National Clearinghouse for Bilingual Education. Washington, DC: National Clearinghouse for Bilingual Education. Online at http://extranet.das.pac.dodea.edu/principal/Daily%20Bulletins,%20Professional%20Articles/Daily%20Bulletin/ESL/Aquiring%20a%20Second%20Language%20for%20School.pdf.

Conchas, G. Q. (2006). *The color of success: Race and high-achieving urban youth.* New York: Teachers College Press.

Connell, B., Jones, M., Mace, R., Mueller, J., Mullick, A., Ostroff, E., Sanford, J., Steinfield, E., Story, M., & Vanderheiden, G. (1997). *The principles of universal design (Version 2.0).* Retrieved January 25, 2005, from www.design.ncsu.edu.8120/cud/univ_design/principles/udprinciples.htm.

Connor, M. H., & Boskin, J. (2001). Overrepresentation of bilingual and poor children in special education classes: A continuing problem. *Journal of Children and Poverty, 7*(1), 23–32.

Cooter, R. D., Flynt, E. S., & Cooter, K. S. (2006). *Cooter Flynt Cooter Comprehensive Reading Inventory: Measuring reading development in regular and special education classrooms.* Upper Saddle River, NJ: Prentice Hall.

Cook, V. (1999). Going beyond the native speaker in language teaching. *TESOL Quarterly, 33*(2), 185–209.

Copeland, L. (2008, March 3). Cold realities take back seat in this classroom. *USA Today,* 9D.

Corley, M. A. (2003). *Poverty, racism, and literacy.* ERIC Digest EDO-CE-02-243. ERIC Clearinghouse on Adult, Career, and Vocational Education.

Corson, D. (1990). *Language policy across the curriculum.* Clevedon, Eng.: Multilingual Matters.

Corson, D. (1999). *Language policy in schools: A resource for teachers and administrators.* Mahwah, NJ: Erlbaum.

Cortés, C. (1993). Acculturation, assimilation, and "adducation." *BEOutreach, 4*(1), 3–5.

Cortés, C. (2013). Personal communication, March 9.

Cosentino De Cohen, C., &Clewell, B. C. (2007). *Putting English language learners on the educational map: The No Child Left Behind Act implemented.* Washington, DC: Urban Institute.

Cotton, K. (1989). *Expectations and student outcomes.* Retrieved April 6, 2005, from educationnorthwest.org/webfm_send/562.

Council for Exceptional Children (2011). Improving executive function skills: An innovative strategy that may enhance learning for all children. Online at http://www.cec.sped.org/

AM/Template.cfm?Section=Home&CONTE NTID=10291&TEMPLATE=/CM/Content Display.cfm.

Council of Chief State School Officers (CCSSO). (2011). *Roadmap for next generation state accountability systems*. Online at http://www .ccsso.org/documents/Roadmap.pdf.

Council of Chief State School Officers (CCSSO). (2012). Standards, assessment & accountability. Online at www.ccsso.org/What_We_Do/ Standards_Assessment_and_Accountability .html.

Coutinho, M. J., & Oswald, D. P. (2004). *Disproportionate representation of culturally and linguistically diverse students in special education: Measuring the problem*. National Center for Culturally Responsive Educational Systems. Retrieved July 12, 2008, from www .nccrest.org/publications.html.

Crago, M. (1993). Communicative interaction and second language acquisition: An Inuit example. *TESOL Quarterly, 26*(3), 487–506.

Crawford, J. (1997). *Best evidence: Research foundations of the bilingual education act*. Washington, DC: National Clearinghouse for Bilingual Education. Online at http://www .ncela.gwu.edu/files/rcd/BE020829/Best_ Evidence_Research.pdf.

Crawford, J. (1999). *Bilingual education: History, politics, theory, and practice* (4th ed.). Los Angeles: Bilingual Educational Services.

Crawford, J. (2003). *Language legislation in the U.S.A.* Retrieved March 19, 2005, from http:// ourworld .compuserve.com/homepages/JW CRAWFORD/langleg.htm.

Crawford, J. (2004a). *Educating English learners: Language diversity in the classroom* (formerly *A bilingual education: History, politics, theory, and practice*). Los Angeles: Bilingual Educational Services.

Crawford, J. (2004b). Has two-way been oversold? *Bilingual Family Newsletter* (Multilingual Matters), *21*(1), 3.

Crawford, L. (1993). *Language and literacy learning in multicultural classrooms*. Boston: Allyn & Bacon.

Crissey, S. R. (2009). *Educational attainment in the United States: 2007*. Washington, DC: U.S. Census Bureau. Online at www.census.gov/pr od/2009pubs/p20–560.pdf.

Cronin, J., Dahlin, M., Adkins, D., & Kingsbury, G. G. (2007). *The proficiency illusion*. Thomas B. Fordham Institute. Retrieved June 27, 2008, from www.edexcellence.net/detail/news.cfm? news_id=376.

Crosby, H. H., & Emery, R. W. (1994). *Better spelling in 30 minutes a day*. New York: Barnes and Noble Books.

Cummins, J. (1979). Cognitive/academic language proficiency, linguistic interdependence, the optimum age question and some other matters. *Working Papers on Bilingualism, 19*, 121–129.

Cummins, J. (1980). The cross-lingual dimensions of language proficiency: Implications for bilingual education and the optimal age issue. *TESOL Quarterly, 14*(2), 175–187.

Cummins, J. (1981a). Age on arrival and immigrant second language learning in Canada: A reassessment. *Applied Linguistics 2*(2), 132–149.

Cummins, J. (1981b). The role of primary language development in promoting educational success for language minority students. In *Schooling and language minority students: A theoretical framework* (pp. 3–49). Sacramento: California State Department of Education.

Cummins, J. (1984). *Bilingualism and special education: Issues in assessment and pedagogy*. San Diego: College-Hill.

Cummins, J. (1986). Empowering minority students: A framework for intervention. *Harvard Educational Review, 56*(1), 18–36.

Cummins, J. (1989). *Empowering minority students*. Sacramento: California Association for Bilingual Education.

Cummins, J. (2001). *Negotiating identities: Education for empowerment in a diverse society*. Los Angeles: California Association for Bilingual Education.

Cummins, J. (2003). Reading and the bilingual student: Fact and friction. In G. García (Ed.),

English learners reaching the highest level of English literacy (pp. 2–33). Newark, DE: International Reading Association.

Cummins, J. (2010). Biliteracy, empowerment, and transformative pedagogy. Online at http://www.utpa.edu/dept/curr_ins/faculty_fo lders/gomez_l/docs/reading_1.pdf.

Cunningham, C. A., & Billingsley, M. (2006). *Curriculum webs: Weaving the web into teaching and learning.* Boston: Pearson.

Curtain, H., & Dahlberg, C. A. (2004). *Language and children—Making the match: New languages for young learners, grades K–8.* Boston: Allyn & Bacon.

Dale, T., & Cuevas, G. (1987). Integrating language and mathematics learning. In J. Crandall (Ed.), *ESL through content-area instruction: Mathematics, science, social studies.* Englewood Cliffs, NJ: Regents/Prentice Hall.

Dale, T., & Cuevas, G. (1992). Integrating mathematics and language learning. In P. Richard-Amato & M. Snow (Eds.), *The multicultural classroom* (pp. 330–348). White Plains, NY: Longman.

Dalle, T. S., & Young, L. J. (2003). *PACE yourself: A handbook for ESL tutors.* Alexandria, VA: Teachers of English to Speakers of Other Languages.

Darder, A. (1991). *Culture and power in the classroom.* New York: Bergin and Garvey.

Day, E. M. (2002). *Identity and the young English learner.* Clevedon, UK: Multilingual Matters.

Day, F. A. (1994). *Multicultural voices in contemporary literature: A resource for teachers.* Portsmouth, NH: Heinemann.

Day, F. A. (1997). *Latina and Latino voices in literature for children and teenagers.* Portsmouth, NH: Heinemann.

Day, F. A. (2003). *Latina and Latino voices in literature: Lives and works.* Westport, CT: Greenwood Publishers.

Delgado-Gaitan, C., & Trueba, H. (1991). *Crossing cultural borders: Education for immigrant families in America.* London: Falmer Press.

De Valenzuela, J. S., Copeland, S. R., Qi, C. H., & Park, M. (2006). Examining educational equity: revisiting the disproportionate representation of minority students in special education. *Exceptional Children, 72*(4), 425–441.

Dewitz, P., & Dewitz, P. K. (2003). They can read the words, but they can't understand: Refining comprehension assessment. *The Reading Teacher, 56*(3), 422–435.

Diamond, B., & Moore, M. (1995). *Multicultural literacy.* White Plains, NY: Longman.

Díaz-Rico, L. (1993). From monocultural to multicultural teaching in an inner-city middle school. In A. Woolfolk (Ed.), *Readings and cases in educational psychology* (pp. 272–279). Boston: Allyn & Bacon.

Díaz-Rico, L. T. (2000). Intercultural communication in teacher education: The knowledge base for CLAD teacher credential programs. *CATESOL Journal, 12*(1), 145–161.

Díaz-Rico, L. T. (2013). *Strategies for teaching English learners.* Boston: Allyn & Bacon.

Díaz-Rico, L. T., & Dullien, S. (2004). *Semiotics and people watching.* Presentation at the regional conference of the California Teachers of English to Speakers of Other Languages regional conference, Los Angeles.

Dicker, S. (1992). Societal views of bilingualism and language learning. *TESOL: Applied Linguistics Interest Section Newsletter, 14*(1), 1, 4.

Domenech, D. (2008). Upholding standards. *Language Magazine, 7*(8), 24–26.

Dorsey, C. (2009). Teaching beyond the pdf. @ *Concord.Org, 13*(3), 2–5.

Dresser, N. (1993). *Our own stories.* White Plains, NY: Longman.

Dryfoos, J. (1998). *Safe passage: Making it through adolescence in a risky society.* New York: Oxford University Press.

Dudeney, G., & Hockly, N. (2007). *How to… Teach English with technology.* Harlow, UK: Pearson Longman.

Dudley-Marling, C., & Searle, D. (1991). *When students have time to talk.* Portsmouth, NH: Heinemann.

Duran, B. J., Dugan, T., & Weffer, R. E. (1997). Increasing teacher effectiveness with language minority students. *High School Journal, 80*(4), 238–246.

Dutro, S., & Moran, C. (2003). Rethinking English language instruction: An architectural approach. In G. García (Ed.), *English learners reaching the highest level of English literacy* (pp. 227–258). Newark, DE: International Reading Association.

Dyson, M. E. (1996). *Between God and gangsta rap: Bearing witness to black culture.* New York: Oxford University Press.

Echevarria, J., & Graves, A. (2007). *Sheltered content instruction: Teaching English language learners with diverse abilities.* Boston: Allyn & Bacon.

Echevarria, J., Vogt, M. E., & Short, D. (2012). *Making content comprehensible for English language learners: The SIOP model* (4th ed.). Boston: Allyn & Bacon.

Echevarría, J., Vogt, M., & Short, D. J. (2010). *The SIOP model for teaching mathematics to English learners.* Boston: Pearson.

Eckert, A. (1992). *Sorrow in our heart.* New York: Bantam.

Edmonson, M. (1971). *Lore: An introduction to the science of fiction.* New York: Holt, Rinehart and Winston.

EdSource. (2012). Schools under stress: Pressures mount of California's largest school districts. www.edsource.org/pub12-schools-under-stress.html.

Egbert, J. (2004). Access to knowledge: Implications of Universal Design for CALL environments. *CALL_EJ Online, 5*(2). Retrieved October 27, 2008, from www.tell.is.ritsumei.ac.jp/callejonline/journal/5-2/egbert.html.

Egbert, J., & Hanson-Smith, E. (2007). *CALL environments: Research, practice, and critical issues* (2nd ed.). Alexandria, VA: Teachers of English to Speakers of Other Languages.

Ellis, D. (2012). Cursive is unnecessary. *California Educator, 16*(9), 45.

Emanuel, E. J. (2012, June 24). Share the wealth. *New York Times,* SR8.

England, L. (Ed.) *Online language teacher education.* New York and London: Routledge.

Equal Educational Opportunities Act of 1974, Pub. L. No. (93-380), 88 Stat. 514 (1974).

Erickson, F. (1977). Some approaches to inquiry in school-community ethnography. *Anthropology and Education Quarterly, 8*(2), 58–69.

Escalante, J., & Dirmann, J. (1990). The Jaime Escalante math program. *Journal of Negro Education, 59*(3), 407–423.

Esquivel, P., & Becerra, H. (2012, April 24). Migrant wave from Mexico stalls. *Los Angeles Times,* A1, A9.

Fairclough, N. (1989). *Language and power.* New York: Longman.

Fairclough, N. (1997). *Critical discourse analysis: The critical study of language.* Reading, MA: Addison-Wesley.

Faltis, C. J., & Coulter, C. A. (2008). *Teaching English learners and immigrant students in secondary schools.* Upper Saddle River, NJ: Pearson Merrill Prentice Hall.

Farrell, T. S. C. (2006). *Succeeding with English language learners: A guide for beginning teachers.* Thousand Oaks, CA: Corwin.

Feagin, J., & Feagin, C. (1993). *Racial and ethnic relations* (4th ed.). Englewood Cliffs, NJ: Prentice Hall.

Feng, J. (1994). Asian-American children: What teachers should know. *ERIC Digest,* ED 369577.

Figueroa, R. A. (1993). The reconstruction of bilingual special education. *Focus on Diversity, 3*(3), 2–3.

Figueroa, R., Fradd, S. H., & Correa, V. I. (1989). Bilingual special education and this issue. *Exceptional Children, 56,* 174–178.

Finders, M. J., & Hynds, S. (2007). *Language arts and literacy in the middle grades: Planning, teaching, and assessing learning.* Upper Saddle River, NJ: Pearson.

Fisher, D., & Frey, N. (2012, Winter/Spring). Accommodations & modifications with learning in mind. *The Special EDge, 25*(2), 8–10.

Fisher, M. (2005). From the coffee house to the schoolhouse: The promise and potential of spoken word poetry in school contexts. *English Education, 37,* 115–131.

Fitzgerald, J. (1999). What is this thing called "balance"? *Reading Teacher, 53*(2), 100–107.

Fitzgerald, J., & Amendum, S. (2007). What is sound writing instruction for multilingual learners? InS. Graham, C. A. MacArthur, & J. Fitzgerald (Eds.), *Best practices in writing instruction* (pp. 289–307). New York: Guilford.

Florida Department of Education. (2003). *Inclusion as an instructional model for LEP students*. Retrieved February 10, 2005, from www.firn.edu/doe/omsle/tapinclu.htm.

Flynt, E. S., & Cooter, R. B. (1999). *The English–Español reading inventory for the classroom*. Upper Saddle River, NJ: Merrill Prentice Hall.

Ford, D. Y. (1998). The underrepresentation of minority students in gifted education: Problems and promises in recruitment and retention. *Journal of Special Education, 32*(1), 4–14.

Foucault, M. (1979). *Discipline and punish: The birth of the prison*. New York: Vintage Books.

Foucault, M. (1980). *Power/knowledge: Selected interviews and other writings 1971–1977*. New York: Pantheon Books.

Frank, A. (1997). *The diary of Anne Frank* (O. Frank and M. Pressler, Eds.; S. Massotty, Trans.). New York: Bantam.

Fránquiz, M. E., Salazar, M. del C., & DeNicolo, C. P. (2011). Challenging majoritarian tales: Portraits of bilingual teachers deconstructing deficit views of bilingual learners. *Bilingual Research Journal, 34*(3), 279–300.

Fredericks-Malone, C., & Gadbois, N. J. (2005/2006). Assessment, emotional scaffolding, and technology: Powerful allies in the K-12 world language classroom. *The NECTFL Review, 57*, 20–29.

Freeman, R. (2004). *Building on community bilingualism*. Philadelphia: Caslon.

Freeman, Y., & Freeman, D. (1998). *ESL/EFL teaching: Principles for success*. Portsmouth, NH: Heinemann.

Freire, P. (1985). *The politics of education* (D. Macedo, Trans.). New York: Bergin and Garvey.

Freire, P., & Macedo, D. (1987). *Literacy: Reading the word and the world*. South Hadley, MA: Bergin and Garvey.

Frey, N., & Fisher, D. (2007). *Reading for information in the elementary school: Content literacy strategies to build comprehension*. Upper Saddle River, NJ: Pearson.

Friend, M., & Bursuck, W. D. (2006). *Including students with special needs: A practical guide for classroom teachers* (4th ed.). Boston: Allyn & Bacon.

Friend, M., & Cook, L. (1996). *Interactions: Collaboration skills for school professionals*. White Plains, NY: Longman.

Friend, M., Hibbard, K. L., & Moutes, M. (2009) *Instructor's resource manual for including students with special needs: A practical guide for classroom teachers* (p. 95). Upper Saddle River, NJ: Pearson.

From the Classroom. (1991). Teachers seek a fair and meaningful assessment process to measure LEP students' progress. *Teacher Designed Learning, 2*(1), 1, 3.

Fromkin, V., Rodman, R., & Hyams, N. (2010). *An introduction to language* (9th ed.). Boston: Cengage.

Fuller, M., & Olson, G. (1998). *Home-school relations: Working successfully with parents and families*. Boston: Allyn & Bacon.

Funaki, I., & Burnett, K. (1993). *When educational systems collide: Teaching and learning with Polynesian students*. Presentation at the annual conference of the Association of Teacher Educators, Los Angeles.

Gaitan, C. D. (2006). *Building culturally responsive classrooms*. Thousand Oaks, CA: Corwin.

Galindo, R. (1997). Language wars: The ideological dimensions of the debates on bilingual education. *Bilingual Research Journal, 21*(2 & 3). Retrieved February 5, 2005, from http://brj.asu.edu/archives/ 23v21/articles/art5.html# issues.

Gándara, P. (1997). *Review of research on instruction of limited English proficient students*. Davis: University of California, Linguistic Minority Research Institute.

Gándara, P. (2010). Overcoming triple segregation: Latino students often face language, cultural, and economic isolation. *Educational Leadership, 68*(3), 60–65.

Gándara, P., Rumberger, R., Maxwell-Jolly, J., & Callahan, R. (2003). English learners in California schools: Unequal resources, unequal outcomes. *Educational Policy Analysis Archives, 11*(36). Online at: www.usc.edu/dept/education/CMMR/FullText/ELLs_in_California_Schools.pdf.

García, E. (2004). The many languages of art. In M. Goldberg (Ed.), *Teaching English language learners through the arts: A SUAVE experience* (pp. 43–54). Boston: Pearson.

García, E. E., & Jensen, B. (2007). Helping young Hispanic learners. *Educational Leadership, 64*(6), 34–39.

García, H. S. (2012). Hispanic-serving institutions and the struggle for cognitive justice. *Journal of Latinos and Education, 11*(3), 195–200.

García, S. B., & Ortiz, A. A. (2004). *Preventing disproportionate representation: Culturally and linguistically responsive prereferral interventions.* National Center for Culturally Responsive Educational Systems. Retrieved January 25, 2005, from www.nccrest.org/publications.html.

Gardner, H. (1983). *Frames of mind: The theory of multiple intelligences.* New York: Basic Books.

Gardner, R., & Lambert, W. (1972). *Attitudes and motivation in second language learning.* Rowley, MA: Newbury House.

Gass, S., & Selinker, L. (2001). *Second language acquisition.* Mahwah, NJ: Erlbaum.

Gately, S. E., & Gately, F. J., Jr. (2001). Understanding coteaching components. *Teaching Exceptional Children, 33*(4), 40–47.

Gay, G. (1975, October). Cultural differences important in education of black children. *Momentum,* 30–32.

Genesee, F. (Ed.). (1999). *Program alternatives for linguistically diverse students.* Santa Cruz, CA: Center for Research on Education,

Diversity and Excellence. Retrieved April 8, 2005, from www.cal.org/crede/pubs/edpractice/Epr1.pdf.

Gibson, M. (1991). Minorities and schooling: Some implications. In M. Gibson & J. Ogbu (Eds.), *Minority status and schooling. A comparative study of immigrant and involuntary minorities* (pp. 357–381). New York: Garland.

Gilbert, J. B. (2006). *Clear speech: Pronunciation and listening comprehension in North American English.* New York: Cambridge University Press.

Gillen, J. (2003). *The language of children.* London and New York: Routledge.

Gillett, P. (1989a). *Cambodian refugees: An introduction to their history and culture.* Available from New Faces of Liberty/SFSC, P.O. Box 5646, San Francisco, CA 94101.

Gillett, P. (1989b). *El Salvador: A country in crisis.* Available from New Faces of Liberty/SFSC, P.O. Box 5646, San Francisco, CA 94101.

Giroux, H. (1983). Theories of reproduction and resistance in the new sociology of education: A critical appraisal. *Harvard Educational Review, 53,* 257–293.

Giroux, H., & McLaren, P. (1996). Teacher education and the politics of engagement: The case for democratic schooling. *Harvard Educational Review, 56*(3), 213–238.

Goals 2000: Educate America Act Pub. L. No. (103–227), (1994).

Goldenberg, C., & Coleman, R. (2010). *Promoting academic achievement among English learners: A guide to the research.* Thousand Oaks, CA: Corwin.

Goleman, D. (1995). *Emotional intelligence.* New York: Scientific American.

Gollnick, D. M., & Chinn, P. C. (2006). *Multicultural education in a pluralistic society* (7th ed.). Upper Saddle River, NJ: Merrill Prentice Hall.

Gómez v. Illinois State Board of Education, 811 F. 2d 1030 (7th Cir. 1987).

González, N. E., Moll, L., & Amanti, C. (Eds.). (2005). *Funds of knowledge: Theorizing practices in households, communities, and classrooms.* Mahwah, NJ: Erlbaum.

González, V. (1994). Bilingual special voices. *NABE News, 17*(6), 19–22.

Good, T., & Brophy, J. (1984). *Looking in classrooms* (3rd ed.). New York: Harper & Row.

Goodwin, S. P. (2010). Facing autism: A growing challenge for our school system. *California Educator, 15*(3), 8–14.

Gopaul-McNicol, S., & Thomas-Presswood, T. (1998). *Working with linguistically and culturally different children.* Boston: Allyn & Bacon.

Gorman, A., & Pierson, D. (2007, September 13). Not at home with English. *Los Angeles Times,* A1, A17.

Gottlieb, M. (1995). Nurturing student learning through portfolios. *TESOL Journal, 5*(1), 12–14.

Gottlieb, M. (2006). *Assessing English language learners.* Thousand Oaks, CA: Corwin.

Gottlieb, M. (2007). *Teacher's manual for Rigby ELL assessment kit.* Orlando, FL: Harcourt Achieve.

Gottlieb, M. (Prin. Writer). (n.d.). *The language proficiency handbook.* Illinois State Board of Education. Retrieved January 7, 2005, from www.isbe.net/assessment/PDF/lang_pro.pdf.

Graham, C. (1978). *Jazz chants.* New York: Oxford University Press.

Graham, C. (1992). *Singing, chanting, telling tales.* Englewood Cliffs, NJ: Regents/Prentice Hall.

Gramsci, A. (1971). *Selections from the prison notebooks of Antonio Gramsci* (Q. Hoare & G. N. Smith, Trans. and Eds.). New York: International Publishers.

Grant, C. A., & Sleeter, C. (1986). *After the school bell rings.* Philadelphia: Falmer Press.

Greaver, M., & Hedberg, K. (2001). Daily reading interventions to help targeted ESL and non-ESL students. Retrieved September 17, 2004, from www.fcps.k12.va.us/DeerParkES/TR/reading/reading.htm.

Green, A. (2007, March 12). This class is learning to its own beat. *Los Angeles Times,* B3.

Gregory, G. H., & Kuzmich, L. (2005). *Differentiated literacy strategies for student growth and achievement in grades 7–12.* Thousand Oaks, CA: Corwin.

Grenoble, L. A., & Whaley, L. J. (1998). *Endangered languages: Current issues and future prospects.* Cambridge, UK: Cambridge University Press.

Griffin, J., & Morgan, L. (1998). Physical education—WRITE ON! *Strategies, 11*(4), 34–37.

Gunning, T. G. (2005). *Creating literacy: Instruction for all students* (5th ed.). Boston: Allyn & Bacon.

Guth, N. (2002). Community Literacy Day: A new school develops community support. *The Reading Teacher, 56*(8), 234–235.

Gutierrez, K. (1994). How talk, context, and script shape contexts for learning: A cross-case comparison of journal sharing. *Linguistics and Education, 5,* 335–365.

Hadaway, N. L., Vardell, S. M., & Young, T. A. (2002). *Literature-based instruction with English language learners, K–12.* Boston: Allyn & Bacon.

Hakuta, K. (1986). *Mirror of language.* New York: Basic Books.

Hakuta, K., Butler, Y. G., & Witt, D. (2000). *How long does it take English learners to attain proficiency?* Santa Barbara: University of California Linguistic Minority Research Institute Policy Report 2000–2001.

Hall, E. (1959). *The silent language.* New York: Anchor Books.

Halliday, M. (1975). *Learning how to mean: Explorations in the development of language.* London: Edward Arnold.

Halliday, M. (1978). *Language as a social semiotic.* Baltimore: University Park Press.

Hamayan, E. (1994). Language development of low-literacy students. In F. Genesee (Ed.), *Educating second language children* (pp. 278–300). Cambridge, UK: Cambridge University Press.

Hammond, J. (2006). The potential of peer scaffolding for ESL students in the mainstream class. In P. McKay (Ed.), *Planning and teaching creatively within a required curriculum* (pp. 149–170). Alexandria, VA: Teachers of English to Speakers of Other Languages.

Han, Z. (2004). *Fossilization in adult second language acquisition.* Clevedon, Eng.: Multilingual Matters.

Hankes, J. E., & Fast, G. R. (Eds.). (2002). *Changing the face of mathematics: Perspectives on indigenous people of North America.* Reston, VA: National Council of Teachers of Mathematics.

Hansen, J. W. (2000). Parables of technological literacy. *Journal of Engineering Technology, 17*(2), 29–31.

Hanson-Smith, E. (1997). *Technology in the classroom: Practice and promise in the 21st century.* Alexandria, VA: Teachers of English to Speakers of Other Languages.

Hardt, U. (1992, Spring). Teaching multicultural understanding. *Oregon English Journal, 13*(1), 3–5.

Harper, C., & De Jong, E. (2004). Misconceptions about teaching English-language learners. *Journal of Adolescent & Adult Literacy, 48*(2), 162–182.

Harris, P. (2006). Teaching English language learners. *The Council Chronicle* (NCTE) *16*(1), 1, 5–7.

Harris, V. (1997). *Teaching multicultural literature in grades K–8.* Norwood, MA: Christopher-Gordon.

Hart, L. (1975). *How the brain works: A new understanding of human learning, emotion, and thinking.* New York: Basic Books.

Hart, L. (1983). *Human brain, human learning.* New York: Longman.

Hayasaki, E. (2004, December 3). Cultural divide on campus. *Los Angeles Times*, A1, A36–A37.

Haycock, K. (2001). Closing the achievement gap. *Educational Leadership, 58*(6), 6–11.

Hayes, C. (1998). *Literacy con cariño: A story of migrant children's success.* Portsmouth, NH: Heinemann.

Haynes, J. (2004, Winter). What effective classroom teachers do. *Essential Teacher, 1*(5), 6–7.

Heath, S. (1983a). Language policies. *Society, 20*(4), 56–63.

Heath, S. (1983b). *Ways with words.* Cambridge, UK: Cambridge University Press.

Heide, F., & Gilliland, J. (1990). *The day of Ahmed's secret.* New York: Lothrop, Lee, & Shepard.

Helfand, D. (2005, March 24). Nearly half of Blacks, Latinos drop out, school study shows. *Los Angeles Times*, A1, A26.

Henderson, D., & May, J. (2005). *Exploring culturally diverse literature for children and adolescents.* Boston: Pearson.

Henwood, D. (1997). Trash-o-nomics. In M. Wray, M. Newitz, & A. Newitz, (Eds.), *White trash: Race and class in America* (pp. 177–191). New York: Routledge.

Herczog, M. M. (2010). Using the NCSS National Curriculum Standards for Social Studies: A Framework for Teaching, Learning, and Assessment to meet state social studies standards. *Social Education, 74*(4), 217–222.

Hernández, B. (2005, January 12). Numerical grades help schools to measure progress. *Los Angeles Times*, B2.

Hernández, J. C. (2009, October 20). A moo-moo here, and better test scores later. *New York Times*, A1, A25).

Hernandez, H. (2001). *Multicultural education: A teacher's guide to linking context, process, and content* (2nd ed.). Upper Saddle River, NJ: Merrill Prentice Hall.

Herrell, A. (2000). *Fifty strategies for teaching English language learners.* Upper Saddle River, NJ: Merrill.

Herrera, S. G., Murry, K. G., & Cabral, R. M. (2007). *Assessment accommodations for classroom teachers of culturally and linguistically diverse students.* Boston: Pearson.

Hibbard, K. L., & Moutes, M. (2006). *Instructor's resource manual and test bank for Friend and Bursack's* Including students with special needs. Boston: Allyn & Bacon.

Hibbing, A. N., & Rankin-Erickson, J. L. (2003). A picture is worth a thousand words: Using visual images to improve comprehension for middle school struggling readers. *The Reading Teacher, 56*(8), 758–770.

Higgins, D. (2011). The unspoken language: Helping students overcome "wooden" patterns of speaking. *CATESOL News, 43*(1), 12.

Hinton, L., & Hale, K. (Eds.). (2001). *The green book of language revitalization in practice*. Burlington, MA: Elsevier.

Hispanic Concerns Study Committee. (1987). *Hispanic concerns study committee report*. Available from National Education Association, 1201 Sixteenth Street NW, Washington, DC 20036.

Hispanic Dropout Project. (1998). *No more excuses: The final report of the Hispanic Dropout Project*. Washington, DC: U.S. Department of Education, Office of the Under Secretary. Online at http://www.wcer.wisc.edu/archive/ccvi/pub/manuscript/Secada-No_More_Excuses.pdf.

Honig, B., Diamond, L., & Gutlohn, L. (2008). *Teaching reading sourcebook*. Novato, CA: Arena Press and Berkeley, CA: Consortium on Reading Excellence.

Howard, G. R. (2007). As diversity grows, so must we. *Educational Leadership, 64*(6), 16–22.

Hruska-Riechmann, S., & Grasha, A. F. (1982). The Grasha-Riechmann Student Learning Scales: Research findings and applications. In J. Keefe (Ed.), *Student learning styles and brain behavior* (pp. 81–86). Reston, VA: National Association of Secondary School Principals.

Hughes, J. (2004). Personal communication.

H.S. 555 Newcomers High School: Academy for new Americans. Online at http://insideschools.org/high/browse/school/1265.

Hunter, J. (1997). Multiple perceptions: Social identity in a multilingual elementary classroom. *TESOL Quarterly, 31*(3), 349–369.

Hymes, D. (1961). The ethnography of speaking. In T. Gladwin & W. Sturtevant (Eds.), *Anthropology and human behavior* (pp. 13–53). Washington, DC: Anthropological Society of Washington.

Idaho Migrant Council v. Board of Education, 647 F. 2d 69 (9th Cir. 1981).

Improving America's Schools Act (IASA). 1994 (P.L. 103-382).

Institute for Education in Transformation. (1992). *Voices from the inside: A report on schooling from inside the classroom*. Available from the Institute for Education in Transformation, Claremont Graduate School, 121 East Tenth St., Claremont, CA 91711-6160.

Intercultural Communication Institute. (2013). The *Intercultural Effectiveness Scale (IES)*. Online at www.intercultural.org/kozai.php.

Ishii, S., & Bruneau, T. (1991). Silence and silences in cross-cultural perspective: Japan and the United States. In L. Samovar & R. Porter (Eds.), *Intercultural communication: A reader* (6th ed., pp. 314–319). Belmont, CA: Wadsworth.

Jacobs, V., Goldberg, M., & Bennett, T. (2004). Experiencing science through the arts. In M. Goldberg (Ed.), *Teaching English language learners through the arts: A SUAVE experience* (pp. 87–98). Boston: Pearson.

Jenks, C., Lee, J. O., & Kanpol, B. (2002). Approaches to multicultural education in preservice teacher education: Philosophical frameworks and models for teaching. In F. Schultz (Ed.), *Annual editions: Multicultural education 2002–2003* (pp. 20–28). Guilford, CT: McGraw-Hill/Dushkin.

Jensen, E. (1998). *Teaching with the brain in mind*. Alexandria, VA: Association for Supervision and Curriculum Development.

Jesness, J. (2004). *Teaching English language learners K–12*. Thousand Oaks, CA: Corwin.

Jewell, M. (1976). Formal institutional studies and language. In W. O'Barr & J. O'Barr (Eds.), *Language and politics* (pp. 421–429). The Hague, Netherlands: Mouton.

Jitendra, A. K., & Rohena-Diaz, E. (1996). Language assessment of students who are linguistically diverse: Why a discrete approach is not the answer. *School Psychology Review, 25*(1), 40–56.

Johnson, D. W., & Johnson, R. T. (1979). Conflict in the classroom: Controversy and learning. *Review of Educational Research, 49*(1), 51–70.

Johnson, D. W., & Johnson, R. T. (1987). *Learning together and alone*. Englewood Cliffs, NJ: Prentice Hall.

Johnson, D. W., & Johnson, R. T. (1994). Constructive conflict in the schools. *Journal of Social Issues, 50*(1), 117–137.

Johnson, D. W., & Johnson, R. T. (1995). Why violence prevention programs don't work—and what does. *Educational Leadership, 52*(5), 63–68.

Johnson, D. W., Johnson, R. T., Dudley, B., & Acikgoz, K. (1994). Effects of conflict resolution training on elementary school students. *Journal of Social Psychology, 134*(6), 803–817.

Jonassen, D. H. (2006). *Modeling with technology: Mindtools for conceptual change* (3rd ed.). Upper Saddle River, NJ: Pearson/Merrill/Prentice Hall.

Jones, J. (1981). The concept of racism and its changing reality. In B. Bowser & R. Hunt (Eds.), *Impacts of racism on white Americans* (pp. 27–49). Beverly Hills, CA: Sage.

Jones-Correa, M. (2012). *Contested ground: Immigration in the United States.* Washington, DC: Migration Policy Institute.

Julian, L. (2007, October 28). TAKS: Bar set so low, it hurts kids. *Houston Chronicle,* E1, E4.

Jussim, L. (1986). Self-fulfilling prophecies: A theoretical and integrative review. *Psychological Review, 93*(4), 429–445.

Kagan, S. (2007). *Differentiated instruction* (smart card). San Clemente, CA: Kagan Publishing.

Kamberelis, G., & de la Luna, L. (2004). Children's writing: How textual forms, contextual forces, and textual politics co-emerge. In C. Bazerman & P. Prior (Eds.), *What writing does and how it does it* (pp. 239–277). Mahwah, NJ: Erlbaum.

Kandel, W., & Cromartie, J. (2004). *New patterns of Hispanic settlement in rural America.* Retrieved January 16, 2005, from www.ers.usda.gov/publications/rdrr99.

Kang, H-W., Kuehn, P., & Herrell, A. (1996). The Hmong literacy project: Parents working to preserve the past and ensure the future. *The Journal of Educational Issues of Language Minority Students, 16.* Online at http://www.ncela.gwu.edu/files/rcd/BE020629/JEILMS_Summer_1996_Volume162.pdf.

Karchmer-Klein, R. (2007). Best practices in using the Internet to support writing. In S. Graham, C. A. MacArthur, & J. Fitzgerald (Eds.), *Best practices in writing instruction* (pp. 222–241). New York: Guilford.

Kaufman, P., Alt, M. N., & Chapman, C. D. (2004). *Dropout rates in the United States: 2001.* Washington, DC: National Center for Education Statistics.

Kea, C., Campbell-Whatley, G. D., & Richards, H. V. (2004). *Becoming culturally responsive educators: Rethinking teacher education pedagogy.* National Center for Culturally Responsive Educational Systems. Retrieved January 29, 2005, from www.nccrest.org/publications.html.

Keefe, M. W. (1987). *Learning style theory and practice.* Reston, VA: National Association of Secondary School Principals.

Kennett. D. (2008). *Pharaoh: Life and afterlife of a god.* New York: Walker & Co.

Keyes v. School District Number One, Denver, Colorado, 576 F. Supp. 1503 (D. Colo. 1983).

Kim, E. Y. (2001). *The yin and yang of American culture.* Yarmouth, ME: Intercultural Press.

Kleinfeld, J. (1988, June). Letter to the editor. *Harvard Education Letter, 4*(3).

Klentschy, M. (2005). Science notebook essentials. *Science and Children, 43*(3). 24–27.

Knobel, M., & Lankshear, C. (2006). Profiles and perspective: Discussing new literacies. *Language Arts, 84*(1), 78–86.

Kohn, A. (2007, June 1). Too destructive to salvage. *USA Today,* 7A.

Kosciw, J. G., Greytak, E. A., Díaz, E. M., & Bartkiewicz, M. J. (2010). *The 2009 National School Climate Survey: The experiences of lesbian, gay, bisexual and transgender youth in our nation's schools.* New York: Gay, Lesbian and Straight Education Network.

Krashen, S. (1981). Bilingual education and second language acquisition theory. In C. F. Leyba (Ed.), *Schooling and language minority students: A theoretical framework* (pp. 51–79).

Los Angeles: Evaluation, Dissemination and Assessment Center, California State University, Los Angeles.

Krashen, S. (1982). *Principles and practice in second language acquisition.* Oxford, UK: Pergamon.

Krashen, S. (1985). *The input hypothesis: Issues and implications.* New York: Longman.

Krashen, S., & Terrell, T. (1983). *The natural approach: Language acquisition in the classroom.* Oxford: Pergamon.

Kress, G. R., & Van Leeuwen, T. (1995). Reading images: The grammar of visual design. London: Routledge.

Kress, J. (1993). *The ESL teacher's book of lists.* West Nyack, NY: Center for Applied Research in Education.

Labbe, J. R. (2007, September 1). Losing literacy. *The [Riverside, CA] Press-Enterprise*, B11.

Labov, W. (1972). *Sociolinguistic patterns.* Philadelphia: University of Pennsylvania Press.

Lambert, W. (1984). An overview of issues in immersion education. In California Department of Education, *Studies on immersion education* (pp. 8–30). Sacramento: California Department of Education.

Lapkoff, S., & Li, R. M. (2007). Five trends for schools. *Educational Leadership, 64*(6), 8–15.

Laturnau, J. (2001). Standards-based instruction for English language learners. Retrieved April 9, 2005, from www.prel.org/products/pc_standards-based.htm.

Lau v. Nichols. (1974). 414 U.S. 563.

Lee, H. (1960). *To kill a mockingbird.* New York: Lippincott.

Lee, J. (2000). Success for all? *American Language Review, 4*(2), 22, 24.

Leff, L. (2012, May 10). State wants waiver on "No Child" penalties. *Associated Press.* Online at www.chron.com/news/article/California-to-apply-for-waiver-to-US-education-law-3550002.php.

Lemberger, N. (1999). Factors affecting language development from the perspectives of four bilingual teachers. In I. Heath & C. Serrano (Eds.), *Annual editions: Teaching English as a second language* (2nd ed., pp. 30–37). Guilford, CT: Dushkin/McGraw-Hill.

Lenneberg, E. (1967). *Biological foundations of language.* New York: Wiley.

Lessow-Hurley, J. (2009). *The foundations of dual language instruction* (5th ed.). Boston: Allyn & Bacon.

Lewis, B. (1998). *The kid's guide to social action: How to solve the social problems you choose—and turn creative thinking into positive action.* Minneapolis, MN: Free Spirit Publishing.

Lin, S. (2002). *Remembering the contributions and sacrifices Chinese Americans have made to America: A time to give back.* Retrieved October 27, 2007, from www.scanews.com/spot/2002/august/s623/memory/ca.html.

Lindholm, K. (1992). Two-way bilingual/immersion education: Theory, conceptual issues and pedagogical implications. In R. Padilla & A. Benavides (Eds.), *Critical perspectives in bilingual education research* (pp. 195–220). Tucson, AZ: Bilingual Review/Press.

Litowitz, B. (1997). Just say no: Responsibility and resistance. In M. Cole, Y. Engeström, & O. Vasquez (Eds.), *Mind, culture, and activity* (pp. 473–484). New York: Cambridge University Press.

Lockwood, A. T. (2000). *Transforming education for Hispanic youth: Broad recommendations for teachers and program staff.* Washington, DC: National Clearinghouse for Bilingual Education, 4. Online at http://www.infoxnet.org/myweb_edu/clase/resources/hispanic%20dropout%20issue%20brief1.pdf.

Lockwood, A. T., & Secada, W. G. (1991). *Transforming education for Hispanic youth: Exemplary practices, programs, and schools.* Accessed July 12, 2008, from http://citeseer.ist.psu.edu/lockwood99 transforming.html.

Loewen, J. (1995). *Lies my teacher told me.* New York: Touchstone.

Loop, C., & Barron, V. (2002). *Which states have statewide ELD standards and language proficiency assessments?* Retrieved March 22, 2005, from www.ncela.gwu.edu/expert/faq/eldstandardsdraft.htm.

López, E. C. (2002). *Tips for the use of interpreters in the assessment of English language learners.* Retrieved February 14, 2005, from http://66.102.7.104/search?q=cache:8COtfXfYi-IJ: www.nasponline.org/culturalcompetence/recommend.pdf+working+with+an+interpreter&hl=en.

Los Angeles Times. (2008). Letters. January 6, p. M2.

Lucas, T., & Wagner, S. (1999). Facilitating secondary English language learners' transition into the mainstream. *TESOL Journal, 8*(4), 6–13.

Luthar, S. S., & Zelazo, L. B. (2003). Research on resilience: An integrative view. In S. S. Luthar (Ed.), *Resilience and vulnerability: Adaptation in the context of childhood adversities* (pp. 510–549). New York: Cambridge University Press.

Lyons, C. A., & Clay, M. M. (2003). *Teaching struggling readers: How to use brain-based research to maximize learning.* Portsmouth, NH: Heinemann.

Maceri, D. (2007). America's languages: Tower of Babel or asset? *Language Magazine, 6*(8), 15. Available at: www.languagemagazine.com.

Maciejewski, T. (2003). *Pragmatics.* Retrieved August 31, 2004, from www.lisle.dupage.k12.il.us/maciejewski/social.htm.

Macmillan, D. L., & Reschly, D. J. (1998). Overrepresentation of minority students: The case for greater specificity or reconsideration of the variables examined. *Journal of Special Education, 32*(1), 15–24.

Majors, P. (n.d.). *Charleston County School District, Charleston, SC, sample standards-based lesson plan.* Retrieved September 29, 2004, from www.cal.org/eslstandards/Charleston.html.

Malavé, L. (1991). Conceptual framework to design a programme intervention for culturally and linguistically different handicapped students. In L. Malavé & G. Duquette (Eds.), *Language, culture and cognition* (pp. 176–189). Clevedon, Eng.: Multilingual Matters.

Malkina, N. (1996). Fun with storytelling. In V. Whiteson (Ed.), *New ways of using drama and literature in language teaching* (pp. 41–42). Alexandria, VA: Teachers of English to Speakers of Other Languages.

Mandlebaum, L. H., & Wilson, R. (1989). Teaching listening skills in the special education classroom. *Academic Therapy, 24,* 451–452.

Manning, M. L. (2002). Understanding diversity, accepting others: Realities and directions. In F. Schultz (Ed.), *Annual editions: Multicultural education 2002/2003* (pp. 206–208). Guilford, CT: McGraw-Hill/Dushkin.

March, T. (2007). The new WWW: Whatever, whenever, wherever. In F. Schultz (Ed.), *Annual editions 10/08: Education* (pp. 213–216). Dubuque, IA: McGraw-Hill Contemporary Learning Series.

Marinova-Todd, S., Marshall, D., & Snow, C. (2000). Three misconceptions about age and L2 learning. *TESOL Quarterly, 34*(1), 9–34.

Marshall, C., & Oliva, M. (2006). *Leadership for social justice: Making revolutions in education.* Boston: Pearson.

Martin, B., & Ringham, F. (2006). *Key terms in semiotics.* London: Continuum.

Martin, D. (2011). The safe zone. *California Educator, 15*(6), 9–13.

Martínez, E. (2010). *500 years of Chicana women's history (500 años de la mujer Chicana)* (5th ed.). New Brunswick, NJ: Rutgers University Press.

Martínez, M. (2013). Personal communication.

Matheson, K. (2009). School's racial tension boils over into fights. Online at http://www.accessmylibrary.com/article-1G1-213640674/us-school-racial-tensions.html.

McCabe, K., & Meissner, D. (2010). *Immigration and the United States: Recession affects flows, prospects for reform.* Washington, DC: Migration Policy Institute.

McCarty, T. L. (2005). Tending the language garden-Lessons from native America. *English Language Learner,* September/October, 10-13, 17.

McClintock, M. (2000). How to interrupt oppressive behavior. In M. Adams, W. J. Blumenfeld,

R. Casteñeda, H. W. Hackman, M. L. Peters, & X. Zúñiga, *Readings for diversity and social justice* (pp. 483–485). New York and London: Routledge.

McGovern, A. (1969). *If you sailed on the Mayflower in 1620.* New York: Scholastic.

McIntosh, P. (1996). White privilege and male privilege: A personal account of coming to see correspondences through work in women's studies. In M. Anderson & P. Collins (Eds.), *Race, class, and gender: An anthology* (2nd ed., pp. 76–87). Belmont, CA: Wadsworth.

McKay, J. (2000). Building self-esteem in children. In M. McKay & P. Fanning, *Self-esteem* (3rd ed., pp. 279–313). New York: Barnes and Noble Books.

McKay, S., & Wong, S. (1996). Multiple discourses, multiple identities: Investment and agency in a second-language learning among Chinese adolescent immigrant students. *Harvard Educational Review, 66*(3), 577–609.

McKeon, D. (1994). When meeting common standards is uncommonly difficult. *Educational Leadership, 51*(8), 45–49.

McLeod, B. (1996). *School reform and student diversity: Exemplary schooling for language minority students.* Online at http://www.eric .ed.gov/ERICWebPortal/search/detailmini .jsp?_nfpb=true&_&ERICExtSearch_Search Value_0=ED392268&ERICExtSearch_Search Type_0=no&accno=ED392268.

McShay, J. C. (2010). Digital stories for critical multicultural education. In S. May & C. E. Sleeter (Eds.), *Critical multiculturalism: Theory and praxis.* New York and London: Routledge.

McVey, D. C. (2007). Helping ESL students improve their grammar. *ESL Magazine, 56,* 16–18.

Mehan, H., Hubbard, L., Lintz, A., & Villanueva, I. (1994). *Tracking untracking: The consequences of placing low-track students in high-track classes.* Online at http://escholarship. org/uc/item/7cq7475x.

Mercer, N. (2000). *Words and minds: How we use language to think together and get things done.* London: Routledge.

Merino, B. (2007). Identifying critical competencies for teachers of English learners. *University of California Linguistic Minority Research Institute (LMRI) Newsletter, 16*(4), 1–7.

Mermelstein, L. (2006). *Reading/writing connections in the K–2 classroom.* Boston: Pearson.

Meyer v. Nebraska, 262 U.S. 390 (1923).

Milambiling, J. (2002). Good neighbors: Mainstreaming ESL students in the rural Midwest. In E. P. Cochran, *Mainstreaming* (pp. 21–30). Alexandria, VA: Teachers of English to Speakers of Other Languages.

Miller, G. (1985). Nonverbal communication. In V. Clark, P. Eschholz, & A. Rosa (Eds.), *Language: Introductory readings* (4th ed., pp. 633–641). New York: St. Martin's Press.

Miller, W. H. (1995). *Alternative assessment techniques for reading and writing.* West Nyack, NY: Center for Applied Research in Education.

Mills, S. C. (2006). *Using the Internet for active teaching and learning.* Upper Saddle River, NJ: Pearson/ Merrill/Prentice Hall.

Mintz, E., & Yun, J. T. (1999). *The complex world of teaching: Perspectives from theory and practice.* Cambridge, MA: Harvard Educational Review.

Molina, R. (2000). Building equitable two-way programs. In N. Cloud, F. Genesee, & E. Hamayan (Eds.), *Dual language instruction* (pp. 11–12). Boston: Heinle and Heinle.

Moore, L. (2013). Personal communication.

Moore, M. S., & Panara, R. F. (1996). *Great deaf Americans* (2nd ed.). New York: DeafLife Press.

Moorman, C., & Haller, T. (2011). *A safe and orderly environment.* National Education Association. Online at www.nea.org/tools/a-safe-and-orderly-environment.html.

Moran, R. F. (2004). Undone by law: The uncertain legacy of *Lau v. Nichols. UC-LMRI Newsletter, 13*(4), 1, 3.

Moras, S. (2001). *Teaching vocabulary to advanced students: A lexical approach.* Accessed May 11, 2010, from www3.telus.net/linguisticsissues/teachingvocabulary.html.

Morey, A., & Kilano, M. (1997). *Multicultural course transformation in higher education: A broader truth*. Boston: Allyn & Bacon.

Morley, J. (2001). Aural comprehension instruction: Principles & practices. In M. Celce-Murcia (Ed.), *Teaching English as a second or foreign language* (3rd ed.). Boston: Heinle and Heinle.

National Center in Educational Outcomes (2011). Accommodations for students with disabilities. Online at www.cehd.umn.edu/NCEO/TopicAreas/Accommodations/Accom-topic.htm.

National Center for Educational Statistics (2011). *State education reforms, Table 2.10. State high school exit exams, by exam characteristics and state: 2010–11*. Online at http://nces.ed.gov/programs/statereform/tab2_10.asp.

National Center for Education Statistics (NCES). (2002). *Percentage distribution of enrollment in public elementary and secondary schools, by race/ethnicity and state: Fall 1986 and fall 2000*. Retrieved January 14, 2005, from nces.ed.gov/programs/digest/d02/dt042.asp.

National Center for Education Statistics (NCES). (2003). *Employees in degree-granting institutions, by race/ethnicity, primary occupation, sex, employment status, and control and type of institution: Fall 2001*. Retrieved March 20, 2005, from http://nces.ed.gov/programs/digest/d03/tables/dt228.asp.

National Center for Education Statistics (NCES). (2007). *Status and trends in the education of racial and ethnic minorities*. Retrieved October 24, 2008, from http://nces.ed.gov/pubs2007/minoritytrends/ ind_4_16.asp.

National Center for Educational Statistics (2011). *Table A-6-2. Number and percentage of children ages 5–17 who spoke a language other than English at home and who spoke English with difficulty, by age and selected characteristics*. Online at http://nces.ed.gov/programs/coe/tables/table-lsm-2.asp.

National Clearinghouse for English Language Acquisition (NCELA). (1996). *Ask NCELA #7 What court rulings have impacted the education of language minority students in the U.S.?* Retrieved March 19, 2005, from www.ncela.gwu.edu/expert/askncela/07court.htm.

National Clearinghouse for English Language Acquisition (NCELA). (2002). *Ask NCELA #3 How has federal policy for language minority students evolved in the U.S.?* Retrieved March 19, 2005, from www.ncela.gwu.edu/expert/faq/03history.htm.

National Clearinghouse for English Language Acquisition and Language Instruction Educational Programs (2007). *2005–2008 Poster*. Retrieved July 3, 2008, from http://www.ncela.gwu/stats/2_nation .htm.

National Clearinghouse for English Language Acquisition (NCELA). (2009). The growing numbers of English learner students. Online at www.ncela.gwu.edu/files/uploads/9/growingLEP_0708.pdf.

National Commission on Teaching and America's Future. (1996). *What matters most: Teaching and America's future*. New York: Author.

National Council for the Social Studies (NCSS) (2010). *National Curriculum Standards for Social Studies: A Framework for Teaching, Learning, and Assessment*. Silver Spring, MD: Author.

National Council of Teachers of English (NCTE) & International Reading Association (IRA). (1996). *Standards for the English language arts*. Urbana, IL & Newark, DE: Authors.

National Council of Teachers of Mathematics (NCTM). (2000). *Principles and standards for school mathematics*. Reston, VA: Author.

National Council of Teachers of Mathematics (NCTM). (2007). *Mathematics teaching today: Improving practice, improving student learning* (2nd ed., T. Martin, Ed.). Reston, VA: Author.

National Research Council. (1996). *The national science education standards*. Washington, DC: National Academy Press.

Navarrete, C., & Gustke, C. (1996). *A guide to performance assessment for linguistically diverse students*. Online at http://www.ncela

.gwu.edu/files/rcd/BE020484/A_Guide_to_ Performance_Assessment.pdf.

Nelson, B. (1996). *Learning English: How school reform fosters language acquisition and development for limited English proficient elementary school students.* Online at http://escholarship.org/uc/item/1tq5q2p3.

Nelson, C. (2004). Reclaiming teacher preparation for success in high-needs schools. *Education, 124*(3), 475–480.

Nelson-Barber, S. (1999). A better education for every child: The dilemma for teachers of culturally and linguistically diverse students. In Mid-continent Research for Education and Learning (McREL) (Ed.), *Including culturally and linguistically diverse students in standards-based reform: A report on McREL's Diversity Roundtable I* (pp. 3–22). Retrieved April 8, 2005, from www.mcrel.org/PDFConversion/Diversity/rt1chapter2.htm.

Newman, C. M. (2006). *Strategies for test-taking success: Reading.* Boston: Thompson Heinle.

Nguyen, V. (2013). Personal communication.

Nichols, S. L. (1999). Gay, lesbian, and bisexual youth: Understanding diversity and promoting tolerance in schools. *The Elementary School Journal, 99*(5), 505–519.

Niehus, M. Personal communication.

Nieto, S., & Bode, P. (2008). *Affirming diversity* (5th ed.). Boston: Allyn & Bacon.

Nilsen, A. P., & Donelson, K. E. (2009). *Literature for today's young adults* (8th ed.). Boston: Pearson.

No Child Left Behind Act of 2001. (2002). Retrieved October 14, 2004, from www.ed.gov/policy/elsec/leg/esea02/index.html.

Nolan, J. F., & Hoover, L. A. (2008). *Teacher supervision & evaluation* (2nd ed.). Hoboken, NJ: Wiley.

Nunan, D. (1989). *Designing tasks for the communicative classroom.* Cambridge, UK: Cambridge University Press.

Nunan. D. (2012). Introduction. In L. England (Ed.), *Online language teacher education* (pp. vii–xiv). New York and London: Routledge.

O'Malley, J. M., & Pierce, L. V. (1996). *Authentic assessment for English language learners.* Menlo Park, CA: Addison-Wesley.

Oakes, J. (1985). *Keeping track: How schools structure inequality.* New Haven, CT: Yale University Press.

Oakes, J. (1992). Can tracking research inform practice? Technical, normative, and political considerations. *Educational Researcher, 21*(4), 12–21.

Oakes, J., & Lipton, M. (2007). *Teaching to change the world* (3rd ed.). Boston: McGraw-Hill.

Ogbu, J. (1978). *Minority education and caste: The American system in crosscultural perspective.* New York: Academic Press.

Ogbu, J., & Matute-Bianchi, M. (1986). Understanding sociocultural factors: Knowledge, identity, and school adjustment. In *Beyond language: Social and cultural factors in schooling language minority students* (pp. 73–142). Los Angeles: Evaluation, Dissemination and Assessment Center, California State University, Los Angeles.

Olsen, L. (2010). *Reparable harm: Fulfilling the unkept promise of educational opportunity for California's long-term English learners.* Long Beach, CA: Californians Together.

Olson, S., & Loucks-Horsley, S. (2000). *Inquiry and the national science education standards.* Washington, DC: National Academy Press.

Ong, W. (1982). *Orality and literacy.* London: Methuen.

Open Court Reading series. (2003). New York: McGraw- Hill/SRA.

Orfield, G., & Frankenberg, E. (2008). *The last have become first.* Los Angeles: UCLA Civil Rights Project/Proyecto Derechos Civiles.

Ortiz, A. A. (2002). Prevention of school failure and early intervention for English language learners. In A. J. Artiles & A. A. Ortiz (Eds.), *English language learners with special education needs: Identification, assessment, and instruction* (pp. 31–63). Washington, DC: Center for Applied Linguistics and Delta Systems Co.

Osgood, K. W. (2002). It takes a class to teach a child: The challenge program. In E. P. Cochran, *Mainstreaming* (pp. 43–51). Alexandria, VA: Teachers of English to Speakers of Other Languages.

Ovando, C., & Collier, V. (1998). *Bilingual and ESL classrooms: Teaching in multicultural contexts.* Boston: McGraw-Hill.

Oyama, S. (1976). A sensitive period for the acquisition of nonnative phonological system. *Journal of Psycholinguistic Research, 5,* 261–284.

Padilla, E. (1998). *Hispanic contributions to the United States.* Retrieved January 10, 2005, from http:// members.aol.com/pjchacon/aims/contributions.html.

Pandya, C., McHugh, M., & Batalova, J. (2011). *LEP data brief.* Washington, DC: Migration Policy Institute.

Pappamihiel, N. E. (2002). English as a second language students and English language anxiety: Issues in the mainstream classroom. *Research in the Teaching of English, 36,* 327–355.

Parade Magazine. (2007, October 28). Making a profit off kids, 10.

Paradis, M. (2005). *Neurolinguistics of bilingualism and the teaching of languages.* Retrieved January 23, 2005, from www.semioticon.com/virtuals/talks/paradis_txt.htm.

Parla, J. (1994). Educating teachers for cultural and linguistic diversity: A model for all teachers. *New York State Association for Bilingual Education Journal, 9,* 1–6. Retrieved February 7, 2005, from www.ncela.gwu.edu/pubs/nysabe/vol9/model.htm.

Pasternak, J. (1994, March 29). Bias blights life outside Appalachia. *Los Angeles Times,* A1, A16.

Payan, R. (1984). Language assessment for bilingual exceptional children. In L. Baca & H. Cervantes (Eds.), *The bilingual special education interface* (pp. 125–137). St. Louis, MO: Times Mirror/Mosby.

Pearson, R. (1974). *Introduction to anthropology.* New York: Holt, Rinehart and Winston.

Peceimer, D. (2013). Personal communication.

Pennycook, A. (1994). *The cultural politics of English as an international language.* New York: Longman.

Penrod, D. (2008). Web 2.0, meet Literacy 2.0. *Educational Technology, 48*(1), 50–52.

Peregoy, S., & Boyle, O. (2013). *Reading, writing, and learning in ESL* (6th ed.). Boston: Pearson.

Pérez, B., & Torres-Guzmán, M. (2002). *Learning in two worlds* (3rd ed.). New York: Longman.

Pérez, W. (2012). *Americans by heart: Undocumented Latino students and the promise of higher education.* New York: Teachers College Press.

Philips, S. (1972). Participant structures and communicative competence: Warm Springs children in community and classroom. In C. Cazden, V. John, & D. Hymes (Eds.), *Functions of language in the classroom* (pp. 370–394). New York: Teachers College Press.

Phillips, J. (1978). College of, by, and for Navajo Indians. *Chronicle of Higher Education, 15,* 10–12.

Pierangelo, R., & Giuliani, G. A. (2001). *What every teacher should know about students with special needs.* Champaign, IL: Research Press.

Pinnell, G. S. (1985). Ways to look at the functions of children's language. In A. Jaggar & M. Smith-Burke (Eds.), *Observing the language learner* (pp. 57–72). Newark, DE: International Reading Association.

Piske, T., Mackay, I. R. A., & Fiege, J. E. (2001). Factors affecting degree of foreign accent in an L2: A Review. *Journal of Phonetics, 29*(2), 191-215.

Plyler v. Doe, 457 U.S. 202, 102 S. Ct. 2382 (1982).

Pittaway, D. S. (2004). Investment and second language acquisition. *Critical Inquiry in Language Studies: An International Journal, 1*(4), 203–218.

Ponjuan, L. (2011). Recruiting and retaining Latino faculty members: The missing piece to

Latino student success. *Thought and Action,* 99–110.

Pope, D. (2002). *Doing school: How we are creating a generation of stressed-out, materialistic, and miseducated students.* New Haven, CT: Yale University Press.

Porter, C. (2010). English is not enough. *Chronicle of Higher Education, 56*(32), 64.

Porter, P., & Taylor, B. P. (2003). Experience is the best teacher: Linking the MA pedagogical grammar course with the ESL grammar classroom. In D. Liu & P. Master, *Grammar teaching in teacher education* (pp. 151–164). Alexandria, VA: Teachers of English to Speakers of Other Languages.

Porterfield, K. (2002). *Indian encyclopedia wins Colorado book award.* Retrieved October 27, 2008, from www.kporterfield.com/aicttw/arti cles/award.html.

Posnick-Goodwin, S. (2010/2011). Shining lights. *California Educator, 15*(4), 8–15.

Posnick-Goodwin, S. (2011). Gifted students can shine. *California Educator, 15*(8), 18–23.

Potowski, K. (2007). *Language and identity in a dual immersion school.* Clevedon, UK: Multilingual Matters.

Powell, K. C., & Kalina, C. J. (2009). TESOL and constructivism: Language meaning, culture, and usage. *Essential Teacher, 6*(2), 34–36.

Pransky, K. (2008). *Beneath the surface: The hidden realities of teaching culturally and linguistically diverse young learners, K–6.* Portsmouth, NH: Heinemann.

Prothrow-Smith, D. (1994, April). Building violence prevention into the classroom. *The School Administrator, 8*(12), 8–12.

Pruitt, W. (2000). Using story to compare, conclude, and identify. In B. Agor (Ed.), *Integrating the ESL standards into classroom practice: Grades 9–12* (pp. 31–54). Alexandria, VA: Teachers of English to Speakers of Other Languages.

Pryor, C. B. (2002). New immigrants and refugees in American schools: Multiple voices. In F. Schultz (Ed.), *Annual editions: Multicultural education 2002/2003* (pp. 185–193). Guilford, CT: McGraw-Hill/Dushkin.

Public Schools of North Carolina. (2004). *The North Carolina competency tests: A handbook for students in the ninth grade for the first time in 2001–2002 and beyond.* Raleigh: Author. Online at www.ncpublicschools.org/ accountability/testing/competency.

Purcell, D. (2013). Personal communication.

Purcell, K., Heaps, A., Buchanan, J., Friedrich, L. (2013). How teachers are using technology at home and in their classrooms. Pew Research Center's Internet and American Life Project, online at http://pewinternet.org/Reports/2013/ Teachers-and-technology/Summary-of-Find ings.aspx.

Qualls-Mitchell, P. (2008). Reading enhancement for deaf and hard-of-hearing children through multicultural empowerment. *The Reading Teacher, 56*(1), 76–84.

Quinn, Q. (2007). Motivating reading. *Language Magazine, 6*(10), 24–26.

Quiñones, S. (2008, February 25). A different kind of home schooling. *Los Angeles Times,* B4.

Rahilly, M. K., & Weinmann, A. (2007). *An overview of Title III programs.* Presentation at the annual conference of the Teachers of English to Speakers of Other Languages, Seattle.

Raimes, A. (Ed.). (1996). *Identities: Readings from contemporary culture.* Boston: Houghton Mifflin.

Ramírez, J. (1992, Winter/Spring). Executive summary, final report: Longitudinal study of structured English immersion strategy, earlyexit and late-exit transitional bilingual education programs for language-minority children. *Bilingual Research Journal, 16*(1 & 2), 1–62.

Rance-Rooney, J. (2008). Digital storytelling for language and culture learning. *Essential Teacher, 5*(1), 29–31.

Ray, B., & Seely, C. (1998). *Fluency through TPR storytelling: Achieving real language acquisition in school* (2nd ed.). Berkeley; CA: Command Performance Language Institute.

Reckendorf, K., & Ortiz, F. W. (2000). *English and ESL inclusion model.* Unpublished article. Amherst, MA: Amherst Regional Middle School.

Redish, L. (2001). Native languages of the Americas: Endangered language revitalization and revival.Online at www.native-languages.org/revive.htm.

Reece-Miller, P. C. (2010). An elephant in the classroom: LGBTQ students and the silent minority. In M. C. Fehr & D. E. Fehr (Eds.), *Teach boldly: Letters to teachers about contemporary issues in education* (pp. 67–76). New York: Peter Lang.

Reese, D. (2007). Proceed with caution: Using Native American folktales in the classroom. *Language Arts, 84*(3), 245–256.

Reese, S. (2006). When foreign languages are not seen or heard. *The Language Educator, 1*(2), 32–37.

Reeves, D. B. (2002). *Making standards work.* Denver, CO: Center for Performance Assessment.

Reyhner, J. (2007). Linguicism in America. *NABE News, 30*(1), 12–15.

Richard-Amato, P. (2003). *Making it happen* (3rd ed.). White Plains, NY: Longman.

Richards, H. V., Brown, A. E., & Forde, T. B. (2004). *Addressing diversity in schools: Culturally responsive pedagogy.* National Center for Culturally Responsive Educational Systems. Retrieved January 21, 2005, from www.nccrest.org/publications.html.

Ríos-Aguilar, C., Canche-González, M., & Moll, L. (2010). *A study of Arizona's teachers of English language learners.* Los Angeles: Civil Rights Project/Proyecto Derechos Civiles.

Ríos v. Read. 75 Civ. 296 (U.S. District Ct. Ed. NY, 1977).

Rivera, C. (2008, March 10). Strife and solutions at school conferences. *Los Angeles Times,* B1, B 6.

Roberts, C. (1995, Summer/Fall). Bilingual education program models. *Bilingual Research Journal, 19*(3 & 4), 369–378.

Rodríguez, L. (2013). Personal communication.

Rodríguez, R., Prieto, A., & Rueda, R. (1984). Issues in bilingual/multicultural special education. *Journal of the National Association for Bilingual Education, 8*(3), 55–65.

Rolstad, K., Mahoney, K., & Glass, G. V. (2005). The big picture: A meta-analysis of program effectiveness research on English language learners. *Educational Policy, 19*(4), 572–594.

Rosas, A. (2013). Personal communication.

Rosenblum, M. R., & Brick, K. (2011). *US immigration policy and Mexican/Central American migration flows: Then and now.* Washington, DC: Migration Policy Institute.

Rueda, R. (1987). Social and communicative aspects of language proficiency in low-achieving language minority students. In H. Trueba (Ed.), *Success or failure? Learning and the language minority student* (pp. 185–197). Cambridge, MA: Newbury House.

Ruíz, R. (1984). Orientations in language planning. *NABE Journal, 8*(2), 15–34.

Rumberger, R. W., & Palardy, G. J. (2005). Does segregation still matter? *Teachers College Record, 107*(9), 1999–2045.

Runner, J. (2000). *"I don't understand" in over 230 languages.* Retrieved April 8, 2005, from www.elite.net/~runner/jennifers/understa.htm.

Russakoff, D. (2009, December 23). Starting at home. *Los Angeles Times,* A31.

Russell, M. (2008). Solving the crisis of the male teacher shortage. *Teachers of Color, 3*(1), 12–14.

Ryan, M. (2008). *Ask the teacher: A practitioner's guide to teaching and learning in the diverse classroom.* Boston: Pearson.

Sales, F. (1989). *Ibrahim.* New York: Lippincott.

Salovey, P. & Mayer, J. D. (1990). Emotional intelligence. *Imagination, Cognition, and Personality, 9*(3), 185–211.

Saslow, J., & Ascher, A. (2006). *Top Notch 2 Copy & go.* White Plains, NY: Pearson Longman.

Sasser, L., Naccarato, L., Corren, J., & Tran, Q. (2002). *English language development progress profile.* Alhambra, CA: Alhambra School District.

Sarmiento, L. E. (2008). Dancing with languages. *Teaching Tolerance, 34,* 22–25.

Saunders, W., Foorman, B., & Carlson, C. (2006). Is a separate block of time for oral English language development in programs for English learners needed? *Elementary School Journal, 107*(2), 181–198.

Saunders, W., & Goldenberg, C. (2001). Strengthening the transition in transitional bilingual education. In D. Christian & F. Genesee (Eds.), *Bilingual education* (pp. 41–56). Alexandria, VA: Teachers of English to Speakers of Other Languages.

Schachter, J. (2003). *Migration by race and Hispanic origin: 1995 to 2000.* Retrieved January 16, 2005, from www.census.gov/prod/2003 pubs/censr-13.pdf.

Schifini, A., Short, D., & Tinajero, J. V. (2002). *High points: Teacher's edition.* Carmel, CA: Hampton Brown.

Schildroth, A., & Hotto, S. (1994). Inclusion or exclusion: Deaf students and the inclusion movement. *American Annals of the Deaf, 139,* 239–243.

Schmidt, P. (2008, February 20). Asians, not whites, hurt most by race-conscious admissions. *USA Today,* 13A.

Schmitt, T. L. (2009). Working together: Bringing Muslim students into the ESL classroom. *TESOL Intercultural Communication Interest SectionNewsletter, 7*(3). Online at www.tesol .org/s_tesol/tc/documents/3_2010_schmitt.pdf.

Schneidermann, B. (2003). *Leonardo's laptop: Human needs and the new computing technologies.* Cambridge, MA: MIT Press.

Schumann, J. (1994). Emotion and cognition in second language acquisition. *Studies in Second Language Acquisition, 16,* 231–242.

Scieszka, J., & Smith, L. (1992). *The stinky cheese man and other fairly stupid tales.* New York: Viking Juvenile.

Scollon, R., & Scollon, S. W. (2003). *Discourses in place: Language in the material world.* London: Routledge.

Scribner, S., & Cole, M. (1978). Literacy without schooling: Testing for intellectual effects. *Harvard Educational Review, 48,* 448–461.

Seelye, H. (1984). *Teaching culture.* Lincolnwood, IL: National Textbook Company.

Selinker, L. (1972). Interlanguage. *International Review of Applied Linguistics, 10*(3), 209–231.

Selinker, L. (1991). Along the way: Interlanguage systems in second language acquisition. In L. Malavé & G. Duquette (Eds.), *Language, culture and cognition* (pp. 23–35). Clevedon, UK: Multilingual Matters.

Seng, C. (2005). *Teaching English to blind students.* Retrieved February 2, 2005, from www .teachingenglish.org.uk/think/methodology/ blind.shtml.

Serna v. Portales Municipal Schools, 499 F. 2d 1147 (10th Cir. 1972).

Shade, B., & New, C. (1993). Cultural influences on learning: Teaching implications. In J. Banks & C. Banks (Eds.), *Multicultural education: Issues and perspectives.* Boston: Allyn & Bacon.

Shah, N. (2012). Educating immigrant students a challenge in U.S., elsewhere. *Education Week, 31*(16), n.p. Retrieved from http://www .edweek.org/ew/articles/2012/01/12/16popula tions.h31.html?intc=EWQC12-TOC.

Shah, P. (2009). Motivating participation: The symbolic effects of Latino representation on parent school involvement. *Social Science Quarterly, 90*(1), 212-230.

Shin, H. B., & Ortman, J. M. (2011, April). *Language projections: 2010–2020.* Washington, DC: Presentation, Federal Forecasters Conference.

Short, D. (1998). Secondary newcomer programs: Helping recent immigrants prepare for school success. *ERIC Digest.* Retrieved January 28, 2005, from http://searcheric.org/scripts/ seget2.asp?db=ericft&want=http://searcheric .org/ericdc/ED419385.htm.

Short, D., & Echevarria, J. (1999). The sheltered instruction observation protocol: A tool for teacher-researcher collaboration and professional development. *ERIC Digest.* Retrieved

January 28, 2005, from http://searcheric.org/scripts/seget2 .asp?db=ericft&want=http://searcheric.org/ericdc/ ED436981.htm.

Short, D. J., Vogt, M., & Echevarría, J. (2011). *The SIOP model for teaching science to English learners.* Boston: Pearson.

Shuter, R. (1991). The Hmong of Laos: Orality, communication, and acculturation. In L. Samovar & R. Porter (Eds.), *Intercultural communication: A reader* (6th ed., pp. 270–276). Belmont, CA: Wadsworth.

Siccone, F. (1995). *Celebrating diversity: Building self-esteem in today's multicultural classrooms.* Boston: Allyn & Bacon.

Siegel, J. (1999). Stigmatized and standardized varieties in the classroom: Interference or separation? *TESOL Quarterly, 33*(4), 701–728.

SIL International. (2009). *Ethnologue: Languages of the world.* Online at www.ethnologue.com.

Sindell, P. (1988). Some discontinuities in the enculturation of Mistassini Cree children. In J. Wurzel (Ed.), *Toward multiculturalism.* Yarmouth, ME: Intercultural Press.

Singleton, D., & Ryan, L. (2004). *Language acquisition: The age factor* (2nd ed.). Clevedon, UK: Multilingual Matters.

Siskind Susser. (n.d.). *The ABC's of immigration—grounds for asylum and refuge.* Retrieved January 16, 2005, from www.visalaw.com.

Skinner, B. (1957). *Verbal behavior.* New York: Appleton, Century, Crofts.

Skutnabb-Kangas, T. (1981). Bilingualism or not: The Education of minorities. (L. Malmberg & D. Crane, Trans.) *Multilingual Matters.* Clevedon, UK.

Skutnabb-Kangas, T. (1993, February 3). *Linguistic genocide and bilingual education.* Presentation at the annual conference of the California Association for Bilingual Education, Anaheim.

Skutnabb-Kangas, T. (2000). *Linguistic genocide in education—or worldwide diversity and human rights?* Mahwah, NJ: Erlbaum.

Slater, J. (2000, May 12). *ELD standards.* Presentation at the Linguistic Minority Research Institute Conference, Irvine, CA.

Sleeter, C. E. (1986). Learning disabilities: The social construction of a special education category. *Exceptional Children, 53*(1), 46–54.

Smilkstein, R. (2002). *We're born to learn: Using the brain's natural learning process to create today's curriculum.* Thousand Oaks, CA: Sage.

Smith, S. L., Paige, R. M., & Steglitz, I. (1998). Theoretical foundations of intercultural training and applications to the teaching of culture. In D. L. Lange, C. A. Klee, R. M. Paige, & Y. A. Yershova (Eds.), *Culture as the core: Interdisciplinary perspectives on culture teaching and learning in the language curriculum* (pp. 53–91). Minneapolis, MN: Center for Advanced Research on Language Acquisition, University of Minnesota.

Snow, C., & Hoefnagel-Hoehle, M. (1978). The critical period for language acquisition: Evidence from second language learning. *Child Development, 49,* 1114–1118.

Snow, C., Burns, S., & Griffin, P. (Eds.). (1998). *Preventing reading difficulties in young children.* Washington, DC: National Academy Press.

Snow, D. (1996). *More than a native speaker.* Alexandria, VA: Teachers of English to Speakers of Other Languages.

Solórzano, D. G., & Yosso, T. J. (2002). Critical race methodology: Counter-storytelling as an analytical framework for education research. *Qualitative Inquiry, 8*(1), 23–44.

Sonbuchner, G. M. (1991). *How to take advantage of your learning styles.* Syracuse, NY: New Readers Press.

Spandel, V., & Hicks, J. (2006). *WriteTraits advanced sampler.* Wilmington, MA: Houghton-Mifflin.

Spencer, C. (2013). Personal communication.

Stahl, S. A., Duffy-Hester, A. M., & Stahl, K. (1998). Everything you wanted to know about phonics (but were afraid to ask). *Reading Research Quarterly, 33*(3), 338–355.

Stainback, W., & Stainback, S. (1984). A rationale for the merger of special and regular education. *Exceptional Children, 51*(2), 102–111.

Stevik, A., Stevik, C. D., & Labissiere, Y. (2008). South Florida's immigrant youth and civic engagement: Major engagement: minor differences. *Applied Developmental Science, 12*(2), 57–65.

Strehorn, K. (2001). The application of Universal Instructional Design to ESL teaching. *Internet TESL Journal.* Retrieved January 25, 2005, from http://iteslj.org/Techniques/Strehorn-UID.html.

Suárez-Orozco, M., Suárez-Orozco, C., & Todorova, E. (2008). *Learning a new land: Immigrant students in American society.* Cambridge, MA: Harvard University Press.

Suina, J. (1985). . . . And then I went to school. *New Mexico Journal of Reading, 5*(2). (Reprinted in *Outlook, 59,* 20–26).

Sue, D. W. (2010). *Microaggressions in everyday life: Race, gender, and sexual orientation.* New York: John Wiley & Sons.

Suleiman, M. (Ed.). (1999). *Arabs in America: Building a new future.* Chicago: Kazi.

Sutherland, D. E. (1989). *The expansion of everyday life 1860–1876.* New York: Harper & Row.

Takahashi, E., Austin, T., & Morimoto, Y. (2000). Social interaction and language development in a FLES classroom. In J. K. Hall & L. S. Verplaetse (Eds.), *Second and foreign language learning through classroom interaction* (pp. 139–162). Mahwah, NJ: Erlbaum.

Tateishi, C. A. (2007–2008). Taking a chance with words. *Rethinking Schools, 22*(2), 20–23.

Taylor, D. (2000). Facing hardships: Jamestown and colonial life. In K. Samway (Ed.), *Integrating the ESL standards into classroom practice* (pp. 53–81). Alexandria, VA: Teachers of English to Speakers of Other Languages.

Teachers of English to Speakers of Other Languages (TESOL). (2001). *Scenarios for ESL standards-based assessment.* Alexandria, VA: Author.

Teachers of English to Speakers of Other Languages (TESOL). (2006). *PreK–12 English language proficiency standards in the core content areas.* Alexandria, VA: Author.

Teske, M., & Marcy, P. (2007). *Step up: Listening, speaking, and critical thinking.* Boston: Houghton Mifflin.

Tharp, R. (1989a). Culturally compatible education: A formula for designing effective classrooms. In H. Trueba, G. Spindler, & L. Spindler (Eds.), *What do anthropologists have to say about dropouts?* (pp. 51–66). New York: Falmer Press.

Tharp, R. (1989b, February). Psychocultural variables and constants: Effects on teaching and learning in schools. *American Psychologist, 44*(2), 349–359.

Thomas, W., & Collier, V. (1997). *School effective-ness for language minority students.* Retrieved April 8, 2005, from www.ncela.gwu.edu/pubs/resource/effectiveness/index.htm.

Thompson, S., & Thurlow, M. (2002). Universally designed assessments: Better tests for everyone! *Policy Directions, No. 14.* Minneapolis, MN: National Center on Educational Outcomes.

Thonis, E. (2005). *The English-Spanish connection.* Miami: Santillana.

Tileston, D. W., & Darling, S. K. (2008). Why culture matters. *Teachers of Color, 3*(1), 58, 60.

Tinker Sachs, G., & Ho, B. (2007). *ESL/EFL cases: Contexts for teacher professional discussions.* Hong Kong: City University of Hong Kong Press.

Tollefson, J. W. (1991). *Planning language, planning inequality.* London: Longman.

Tollefson, J. W. (Ed.). (1995). *Power and inequality in language education.* Cambridge, UK: Cambridge University Press.

Tollefson, J. W. (Ed.). (2002). *Language policies in education: Critical issues.* Mahwah, NJ: Erlbaum.

Tompkins, G. (2009). *Literacy for the 21st century: A balanced approach* (5th ed.). Upper Saddle River, NJ: Prentice Hall.

Toohey, K., & Norton, B. (2003). Learner autonomy as agency in sociocultural settings. In D. Palfreyman and R. C. Smith (Eds.), *Learner autonomy across cultures: Language education perspectives* (pp. 58–74). London: Palgrave Macmillan.

Tran, M-T (2008, December 1). Keeping their Vietnamese heritage alive. *Los Angeles Times,* B3.

Triandis, H. C. (1995). *Individualism & collectivism.* Boulder, CO: Westview Press.

Trounson, R. (2012, March 23). Number of Asians in U.S. surges. *Los Angeles Times,* AA2.

Trueba, H. (1989). *Raising silent voices.* Boston: Heinle and Heinle.

Trueba, H., Cheng, L., & Ima, K. (1993). *Myth or reality: Adaptive strategies of Asian Americans in California.* Washington, DC: Falmer Press.

Tunnell, M. O., & Jacobs, J. S. (2000). *Children's literature, briefly* (2nd ed.). Upper Saddle River, NJ: Merrill Prentice Hall.

Ukpokodu, N. (2002). Multiculturalism vs. globalism. In F. Schultz (Ed.), *Annual editions: Multicultural education 2002–2003* (pp. 7–10). Guilford, CT: McGraw-Hill/Dushkin.

U. S. Census Bureau, American Community Survey (ACS). (2011). Selected social characteristics in the United States, http://factfinder2.census.gov/faces/tableservices/jsf/pages/productview.xhtml?pid=ACS_10_1YR_DP02&prodType=table.

U.S. Census Bureau. (2004a). *Educational attainment in the U.S.: 2003.* Retrieved January 12, 2005, from www.census.gov/population/www/socdem/educattn.html.

U.S. Census Bureau. (2004b). *Health insurance data.* Retrieved January 12, 2005, from www.census.gov/hhes/www/hlthins/hlthin03/hlthtables03.html.

U.S. Census Bureau. (2004c). *Poverty tables 2003.* Retrieved January 12, 2005, from www.census.gov/hhes/poverty/poverty03/tables03.html.

U.S. Census Bureau. (2010). *Current population survey.* Unpublished data. Retrieved from www.census.gov/population/www/socdemo/school.html.

U.S. Census Bureau. (2012). *2012 Statistical abstract.* Online at www.census.gov/compendia/statab/cats/education/educational_attainment.html.

U.S. Department of Education (2011). *Winning the future: Improving education for the Latino community.* Washington, DC: Author.

U.S. Department of Education (2012). *Teacher shortage areas nationwide listing 1990–1991 through 2012–2013.* Washington, DC: Author.

U.S. Department of State, Bureau of Consular Affairs. (2004). *Visa Bulletin, 8*(76). Washington, DC: Author. Retrieved January 18, 2005, from http:// travel.state.gov/visa/frvi/bulletin/bulletin_1343.html.

U.S. Government Accounting Office. (2002). *Per-pupil spending differences between selected inner city and suburban schools varied by metropolitan area.* Retrieved January 14, 2005, from www.gao.gov/new.items/d03234.pdf.

U.S. Office for Civil Rights. (1970). *May 25 memorandum.* Retrieved March 19, 2005, from www.ed.gov/about/offices/list/ocr/docs/lau1970.html.

U.S. Office for Civil Rights. (1976). Office for Civil Rights guidelines: Task force findings specifying remedies available for eliminating past educational practices ruled unlawful under *Lau v. Nichols.* In J. Alatis & K. Twaddell (Eds.), *English as a second language in bilingual education* (pp. 325–332). Washington, DC: Teachers of English to Speakers of Other Languages.

U.S. Office for Civil Rights. (1999). *Programs for English language learners.* Retrieved from www.ed.gov/offices/OCR/ELL.

Unrau, N. (2008). *Content area reading and writing: Fostering literacies in middle and high school cultures.* Upper Saddle River, NJ: Merrill Prentice Hall.

Uribe, D. (2008). Crazed on phonics. *Language Magazine, 7*(8), 37. Available at: www.languagemagazine.com.

Urow, C., & Sontag, J. (2001). Creating commuity—*un mundo entero*: The Inter-American experience. In D. Christian &

F. Genesee (Eds.), *Bilingual education.* Alexandria, VA: Teachers of English to Speakers of Other Languages.

Vacca, J. A. I., Vacca, R. T., Gove, M. K., Burkey, L. C., Lenhart, L. A., & McKeon, C. A. (2011). *Reading and learning to read* (8th ed). Boston: Allyn & Bacon.

Valdes, A. (2007). Top 10 immigration myths. *Colors^NW Magazine, 6*(12), 21–32, 43.

Valencia, R. R., & Villareal, B. J. (2003). Improving students' reading performance via standards-based school reform: A critique. *The Reading Teacher, 56*(7), 612–621.

Valles, E. C. (1998). The disproportionate representation of minority students in special education: Responding to the problem. *Journal of Special Education, 32*(1), 52–54.

Veeder, K., & Tramutt, J. (2000). Strengthening literacy in both languages. In N. Cloud, F. Genesee, & E. Hamayan (Eds.), *Dual language instruction* (p. 91). Boston: Heinle and Heinle.

Verdugo Hills High School. (2004). *Redesignated students.* Retrieved February 2, 2005, from www.lausd.k12.ca.us/Verdugo_HS/classes/esl/redes.htm.

Villa, R. A., Thousand, J. S., & Nevin, A. I. (2004). *A guide to co-teaching.* Thousand Oaks, CA: Corwin.

Villaseñor, V. (1992). *Rain of gold.* New York: Dell.

Villaume, S., & Brabham, E. (2003). Phonics instruction: Beyond the debate. *The Reading Teacher, 56*(5), 478–482.

Villegas, A. M., & Lucas, T. (2002). Preparing culturally responsive teachers: Rethinking the curriculum. *Journal of Teacher Education, 53*(1), 20–32.

Villegas, A. M., & Lucas, T. (2007). The culturally responsive teacher. *Educational Leadership, 64*(6), 28–33.

Vygotsky, L. (1978). *Mind in society.* Cambridge, MA: Harvard University Press.

Wadsworth, D., & Remaley, M. H. (2007). What families want. *Educational Leadership, 64*(6), 23–27.

Wallach, G. P., & Miller, L. (1988). *Language intervention and academic success.* Boston: Little, Brown.

Walqui, A. (1999). Assessment of culturally and linguistically diverse students: Considerations for the 21st century. In Mid-continent Research for Education and Learning (McREL) (Ed.), *Including culturally and linguistically diverse students in standards-based reform: A report on McREL's Diversity Roundtable I* (pp. 55–84). Retrieved March 17, 2005, from www.mcrel.org/topics/productDetail.asp?topicsID=3&productID=56.

Ward, A. W., & Murray-Ward, M. (1999). *Assessment in the classroom.* Belmont, CA: Wadsworth.

Weber, A. (2001). An international school in Indiana, USA. In D. Christian & F. Genesee (Eds.), *Bilingual education* (pp. 151–165). Alexandria, VA: Teachers of English to Speakers of Other Languages.

Weber, G. (2008). A proud history: New African-American curriculum helps students realize cultural pride. *Teachers of Color, 3*(1), 44–45.

Wells, M. C. (1996). *Literacies lost: When students move from a progressive middle school to a traditional high school.* New York: Teachers College Press.

West, J. F., & Idol, L. (1990). Collaborative consultation in the education of mildly handicapped and at-risk students. *Remedial and Special Education, 11*(1), 22–31.

Wiese, A. M., & García, E. (1998). The Bilingual Education Act: Language minority students and equal educational opportunity. *Bilingual Research Journal, 22*(1). Retrieved April 9, 2005, from http:// brj.asu.edu/v221/articles/art1.html.

Wiggins, G. (2005). What is understanding by design? *Understanding by design.* Retrieved March 23, 2005, from www.grantwiggins.org/ubd.html.

Wilber, D. (2010). *iWrite: Using blogs, wikis, and digital stories in the English classroom.* Portsmouth, NH: Heinemann.

Willard, N. E. (2007). *Cyberbullying and cyber-threats: Responding to the challenge of online social aggression, threats, and distress*. Champaign, IL: Research Press. 367C.

Willet, J. (1995). Becoming first graders in an L2: An ethnographic study of L2 socialization. *TESOL Quarterly, 29*(3), 473–503.

Williams, B. T. (2007). Standardized students: The problems with writing for tests instead of people. In Schultz, F. (Ed.), *Annual editions 10/08: Education* (pp. 71–75). Dubuque, IA: McGraw-Hill Contemporary Learning Series.

Wilner, L. K., & Feinstein-Whitaker, M. (2008). Accenting the positive. *Language Magazine, 7*(8), 34.

Wilton, D. (2003). *How many words are there in the English language?* Retrieved August 30, 2004, from www.wordorigins.org/number.htm.

Wolfenbarger, C. D., & Sipe, L. R. (2007). A unique and literary art form: Recent research on picture books. *Language Arts, 84*(3), 273–280.

Woolfolk, A. (2007). *Educational psychology* (10th ed.). Boston: Allyn & Bacon.

Woolfolk, A., & Brooks, D. (1985). The influence of teachers' nonverbal behaviors on students' perceptions and performance. *Elementary School Journal, 85,* 514–528.

Worthen, B., & Spandel, V. (1991). Putting the standardized test debate in perspective. *Educational Leadership, 48*(5), 65–69.

Worthy, J., Moorman, M., & Turner, M. (1999). What Johnny likes to read is hard to find in school. *Reading Research Quarterly, 14,* 12–27.

Wray, M., & Newitz, A. (1997). *White trash: Race and class in America*. New York: Routledge.

Yamauchi, L., & Wilhelm, P. (2001). *e Ola Ka Hawai'i I Kona 'Olelo:* Hawaiians live in their language. In D. Christian & F. Genesee (Eds.), *Bilingual education* (pp. 83–94). Alexandria, VA: Teachers of English to Speakers of Other Languages.

Yao, E. (1988). Working effectively with Asian immigrant parents. *Phi Delta Kappan, 70*(3), 223–225.

Yates, S. (1996). English in cyberspace. In S. Goodman & D. Graddol (Eds.), *Redesigning English: New texts, new identities* (pp. 106–140). London: Routledge.

Yep, L. (1975). *Dragonwings*. New York: Harper & Row.

Yi, Y. (2009) Adolescent literacy and identity construction among 1.5 Generation students from a transnational perspective, *Journal of Asia Pacific Communication, 19*(1), 100–129.

Young, M., & Helvie, S. (1996). Parent power: A positive link to school success. *Journal of Educational Issues of Language Minority Students, 16*. Online at http://www.ncela.gwu.edu/files/rcd/BE020638/JEILMS_Summer_1996_Volume1611.pdf.

Zacarian, D. (2004). Keeping Tren in school. *Essential Teacher, 1*(2), 12–13.

Zacarian, D. (2004). Personal communication.

Zacarian, D. (2011). *Transforming schools for English learners: A comprehensive framework for school leaders*. Thousand Oaks, CA: Corwin.

Zanger, V. V. (1994). "Not joined in": The social context of English literacy development for Hispanic youth. In B. M. Ferdman, R.-M. Weber, & A. G. Ramírez (Eds.), *Literacy across languages and cultures* (pp. 171–198). Albany: SUNY Press.

Zarate, M. E. (2007). *Understanding Latino parental involvement in education, #2069.* Los Angeles: The Tomás Rivera Policy Institute.

Zarate, M. E., Bhimji, F., & Reese, L. (2005). Ethnic identity and academic achievement among Latino/a adolescents. *Journal of Latinos in Education, 4*(2), 93–114.

Zehler, A., Hopstock, P., Fleischman, H., & Greniuk, C. (1994). *An examination of assessment of limited English proficient students*. Arlington, VA: Special Issues Analysis Center. Online at http://www.ncela.gwu.edu/files/rcd/BE02

0221/Examination_of_Assessment_of_LEP .pdf.

Zehler, A. M., Fleischman, H. L., Hopstock, P. J., Stephenson, T. G., Pendzick, M. L., & Sapru, S. (2003). *Descriptive study of services to LEP students and LEP students with disabilities* (Vol. 4). Washington, DC: US Department of Education, Office of English Language Acquisition, Language Enhancement, and Academic Achievement for Limited English Proficient Students. Online at http://www.ncela.gwu .edu/files/rcd/BE021199/special_ed4.pdf.

Zeiler, H. (2007). Successful interventions. *Language Magazine, 6*(9), 32–35.

Zemach, D. (2007). Picture this. *Essential Teacher, 4*(2), 12–13.

Zemach, D. (2009). The mystery of the perfect method. *Essential Teacher, 6*(3–4), 15–16.

Name Index

Subject Index

Chicano/a(s), 249
  history of Chicanas, 273
  power movement, 224
  terms denoting, xvii, 240
Chinese, Chinese American(s). *See also* Asian American(s)
  academic achievement of, 161
  attitudes towards standardized testing, 247
  contributions of, 225
  culturally supported or limiting attitudes and abilities, 282–292
  demography of, 226
  exploitation of, 228
  immigration, 234, 235, 237
  immigration laws/policies about, 234, 237
  in Monterey Park, 326
  parental involvement, 302
  speakers (Mandarin) and English syntax, 36
Chinese Exclusion Act, 234, 237
Chinese language. *See* Mandarin
Chinese characters, 302
Civil Rights Act of 1964, 153
Class bias, in testing, 212
Class discussions, 288
Classism, 263–264
Classroom learning community, 110
Classroom(s)
  discourse, 41, 284
  environment of, 118
  organization of, 287
  practices that validate identity, 280
  resolving conflict in, 266
  volunteers, 179
Clipping, as a word-formation process, 35
Code switching, 51, 176
Cognitive approaches to language learning, 52–53, 57–58
Cognitive Academic Language Learning Approach (CALLA), 52
Cognitive academic language proficiency (CALP), 59–61

Cognitive factors. *See* Psychological factors, cognitive
Cognitive justice, struggle for, 231
Cognitive strategies, 52
Cognitive style, 7, 15–16
Collaboration with colleagues, 322
Collaborative teaching, 178
Colloquial usage, 36
Common Core
  assessments, 190, 203
  standards, 186
Common underlying proficiency (CUP), 59
Communication
  abilities, increased by CALL and CMC, 108
  listening for, 77–78
  nonverbal, 41–44
  role of silence in, 284
  strategies, 50–51
  verbal and nonverbal, 283–284
Communicative competence, 62–64
  discourse competence, 63
  grammatical competence, 63
  sociolinguistic competence, 63
  strategic competence, 63
Communicative distance, 43
Community advocates, 301–302
Community-based organizations (CBOs), 307
Community organizations, 326–327
Community partnerships, 303–307
Community support for schooling, 295–303
Compensatory education, 150, 151
Competency tests, 198
Complex Instruction, 177
Complexity of language, 30
Comprehensibility, 116, 117, 125–126, 131, 133–134, 137–138, 141–142
  contextualizing instruction, 124, 131

into, through, and beyond, 133–134
  strategies for, 126
Comprehensible input, 58
Comprehension checks, 125
Computer, texting shorthand, 35
Computer-Assisted Language Learning (CALL), 105–112
  and classroom learning community, 110
  enhances creativity, 109
  impacts literacy instruction, 106
  increases communicative abilities, 108
  supports learner autonomy, 108–109
  supports strategic learning, 107
Computer-Mediated Communication (CMC), 105, 108, 111
Computers, 105–112
Concurrent-translation model, 175
Concurrent validity, 213
Conductive hearing loss, 357
Conflict resolution, 264–266
Constructivist learning, 62
  social constructivist, 64
Content-area instruction
  application, 129–144
  comprehensibility in, 116, 117, 125–126, 131, 133–134, 137–138, 141–142
  connections in, 116, 117, 122–123, 130, 133, 137, 141
  explanatory models in, 129
  flexible, thematic curricula in, 130
  in history, 130
  instructional needs beyond the classroom, 144
  interaction in, 131, 134, 138
  in literature, 132–135
  in mathematics, 135–139
  learning strategies in, 137
  modeling technology, 137
  in physical education, 143–144
  primary language use in, 135